CW00825421

Digital Education and Learning

Series Editors

Michael Thomas
University of Central Lancashire
Preston, UK

John Palfrey
Phillips Academy
Andover, MA, USA

Mark Warschauer
University of California
Irvine, CA, USA

Much has been written during the first decade of the new millennium about the potential of digital technologies to produce a transformation of education. Digital technologies are portrayed as tools that will enhance learner collaboration and motivation and develop new multimodal literacy skills. Accompanying this has been the move from understanding literacy on the cognitive level to an appreciation of the sociocultural forces shaping learner development. Responding to these claims, the Digital Education and Learning Series explores the pedagogical potential and realities of digital technologies in a wide range of disciplinary contexts across the educational spectrum both in and outside of class. Focusing on local and global perspectives, the series responds to the shifting landscape of education, the way digital technologies are being used in different educational and cultural contexts, and examines the differences that lie behind the generalizations of the digital age. Incorporating cutting edge volumes with theoretical perspectives and case studies (single authored and edited collections), the series provides an accessible and valuable resource for academic researchers, teacher trainers, administrators and students interested in interdisciplinary studies of education and new and emerging technologies.

More information about this series at
http://www.springer.com/series/14952

Grete Jamissen • Pip Hardy • Yngve Nordkvelle • Heather Pleasants
Editors

Digital Storytelling in Higher Education

International Perspectives

Editors
Grete Jamissen
Oslo and Akershus University College
of Applied Sciences
Oslo, Norway

Yngve Nordkvelle
Inland Norway University of
Applied Sciences
Lillehammer, Norway

Pip Hardy
Pilgrim Projects
Cambridge, UK

Heather Pleasants
University of Alabama
Tuscaloosa, AL, USA

Digital Education and Learning
ISBN 978-3-319-51057-6   ISBN 978-3-319-51058-3   (eBook)
DOI 10.1007/978-3-319-51058-3

Library of Congress Control Number: 2017934103

Cover image © ArtesiaWells / Alamy Stock Photo

Printed on acid-free paper

This Palgrave Macmillan imprint is published by Springer Nature
The registered company is Springer International Publishing AG
The registered company address is: Gewerbestrasse 11, 6330 Cham, Switzerland

FOREWORD

Twenty years ago, in the fall of 1996, I made a trip to Europe. To Bristol, England. To hold what would be the first of many digital storytelling (DS) workshops in the UK and Europe over the next several years.

Our sponsor in Bristol was Hewlett Packard (HP) Labs, the research and development wing of the US technology company. They wanted us working in a partnership between the Watershed, a media arts cen-tre down on the quay in central Bristol and the University of the West of England (UWE). A graduate student who also worked at HP Labs, Clodagh Miskelly, would be part of one of those first workshops, as would a number of local academics.

It was our first academic partnership in the UK. During the next couple of years, we came back to UWE. These initial workshops in Europe were quite important to us; we were not at all sure that the populist ethos of our work would translate to contemporary Europe, particularly as a new genre of media communications in an educational context.

I think it would be fair to say that the European academic world did not quite know what to make of our project. Media arts educa-tion and media literacy were well-established fields in the UK and the rest of Europe. And while computer-based media work was still a fresh idea, there was nothing particularly compelling about our model from a media arts standpoint. The little pieces made in these short workshops were not going to be the kind of work that would end up circulating at local video centres or annual educational video festivals, or appearing in some corner of local television. Video on the internet was still years from being practical, so what do you do with a media practice that was not about some form of broadcast?

Nor was it conceivable for people to think of this work as a new type of multi-modal composition. Despite our insistence that we were re-purposing oral tradition and popular literacy for the digital age, a sort of practicum to Walter Ong's perspectives on orality, literacy and electronic media, that it had a potential as a part of all sectors of academic work, our personal, non-expository approach seemed suspect.

I am sure we felt, even if it was never spoken, the 'well that's quite nice, darling, but really...' dismissal of our post-modern pals working at their academic institutions. I remember at one of our early workshops in the Netherlands, a Dutch colleague commented, 'this is like Oprah Winfrey!' That was not good. I assumed our future in Europe was limited, as no one seemed to understand what we were trying to achieve.

We were very fortunate in 1998 to be invited to make our residence at the School of Education at the University of California, Berkeley. Dr Glynda Hull, the College Writing Program, and a group of her graduate students assisted in a reinterpretation of our practice as a form of communicative engagement different from the 'multimedia' authoring (Educational Powerpoint and Hypercard stacks on CD ROMS) and concern about hypertext composition; that was how 'digital' composition was being discussed at the time.

Our approach had us taking the tool of digital video editing and, to a lesser extent, photo manipulation and re-composition in Photoshop, and inviting a populist voice to emerge from a simple, direct method of telling a brief, personal story. Hull and others recognized the potential of such a method to integrate processes of identity construction with the digital literacy concern, and information technology strategies, of contemporary curricula.

Other educators around the world began to take note, and we found ourselves bouncing around Scandinavia, Germany, the Netherlands, Belgium and, of course, all around the USA presenting the idea to educational professionals. In 2002, I spoke, as someone introducing an idea, at the 'Society for Information Technology in Education' Conference about DS. By 2006, there were 33 separate presentations on DS. DS had arrived on the college campus as a valuable new way to encourage all students to compose for the screen.

What we have seen as a community over the last two decades is the expansion of the utility of DS into every corner of higher education. In our collaborations in the field, we have assisted campuses in dozens of different applications including communities of practice using DS across the curriculum, new forms of expression in writing and visual methods, reflective observation in service learning and study abroad, negotiating cultural difference and dialogue, as engagement and distribution of concepts in health and social work, to name a few. But in a broad sense, as editors and educators in the wider sense, and in our small contribution to this volume, while the tool, the brand, the genre or the idea of DS is broadly disseminated, the underlying theoretical work, the underlying value system and foundational perspectives are still very much in development.

So, all these years later, a cross section of European, African, Asian/Pacific Island and American academics and practitioners have come together in *Digital Storytelling in Higher Education* edited by Grete Jamissen, Pip Hardy, Yngve Nordkvelle and Heather Pleasants.

The editors are situating DS as a vital tool in the larger humanistic, value-centred educational project. They suggest that we use the integrative arguments of American educator Ernest Boyer from the late 1980s and early 1990s about rethinking how we assess scholarship in higher education. They use Boyer's four-pillar perspective on scholarly activity as the frame for our understanding of DS's potential in higher education.

I am not a professional academic nor do I pretend to grasp the evolution of the various ways of defining the purpose of academic institutions and scholarship as a whole. But when I look at the four pillars, the encouragement of original research (discovery), the ability to synthesize knowledge in an interdisciplinary and historical manner (integration), the ability to take one's academic effort and extend that work into local community, or greater society, in a demonstrable way (application), and the ability to take one's scholarship and advance how we imagine teaching and learning occur in a broadly understood, and evaluated, way (teaching), I recognize how useful this framework is to encompass all the ways our colleagues around the world want to use this tool in higher education.

In 2016, we are years beyond the conceptualization of DS as a 'nice' way to share personal stories. We are beyond the view of this work as a doorway to media technology literacy and even a perspective that the work simply posits a mechanism of multi-modal composition. DS, as practiced by the practitioners and educators included in this volume, is a transformative learning process that has broad implications for all of the four 'scholarships' described by Boyer.

As you look across the contributions, you are made aware of the depth of commitment of the authors to understanding the strengths, limitations and opportunities of DS as composition, as connection and as building respectful, healthy educational communities and informed responsible citizens.

Along with all these contributors, we share a commitment to bring the whole person into the educational experience. We are not on this planet as educators to stack the lives of our learners into tiers of success. We are here to awaken the sense that scholarship and learning should be, in every sense of the word, a healthy endeavour. It should create whole people, who can address complicated issues, to make a more whole, safe, sustained and sustainable world.

Joe Lambert

Series Foreword

Much has been written during the first decade of the new millennium about the potential of digital technologies to radically transform education and learning. Typically, such calls for change spring from the argument that traditional education no longer engages learners or teaches them the skills required for the twenty-first century. Digital technologies are often described as tools that will enhance collaboration and motivate learners to re-engage with education and enable them to develop the new multi-modal literacy skills required for today's knowledge economy. Using digital technologies is a creative experience in which learners actively engage with solving problems in authentic environments that underline their productive skills rather than merely passively consuming knowledge. Accompanying this argument has been the move from understanding literacy on the cognitive level to an appreciation of the socio-cultural forces shaping learner development and the role communities play in supporting the acquisition of knowledge.

Emerging from this context, the Digital Education and Learning series was founded to explore the pedagogical potential and realities of digital technologies in a wide range of disciplinary contexts across the educational spectrum around the world. Focusing on local and global perspectives, the series responds to the shifting demands and expectations of educational stakeholders, looks at the ways new technologies are actually being used in different educational and cultural contexts, and examines the opportunities and challenges that lie behind the myths and rhetoric of digital age education. The series encourages the development of evidence-based research that is rooted in an understanding of the history of technology, as well as open to the potential of new innovation, and adopts critical perspectives on technological determinism as well as techno-scepticism.

While the potential for changing the way we learn in the digital age is significant, and new sources of information and forms of interaction have developed, many educational institutions and learning environments have changed little from those that existed over 100 years ago. Whether in the form of smartphones, laptops or tablets, digital technologies may be increasingly ubiquitous in a person's social life but marginal in his or her daily educational experience once the person enters a classroom. Although many people increasingly invest more and more time on their favourite social media site, integrating these technologies into curricula or formal learning environments remains a significant challenge, if indeed it is a worthwhile aim in the first place. History tells us that change in educational contexts, if it happens at all in ways that were intended, is typically more 'incremental' and rarely 'revolutionary'. Understanding the development of learning technologies in the context of a historically informed approach therefore is one of the core aspects of the series, as is the need to understand the increasing internationalization of education and the way learning technologies are culturally mediated. While the digital world appears to be increasingly 'flat', significant challenges continue to exist, and the series will problematize terms that have sought to erase cultural, pedagogical and theoretical differences rather than understand them. 'Digital natives', 'digital literacy', 'digital divide' and 'digital media'—these and such mantras as 'twenty-first-century learning'—are phrases that continue to be used in ways that require further clarification and critical engagement rather than unquestioning and uncritical acceptance.

The series aims to examine the complex discourse of digital technologies and to understand the implications for teaching, learning and professional development. By mixing volumes with theoretical perspectives with case studies detailing actual teaching approaches, whether on or off campus, in face-to-face, fully online or blended learning contexts, the series will examine the emergence of digital technologies from a range of new international and interdisciplinary perspectives. Incorporating original and innovative volumes with theoretical perspectives and case studies (single-authored and edited collections), the series aims to provide an accessible and valuable resource for academic researchers, teacher trainers, administrators, policymakers and learners interested in cutting-edge research on new and emerging technologies in education.

Series Editors
Michael Thomas
James P. Gee
John G. Palfrey

PREFACE

We, the editors of this book, and probably you, if you are also engaged in the lofty pursuit of higher education, will be concerned with the kindling of flames in your students.

It is Pascal who is credited with saying: 'We tell stories to entertain and to teach'. We believe that we also tell stories to learn, and we know that the telling and sharing of stories are among the best ways to kindle that flame.

We have been inspired by the potential of DS to inspire our students and teach them how to learn—about the subjects they are studying, how they are studying them, how to present their learning to others and how to use new technologies to perform the most ancient of tasks: the expression and sharing of experience. Our own experiences of creating digital stories with students are that they learn about all of these things and much more: they learn about the communities in which they live, study and work; they learn about their own potential to overcome adversity and sorrow; they learn to see the future as a bright opportunity to which they belong and which belongs to them and, above all, they learn about themselves.

This book began as a twinkle in the eye of Grete Jamissen. Grete's determination to transform her own university into 'a digital storytelling university' extended to her vision of a book about the myriad uses for DS in higher education. Needless to say, she infected the rest of us editors with her enthusiasm and commitment to the growing potential of DS as a valuable tool for teaching and learning and research as well as for community engagement and the integration of new knowledge across disciplines. DS is nothing if not interdisciplinary, spanning the fields of community theatre, creative writing, photography, film and video editing, group work, drama and beyond, and fitting comfortably into the more established disciplines of education, medicine and healthcare, social work, history, anthropology and many more.

The twinkle in Grete's eye sparked Yngve Nordkvelle to propose the use of Ernest Boyer's model of the four scholarships to provide a framework for this book. It was at this point that the twinkle began to take form, and in September 2015, at the sixth international DS conference in Massachusetts, we presented our vision of the book, together with a model illustrating the impact of DS in each and all of the four scholarships (Fig. 1).

Colleagues were eager to contribute to the first ever book about DS in higher education, and so a little over a year later, we are proud to present what we consider to be an outstanding collection of chapters from around the world about the impact of DS in higher education.

Before letting readers loose on the rest of this book, however, there are some important messages to convey and a few points to clarify.

The term 'digital storytelling' has become ubiquitous in the twenty-first century, where almost everything is digital. It wasn't always like that. In mid-1990s' California, the explosion in digital technologies resulted in the development of multimedia tools that even ordinary people could

Fig. 1   Digital storytelling and the four scholarships (Hardy, Jamissen, Nordkvelle and Pleasants 2015 (after Boyer and Rice))

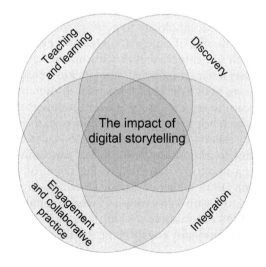

use. A small group of community theatre types were inspired to combine traditional storytelling methods with some of these cool, new technologies to develop a workshop model that would make it possible for anyone who could use a computer to create a short movie about something that mattered to them.

And so, the model of DS upon which the chapters in this book are based is the model developed by Joe Lambert, Dana Atchley and the Center for Digital Storytelling (now StoryCenter) in that particular hotbed of West Coast creativity. It relies on a carefully facilitated workshop process during which participants share their story ideas, develop a script, record a voice-over, select images, use video editing software to assemble all these elements into a short video about something of importance to the storyteller and then watch the finished stories together. While the chapters in this book describe many different adaptations for use in a wide variety of contexts, there are some commonalities, and it will be helpful if you, the reader, are aware of these.

The Story Circle is at the core of our practice. This safe space offers an opportunity for storytellers to share their story ideas and receive comments, questions and feedback from the other people in the circle. The Story Circle is conducted in an air of respectful listening, usually guarded by an agreement to preserve the confidentiality of the words spoken there. In our busy world, the Story Circle affords an unusual and welcome forum to share—and to listen—deeply.

To support the development of digital stories in the StoryCenter tradition, The Seven Elements of Digital Storytelling, now the Seven Steps of Digital Storytelling, offer guidance to novice storytellers, steering them gently through literary theory towards the quest for personal meaning and the ultimate goal of presenting something that will be, as Pascal might have said, both entertaining and instructive.

At the heart of every chapter included in this volume is respect for the potential of every person to create something of lasting value in a new media format. Many people who participate in these workshops find the experience transformative, as you will read, while the stories themselves can be used to great effect in a wide variety of contexts, as you will discover.

We are deeply indebted to Joe Lambert, the father of DS. Without his vision, inspiration and dedication to the notion that every story matters, there would be no book.

There would also be no book without the wisdom, knowledge, generosity and patience of all the contributors who have so graciously written the chapters contained herein.

We must also thank our many colleagues and friends in the international DS world, with whom we have shared hopes and dreams, successes and failures, stories and conversations, aspiration and inspiration and glasses of wine too numerous to mention during the course of DS conferences in Portugal, Norway, Greece, Turkey, Spain, Australia, the UK and the USA.

We, the editors, would also like to express our heartfelt thanks to all those who have shared their stories with us and, in so doing, opened our eyes to the educational and transformative potential of DS at individual, group, organization and societal levels.

We are grateful to our publisher, Palgrave Macmillan, for taking on the task of publishing our work and to our editor, Laura Aldridge, who has unfailingly answered even the smallest of queries with speed and good humour.

We would also like to acknowledge the support we have received from our families, our partners and our institutions as we have grappled with the multitude of tasks involved in creating a book such as this one.

We hope that this book will kindle the flames of curiosity and enthusiasm and that you will be inspired to learn more about—and experiment with—DS in your own educational endeavours.

1 November 2016

Pip Hardy
Cambridge, UK

Grete Jamissen
Oslo, Norway

Yngve Nordkvelle
Lillehammer, Norway

Heather Pleasants
Tuscaloosa, USA

CONTENTS

CONTRIBUTORS

Darcy Alexandra Darcy Alexandra specializes in documentary storytelling and the politics of voice and listening. She holds a PhD from the Centre for Transcultural Research and Media Practice, Dublin Institute of Technology and an MA from the University of Arizona. Since 2007, she has designed and facilitated participatory media research that centres co-creative audiovisual production as a means of inquiry and public engagement. She has conducted audiovisual research in the US-Mexico borderlands, El Salvador, Uruguay, Cuba and Ireland and taught DS in collaboration with university, non-governmental and governmental agencies including the Forum on Migration and Communications, the Dublin City Council and the Swiss Agency for Development and Cooperation. She is a guest lecturer at the Institute for Social Anthropology, University of Bern.

Kim Anderson Kim Anderson, PhD, is a professor in the School of Social Work and the Public Affairs Doctoral Program at the University of Central Florida in Orlando, Florida. For 25 years, she has practised and conducted research in the trauma field. Her book, *Enhancing Resilience in Survivors of Family Violence* (Anderson, 2010), provides empirical findings and conceptual insights for professionals to assist people affected by violence and oppression to cultivate their strengths and resilient capacities. Dr Anderson has also created a digital story curriculum for youth and adults impacted by violence and trained helping professionals on this innovative narrative method.

Ana Oskoz Ana Oskoz is an associate professor in Modern Languages, Linguistics and Intercultural Communication and the director of the Humanities Scholars Program at the University of Maryland, Baltimore County (UMBC). In her research, Ana Oskoz has examined the use of different social digital tools and social media platforms whether for developing second language students' writing skills, enhancing their digital literacies or developing their intercultural communication.

Beverly Bickel Beverly Bickel is a clinical associate professor in the Language, Literacy, and Culture Doctoral Program and affiliate associate professor of Gender & Women's Studies at the University of Maryland, Baltimore County (UMBC). Her interdisciplinary scholarship focuses on the production, exchange, and dissemination of transformational knowledge for changing cultural practices in social justice and participatory democracy efforts on and beyond campus.

Elaine Bliss Elaine Bliss is a senior tutor in Geography at the University of Waikato, Aotearoa New Zealand. Elaine received her PhD in 2015 from the University of Waikato for her thesis titled 'Performative Methodologies: Geographies of Emotion and Affect in Digital Storytelling Workshops'. Elaine developed the first interdisciplinary DS paper in a Aotearoa New Zealand University and has been teaching it since 2013.

Karen Diaz Karen Diaz was a founding member of the Digital Storytelling Program at Ohio State University (OSU). This programme was a cross-campus collaboration that began in 2006 and continues today, even though she is no longer with the programme. Karen spent 15 years focused on work that advanced the information literacy of students on the campus through the DS programme, managing an information literacy grant programme, teaching credit courses, designing learning opportunities and managing the instructional work of the OSU Libraries Teaching and Learning Department. She is currently the associate dean of Libraries at West Virginia University.

Yvonne Fritze Yvonne Fritze (born 1962) is an associate professor of education at Lillehammer University College since 2003 and has recently been vice-rector for research. Trained as an MA in media studies at Copenhagen University, she holds a PhD in distance education from the University of Southern Denmark. She has published on issues like distance education, use of visual materials in teaching, online dating as well as e-publishing. She is co-editor on Seminar.net (http://seminar.net), an international e-journal about media, technology and lifelong learning.

Daniela Gachago Daniela Gachago is a senior lecturer in the Centre for Innovative Educational Technology at the Cape Peninsula University of Technology. Her research interests lie in the potential of emerging technologies to improve teaching and learning in higher education, with a particular focus on using social media and DS for social change. She completed a PhD at the University of Cape Town School of Education, where she explored the role of emotions in transforming students' engagement across difference and a Master's in Adult Education at the University of Botswana.

Carol Haigh Carol Haigh has over 30 years of experience of academia and healthcare settings within the UK. She has acted as an expert advisor to the Royal

College of Nursing and other health related charities, is vice-chair of a local ethics committee and maintains strong links with the wider clinical disciplines facilitating improvements in patient engagement and experience using technology and social media. She has a special interest in ethics and health technology from a user perspective. Contact her on c.haigh@mmu.ac.uk and find her CV here http://mmu.academia.edu/CarolHaigh or follow her on twitter @loracenna

Satu Hakanurmi Satu Hakanurmi works at the University of Turku, Faculty of Education, and is associated with The Finnish Society for Research on Adult Education. Her research interests are in adult education, workplace learning, professional development, storytelling and narratives, identity and online learning.

Tony Hall Tony Hall is a lecturer in Educational Technology, School of Education, National University of Ireland, Galway (NUIG). Tony's research interests include educational innovation; narrative theory and technology in education, including DS; and practitioner methodology through design-based research. At NUIG, Tony jointly leads—with Drs Michael Hogan, John Breslin and Bonnie Thompson Long—the EU Horizon 2020 Q-Tales Project to design educational e-books: http://www.qtales.com/. Tony is also co-principal investigator for the REX Project to design an online portal to support teacher research: http://www.researchexpertiseexchange.com/. Tony is a fellow of the International Society for Design and Development in Education: http://www.isdde.org.

Pip Hardy Pip Hardy is a director of Pilgrim Projects, UK, an education consultancy specializing in open learning and healthcare quality improvement, and a co-founder of Patient Voices (www.patientvoices.org.uk). With a BA in English Literature and an MSc in Lifelong Learning, Pip has a keen interest in how stories can promote learning, understanding and insight. Her PhD investigates the potential of DS to transform healthcare and healthcare education.

Geir Haugsbakk Geir Haugsbakk (born 1956) is an associate professor of education at Lillehammer University College. He worked in the Centre for Lifelong Learning for a decade and is now Head of Department of Education. His PhD from the University of Tromsø was on the politics and rhetoric of implementing ICT in schools in Norway. His primary interests are in language, media, technology and education. He is currently working on a research project focusing on 'Digital Bildung'. He is also co-editor of seminar.net.

Brooke Hessler Brooke Hessler is a professor of writing and director of Learning Resources at California College of the Arts. An award-winning teacher of experiential and arts-integrated courses, her digital storywork has included long-term collaborations with K-12 educators, community arts activists and survivors of natural disasters and domestic terrorism. Her research centres on the uses of participatory media for critical reflection and embodied learning. She is co-author of *A Guide to Composition Pedagogies* (Oxford).

Romy Hübler Romy Hübler coordinates student involvement in Student Life at UMBC and organizes with faculty, staff and students to integrate civic and community engagement into all aspects of education at UMBC. Her research explores engaged pedagogies and scholarship, civic agency and social change.

Ida Hydle Ida Hydle is a Norwegian research professor at NOVA, the Welfare Research Institute, University College of Applied sciences in Oslo and Akershus and adjunct professor at the University of Tromsø, Department of Social Work and Child Protection. She holds PhD degrees in medicine and social anthropology. She has experience from practical work as a medical doctor within social medicine and rehabilitation, geriatrics and mental health work as well as teaching and training at all academic levels, research planning and implementation within social medicine, mental health work, medical and legal anthropology, visual cultural studies and peace studies, restorative justice and restorative practice studies.

Grete Jamissen Grete Jamissen is professor of education at Oslo and Akershus University College and has a previous career in computer industry and Telenor. In addition to learning with technology, she has published on issues like action research and learning organizations. She has led the institutional implementation of DS for learning, communication and collaboration since 2005 and led the organizing group for the fourth world conference on DS in Lillehammer in 2011. She has co-authored two Norwegian books on DS (2012, 2015) and contributed in 'Appraising Digital Storytelling across Educational Contexts', Publicacions de la Universitat de València 2014.

Tricia Jenkins Tricia Jenkins is the co-founder and director of DigiTales Ltd, a research and DS company based in London. She is currently finalizing her PhD at Middlesex University, in which she studied the benefits of DS with older people both as a participatory process and, in the potential of the stories themselves, as rich qualitative data. She has worked extensively across media education, participatory media and the related creative industries.

Joe Lambert Joe Lambert founded the Center for Digital Storytelling (now StoryCenter) in 1994. He and his colleagues developed a computer training and arts programme known as The Digital Storytelling Workshop, which became a broadly adopted model of community-based participatory media and media education. Lambert and his staff have travelled the world to spread the practice of DS to all 50 US states and 48 countries. He is the author of *Digital Storytelling: Capturing Lives, Creating Community* (Routledge) and a more recent work *Seven Stages: Story and the Human Experience* (Digital Diner Press).

Ragnhild Larsson Ragnhild Larsson is a Swedish, independent journalist, science communicator and storyteller. She has worked as a journalist for 30 years and facilitates workshops in DS. Ragnhild Larsson has also developed a method to create digital stories on behalf of researchers and has produced stories for Chalmers University, Gothenburg University, The Hasselblad Foundation and Swedish Foundation of Strategic Research, among others. She also writes articles and has co-authored several books about working life issues. A main theme in all her work is sustainability, whether it is a sustainable working life or environmental and climate change issues.

Brian Leaf Brian Leaf was recruited into the OSU Digital Storytelling Program by his then-supervisor Karen Diaz in 2013. After she left, he succeeded her in coordinating the interdisciplinary programme, discovering his passion for outreach and facilitation. During the five years he worked at OSU, Brian was responsible for redesigning credit courses, tackling information literacy issues and producing instructional media. While involved with the DS programme, he helped develop new partnerships and classroom opportunities. He has taken the lessons he learned to his new position as emerging technologies coordinator for the Regional Medical Library of the National Network of Libraries of Medicine South Central Region, where he is engaged in outreach and finding solutions for healthier communities across the region.

Inger Kjersti Lindvig Inger Kjersti Lindvig is an associate professor in social pedagogy at the University College of Southeast Norway. Her research interests span from interdisciplinary and interprofessional education to international, global and multicultural issues related to health, social and welfare studies. She has broad experience from teaching, development and innovative work in the health, social and educational sector, both nationally and internationally. She has done field work and practical studies in Africa, Asia, South America and Europe. At present, she participates in the Erasmus+ project: *'Common Good First. Digital Storytelling for Social Innovation'*: Cooperation for innovation and the exchange of good practices.

Bonnie Thompson Long Bonnie Thompson Long is an education technologist/multimedia content developer in the Centre for Adult Learning and Professional Development, NUIG. Bonnie's main research interest lies in the use of technology to enhance the learning experience of pre-service teachers. Her PhD research, on which this chapter is based, focused on the use of DS as a method of enhancing student teachers' ability to be reflective practitioners. Related interests include reflective practice, narrative theory in education, DS, multimedia learning theories, autoethnography in teacher education and pre-service teachers' use of technology.

Michael Meimaris Michael Meimaris is the founder of the New Technologies Laboratory in Communication, Education and Mass Media of the National and Kapodistrian University of Athens and currently the director of the University

Research Institute of Applied Communication. He has studied mathematics, statistics and computer-based data analysis. His scientific interests involve the application of new technologies in communication, education and mass media, graphics and computer animation, the new technological communication environment and its design, DS, intergenerational communication and learning, digital game-based learning and open and distance education. He is member of the International Committee and president of the National Committee of the Möbius Awards, member of the scientific board of the Maison des Sciences de l'Homme Paris-Nord of France, as well as of C.I.T.I. of Universidade NOVA de Lisboa (Portugal). He is also the member of the governing board of the UNESCO Institute for Information Technologies in Education (IITE). He was awarded Chevalier de l'Ordre des Palmes Académiques of the French Democracy.

Mari Ann Moss Mari Ann's current affiliation is as the director of Dreamcatcher Enterprise Ltd, where she breeds thoroughbred race horses. Her experience in higher education started in 1996 as manager of Campus Media, providing multimedia services at the University of Waikato in New Zealand. In 2001, Campus Media became the Waikato Innovation Centre for eEducation, supporting online learning. In 2004, they secured venture capital and spun out Ectus Ltd, a commercial company that integrated video conferencing with social media. Ectus won Computerworld's Excellence Awards 2005 for Innovative Use of Technology and in collaboration with the university, won Excellence in the Use of IT in Education—Tertiary & Commercial. The successful sale of Ectus after 18 months to Tandberg ASA in Norway was then the most successful exit of a New Zealand Venture Investment Funded Company. The sale of the company gave Mari Ann an opportunity to do a PhD in the Waikato Management School, which she completed in 2012.

Mike Moulton Mike Moulton is the head of the Learning Center at the Norwegian University of Life Sciences. He has worked for many years with faculty development and the support and enhancement of learning through the integration of digital technologies. Particularly, he has worked to establish DS as an alternative to the traditional term paper in higher education. In addition, Moulton is exploring the use of DS as a means to improve agricultural extension practices in Malawi.

Yngve Nordkvelle Yngve Nordkvelle (born 1955) is a professor of education at Lillehammer University College since 1999 and has published on issues like global and international education, distance education, online dating as well as e-publishing. He has directed the programme for teaching and learning at the college since 2004. He was active in organizing the fourth world conference on DS in Lillehammer in 2011. He is the chief editor of Seminar.net (http://seminar.net), an international e-journal about media, technology and lifelong learning.

Heather Pleasants Heather Pleasants is an associate director of Institutional Effectiveness at the University of Alabama and the director of a five-year project focused on using experiential education to support undergraduates' problem-solving skills. Her scholarship focuses on issues of voice, leadership, literacy/storytelling, mobility and identity. Dr. Pleasants is the co-editor of the 2014 book, 'Community-Based Multiliteracies and Digital Media Projects: Questioning Assumptions, Exploring Realities' (Peter Lang) and is a graduate of the University of Michigan-Flint (BS in Psychology) and Michigan State University (PhD in Educational Psychology, specialization in language, literacy and learning).

Sandra Ribeiro Sandra Ribeiro is a senior lecturer at ISCAP-IPP in the area of Languages and Cultures. She holds a PhD from the University of Aveiro, Portugal, in digital storytelling in higher education. Her research interests include DS as a pedagogical practice to foster student reflection and overall student development; the integration of technology in education; and language-learning, translation and interpreting as acts of intercultural communication.

William Shewbridge William Shewbridge is the professor of the Practice in the Department of Media and Communication Studies at UMBC. He is the founding director and executive producer of UMBC's New Media Studio and has been leading the DS community at UMBC since 2006.

Pam Sykes Pam Sykes is currently a PhD student and fellow in the Centre for Humanities Research at the University of Western Cape. Her PhD will examine how the processes of DS, including the multiple mediations of facilitation, scripting, picture production, voice recording, digital video editing and group dynamics, shape the crafting of stories recalling migrant labour experiences in a South African township. Originally trained as a journalist, she holds an MSc in Science and Technology Studies from the University of Edinburgh and studied facilitation at StoryCenter. She has worked with universities and NGOs to produce stories on topics including HIV/Aids, gender-based violence prevention, teacher education and food security.

LIST OF FIGURES

List of Tables

CHAPTER 1

The Long March: The Origins of Voice, Emotion and Image in Higher Education

Yngve Nordkvelle

INTRODUCTION

This book project was initiated by scholars who have practised digital storytelling in higher education over many years. We, editors and authors alike, have been deeply inspired by the model developed by the Center for Digital Storytelling (now StoryCenter) in Berkeley, California, and have met and discussed common concerns in seminars and conferences over the years. We talked about how our workshops with diverse groups of teachers and researchers in higher education, as well as students and practitioners inside and outside our institutions, share similarities as well as differences. We sought a frame of reference for understanding higher education as a more diverse set of activities. Our question was whether there was a model that would provide space for our concepts of voice, emotion, multimodalities and deep reflection. In Ernest L. Boyer's notion of the four scholarships, we found a common ground on which to land our ideas.

Since its publication in 1990, *Scholarship Reconsidered: Priorities of the Professoriate* has evolved theoretically and continues to shape our thinking

Y. Nordkvelle (✉)
Inland Norway University of Applied Sciences, Lillehammer, Norway

G. Jamissen et al. (eds.), *Digital Storytelling in Higher Education*,
Digital Education and Learning, DOI 10.1007/978-3-319-51058-3_1

about the complexity of the roles and tasks of higher education. As academics in higher education, we assume the responsibility of serving the four scholarships of "discovery", "teaching and learning", "integration" and "application". In this book, we have expanded the scholarship of application to a "scholarship of engagement and collaborative action". We will now go on to justify the use of Boyer's model as a way of understanding how and why digital storytelling can be successfully used in higher education.

How often is higher education referred to as solely "bookish" studies, where reading and writing are the only media students get really involved with, and where distant and disengaged "reason" rules? The history of education offers many examples of how teachers have designed teaching differently, building on emotions and engagement, with the aim of empowering students and developing their voice, not only in text but also through the use of images. However, the sources are scattered, and there has been no coordinated effort in this regard. In this book, we will look specifically at examples of openness to voice, emotion and image in higher education and beyond. The classification offered in Boyer's book has evolved as a strong narrative about the function and meaning of higher education in modern society. Our argument is that placing digital storytelling at the heart of the story of the four scholarships is vital for improving higher education in the digital era.

A visual introduction is appropriate here. From Laurentius de Voltolina's painting (circa 1350) of a lecture hall at the University of Bologna, we can see Henricus, the German professor of ethics, talk to his students. His book on the subject is placed on the lectern in front of him, from which he reads or tells stories about the subject. Professor Henricus was a scholar who excelled in the area of Law, and he had compiled his research into a book. The picture illustrates the close historical links between *the scholarship of discovery* and *the scholarship of teaching and learning*. It is still an ideal that practising researchers also teach undergraduate as well as postgraduate students. In the painting, we also see students chatting, probably arguing about something the professor said, or relating it to an observation. The students' activities show how *the scholarship of integration* is also apparent: students discuss matters presented by a teacher to make sense for their future. Last, *the scholarship of engagement and collaborative action* is demonstrated by these background facts: in Bologna, the students hired the teachers, retaining them as long as they were considered useful to the students, while the community checked for the relevance and applicability of the wisdom provided by the professors.

We also think the painting shows us that higher education was not always conceived of as an arena mainly defined by the written word. In fact, texts were difficult to get hold of, and teaching in mediaeval universities was based on teachers reading, or discussing quotes, from texts. Teaching did not rely on the spoken word alone, but incorporated body language and student participation. Students needed both visual and aural competencies for a full understanding of what was being taught.

There is a long way to go from fourteenth-century Bologna to the higher education classrooms of today. Today, Henricus' stories would be taped, streamed or even exposed to reiterating practices of "student-response-systems"; we could even imagine students being invited to create digital stories in order to engage with the puzzles of legal ethics that were Professor Henricus' speciality.

TEACHING WITH ENGAGEMENT AND EMOTION

We know that the students of Bologna hired their own teachers. To survive for more than one term, they needed to communicate well and engage their students. One of the first authors of handbooks for teachers, Hugo St Victor (1096–1141), complained that too many teachers failed to stick to their topic when they taught. They were far too tempted to talk beside the topic with stories and digressions. His complaint goes back to AD 1128, in the cloister school of St Victor in Paris. The philosopher Immanuel Kant (1724–1804) was a teacher more to Hugo's liking: cool, analytical and logical, talking almost like a robot to his students. Kant's former teaching assistant at the University of Kønigsberg (now Kaliningrad), Johann Herder (1744–1803), however, was his direct opposite. He took the idea of evoking students' emotions in his teaching to a peak. His topic was ethnology and folklore, and he taught with fire and thunder, reading poetry, singing and chanting, putting up tableaus for drama and so on. Being a student under Herder meant identifying with the people and cultures in question, seeing it their way. Herder became the most influential intellectual inspiration for the development of the Nordic Folk High School, which emphasises the "living word", the use of body *and* mind, experiential learning and the formation of students' character over the learning of facts. Combining logic with emotion, overview with empathy and mission with clarity are clearly historical origins of the "scholarship of integration". In particular, Immanuel Kant's essay on Enlightenment was a clear argument for the ethical commitment to truth, to the quest for certainty and involving the whole person in pursuit of progress for mankind.

IDENTIFYING A VOICE

The result of learning to be an engaged member of the academic community would be to produce significant contributions. Historically, the academic product would be the oral defence of a thesis. Academics would, if they were diligent, be happy to produce a collection of quotes from the classics as their "book". The art of writing entered the academic curriculum in the fourteenth century as a result of demands from the Merchants' Guild. Trade relations between merchant cities like Genoa and remote places like Iceland relied on the ability to communicate in a friendly and diplomatic way, at a distance and in Latin, so that mutual trust could be built. Teaching the *ars dictaminis*—that is, the art of prose composition— relied on a particular set of rules and so ancient rhetoric from Aristotle, Cicero and Quintilian became essential reading and formed the basis for practice. Impressive writing and overt politeness were necessary to build a strong sense of trust when money was not easily sent. The voice of the writer was shaped by his eloquence and mastery of the rhetorical rules, while trustworthiness was built through knowledge of the classics and the provision of ample quotes. Umberto Eco captured this fascination with good writing in *The Name of the Rose*.

This is still an important part of academic writing, with a great deal of emphasis on finding a suitable and individual tone and voice. One might say that elaborating the voice of young students started in the Renaissance. Mornings were spent listening to formal lectures delivered by expert professors; after lunch, junior teachers took over and led more informal talks. In these sessions, students discussed the contexts and relevance of the expert utterances. Generally, students lacked access to university libraries until the late seventeenth century and so these discussions offered them an opportunity to memorise facts and figures in a familiar, accessible language.

When the Halle University of Germany was established in the late seventeenth century, the theologist August Hermann Franke (1663–1727) assisted poor students by hiring them to teach orphaned children in the Waisenhaus. He spent evenings with the student teachers, inviting them to tell about their experiences through the day, wove the stories together, prompted reflection and developed ideas about how to improve their practice. He called this activity a "seminar", meaning a "seedbed" or "nursery" where ideas of the students met the opinions of the elder and more experienced people, and they reflected together. These seminars became influential learning contexts in German universities from the early nineteenth century onwards and were brought to the USA by the founders of the Johns Hopkins University, where John Dewey graduated in 1884 (Dykhuizen 1961). The seminar model spread out through the USA via the progressive idea of Dewey and his followers.

Educational institutions have traditionally been *fora* for free speech, and the students of University of California, Berkeley, had to fight for their right to speak freely against local government, Governor Reagan and police forces as late as in 1962. The student uprising against suppression of free speech was part of a global movement. It was no accident that bringing free speech into new media also took place in the San Francisco Bay area, where media technologies developed rapidly in the 1970s, 1980s and 1990s.

Free speech and creative writing were closely linked historically while inclusion of the student voice was also an important aspect of the Anglo-American tradition of higher education. The philosopher George Jardine (1742–1827), who worked at the University of Glasgow from 1774, had many poor students who were unable to buy books. The logical thing was to make students write notes from their lectures, develop these notes into essays and then let students read and comment on each other's work. Gaillet (1994) sees his actions as the start of "creative writing" in the curriculum, a trend that was successfully transferred to secondary and tertiary education in the USA. The first writers' school was established in the Soviet Union at the Maxim Gorkij Institute in 1933; creative writing is now commonplace in higher education.

LEARNING WITH IMAGES

While we easily can justify the claim that emotions and voice have historically been important dimensions in higher education, the importance of *the visual* is less obvious. One way of arguing for its importance is to start with medical education. For centuries, medical education was the province of wise women or men who passed on their wisdom to their apprentices; war offered plenty of opportunity to practise surgery. The body was visualised in an illustrated textbook depicting the anatomy of apes, because religion forbid the use of human bodies for these purposes. It was not until 1543 that the doctor Vesalius (1514–1554) had the nerve to break the taboo of dissecting a dead body and let draw what he saw therein. In the Rembrandt (1606–1669) painting, *Dr. Tulp's Anatomy*, the textbook lying at the feet of the dead body is Vesalius' book. The visual verification of what Dr Tulp revealed and the spectators witnessed was compared with the book made 80 years before.

The use of visual aids in academic teaching was further developed by Petrus Ramus (1515–1572) at the University of Paris in the 1550s. Ramus produced tables and figures and included them, together with written material, in textbooks produced for students. The art of teaching gradually turned towards consideration of how students learn, that is, by visualising, speaking eloquently, supporting the acquisition of new information, as the great Czech educator Comenius (1592–1670) developed the "art of teaching", called "Didactics". The textbook that demonstrated his principles, *Orbis pictus*, was published in 1670. Comenius postponed the publication of the book by 30 years until he could find a proper printer who could do justice to the artwork.

The oldest institution for training visual artists has been found in China, dating back to 1104 (Stankiewicz 2007, p. 10), while in Europe, the art academy of Medici was established in 1488. The Accademia del Disigno, established in 1563 in Florence, was both an art education institution and a Guild, but with an emphasis on theoretical perspectives, while most Guilds gave precedence to practice (Stankiewicz 2007, p. 12). Technical and vocational training was initially restricted to the Guilds, where training for the apprentice was a matter of copying the master, being under his tutoring and guidance. Being a "journeyman" meant that, to become a master in your own right, you needed to dissociate yourself from the master and earn your own mastery.

The Guilds became formal settings for training where young artisans studied under the master, undergoing tests to demonstrate that mastery was, eventually, well deserved. Many countries in Europe established national art academies throughout the eighteenth century, first and foremost to celebrate a national tradition and also to counter the strong Italian influence. According to Stankiewicz, the government interest in controlling the style and purpose of the arts was a strong argument for the State to finance and supervise the training of artists (2007, p. 13). In the *conservatoire* model, higher education found a form with important commonalities between all the arts: techniques were learned and practised, and students were also taught aesthetics, art criticism, art history and philosophy. Schools of fine art, music, painting, sculpture, architecture and design were based on such activities. The famous art school in Berlin, the *Bauhaus*, established in 1920, was an example of an art education which merged conflicting ideas about theory versus practice into a consistent workshop method (Christie 2012). In the USA alone today, more than 600 colleges offer programmes that include some elements of media production. Making audio–visual products is now a widespread activity in higher education, and across a broad range of subjects.

The training of engineers and architects was also performed by the Guilds. Masters were contractors who designed and built massive constructions. Michael Knoll explains how the Guilds found it fruitful to create different teams of talented apprentices; these teams would compete with bids to determine how the next section of the building would be built. The *progetti* or project plan required the students to plan, draw, design and make calculations that would result in a solution to the problem at hand. The method of solving problems this way spread across Europe, as well as to the USA, with a strong influence on agricultural colleges, from which John Dewey found great inspiration to formulate the ideas of the "project method" (Knoll 1997). The workshop and the laboratory provided similar spaces in which to test, modify and retest objects and tools, chemical solutions or temperatures. When technical schools and universities started to teach students, they did so in workshops, relying heavily on experienced practitioners as tutors, and with students producing material that was genuinely useful. Massachusetts Institute of Technology was, for a hundred years or so, a collection of workshops, before the emphasis shifted towards the academic and theoretical ways of working after World War I.

HIGHER EDUCATION AND NEW LITERACIES

We fail to understand higher education if we see it as a place where emotions and voice have been excluded, and where images have been shunned. We can, however, argue that emotions, voice and image deserve more space and sharper focus in the curriculum. First and foremost, we have institutions whose main purpose is to train artists to work systematically with emotions and voice as expression in various types of artefacts. In modern film schools, for instance, voice, image and emotions are crucial elements of the curriculum. In many instances, digital storytelling is a way of expressing the unity of these three elements in a similar way.

The visual and the auditory, the emotional and the meaningful are elements of higher education that we will explore further within this book. We believe that making stories digitally and airing them in an educational institution is a profound way of training students to become literate in new media. But, more importantly, it also connects students to the realms of meaning and purpose of higher education that are vital for transforming ordinary literacies into deep engagement and concern for the social consequences of our actions. We can point to some of the historical roots of opportunities to learn via all the senses and apply skills in seeing, drawing, photography, storytelling, essay writing, lab-work and art work in many forms; but these roots have not grown to be considered a normal or necessary element in what we usually think of as higher education.

Cary Jewitt (2008) points out that media literacy and "multi-literacies" originated from radical adult educators in the tradition of Paolo Freire (1921–1997), the Brazilian lawyer and social entrepreneur, who wished to capture the complexity that children and adults experience in meeting so many forms of visual expression. Learning to read them in the classroom or in other situations was their road to liberation. Within this tradition, to be literate means to master the art of reading words on a page. But contemporary theories of multimodal literacies include reading images, video, facial expressions and textual forms that extend to the classroom, the built environment, emotions and moods and beyond.

Theories about the expertise (or "literacy") required in order to read and interpret these different modalities was first expressed by the New London Group, named after the town in which they met. In 1996, in New Hampshire, USA, the group formulated a manifesto for "multiliteracy". The inspiration from Freire gave adult education around the world a strong injection of cultural and social radicalism, which echoed in the student uprisings that continue to take place around the world.

THE FOUR SCHOLARSHIPS, DIGITAL STORYTELLING AND MULTILITERACY

In the rest of this book, we aim to show how digital storytelling might fill important roles in taking higher education into the context of new media. In the section on "The Scholarship of Teaching and Learning", the chapters deal with what the essence of a digital story is and how the boundaries of the genre should be described. They also present projects and experiences relating to how reflection is taught and promoted in teacher education and in the health professions.

In the section on "The Scholarship of Discovery", we present chapters on how digital stories are used in research in medical care, in migration and refugee studies, science communication and establishing understanding in the public regarding research projects. Finally, the section presents a research project in which the process of making digital stories fills an important role as a participatory action research strategy.

The third section, on "The Scholarship of Integration", gives readers an opportunity to look more closely into the intended effects of digital storytelling in training nurses and nursing teachers to become more attentive to the needs of elderly patients. It also presents a case in which students' identity and self-presentation can be interpreted in existential terms. Meanwhile, researchers need to work together when they create new programmes, and one chapter shows how digital stories can clarify and communicate the meanings and identities of researchers in their work. A chapter about how libraries work with students to identify their ways of finding information is another example of how producing audio–visual stories supports students in deriving meaning from complex situations. Another chapter in this section offers a theoretical reflection on how theories of pedagogy and didactics relate to Boyer's notion of "integration" and the European continental tradition of *Bildung* (or self-cultivation) as the aim of higher education.

In the final section, we present chapters on how digital stories can be used to connect with the world outside our colleges and universities. One case study from New Zealand demonstrates how digital stories were used as part of a process of empowering voluntary social work organisations to make a stronger impact on those with whom they worked. In the next chapter, the author discusses how longitudinal storytelling work helps us understand how we might (re)define our notions of engaged scholarship within a community of practice. Digital storytelling as an engaged scholarship practice is considered at the programmatic level in Greece, and in the final chapter, scholars from Baltimore show how digital storytelling is a tool for connecting students and communities with the university.

Sometimes we are challenged by faculty who think learning to teach with new media is too modern or outside of the scope of what teachers in higher education normally are supposed to do. We think differently. Audio–visual expression has always had a space in higher education—and this space is vastly expanded by the current influence of new media. We speak today about living in "the mediatized society", in which communication in general is more and more a multimodal phenomenon (Lundby 2008). Media theorists explain that living a mediatised life demands that we develop new skills and competencies in mastering media, as both producers and consumers of media. Communicating through media substitutes actions formerly performed face to face and alters patterns of communication in daily life. This changes the ways in which people relate to each other and opens new possibilities for communication as well as closing down or hampering some established ways of communication (Hjarvard 2008).

We hope this book will demonstrate that digital stories have relevance for many other dimensions of higher education and that it will illuminate how visual, auditory and emotional communication play together in the process of mediatising higher education. Digital storytelling has the potential to include young and elderly students, teachers of all ages and positions, as well as members of the wider community. This is an essential part of what we understand as the heart of scholarship today.

REFERENCES

Boyer, E. L. (1990). *Scholarship reconsidered. Priorities of the professoriate.* The Carnegie Foundation for the Advancement of Teaching: Princeton.

Christie, I. (2012). From Bauhaus to arthouse. *Sight & Sound, 22*(6), 12–13.

Dykhuizen, G. (1961). John Dewey at Johns Hopkins (1882–1884). *Journal of the History of Ideas, 22*(1), 103–116.

Gaillet, L. L. (1994). An historical perspective on collaborative learning. *Journal of Advanced Composition, 14*(1). Available at: https://www.jstor.org/stable/20865949?seq=1#page_scan_tab_contents. Accessed 31 Oct 2016.

Hjarvard, S. (2008). The mediatization of society. "A theory of the media as agents of social and cultural change". *Nordicom Review, 29*(2), 105–134.

Jewitt, C. (2008). *Technology, literacy, learning: A multimodality approach.* London: Routledge.

Knoll, M. (1997). The project method: Its vocational education origin and international development. *Journal of Industrial Teacher Education, 34*(3), 59–80.

Lundby, K. (Ed.) (2008). *Digital storytelling, mediatized stories: Self-representations in new media.* New York: Peter Lang.

Stankiewicz, M. A. (2007). Capitalizing art education: Mapping international histories. In L. Bresler (Ed.), *International handbook of research in arts education* (pp. 7–30). New York: Springer.

PART 1

The Scholarship of Teaching and Learning

CHAPTER 2

Introduction to the Scholarship of Teaching and Learning

Pip Hardy

In his 1994 report on scholarship, Ernest Boyer contends that research is useless unless it is informed by, and integrated with, practice. Furthermore, he suggests that research should be creatively communicated to others and be applicable in the service of individuals, communities and societies in such a way that theory both informs and is informed by practice (Boyer 1994).

Boyer's scholarship of teaching describes activities that not only transmit knowledge but also transform and extend that knowledge. In this way, teaching and learning become what Parker Palmer describes as "communal activities" (Palmer 1983). Teaching and learning should not be separated. Teachers must use their understanding, their creativity and all the tools of pedagogy available to them to convey their knowledge and understanding to their students. In order to do this well, teachers must be continuous

P. Hardy (✉)
Pilgrim Projects, Cambridge, UK

© The Author(s) 2017
G. Jamissen et al. (eds.), *Digital Storytelling in Higher Education,*
Digital Education and Learning, DOI 10.1007/978-3-319-51058-3_2

learners themselves, constantly searching for the most appropriate ways to connect their own knowledge and insight with the needs of their students.

One of these needs, in a world characterised by complexity and uncertainty, is to recognise that *knowing* must contend with *being* for a place at the core of pedagogy (Barnett 2012). A more holistic pedagogic approach that is inclusive of everyone within the academy will address the vision of developing wisdom that addresses hearts *and* minds, providing individuals and communities with the capacity for flexibility and creativity, and the ability to *be* as well as to *know*. Cognitive psychologist Jerome Bruner describes this as incorporating the science of the concrete (*logico scientific*) as well as the science of the imagination (*narrative*) (Bruner 1986).

Stories enable us to go beyond facts that can easily be counted and measured, and cultivate the capacity to tap into imaginations and narratives in order to gain insight and wisdom. Digital stories and digital storytelling (DS) exemplify Illich's idea of convivial tools, that is, those items or practices that "give each person who uses them the greatest opportunity to enrich the environment with the fruits of his or her vision" (Illich 1973).

In addition to educating people who will be able to "enrich the environment", it behoves those of us engaged in the pursuit of higher education to remember that one of the characteristics of a professional is the ability to reflect on and learn from practice (Schön 1983). Studying the links between higher education and professional practice, Richard Winter (Winter 1992) proposed that the professional role should include:

- A requirement that understanding should continually develop through reflection upon practice
- Interpretive responsibility towards an always incomplete body of knowledge
- A basis in a complex set of ethical principles
- An understanding of the importance of affective dimensions (conscious and unconscious)

The chapters in this section bear testament to the centrality of reflection in education for professional practice and to the potential of classical DS to encourage and support the skills necessary to creatively interpret knowledge while also attending to the ethical and affective dimensions of the work.

We begin, then, in Chap. 3, with an invitation from Joe Lambert and Brooke Hessler to explore DS through the analytical lens of Meyer and

Land's *threshold concepts*, that is, those ideas that challenge us to see things in new ways by pushing us just beyond the threshold of our existing knowledge.

> A threshold concept can be considered as akin to a portal, opening up a new and previously inaccessible way of thinking about something. It represents a transformed way of understanding, or interpreting, or viewing something without which the learner cannot progress. (Meyer and Land 2003)

Hessler and Lambert draw on their many years of experience in community engagement and participatory media pedagogies to share some of what they consider to be the essential qualities of DS as a practice of critical literacy. They then situate DS within the framework of threshold concepts, arguing that, as a practice, DS is transformative, probably irreversible, integrative and (often) bordering on other thresholds to new areas of discovery. Readers are then invited to engage in an ongoing dialogue about threshold concepts of digital storywork and its potential as a transformative pedagogy.

Chapter 4 turns to the use of DS with medical students. The UK General Medical Council requires doctors to "systematically reflect on practice" (GMC 2009). However, reflection in medical school is often taught in a formulaic way that doesn't always make sense to students; nor does it result in deep or meaningful reflection. "Soft" skills, such as reflection and communication are considered secondary to clinical skills and are accorded little time or attention in the crowded clinical curriculum.

The degree to which the students were able to integrate their clinical knowledge with their ability to empathise and contemplate meeting challenges in new and creative ways is apparent in the stories they produced, while the implications for further practice are clearly articulated in their reflective statements about the process. The chapter also touches on some of the challenges inherent in assessing DS and digital stories and describes the construction of an approach that was intended to be itself reflective, thoughtful, innovative and rigorous.

In Chap. 5, Bonnie Thompson Long and Tony Hall extend the discourse on reflection using Barrett's and Moon's ideas about creative and novel representations of reflection (Barrett 2006; Moon 2004), including DS in their work with education students. Their longitudinal research study set out to discover whether integrating storytelling with digital technologies would result in deeper reflection. In addition, they wondered whether this approach could move teachers beyond the role of technician and enable them to respond to challenges in more holistic ways, with intuition, emotion and passion, as well as technical, pedagogical knowledge skills. Clearly, this process both requires, and cultivates the capacity for, deep reflection, practical knowledge and the ability to learn from experience.

Using Design Based Research methodology, Long and Hall's research has resulted in the R-NEST model encompassing five main themes: reflection, narrative, engagement, sociality and technology in a model that enumerates key criteria and principles for developing and utilising DS to deepen reflection.

In Chap. 6, Kim Anderson describes using DS with postgraduate social work students to give them insight into the use of DS as a therapeutic tool with clients. Students created, and subsequently analysed, stories of adversity, particularly in relation to race, victimisation, poverty, disability and death. Analysis of themes revealed two of Schön's reflective patterns (Schön 1983). Firstly, reflection-in-action involved connecting with feelings, emotions and prior experiences while attending to the technical and narrative aspects of digital story creation and dissemination. Secondly, reflection-on-action took place during the analysis of how the DS process impacted students' personal and professional learning. Anderson's project suggests that DS can be an effective form of experiential learning to help students increase their technical and therapeutic self-efficacy while also providing an avenue for them to engage in deep reflective practice.

In the last chapter in this section, Daniela Gachago and Pam Sykes explore the ethical challenges of introducing a highly personal, emotional and process-oriented approach into the educational curriculum in South Africa. Drawing on their own experiences and utilising a dialogic approach, the authors offer "snapshots" that capture their responses to ethical issues such as the need for emotional support and follow-up, appropriate processes for assessment, handling strong emotions and difficult dialogues, circumstances around public sharing of stories, safety and the possibilities of triggering post-traumatic stress responses. The authors' openness and generosity in speaking about their personal and professional responses to these issues offer new insights into both the challenges and possible responses to some of the complex ethical dilemmas faced by anyone who facilitates DS workshops.

References

Barnett, R. (2012). Learning for an unknown future. *Higher Education Research & Development, 31,* 65–77.

Barrett, H. (2006). Researching and evaluating digital storytelling as a deep learning tool. *Technology and Teacher Education Annual, 1,* 647.

Boyer, E. L. (1994). *Scholarship reconsidered: Priorities of the professoriate.* Princeton: The Carnegie Foundation for the advancement of teaching.

Bruner, J. (1986). *Actual minds, possible worlds.* Cambridge, MA/London: Harvard University Press.

GMC. (2009). *Tomorrow's doctors: Outcomes and standards for undergraduate medical education.* Manchester: General Medical Council.

Illich, I. (1973). *Tools for conviviality.* New York: Harper and Row.

Meyer, J. H. F., & Land, R. (2003). Threshold concepts and troublesome knowledge: Linkages to ways of thinking and practising. In C. Rust (Ed.), *Improving student learning – Theory and practice ten years on.* Oxford: Oxford Centre for Staff and Learning Development (OCSLD).

Moon, J. (2004). *Handbook of reflective and experiential learning: Theory and practice.* Abingdon: Routledge and Falmer.

Palmer, P. J. (1983). *To know as we are known.* New York: Harper & Row.

Schön, D. (1983). *The reflective practitioner: How professionals think in action.* New York: Basic books.

Winter, R. (1992). The assessment Programme – Competence-based education at professional/Honours degree level. *Competence and Assessment, 20,* 14–18.

CHAPTER 3

Threshold Concepts in Digital Storytelling: Naming What We Know About Storywork

Brooke Hessler and Joe Lambert

INTRODUCTION

"If it looks like a duck and sounds like a duck, then it's a duck." As former Texans (if such a thing is possible), we basically agree that this statement is one of the things wrong with Texas. Sometimes things look and sound like ducks but are not ducks. Sometimes things are ducks that neither look nor sound like them. And a lot of the time what matters most isn't whether the thing is a duck but whether it has an essential "duckness," if you will: a quality of swimming or waddling or brooding or deliciousness that especially intrigues or delights us.

And so it goes with digital storytelling.

Or at least that is what we hope to explore in this chapter. With more than 20 years each using participatory media pedagogies in and beyond college classrooms, we find ourselves (as will many of our co-contributors in this volume) observing what digital storytelling has become and considering what, in essence, it distinctively retains and can more deeply be.

B. Hessler (✉)
California College of the Arts, Oakland, CA, USA

J. Lambert
StoryCenter, Berkeley, CA, USA

© The Author(s) 2017   19
G. Jamissen et al. (eds.), *Digital Storytelling in Higher Education*,
Digital Education and Learning, DOI 10.1007/978-3-319-51058-3_3

Consider this: two videos of similar quality in terms of format, topic, and style; each three minutes long, telling a first-person story through voiceover narration and a sequence of images. Both done as academic homework assignments. One was produced through a process of guided critical reflection, story-sharing, and collaborative making; the other was assembled in a rush to meet a deadline—the student read the assignment, was skillful enough as a writer and video editor to compose a nice project on her own, and completed the whole thing in a few hours—the same as she might crank out any other homework task. Are both projects digital stories? Yes. Are both projects examples of digital storytelling? Yes and no. If we consider digital storytelling a genre, and if we define genre simply as a recognizable literary format, then yes both students did the work of digital storytelling. And if we consider digital storytelling a tool for pedagogy we may come to a similar conclusion: in both cases, the instructor assigned digital storytelling to achieve a set of learning objectives. But if you are reading this chapter, you have likely concluded that digital storytelling—as a genre and as a pedagogy—is more than the homeworking of reflective videos. The task of the scholarship of teaching and learning (SOTL) is to help us acquire a more sensitive understanding of the principles and practices that make digital storytelling a potentially transformative educational experience—principles and practices of storywork that may not always conform to the kinds of projects typically viewed as digital stories. Indeed, such storywork need not be digital at all.

What's in a Name? Digital Storytelling as Genre and Pedagogy

As we collaborate with SOTL researchers worldwide to understand how digital storytelling works, it is helpful to clarify our terms. For years, some pedagogical scholars foregrounded digital storytelling as a way to teach and practice media literacy in relationship to dominant media institutions and representations. In 1998, for example, Kathleen Tyner argued for the relevance of digital storytelling and other participatory media practices:

> The central objective for the study of media representation as a cognitive approach to media production is that of voice. Voice is a concept that transcends the vagaries of the image or even the politics of identity. Specifically, media production gives voice to students who are otherwise silenced in their schools and communities. It allows students to represent their experiences

and their communities as cultural insiders, instead of the incessant misrepresentation of them by media producers outside their communities. (p. 185)

This emphasis on voice, on democratization of media production, was contrasted with an emphasis on a creative genre, an arts practice, within the developing range of arts practices made possible by broad access to information technologies. Several of us as early proponents and practitioners of the work (including Dana Atchley, Daniel Meadows, Pedro Meyer, Abbe Don) saw the digital short film as a new genre, as "sonnets from the people" as Daniel Meadows described it (Kidd 2005, pp. 66–85). Still others, particularly in the academic realm, wanted to contextualize the work within the broad ecology of media production and consumption (including the original Queenstown University of Technology group of John Hartley, Helen Klaebe, Jean Burgess, Kelly McWilliam, and Kristina Spurgeon; Norway's Knut Lundby and Grete Jamissen; and more recent scholars Pip Hardy, Bryan Alexander, Nancy Thumim, Mark Dunford, and Tricia Jenkins), situating the various models growing out of the Center for Digital Storytelling (CDS) methods as an encompassing genre.

As a genre, we would argue that digital storytelling is better understood through the lens of theorists like Carolyn Miller who assert that genres in all media, old and new, develop as situated forms of social action. Miller was concerned with the formulation of genre as a social construction motivated by the pressing understandings and needs, the exigencies, of both audience and speaker. In what became a seminal essay for the public turn in college writing, Miller argued that exigencies are "a form of social knowledge—a mutual construing of objects, events, interests, and purposes that not only links them but also makes them what they are: an objectified social need" (1984, p. 157). Genres arise from recurrent rhetorical situations (p. 159). In other words, whether we are examining a haiku or a business memo or an Instagram selfie, the familiar format, style, and content evolved from a repeated need to communicate in that particular way to or with a particular audience. So a business memo looks and functions as it does because that method has proven effective for many years within that environment. And its kindred genre, the email message, looks a lot like a memo (even retaining rhetorical remnants like "cc:" for "carbon copy") because busy professionals still find it effective to communicate in de facto memos.

Likewise, digital storytelling arose as a genre because participatory media needed to happen. Everyday people—whose lives were increasingly

influenced by media—needed to see their own stories on screens; they
needed to see their points of view broadcast along with everyone else's.
They needed the opportunity to compose and communicate and replicate
and challenge the stories told to and about them through videos and other
media—only in this way can social media be inclusive in fact and not just
in name. Tweets, blogs, and digital stories are kindred genres performing
personal and public expression and connection.

Around the same time that participatory media/community arts activists were devising ways to make multimedia composing more accessible
to ordinary people, researchers of teaching and learning were experi-
menting with ways to incorporate mass media into college communication classes—and they were debating the extent to which ideology and
social criticism were essential to academic writing instruction, given its
status as a gateway to educated citizenship (see, e.g., McComiskey 2002).
Multimedia social–epistemic rhetoric pedagogies arose whereby scholars
such as James Berlin built upon Marshal McLuhan and Paolo Freire to
argue that responsible pedagogy must train college students to critique
media from the inside out—as makers of television scripts and video
recordings, for example—because their full citizenship in a global society
depends on their ability to master the media that most influence their lives
(Berlin 1996, pp. 123–56). A key principle of social–epistemic rhetoric is
that knowledge itself exists as a dialectic between the individual, a community, and their material conditions—educators who assign new media
projects are potentially engaging students in digital genres not only to
build their digital literacy skills but also to immerse them in a process
of interdependent, interactive meaning-making. The digital-storytelling-
as-social-activism movement, with its public workshops and educational
programming, coinciding with the increasing accessibility of digital media,
gave teachers the training, tools, models, and communities of practice
needed to realistically assign digital storytelling projects that foster critical
digital literacy, civic literacy, and greater self-awareness.

In this regard, digital storytelling is a pedagogical tool, yes, but it is also
pedagogy—not just a *tool* for pedagogy. And pedagogy itself is not merely
a method of teaching; it is a considered perspective on what teaching and
learning can be. To adapt a definition by Nancy Myers, we view pedagogy as

> an ethical philosophy of teaching that accounts for the complex matrix of
> people, knowledge, and practice within the immediacy of each [encounter] ….
> [T]he regular, connected and articulated choices made from within a realm

of possibilities and then acted on. Historically, it accounts for the goals of the institution and to some extent society: it manifests in the goals of the individual teacher [facilitator], which may include an agenda to help students [storytellers] learn to critique both the institution and society; and it makes room for the goals of the individual students. (Tate et al. 2013, p. 3)

As we proceed through this reflection on the pedagogical ethos of digital storytelling, we are intentionally foregrounding the approach that evolved through CDS because of its broad influence on academic adaptations of digital storytelling (as documented by, e.g., Alexander 2011; Hull and Katz 2006; Gregori-Signes and Brigido-Corachan 2014; Jamissen and Skou 2010; Lambert 2013) and because, of course, it is the narrative we know best.

The CDS approach to digital storytelling was informed by the traditions of community arts and community-based media practices representing a half-century of social activist, grassroots arts making. The concepts and pedagogical perspectives of these practitioners were aligned with critical pedagogy/liberationist educational practices. A central aspect of these perspectives was *consciencization*, the ability of the learner/storyteller to grasp their own metacognitive process within the context of their social situation (Freire 1970). This underscores why digital storytelling has always been, at heart, an approach that is potentially transformative rather than narrowly instrumental. Granted, teaching someone the basic skills of making a video from scratch can be an empowering and perhaps transformative lesson, but that functional literacy is opening a door to a much richer array of literate practices and interactions. Digital storytelling has been an especially good fit for service-learning educators because of its kindred heritage in experiential and liberatory pedagogies and its shared commitment to transformative learning principles such as critical reflection, collaboration, and reciprocal exchanges of expertise between participants (Eyler and Giles 1999; Hessler and Taggart 2004; Hull 2003).

Treating digital storytelling as both individual and social transformation helps to situate the practice appropriately. As Jack Mezirow established in his arguments on transformative processes in education, students' deep learning emerges from an epistemological shift in their frame of reference (1997). When practiced as a transformative rather than summative process, digital storytelling helps storytellers look at events or issues through the lens of personal experience, but then also to look at the way they are looking, on how they are working toward a process of discovery.

How does this self-reflexivity happen? How can we facilitate learning in a way more likely to give storytellers a transformative experience? This chapter is our initial attempt to clarify and articulate the ways expert facilitators approach digital storytelling as a potential transformative learning experience—to name what we know—or what we believe to be true—about the principles and practices of storywork. The book that inspired this essay, *Naming What We Know: Threshold Concepts of Writing Studies* makes 37 assertions that serve as threshold concepts within that discipline, "foundational assumptions that inform student learning across time," such as: "Writing Enacts and Creates Identities and Ideologies" and "All Writers Have More to Learn" (Adler-Kassner and Wardle 2015). Our present ambition is more modest: to offer a set of assertions that we believe are ripe for further discussion within the digital storytelling community of practice. While we note that the work of digital storytelling, especially when done within first-year seminars, is sometimes viewed as a subspecialty of writing studies—and therefore arguably subject to the same threshold concepts as that discipline—we approach digital storytelling as yet another hippogriff, a category of rhetorical, aesthetic, social, and cultural studies that is more complex (and more magical) when viewed in terms of what it can afford the imaginative narrator. Given the diversity of the contexts and curricula where digital storytelling is taught, we believe that threshold concepts can give us some of the language needed to talk in more precise ways about the epistemological, metacognitive, and pedagogical dimensions of digital storytelling.

Threshold Concepts, Once Over Lightly

Over the last decade, the study of threshold concepts has become an international movement in the SOTL. The work began as part of a UK-based study of undergraduate learning environments by the Higher Education Academy, paying special attention to ways that students get stuck trying to understand complex topics within their disciplines. In their analysis of Economics students, Meyer and Land observed a pattern in the ways students worked through "troublesome knowledge"—ideas they might learn superficially to pass a test but never fully understand, partly because the ideas themselves demand a radically different way of viewing the world, or themselves, or how things appear to function in everyday life (Meyer and Land 2006; Meyer et al. 2010). An example is the term "depreciation"—an idea that makes sense to economists but is experienced by ordinary consumers as a frustrating rationale for why a new car loses 10 percent of its value the moment you drive it off the dealer's lot. Understanding depreciation means understanding how an array of financial, psychological, environmental, and cultural factors can make something measurably less valuable even if the thing itself hasn't actually changed. It's a conceptual gateway essential for thinking like an economist. Every craft and academic discipline has such concepts; they are ideas to master as well as critical perspectives on the kinds of problem-solving done in and beyond the studio or classroom.

Scholars compiling threshold concepts often present them as key terms like "depreciation" above; other times, the concepts may take the form of assertions, such as "Writing is a social and rhetorical activity" (Adler-Kassner and Wardle 2015). As Chris Anson notes, when a threshold concept is phrased as an assertion, it becomes less of a buzzword and more of a heuristic, an invitation to discussion among reflective practitioners (2015). In this spirit, we composed our initial set of threshold concepts as assertions worthy of further reflection and dialogue at and beyond our wiki: dsconcepts.wikispaces.com.

THRESHOLD CONCEPTS OF [DIGITAL] STORYWORK

According to Meyer and Land (2006, pp. 7–8), a threshold concept in any field of endeavor will be:

- Transformative: once understood, its potential effect is a significant shift in the student's perception of the subject.
- Probably irreversible: this change of perspective is unlikely to be forgotten.
- Integrative: it exposes the previously hidden interrelatedness of something.
- Possibly often (though not necessarily always) bounded in that any conceptual space will have terminal frontiers, bordering with thresholds into new conceptual areas.
- Potentially (though not necessarily) troublesome: because they seem counterintuitive, butting up against the student's current ways of knowing—ritual knowledge, tacit knowledge, and so on.

We are especially interested in concepts which may on the surface seem self-evident, but from a critical perspective become a more nuanced set of core assumptions that permeate storywork. In the next section, we briefly introduce eight potential threshold concepts, landing on one that undergirds the rest: every story matters.

Concept 1: Intimacy and Safety Inform Narrative

As digital storytelling methods grew from their community arts and technology literacy origins, both practitioners and researchers around the world began to see potential applications for healing and personal growth (see, e.g., Bailey 2011; Goodman and Newman 2014; Haigh and Hardy 2011; Jamissen and Haug 2014). Personal narratives that disclose intimate or painful details may be viewed as inappropriate for some contexts and cultures; however, when responsibly scaffolded, storytelling can foster a level of supportiveness and mutual respect that brings people together in ways that are fundamental to our humanity. As many experienced practitioners can attest, it matters little if you ask people to tell you a story about a subject from a safe distance, for if they sense the opportunity to explore unconsidered, or unprocessed, life experience, at least one person in ten will choose to disclose something that carries great emotional weight. The troublesome aspect of this concept is that a willingness to "look at the dragon" of one's experience is precisely what leads to a potential transformation—for the storyteller and for the perceived quality of the final story.

Concept 2: Collaborative Making Is a Means of Communication and Communion

Digital storytelling was conceived as a group dynamic informed by skillful facilitation. While many software designers, educators, and other professionals continue to experiment with ways to scale the method as a "do-it-yourself" activity, the stories arising from these methods miss an important dimension of the process and may hold less power for the storyteller and intended audience. The emphasis on a group dynamic in the classroom or workshop, the story circle, the joint tutorial process, the encouragement of participants assisting each other through the process, and the final screening, is precisely what makes the experience effective for participants. Participant storytellers recognize one another as peers as they move through a shared creative struggle and culminating experience. The collaborative environment not only allows for the stories' communicative power to be considered and improved, but for a deeper level of communion to take place. This is critical to the transformative change that many storytellers experience coming through a workshop or classroom implementation that distinguishes the practice from other forms of media and writing experiences.

Concept 3: Digital Storytelling Is a Form of Critical Literacy

This is the kind of statement that may seem obvious to facilitators, but not so obvious to people outside our community of practice who experience mostly the end product, the video, and reasonably conclude that we are foremost teaching a form of *functional* media literacy: the making of videos for social media. What makes the assertion a potential threshold concept is an understanding of the idea of *critical literacy*—an ability to deploy language to examine our ongoing development, to reveal the subjective positions from which we make sense of the world and act in it (Shor 1999)—and how the process of making and sharing digital stories about pivotal moments can foster that level of critical reflection.

The structure of the well-traveled Seven Steps introductory presentation by CDS/StoryCenter grew from framing the story process as a metacognitive event: having storytellers ask themselves not just "What is the story about?" but "Why does it matter right now?" often leads them to make objects of the feelings, memories, influences, ideas, and ideologies that they may or may not have considered prior to the storytelling experience. This critically reflective aspect of the storywork process is yet another component of the transformative potential of the practice.

Concept 4: Constraints Foster Creative Breakthroughs

Digital stories are constrained principally by word count—typically 250–375 words in the practice of CDS/StoryCenter and many other facilitators. This brevity has been critiqued as forcing a mold onto what might be comfortably approached as a more open-ended, participant-centered process of choices. The intuitive argument is that creative choice is expanded by an open-ended process. As many working artists have learned, open-ended choice is not freedom. Choice can be another kind of tyranny, masquerading as opportunity. Constraints (in terms of time, visual artifacts, sound effects, or other elements) challenge the storyteller to become a more ingenious narrator, approaching more carefully the myriad possibilities of video as a creative genre, to unleash or invent a choice. As digital storytelling projects are often the first or early creative experiences in these toolsets for storytellers, the constraints allow for deeper exploration into a limited set of resources.

Concept 5: Multimodal Composition Is a Cognitive Activity

As has been argued about composing academic texts in multiple modalities or media (see, e.g., Brooke 2013; Fleckenstein 2010; Palmeri 2012), composing a digital story requires a complex series of decisions that access multiple intelligences (Gardner 1983), multiple strategies for engaging and interpreting knowledge about oneself and the world. Multimodal composition invites participant storytellers to lean into the unique strengths of their cognition processes. Some people compose in visual sequence to inform their auditory process of narration, while others attach significance and think through the mood of a piece of background music before considering the focus and emphasis of the text and images. The interrelationship of the layers of meaning becomes itself a cognitive process that considers the minute choices moment to moment, as well as the overall feel/impact of the entire work. Film as a communicative genre has its own 100-year discourse about the innumerable ways in which the filmmaker makes choices in design; digital storytelling allows for us now to explore how those lessons can be part of a much broader compositional opportunity for student novices and for the public.

Concept 6: Choices in Design Aesthetics Inform and Are Informed by Literacies, Culture, and Ideology

Some theorists and practitioners in digital storytelling have labored to define aesthetic success in the design of a digital story, in the practical service of rubric-based assessment or for other purposes. While we appreciate (and continue to develop) ways to integrate formative and summative assessment into academically assigned storywork, we are compelled to observe that these attempts usually lead one to learn just as much about who is doing the assessment, and what they are signifying about themselves or their institutional context.

From our perspective, digital storytelling shares with the community arts movement the understanding that aesthetics are fluid constructions that reflect the literacies, culture, and ideological assumptions of those doing a critique. What constitutes cliché and what constitutes aesthetic originality are assessed in light of the storyteller's own exposure to works of art, experience with art making, familiarity with the dynamics of critical assessment, and of course their culturally or ideologically bounded perspectives. Critical self-awareness about what one is indicating about oneself through an artistic choice is itself a highly developed literacy. In many contexts, the facilitator is of a different culture, ideological perspective, and literacy level than her students. Where graded assessments are required for digital stories, we recommend co-constructing a rubric or metric of success alongside students, holding their design perspectives and your own as part of the process, and using this process as an inroad to discussing what aesthetics mean and how diversely they may matter.

Concept 7: Listening Is an Ethic and a Craft

Listening is an activity that considerate people believe they are already doing thoughtfully and fairly—particularly when engaged in a course or workshop that fosters (or strives for) the kind of democratic environment described above. The instructor herself may believe that by virtue of the fact students are sitting in a circle sharing stories, or responding to one another on a discussion board, she is automatically fostering attentive listening. But listening requires self-discipline and self-awareness.

Scholars of transformative learning have documented a taxonomy of listening that is helpful for explaining why listening is more than meets the ear. Extending communication studies by Peter Senge and others, Otto Scharmer notes four main types of listening: (1) downloading (listening for confirmations of what you already expect or believe); (2) factual listening (noting new and novel information that compares or contrasts with what you believe you know); (3) empathic listening (concentrating on aspects of the speaker's story to which you can emotionally connect, and in that way making the other person's story align with your own); and (4) generative listening (seeking to understand what the speaker is trying to say, to know his or her story at a deeper level, often by attending to body language or other cues that transcend the information being spoken) (Scharmer 2009).

In storywork, generative listening is essential for a co-creative experience, for everyone's story to be heard. When we speak of "deep listening," we are speaking about the interplay of someone working out an idea
before an audience, and how that audience demonstrably holds that idea,
works through it, and provides insightful commentary and reflection on
the idea. The quality of listening is both somatic, in terms of attentive-
ness and body language, and as importantly, cognitive and metacognitive, in demonstrating how the speaker's words were absorbed, held, and
thoroughly considered, before a response was made. Sometimes this is
evinced by how accurately someone remembers certain phrases expressing
a concept, and sometimes in how well they re-summarize the gist of the
storyteller's meaning. Such listening takes practice, and a sincere conviction that every story matters.

Concept 8: Every Story Matters

This is our most radical assertion. Acknowledging that every story matters—in our classroom, in a public workshop, in a community literacy
center—may seem sweetly self-evident. Inviting people from rival perspectives to compose and communicate their views is, after all, what engaged
educators most consistently attempt to do, whether mentoring students
as teaching artists or as city planners or as oral historians or as digital storytellers. But an interesting shift arises, particularly in higher education,
when we frame story-sharing as a means of diversity training or intercultural inquiry: stories seem to become important because of who or what
the teller represents—an unconventional point of view, a source of wisdom
on a particular episode in history, a spokesperson for a marginalized community. Such encounters help us achieve important academic aims, such
as giving students an opportunity to cultivate empathy and openness, for
example (AAC&U 2015). But as the Museum of the Person's founder
Karen Worcman reminds us, "Every person's story matters because every
person matters," and not because of what the story may represent or how
it might be used (Misorelli and Worcman 2016). Storyworkers may indeed
become story curators, and some stories will connect with a particular purpose or audience more than others, but every person's narrative deserves
equal care and consideration. The digital storytelling educator bears an
extra responsibility to reinforce this principle among participants who may
become storyworkers themselves.

CROSSING THE THRESHOLD: GETTING INTO TROUBLE

What are the consequences of believing—or acting upon, or teaching—those eight assertions about digital storywork? For starters, perhaps clarity of purpose. As we wrote our way through the initial list, we found our paragraphs evolving from a relatively conventional scholarly synthesis to a tone rather like a manifesto. We think this is a good thing. As we grappled with the transformative and troublesome dimensions of each threshold concept, we found, as we hope you will too, opportunities for critical reflection about our mission as educators.

We are committed to universal access to the production of a digital story as a human right. We view this as a core condition to a sense of agency in each individual in relationship to the larger social project. Like our colleagues in organizations like the Museum of the Person in Brazil, StoryCorps in the United States, and countless local, regional, and international organizations that emphasize the representation of ordinary people, we see a relationship between signifying every citizen with a story and creating the basis for healthy democracy.

In this sense, one's first digital story is a form of membership, a representation of your deeply considered insights and voice into a society greatly dominated by the screens of social media, film, and television. As Guillermo Gomez Peña once said in performance, "the existential question for us as citizens in the twenty-first century is TV or not TV." We realize the power of the moving image to validate experience, and we want everyone to share in the power of media publication, even if that publication only reaches the moment of being projected on a wall of a workshop.

This perspective is troubling because it suggests that, in the long run, any formal, or informal, ways that we segregate media producers from media consumers is unhealthy and counterproductive for society. In cultures that thoroughly accept media consumption as central to civic life, we are suggesting that citizens should feel empowered to speak back with their own stories, extending their experiences, memories, and perspectives into the media landscape. Put another way, we worry less about the "mediocrity" of the masses making media than the single voice being silenced—one by which a small or large transformation might be made possible.

For many, the decentralization of authority, both political and artistic, that comes from this process is implicitly troubling, and they would prefer to separate the social justice component of digital storytelling from the more general educational concern. However, lacking the impulse to extend these literacies to every single person inevitably privileges those with aptitudes or proclivities in the technical toolsets, with strong and well-formed insights, with a flair for language and narrative construction. Creating environments where all those differences and capabilities are appreciated, but where none are overly privileged, becomes the distinct challenge for the educator.

In our conception of storywork, we start with encouraging the storytellers' sense of fundamental authority on their own personal experience. Even as they may be framing a subject, or addressing a broader issue, their starting point is how they understand their own awareness of the way the story works, where it currently works *upon them*, and where with group reflection and individual feedback, they would like to transform those understandings. Note that we can borrow the subject–object perspective via Kegan's integration of Piaget/Erickson in the field of psychology to suggest that these processes can be viewed as significant developmental epistemological shifts. *The story that has been telling you*, to which you have been subject, becomes *the story you can tell*, that which you can now make object (Kegan 1983, 1994). The process is both to listen deeply to the way in which the storyteller initially presents their concept and to encourage group and individual inquiry into the how and why of the storyteller's initial enthusiasm or reticence in telling that story.

While this may seem obvious as a condition of progressive educational practice, this perspective is, again, "troublesome" in scenarios where the professor or facilitator is perceived as the storytelling expert—particularly when that expert is assigning an academic grade for the story. If our pedagogy is rooted in the belief that every story matters, we must teach in a way that ensures students approach each step in the process as democratic and collaborative, not just for the sake of politeness but because the stories being shared have valuable insights for everyone in the room. This means that the story circle, for example, is not a generic form of peer review. The purpose of that sharing of story drafts is not just to get the story done, nor revised into a form that entertains or impresses the group, nor edited well enough to earn a decent grade; the purpose is to support the telling of the story and the listening to the story—which, in turn, may help participants to become more empathetic, attentive, and collaborative learners.

We understand that in an academic environment with larger class sizes and a curriculum distributed over many weeks it can be challenging to replicate the level of interpersonal care that we try to foster in small group intensive workshop environments. But coaching students to serve as deputy co-facilitators and practicing the ritual of holding space and allocating minutes of silence, if needed, to help a storyteller think through and articulate an idea, are ways that we can begin to teach listening as a discipline and as a way to demonstrate mutual respect. Every comment, every decision about how we engage participants, every way that we organize and manage the production process, we are making sure participants are aware of their own creative choices, and power, in the situation.

Informed by this perspective, we have found that not only does the experience of the learning environment improve but so do the stories.

Those of us working as practitioners can easily look back at our last workshop or classroom experience and recognize the complexity of holding these concepts while simply trying to survive getting a group of stories to completion. The average classroom teacher, or community-based facilitator, much less the participant storytellers, is not constructing his or her efforts with a checklist of threshold concepts. But as scholars of teaching and learning, we can use these concepts to illuminate the ways in which transformative learning is constructed not just of methods and techniques but also of values, ethics, and social and self-awareness. We look forward to expanding this discussion with our colleagues and friends in the field.

REFERENCES

Adler-Kassner, L., & Wardle, E. (2015). *Naming what we know: Threshold concepts of writing studies*. Boulder: University of Colorado Press.

Alexander, B. (2011). *The new digital storytelling: Creating narratives with new media*. Santa Barbara: Praeger.

Anson, C. (2015). Crossing thresholds: What's to know about writing across the curriculum? In L. Adler-Kassner & E. Wardle (Eds.), *Naming what we know: Threshold concepts of writing studies* (pp. 203–219). Boulder: University of Colorado Press.

Association of American Colleges & Universities (AAC&U). (2015). *VALUE: Valid assessment of learning in undergraduate education*. Retrieved August 1, 2016, from https://www.aacu.org/value

Bailey, B. (2011). "When I make a film, it's out of my head": Expressing emotion and healing through digital filmmaking in the classroom. *Digital Culture and Education (3)*. Retrieved from http://www.digitalcultureandeducation.com/volume-3/

Berlin, J. A. (1996). *Rhetorics, poetics, and cultures: Refiguring college English studies*. West Lafayette: Parlor Press.

Brooke, C. (2013). New media pedagogy. In G. Tate, A. Rupiper Taggart, K. Schick, & H. B. Hessler (Eds.), *A guide to composition pedagogies* (2nd ed., pp. 177–193). New York: Oxford University Press.

Dunford, M., & Jenkins, T. (2015). Understanding the media literacy of digital storytelling. *Media Education Research Journal, 5*(2), 26–41.

Eyler, J., & Giles Jr., D. E. (1999). *Where's the learning in service-learning?* San Francisco: Jossey-Bass.

Fleckenstein, K. S. (2010). *Vision, rhetoric, and social action in the composition classroom.* Carbondale: Southern Illinois University Press.

Freire, P. (1970). *Pedagogy of the oppressed.* New York: Bloomsbury.

Gardner, H. (1983). *Frames of mind: The theory of multiple intelligences.* New York: Basic Books.

Goodman, R., & Newman, D. (2014). Testing a digital storytelling intervention to reduce stress in adolescent females. *Storytelling, Self, Society, 10*(2), 177–193.

Gregori-Signes, C., & Brigido-Corcachan, A. M. (Eds.). (2014). *Appraising digital storytelling across educational contexts.* Valencia: University of Valencia Press.

Haigh, C., & Hardy, P. (2011). Tell me a story—A conceptual exploration of storytelling in healthcare education. *Nurse Education Today, 31*(4), 408–411.

Hessler, H. B., & Rupiper Taggart, A. (2004). Reciprocal expertise: Community service and the writing group. In B. J. Moss, N. P. Highberg, & M. Nicolas (Eds.), *Writing groups inside and outside the classroom* (pp. 95–112). Mahwah: Lawrence Erlbaum Associates.

Hull, G. A. (2003). At last: Youth culture and digital media: new literacies for new times. *Research in the Teaching of English, 38*(2), 229–233.

Hull, G. A., & Katz, M. (2006). Crafting an agentive self: Case studies of digital storytelling. *Research in the Teaching of English, 41*(1), 43–81.

Jamissen, G., & Holte Haug, K. (2014). Towards the digital storytelling university. In C. Gregori-Signes & A. M. Brigido-Corcachan (Eds.), *Appraising digital storytelling across educational contexts* (pp. 93–113). Valencia: University of Valencia Press.

Jamissen, G., & Skou, G. (2010). Poetic reflection through digital storytelling: A methodology to foster professional health worker identity in students. *International Journal of Media, Technology and Lifelong Learning, 6*(2), 177–191.

Kegan, R. (1983). *The evolving self: Problem and process in human development.* Cambridge: Harvard University Press.

Kegan, R. (1994). *In over our heads: The mental demands of modern life.* Cambridge: Harvard University Press.

Kidd, J. (2005). *Capture Wales:* Digital storytelling at the BBC. *Wales Media Journal, 2,* 66–85.

Lambert, J. (2013). *Digital storytelling: Capturing lives, creating community* (4th ed.). New York: Routledge.

McComiskey, B. (2002). Ideology and critique in composition studies. *JAC*, *22*(1), 167–175.

Meyer, J. H. F., & Land, R. (2006). *Overcoming barriers to student understanding: Threshold concepts and troublesome knowledge*. London: Routledge.

Meyer, J. H. F., Land, R., & Baillie, C. (Eds.). (2010). *Threshold concepts and transformational learning*. Rotterdam: Sense.

Mezirow, J. (1997). *Transformative learning in action: Insights from practice*. San Francisco: Jossey-Bass.

Miller, C. (1984). Genre as social action. *Quarterly Journal of Speech, 70*, 151–167.

Misorelli, C., & Worcman, K. (2016). *People, stories, and museums: Museu da Pessoa, Sao Paolo, Brazil*. International Digital Storytelling Festival. Cape Town Peninsula University of Technology. Cape Town, South Africa.

Palmeri, J. (2012). *Remixing composition: A history of multimodal writing pedagogy*. Carbondale: Southern Illinois University Press.

Scharmer, C. O. (2009). *Theory U: Leading from the future as it emerges*. Oakland: Berrett-Koehler.

Shor, I. (1999). What is critical literacy? *The Journal of Pedagogy, Pluralism, and Practice, 1*(4). Retrieved from http://www.lesley.edu/journal-pedagogy-pluralism-practice/ira-shor/critical-literacy/

Tate, G., Rupiper Taggart, A., Schick, K., & Hessler, H. B. (2013). *A guide to composition pedagogies* (2nd ed.). Oxford: Oxford University Press.

Tyner, K. (1998). *Literacy in a digital world: Teaching and learning in the age of information*. New York: Routledge.

CHAPTER 4

Physician, Know Thyself: Using Digital Storytelling to Promote Reflection in Medical Education

Pip Hardy

THE NEED FOR REFLECTION IN HEALTHCARE

Reflection is one of the hallmarks of a true professional (Winter 1992; Boud et al. 1985) and its value in professional development across many fields of practice has grown since John Dewey pointed out that "we do not learn from experience; we learn from reflecting on experience" (Dewey 1938). Forty-five years later, Donald Schön attempted to reform professional knowledge by giving prominence to the "competence and artistry already embedded in skilful practice, especially "reflection-in-action" (the "thinking what they are doing while they are doing it") that practitioners sometimes bring to situations of uncertainty, uniqueness and conflict" (Schön 1983, 1987).

This ability to reflect in action is paramount in the practice of healthcare, where the ability to make swift decisions in the face of this "uncertainty, uniqueness and conflict" is critical and where the wrong decision can cost a life.

P. Hardy (✉)
Pilgrim Projects, Cambridge, UK

© The Author(s) 2017
G. Jamissen et al. (eds.), *Digital Storytelling in Higher Education*,
Digital Education and Learning, DOI 10.1007/978-3-319-51058-3_4

In addition to the clinical skills they must acquire, nurses, doctors and allied health professionals are encouraged to become reflective practitioners, in the expectation that the ability to reflect on and in practice—and to learn from that reflection—will contribute to better care for patients. Despite growing attempts to promote reflection in the curriculum and numerous books advocating different approaches and models, it seems that the teaching of reflection, although universally acknowledged as important by schools of medicine and healthcare globally, may be easier said than done (Mann et al. 2009).

While the United Kingdom General Medical Council (GMC) requires doctors to be reflective practitioners (GMC 2009), reflection in medical school is often taught in a prescriptive and formulaic way—a tickbox exercise signifying little other than students' ability to answer a pre-set list of questions. In the words of one student, "We reflect all the time and then we reflect on our reflections until we're sick of it" (Corry-Bass et al. 2014). Furthermore, pressure to accumulate clinical practice sign-offs trumps most other activities and so the development of reflection, self-awareness, emotional intelligence and resilience, and the cultivation of empathy and compassion remain secondary to the acquisition of clinical skills. This presents a dilemma: medical students are expected to reflect but the opportunity to develop the necessary skills is not prioritised.

Medical and healthcare educators in the United Kingdom and elsewhere have been challenged to support reflection in their students. This may relate to a trend towards linking reflective skills with diagnostic ability (Sobral 2000) and the requisite objective testing to measure this ability; although other approaches seek to develop reflective skills as part of the development of well-rounded, humane and caring professionals (Wald et al. 2015). Some programmes and initiatives attempt to improve reflection through the introduction of the arts and humanities and the use of stories. In the second half of the twentieth century, Robert Coles championed the importance of stories in medical education, responding to his mentor's plea for "more stories, less theory," urging Coles to "err on the side of each person's particularity and only later add a more general statement" (Coles 1989, p. 27). More recently, medical educators have advocated the use of music (Janaudis et al. 2011), film (Blasco et al. 2006), literature and narrative (Charon and Montello 2002), reflective writing (RW) (Wald et al. 2015) and even digital storytelling (Sandars 2009;

Jamissen and Skou 2010; Stacey and Hardy 2011; Anderson and Kinnair 2014). Some of these more creative approaches have encouraged deeper and more emotionally engaged responses to practice and patients, but they are still not widely used.

PATIENT VOICES AND REFLECTION

Reflection lies at the heart of the Patient Voices Programme. Prior to its inception, the founders had spent many years imparting the skills and attitudes of reflection to professionals in various fields, including healthcare, through the design and development of open, distance and work-based learning programmes. The particular challenges faced by those working in healthcare—illness, pain, trauma, fear and death—make it important for clinicians to be able to integrate their feelings rather than simply defending against the anxieties inherent in their work (Hardy 2007; Menzies-Lyth 1988). This requires a commitment to the practice of reflection, the cultivation of self-awareness, the development of resilience and an enhanced capacity to care—all aspects of professional identity formation (Wald et al. 2015) as well as being hallmarks of a true professional (Winter 1992).

The Patient Voices Programme (www.patientvoices.org.uk) was founded with the intention of promoting deep reflection by means of watching and responding to digital stories created by patients, carers and clinicians. Our belief that telling and listening to stories was and is a cornerstone of reflective learning, experiential learning and community learning is supported by a number of theorists (Dewey 1938; Wenger 1999; Moon 1999) and borne out by research into the use of digital stories as prompts to reflection (Hardy 2007).

The Patient Voices approach to digital storytelling is based in the "classical" digital storytelling model developed by StoryCenter but adapted to, and with a clear focus on, healthcare. These digital stories are, effectively, short, facilitated auto-ethnographies (Sumner 2015), created through a hermeneutic process designed to illuminate understanding of a particular event or experience. Patient Voices was established in an attempt to align hearts and minds with respect to the design and delivery of healthcare through the creation and dissemination of stories that would prompt reflection on practice, promote greater empathy and humanity and, ultimately, lead to more compassionate, as well as safer, care (Hardy 2004).

How the Project Came About

The Director of Educational Research and Innovation at Kings College London (KCL) had participated in a Patient Voices workshop in 2008 and wanted to explore the use of digital storytelling within the medical school to deepen reflective skills, increase self-knowledge and awareness, promote greater creativity and contribute to the formation of professional identity. She approached Patient Voices to develop a Student Selected Component (SSC) that built on a model previously piloted at the University of Leicester (Anderson et al. 2012) and would be capable of assessment.

It was important to decision-makers at KCL that the SSC would be based on the Patient Voices approach to reflective practice internationally recognised by the *British Medical Journal* and others for supporting culture change and improving service delivery in healthcare (BMJ 2010); it was equally important for them that the Leicester medical students had benefited from the experience of creating digital stories (Anderson et al. 2012). Reflecting on the experience, some years later, one of the Leicester junior doctor/storytellers reported that "the digital storytelling workshop was "one of the most memorable experiences I had at Medical School" and has heavily influenced my attitude and approach to reflective practice," while another said that the workshop "served as an opportunity to develop as an individual, and as a reflective practitioner in my own right, building on my own professional identity" (Corry-Bass et al. 2014). Students exposed to the stories report a deeper understanding of themselves and the realities of providing care (Anderson and Kinnair 2014).

An application was submitted to KCL based on the following aims and learning outcomes:

> The aim of this Student Selected Component is to support and enhance your future professional practice by developing skills of reflection and learning from experience in the clinical setting through the creation of a personal digital story. Focusing upon the human experience of healthcare, this experience will provide opportunities to explore the practical realities of providing professional, empathic and compassionate healthcare.
>
> By the end of the SSC, you will be able to:

> - articulate and reflect on your learning from experience in the clinical setting
> - appreciate the power of personal stories
> - create a digital story
> - reflect on the creation of the digital story

- develop empathy and compassion
- enhance your presentation skills.

(From *Physician, know thyself: Tomorrow's doctors reflected in today's technology* module guide)

The submission was successful and so we began our work with four third-year medical students.

METHOD AND APPROACH

Development of a module guide ensured the integrity of the classical digital storytelling process whilst meeting the needs of the students and their busy schedules; some adaptations were necessary in order to suit the ten-week SSC format, increase independent and/or virtual learning and meet formal assessment requirements.

The schedule included a mix of face-to-face, virtual and independent learning. A key requirement of the SSC was the creation of the summative reflective statement of formative, weekly, reflective tasks that are not included in the timetable below (Table 4.1).

Table 4.1 From the module guide

Week 1	Group session to introduce the SSC and digital storytelling in healthcare Independent learning tasks (to be completed in own time): watch some Patient Voices digital stories and evaluate according to agreed framework. Begin thinking of story ideas
Week 2	Group session to explore ideas for stories (Story circle 1) Discuss and agree reflective framework to support development and construction of the story and the reflective statement Co-create and agree criteria for assessing your digital stories Independent learning task (to be completed in own time): develop story ideas and begin scripting
Week 3	Independent learning: develop story scripts, begin to think about images
Week 4	Group session to share scripts and obtain feedback. (Story circle 2)
Week 5	Photography and image editing tutorial and recording of voiceovers
Week 6	Independent learning to be completed in own time: select and edit images, prepare storyboards
Week 7	Group introduction to video editing programme (hardware and software provided)
Week 8	Group session to continue video editing and review images
Week 9	Group session to continue video editing, finalise stories
Week 10	Premier of stories
Week 11	Reflection and peer review

Ethics: Care and Consent and a (Trigger) Warning

The module guide also included information about the potentially emotional nature of digital storytelling, alerting students to its potential to arouse sometimes-painful memories and feelings. It was suggested that, if they found themselves in distress, students should seek help from a friend or mentor or from the Patient Voices facilitators, one of whom is a trained counsellor. None of the students requested additional support.

The students signed consent forms, agreeing to participate in the workshop and to the use of their reflective statements as potential data for research, and acknowledging that further consent would be sought before any stories they created were released (Hardy 2015).

PREPARATION

The students were contacted by email before the first session and invited to read the module guide, which included several reflective frameworks and encouragement to watch some stories, including those created by the Leicester Medical students (www.patientvoices.org.uk/lssc.htm). They were asked to reflect on the stories using the Patient Voices "EAR" (Effective, Affective, Reflective) framework (Sumner 2009), and to deconstruct the stories using the Seven Elements of Digital Storytelling (Lambert 2002) according to the *schema* below. Note: for discussing the construction of stories and considering digital storytelling as a distinct genre, we have found the Seven Elements provides a more useful framework than the Seven Steps later introduced by StoryCenter (Lambert 2010), and so it was more suitable for our purpose here (Fig. 4.1).

Working with students over ten weeks rather than three days gave us the luxury of time and we were able to help them "limber up" their storytelling muscles with a variety of writing activities and paired storytelling exercises during the first two sessions. Initial concerns about how "personal" the stories could be, gave way to a willingness to be open and transparent about their personal—and professional—lives.

Assessment

Gaining formal credit for the SSC required a form of assessment that would gain institutional approval. The solution that was robust enough to meet the KCL standard marking scheme and assessment criteria, appro-

Element	1	5
Point of view	There appears to be no clear point or purpose to the story and little awareness of the audience.	There is a clear purpose to the story, with consistent focus, and the storyteller's point of view is obvious. There is a strong awareness of audience.
Dramatic question	There is little or no suspense, the resolution of the story is predictable; there may not really be a story at all.	A tension is created so that we are desperate to know what's going to happen; there may be an element of surprise and the resolution may differ from our expectation.
Emotional content	There is little or no emotional engagement; we may not really care what happens.	There is deep and strong emotional engagement – we really *care* about what happens.
Voice	Little consistency, poor inflection, more like a monologue than a conversation.	Good, clear and consistent use of voice, with varied inflection, and a slow, clear, conversational style.
Soundtrack	There is no music, it is inappropriate, distracting, used indiscreetly or simply adds nothing to the story.	Music is used to stir an emotional response, clearly sets the tone of the story.
Economy	The story is too long (losing our interest); the words and pictures may duplicate rather than enhance one another; images may be very literal and add little to the spoken words.	Images and words work well and succinctly together to convey the story and the atmosphere; images may be symbolic or metaphorical.
Pacing	Mechanical rhythm with limited vitality, and limited 'punctuation' either through use of voice or images. The pacing may not fit the story line.	Engaging, interesting, varied, vital and appropriate rhythm and pacing; using pauses to convey emotion or emphasis and allowing the story to breathe

Fig. 4.1 Schema for deconstructing and assessing stories

priate to the reflective nature of the work, innovative enough to suit the teaching methods and learning outcomes and co-designed with the students was as follows (Table 4.2):

The challenges of marking such subjective work had to be balanced with KCL's requirement that marking schemes be consistent across the School. Standardised marking schemes guide examination of written work but offer little help in assessing audio-visual work, but we found it possible to apply some of the guidance for written work to the assessment of the digital stories. Work that would receive a mark of 70–100%, for example, would be well written, logical, accurate and comprehensive in its coverage of the topic; the student would have to provide evidence of independent study and critical evaluation and, overall, there would have to be a high standard of presentation and analysis.

Criteria were agreed with the students, based on the Seven Elements, on which to assess their own and each other's digital stories. This collaborative involvement in designing the assessment contributed to their understanding of key features of the reflective process and how that would be evidenced.

All students received high marks for the SSC, capped by KCL at 85%. A request to provide a justification for each mark gave us an opportunity to describe changes we observed in students' skills of reflection, written

Table 4.2   From the module guide

Students will be assessed on the creation of a digital story about an experience of clinical practice, together with a reflective statement describing the reasons for the choice of story, explaining the choice and juxtaposition of words and images, aesthetic and editorial choices and the experience of editing their own short video.

Students will be involved in co-creating the criteria for assessment of their digital stories at an early stage in the SSC; elements of peer review are intrinsic to the digital storytelling process.

Finally, students will design and participate in a presentation of their digital stories to other third-year students and staff and respond to questions and comments from the audience.

In brief:

1. 2–3-minute digital story (60%)
2. 500–1000-word reflective statement explaining and reviewing the creation of their digital story, including selection of subject, editorial choices and decisions, identifying key personal learning and so on (20%)
3. Formal presentation (screening) of digital stories, open to the third-year students and the public, for SSC students to showcase their work and respond to questions and comments from the audience (20%)

and spoken expression, use of images, analysis of story choice and editorial decisions and the impact of this work on their learning and their clinical practice.

GATHERING AND ANALYSING DATA

The SSC was planned and implemented as an educational intervention rather than as a research project. However, in signing the Patient Voices consent form, storytellers also agree to participate in research; the intention to write a paper based on the SSC was discussed with the students. They were invited to bear this in mind as they wrote their weekly reflective statements and their final, assessed piece of reflection.

The data that informs the discussion below are drawn from these reflective writings. In addition, 18 months after the completion of the SSC, an email was sent to the students designed to evaluate the longer-term impact of the digital storytelling process on their practice. While all responded enthusiastically, only two had time to engage in this longer-term reflection.

The reflective statements were considered and roughly coded in relation to the aims of the SSC and the key theories of reflection that underpin the work of Patient Voices and of this project, resulting in identification of the following themes:

- Learning together (the value of community)
- Deepening reflection
- The value of stories
- Developing personal/professional identity
- Seeing patients as people

RESULTS AND DISCUSSION: A SMALL REVOLUTION

Each student produced two digital stories, indicating their deep engagement with the process and their willingness to spend more time in face-to-face sessions. The students worked well as a group, sharing ideas and experiences openly and honestly and learning from each other. The ability to distil an experience into one 2–3-minute story is no small feat and these students demonstrated determination, sensitivity, intelligence, creativity and a willingness to learn how to look at the world—themselves, their work and their patients—differently, with the potential to work in new and different ways.

Barnett has written about a revolution in pedagogy, one that shifts the focus from *knowledge* as the central focus of education to *being*.

> The key problem of super-complexity is not one of knowledge; it is one of being. Accordingly, we have to displace knowledge from the core of our pedagogies. The student's being has to take centre stage. Feeling uncertainty, responding to uncertainty, gaining confidence to insert oneself amid the numerous counter-claims to which one is exposed, these are matters of being.

> Their acquisition calls for a revolution in the pedagogical relationships within a university. (Barnett 2012)

Learning together

From the outset, it was clear that the medical students found our approach unusual.

> it didn't feel like they were the teachers and we were the pupils; suddenly we were a small group of interesting, diverse and unique people sat in a room each with different experiences and opinions. But it really felt like our opinions, as students, were greatly valued—this (perhaps unfortunately) is something that is relatively unusual when one studies medicine.
> What a refreshing experience it was to feel that our supervisors were even in very small ways learning from us in the same way we were learning from them. DG

The students enjoyed and valued "communal activities" (Palmer 1983)—those educational activities that do not separate teaching and learning but rather seek to extend and transform knowledge through creative use of the tools and technologies available (Boyer 1990), while also acknowledging the value of working and learning together, as these quotes reveal:

> One of the best things about this SSC was working genuinely as a tight-knit group together. DG

The students appreciated being able to learn from one another and recognised that openness and honesty can provide valuable opportunities for learning about themselves and their patients:

> I thoroughly valued the times of group reflection ... listening to others, hearing their point of view and learning from them, other ways to see and think about things. LP

Their experiences echo the finding of Wald and colleagues that interactive RW with medical students has resulted in "a richness of insight in students' RW and small-group reflection, and we observe students gaining a deeper understanding of themselves and their roles as physicians" (Wald et al. 2015), as the following quote shows:

> The small group session also allowed for us to be quite open with each other and all the feedback received was in a positive direction, that is, how something could be better rather than how something was done badly. MM

Deepening Reflection

Although learning about reflection might not have been the students' primary motivation for electing this SSC, it became evident that reflective skills had value:

> My reasons for choosing [the SSC] had been much more to do with the opportunity to make a film than to enhance my appreciation of reflection. However very soon ... I realised that the real thing I was going to gain from the module was a new insight into the importance of reflection. DG

All students made progress in their ability to reflect deeply and meaningfully on an experience and to apply that learning to practice (Kolb 1983). The students felt they had learned about reflection in a way that was of practical benefit as well as being enjoyable:

> This experience has been incredibly useful. The teaching itself has taught me the practical aspects for how to reflect, and more than that how to do this in a scientific manner. This allows for a practical way to apply a thought process to an experience that it's usually hard to work out. MM

> During the SSC, through the process of developing an idea, writing a script and making a film about an incident you couldn't help but reflect. Sometimes it was disguised under the cover of fun and exciting "filmmaking" but essentially what we did for 12 weeks was solid deep reflecting. I loved it. I realised how enjoyable, interesting and useful reflection is. DG

In some cases, the reflection went deeper, resulting in profound realisations and clear development of moral imagination (Coles 1989).

> After taking a substandard history (when I reflect back) ... I was subsequently brought to the grave realisation that she had cancer which was spreading; and all of a sudden my [personal] concerns were minute specks of dust. ... From that day forwards, I have endeavoured to put my life into perspective with the patient's life and recognise that any complaint from a patient (no matter how small it may seem) should be acknowledged, as well as recognising that my interaction with patients should never be tainted by my day's experiences. CA

The Value of Stories

The students also grew in self-awareness, creativity, imagination and competence in the use of narrative and audio-visual storytelling as "convivial tools," that is, items or practices that "give each person who uses them the greatest opportunity to enrich the environment with the fruits of his or her vision" (Illich 1973). One student writes about an exercise during one early session:

> This was an activity that allowed me to start thinking critically about which clinical experiences I could translate into a story. I noticed that as we carried out the activity a second time, my ability to condense detail and convey the salient points was strengthened and this would prove to be extremely advantageous when I started putting my story together, especially because it reaffirmed the reality that the best stories are "effective, affective and reflective." CA

As well as valuing the practical aspects of digital storytelling, one student notes the value of learning from the stories of the other students, recognising a small community of practice (Wenger 1999).

> My classmates were also fantastic at storytelling and due to the group nature of the project it was possible to learn from them as well as from the teaching. The story circles where we produced a story without previous preparation and then cutting this story down to the fine points showed us the correct way to be economic with our timings and helped in the finalised production of our stories. MM

Another describes how watching other students' stories enabled her to think about the difference between reflection and "just thinking":

> Watching the videos made me think about reflection and question if I reflect after I have seen a patient? It's easy to think that just thinking over their

case, presenting to a consultant or explain to a friend about a condition counts as reflections but did I actually think about the patient as a person? The fact that we are just two human beings in a situation? LP

Developing Professional Identity

Recognising the value of both watching and creating stories feeds into developing professional identity:

> It strikes me that if all medical students made—or even watched—these [stories] perhaps we would all feel more empowered and actually more energised to learn as we would feel part of a team, we would feel we had an important role and we would feel we could actually be "producers" of patients' good health and happiness. DG

The students changed from being passive recipients of knowledge "sitting open-eyed and open-booked to consume information from our lecturers, tutors or consultants," as one student commented, to people aware of their own value, and the importance of their relationships with patients.

> It helped me to realise that every medical problem doesn't require a book-smart doctor with no social skills but instead often requires a personal touch. From this experience I have tried to carry out all my exams and histories by listening to my patients about what they say and how this affects them rather than trying to follow a flowchart through to arrive at a diagnosis. MM

All students expressed a growing awareness of the human (as opposed to the clinical) nature of healthcare:

> Something that always strikes me when I watch the stories is the breakdown of any division between clinicians and patients, when a clinician or patient talks of their own experience you no longer see clinicians and patients but just two human beings trying to help each other. For me many of the stories are a true reminder that at the times when we are most vulnerable or even close to death we no longer want "doctors" or "nurses" around us, we simply want other human beings around us. DG

People want to be treated as individuals rather than diseases:

> [Making my story] allowed me to realise how all patients want to be treated as individuals with an illness, and how I should not attempt to trivialise my patient by seeing them as a defining problem that requires treatment. MM

The students' responses have important implications for teaching, learning and practice; opportunities for creative expression in an atmosphere of non-judgemental appreciation can promote the development of professional identity characterised by humanity and self-awareness that arises from meaningful reflection on practice.

Seeing Patients as People

A key aspect of developing as a healthcare professional is the ability to see patients as human beings; this theme was at the core of all the students' reflective statements.

> I take time now. I stop and think now. I've learnt medicine isn't about passing exams; it isn't about getting the best marks or impressing your consultant the most. It's about people. Sick people who need to know you're there, that they aren't alone. They aren't just another case study or Grand Round patient; they are a father, a mother, a daughter, a son. ... Another person just like me in this dangerous world. LP

Students reported shifting away from regarding patients as collections of symptoms or interesting opportunities for practice, to seeing them as people.

> I have truly been challenged to think more holistically of each patient that I am privileged to talk with. Finally, for every single patient I speak with now and in the future, this SSC has taught me (in an unorthodox way) to recognise that each patient is a human person with a human life full of human experiences and stories and thus it would only make sense to approach each one as a human person and not as a potential sign up, grand round presentation or practical skills opportunity. CA

Students also found value in other Patient Voices stories:

> One of the previous stories has also helped to show me how while for us the "sign off" culture is acceptable and common, we need to remember not to treat our patients as conditions and sign offs. We need to always remember to treat our patients with the respect they deserve and not break them down to their condition or the task that they need done. MM

One student had a profound realisation about patients:

Through the better reflection that came about through this module it became so clear to me that all patients should be seen as equal to us. They are not just tools for our own education; they are human beings—some of whom are going through terrible periods of their life and we should treat every single patient the same. DG

Longer-Term Impact

In healthcare, as in digital storytelling, there is increasing emphasis on impact—impact of treatment, of intervention, of research, of education and training. To assess the longer-term impact of creating a digital story, the students were invited to offer their reflections on whether and how the SSC had affected them in the 18 months following its completion. Two responded, offering indications as to the ongoing benefits of the classical digital storytelling process, with implications for its use in medical education. They wrote about how the process of creating their own stories had contributed to their development as professionals, to becoming better doctors and seeing their patients as people, and of how reflection contributes to greater resilience in the face of the inevitable stresses of delivering healthcare.

> Over a year on, this appreciation for reflection very much remains. I still find myself at the end of the day taking time to pause, think and reflect on my experiences of that day, either privately or with others, telling them the story of what had happened. This allows me to make sense of any difficulties I encounter and allows me to see what I could have done differently.
>
> Being better at reflection has had a huge impact on me personally in terms of my psychological well-being and on how I interact with patients. Firstly for me being able to look back on situations and think "why was I stressed?," "why was I really anxious?" and actually find answers to it has reduced my levels of stress and anxiety dramatically. DG

Perhaps the most valuable learning of all is summed up in CA's recognition of the "gift of a listening ear and heart."

> I found myself on the wards in my final rotation of Year 3 and all of Year 4 looking far beyond the physical or mental illness which human beings in hospitals had. I was now seeing each one as an individual and deeply reflecting on their story, their experience and truly empathising with sincerity.

This is a great achievement for an SSC which I never thought would offer as much as it has done! It went beyond my expectations and has equipped me with skills—the ones which may not pass contribute to the passing of exams as we're so conditioned to think—but the ones which will make me a better doctor.

I look forward to engaging with all my patients from this new-found vantage point. It brought to light the fundamental truth that I am not just a doctor with patients; I am a fellow human being. Just as I would expect to be respected as such, I should and will continue to go beyond the confines of a checklist giving the intangible gift of a listening ear and heart. CA

Conclusion and Recommendations

The process of creating reflective digital stories was experienced as transformational by these medical students, offering them new ways of seeing themselves and their patients. The students' ability to reflect improved in ways that affected their clinical work with patients and peers as well as their emotional well-being. The opportunity to think deeply about an experience and reflect on its meaning, while working in a respectful environment of equals contributed to greater confidence and deeper insights as well as an appreciation of the need for humanity and empathy in the practice of medicine.

On the basis of this study, digital storytelling has the potential to enhance skills of reflection, increase self-awareness, deepen insight, strengthen professional identity and contribute to a new, more humane way of approaching learning and practice. Further research could usefully be conducted with more or larger cohorts of medical and other healthcare students.

The medical students' stories can be seen at www.patientvoices.org.uk/pkt.htm

References

Anderson, E., & Kinnair, D. (2014). Reflection – They just don't get it! Digital stories from junior doctors. In P. Hardy & T. Sumner (Eds.), *Cultivating compassion: how digital storytelling is transforming healthcare*. Chichester: Kingsham Press.

Anderson, L., Kinnair, D., Hardy, P., & Sumner, T. (2012). They just don't get it: Using digital stories to promote meaningful undergraduate reflection. *Medical Teacher, 34*, 597–598.

Barnett, R. (2012). Learning for an unknown future. *Higher Education Research & Development, 31,* 65–77.

Blasco, P. G., Moreto, G., Roncoletta, A. F., Levites, M. R., & Janaudis, M. A. (2006). Using movie clips to foster learners' reflection: Improving education in the affective domain. *Family Medicine-Kansas City, 38,* 94.

BMJ. 2010. *Patient Voices: Excellence in Healthcare Education 2010 winners.* London: British Medical Association. Available: http://groupawards.bmj. com/excellence-in-healthcare-education-2010-winners. Accessed 2012.

Boud, D., Keogh, R., & Walker, D. (1985). *Reflection: Turning experience into learning.* London: Kogan Page.

Boyer, E. L. (1990). *Scholarship reconsidered: Priorities of the professoriate.* Princeton: The Carnegie Foundation for the advancement of teaching.

Charon, R., & Montello, M. (2002). *Stories matter: The role of narrative in medical ethics (reflective bioethics).* London: Routledge.

Coles, R. (1989). *The call of stories: Teaching and the moral imagination.* Boston: Houghton Mifflin.

Corry-Bass, S., Critchfield, M., & Pang, W. (2014). Reflection – Now we get it! In P. Hardy & T. Sumner (Eds.), *Cultivating compassion: How digital storytelling is transforming healthcare.* Chichester: Kingsham Press.

Dewey, J. (1938). *Experience and education.* New York: Collier.

GMC. (2009). *Tomorrow's doctors: Outcomes and standards for undergraduate medical education.* Manchester: General Medical Council.

Hardy, P. 2004. *Patient Voices: The rationale.* Cambridge: Pilgrim Projects. Available at: http://www.patientvoices.org.uk/about.htm. Accessed 2 Oct 2016.

Hardy, P., 2007. *An investigation into the application of the Patient Voices digital stories in healthcare education: Quality of learning, policy impact and practice-based value.* MSc in Lifelong Learning MSc dissertation, University of Ulster.

Hardy, P., 2015. First do no harm: Developing an ethical process of consent and release for digital storytelling in healthcare. *Seminar.net: Media, Technology & Life-Long Learning, 11,* 162–169.

Illich, I. (1973). *Tools for conviviality.* Toronto: Harper and Row.

Jamissen, G., & Skou, G. (2010). Poetic reflection through digital storytelling – A methodology to foster professional health worker identity in students. *Seminar. net: Media, Technology & Life-Long Learning, 6*(2), 177–191.

Janaudis, M. A., Fleming, M., & Blasco, P. G. (2011). The sound of music: Transforming medical students into reflective practitioners. *Creative Education, 4*(6), 49–52. Suppl. Special Issue on Medical Education and Health Education; Irvine4.6A (Jun 2013).

Kolb, D. A. (1983). *Expriential learning: Experience as the source of learning.* Hemel Hempstead: Prentice-Hall.

Lambert, J. (2002). *Digital storytelling: Capturing lives, creating community.* Berkeley: Digital Diner Press.

Lambert, J. (2010). *Digital storytelling cookbook* (Rev ed.). Berkeley: Digital Diner Press.

Mann, K., Gordon, J., & MacLeod, A. (2009). Reflection and reflective practice in health professions education: A systematic review. *Advances in Health Sciences Education: Theory and Practice, 14*, 595–621.

Menzies-Lyth, I. (1988). *The functioning of social systems as a defence against anxiety.* In *Containing anxiety in institutions.* London: Free Association Books.

Moon, J. (1999). *Reflection in learning and professional development: Theory and practice.* London: Kogan Page.

Palmer, P. J. (1983). *To know as we are known.* New York: Harper & Row.

Sandars, J. (2009). The use of reflection in medical education: AMEE Guide No. 44. *Medical Teacher, 31*, 685–695.

Schön, D. (1983). *The reflective practitioner: How professionals think in action.* New York: Basic books.

Schön, D. (1987). *Educating the reflective practitioner: Toward a new design for teaching and learning in the professions.* San Francisco: Jossey-Bass.

Sobral, D. T. (2000). An appraisal of medical students' reflection-in-learning. *Medical Education-Oxford, 34*, 182–187.

Stacey, G., & Hardy, P. (2011). Challenging the shock of reality through digital storytelling. *Nurse Education in Practice, 11*, 159–164.

Sumner, T. (2009). *Inspiring innovation through Patient Voices: Presentation at Innovation Expo.* London: Edexcel London.

Sumner, T., 2015. Inverting the pyramid of voice: Digital storytellers creating activist memes of care experiences. *DS9.* Cardiff.

Wald, H. S., Anthony, D., Hutchinson, T. A., Liben, S., Smilovitch, M., & Donato, A. A. (2015). Professional identity formation in medical education for humanistic, resilient physicians: Pedagogic strategies for bridging theory to practice. *Academic Medicine, 90*, 753–760.

Wenger, E. (1999). *Communities of practice: Learning, meaning and identity.* Cambridge: Cambridge University Press.

Winter, R. (1992). The assessment Programme – Competence-based education at professional /Honours degree level. *Competence and Assessment, 20*, 14–18.

CHAPTER 5

From Dewey to Digital: Design-Based Research for Deeper Reflection Through Digital Storytelling

Bonnie Thompson Long and Tony Hall

INTRODUCTION

The research reported in this chapter was undertaken on a longitudinal basis, over a period of four years, involving 323 pre-service teachers. Designing digital storytelling (DS) with and for pre-service teachers enabled the authors to examine how it might be conceptualised and implemented to support and enhance learning from practice, especially in their formative and sensitive, early-stage transition into the professional career of teaching in post-primary schools. In this DS research, the authors worked with student teachers from across all subject areas of the Irish post-primary school curriculum, including mathematics, science, history, geography and languages.

From a methodological perspective, we employed design-based research (DBR). We chose DBR because it is itself a reflective approach, particularly well suited to the iterative, participatory and principled design

B.T. Long (✉)
National University of Ireland, Galway, Ireland

T. Hall
National University of Ireland, Galway, Ireland

G. Jamissen et al. (eds.), *Digital Storytelling in Higher Education*,
Digital Education and Learning, DOI 10.1007/978-3-319-51058-3_5

of innovations with technology-enhanced learning (Barab and Squire 2004; Reeves et al. 2005; Hofer and Owings Swan 2006).

DBR, action research (AR) and other cognate, change and solution-oriented methodologies belong to the same family of practitioner-based, interventional research modalities in education. In terms of DS, exemplar practitioner-based research is Jamissen and Haug's (2014) longitudinal, multicycle action research to design and develop digital storytelling to support practice learning within early childhood teacher education. Consistent with Jamissen and Haug's (2014) impactful action research, our design-based research process involved three major cycles of design, implementation and evaluation: (1) initial pilot intervention, (2) mainstream/scaling-up of the design and (3) a third, capstone intervention.

THE PROCESS

Through our multicycle, accretive and iterative DBR process, we conceptualised and refined R-NEST (reflection, narrative, engagement, sociality and technology), a bespoke framework for the design of DS to support pre-service teachers in the creation of multimodal narratives embodying deep reflection. We report here key aspects of R-NEST, namely the significant potential of using second-order reflection (Moon 2004) alongside Tripp's (1993) conception of critical incident, in the situated design and deployment of DS to mediate and augment student teachers' reflective practice.

Our Starting Point: An Initial R-NEST Concept Design

Boyer noted that "teaching is/a dynamic endeavour, involving all the analogies, metaphors, and images that build bridges between the teacher's understanding, and the student's learning" (1990, p. 23). This chapter reports design-based research which sought to explore the use of digital storytelling and its augmented, multimedia affordances, "analogies, metaphors, and images" (1990, p. 23) to help student teachers for the second-level sector reflect more deeply on their learning from practice in schools. Our research was originally inspired by Barrett's (2005) and Moon's (1999) ideas about creative and novel representations of reflection, including the potential of combining narrative and storytelling with digital media and technology. Illustrated in Fig. 5.1, the synthesis of our nascent R-NEST design emerged through four main activities: (1) our biographical reflection as teacher educators, including situational analysis of the constraints and possibilities within our own initial teacher education

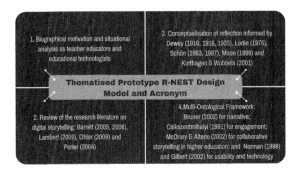

Fig. 5.1 Synthesis of the initial, prototype R-NEST design-based research model

programme in Ireland, (2) review of relevant DS literature, (3) critical conceptualisation of the notion of "reflection", predicated on seminal thinking and writing on the topic, for example, Dewey (1910, 1916, 1933) and (4) the authors' initial theorisation work about digitalising narrative (multi-ontological framework). Our initial conceptualisation of R-NEST encompassed a very broad literature, from Dewey to the digital. We used R-NEST to frame both the design and evaluation of our innovation with digital storytelling over the three cycles.

Five major themes emerged in our initial concept design. Expanding these themes, the guiding principles of the initial R-NEST were:

- the potentially important role of storytelling as a medium for identity development in teacher education;
- the central importance of collaborative learning among pre-service teachers, especially in relation to personal stories of change (Lambert 2009, 2013) and reflection thereon;
- easy-to-use technology and easy to access and use, rich media content; and
- creative engagement in the process.

Each of the three design cycles, pilot, mainstream and capstone, involved iterating through and finessing our DS innovation, informed by the emerging and evolving R-NEST model, continuing review of the extant, relevant research on digital storytelling design, and concepts and theories of educational technology.

From Concept to Pilot: The Emerging R-NEST Digital Storytelling Innovation

Reflecting on practice is a mandatory competency component in many teacher education programmes internationally and constitutes a prevailing paradigm in education globally (Collin et al. 2013). Most reflective assignments required of student teachers are written assignments (Moon 1999). However, as Kajder and Parkes (2012) noted, this might not be the best way for students to evidence their reflection. Similar to findings reported in the literature (see Calderhead 1989; MacLeod and Cowieson 2001; Moon 1999; Moon 2004), there was a lack of depth in our students' reflections, especially when these were expressed through exclusively written formats. Digital storytelling can enhance reflection (Barrett 2005, 2006; Kearney 2009; Matthews-DeNatale 2008). The pilot study was our first step towards designing a DS project to enhance students' reflective practice in our initial teacher education programme.

It is not possible to enumerate all aspects of the design-based research process within the scope and word count of this book chapter. For a complete discussion of the trajectory of the research from initial concept design to full, programme-wide DS implementation, the reader is directed to the doctoral thesis on which this article is based (Thompson Long 2014).

Our DS project was fundamentally inspired by the Center for Digital Storytelling's (CDS), now StoryCenter, Digital Storytelling Workshop Model (Lambert 2010, 2013), and the broad topic for the pilot DS study was in line with other DS exploratory projects reviewed in the literature at the time. These required students to create digital stories based on topics such as, "Why do I want to be a teacher?" (Heo 2009, p. 414) and "What does it mean to me to be a teacher?" (Kearney 2009, p. 1989). After the five weeks of instruction related to the pilot DS concluded, students who had volunteered to complete a digital story had an additional six weeks to work on their DS on their own. While initially 67 students had volunteered to complete a digital story, 18 students submitted a digital story as part of their professional practice portfolio at the end of the academic year.

Materials used to analyse the DS project included the students' completed digital stories, their "working portfolios" (planning materials), an online discussion board, student emails and a post-DS questionnaire. Of the 18 students who completed a digital story, 16 gave permission for their DS materials to be used for research purposes, and 12 completed the questionnaire. The results of this questionnaire showed that the 12 students who completed the survey found the DS process to be a positive, motivating and worthwhile experience. They also found it to be reflective, fun, and engaging (Thompson Long 2014). However, their final digital stories, when analysed using a rubric based on Moon's (2004) generic framework for reflection, did not evidence the depth of reflection we had hoped for. Moon's (2004) scale ranges from the lowest level of "Descriptive" to the highest level of "Reflective (2)". While none of the digital stories received the lowest "Descriptive" rating, the majority of digital stories were rated as only "Descriptive with some reflection" ($n = 8$). Five of the digital stories showed "Reflective (1)" levels, and only three of the digital stories were rated as showing the highest level of reflection, "Reflective (2)" (Thompson Long 2014). Interestingly, further analysis of the digital stories scoring the highest levels of reflection showed that the students who created these diverged from the assignment brief significantly, and instead of giving a "broad assessment of the year", each told a story of a significant aspect of their developing teacher identity.

During our own reflection on the pilot implementation, couched within the R-NEST framework and relevant literature, we realised that the task set for the students, while allowing for some reflection, was too broad. A critical finding from the pilot intervention was that if we wanted students to produce something that was deeply reflective, we needed to set a task that would allow them to delve more deeply into a particular experience, focusing on the thoughts, feelings and motivations that led to and emerged from that experience.

Principles of Redesigning the Digital Storytelling Project for Deeper Reflection

Most of the students who took the post-DS questionnaire felt that the DS process had enhanced their reflection on practice, even though many of them did not create digital stories that evidenced deep reflection. This led us to the realisation that the product, and depth of reflection evident only in the final digital story, might not be of paramount importance. Gravestock and Jenkins (2009) and Sandars et al. (2008) noted that reflection can take place at all stages of the creation of a digital story. These authors placed the emphasis on the process, not exclusively on the product.

A discussion of the pertinent areas of the reflective literature, and their effect on the second DS design implementation led us to focus on characteristics of the reflective process. These included issues such as the intent or disposition of the learner, and how to scaffold and structure the reflective process, in particular as a collaborative narrative process. We also needed to understand degrees of reflection and how to encourage and recognise deep reflection and, perhaps most importantly, its mediation through both the process and product of designing a digital story. Contextualised critically in terms of the R-NEST design model and relevant DS research, we now outline the key aspects we focused on in the redesign of the pilot DS project for the second, mainstream iteration of the DBR process. These included both the processes and products of reflection, framed and organised in a focused manner using Tripp's (1993) concept of critical incident, engaged and positive learner intent/disposition, reflection as structured, social storytelling and the central importance of second-order reflection.

Reflective Products and Processes

After investigating many different types of possible story prompts in the literature, we realised that the possible answer to the focus of the students' digital stories lay in an existing section of the students' coursework: their Professional Practice Portfolio, specifically the critical incident analysis essay. This compares closely with the findings of Jamissen and Skou (2010, p. 187) that "creativity as a quality can be learned and prompted by the conscious use of tools and processes". In particular, Tripp (1993) promotes the use of critical incidents in teaching as ways of developing an understanding of, and control over professional judgement and practice. Tripp sees everything that happens in a classroom as a potential critical incident, indeed: "we just need to analyse it critically to make it one" (Tripp 1993, p. 28).

Our critical incident analysis assignment brief defined a critical incident as "a happening, an incident or an event involving you or observed by you that has made you subsequently think and/or act differently about that particular issue" (NUI Galway School of Education 2010). The critical incident analysis required students to pick an incident from their reflective journal and tell a story about the incident that took place. They had to discuss why this was a defining moment for them. They had to reflect critically on the incident; discuss emotions, feelings and reactions related to it. It also asked them to draw on academic literature germane to the subject of the incident.

We felt that using this task as the basis for the digital story assignment could lead the students through the reflective process as envisioned by Dewey (1933), allowing them to undergo the steps necessary for deeper reflection.

Learner Disposition

Many students can be resistant to participating in reflective assignments (Moon 1999). Boud et al. (1985) emphasised that the intent of the learner has an impact on the reflective process. They stated that "The intent of the learner permeates every stage of the process from the choice to engage in a particular activity to the ultimate results of the reflective process" (Boud et al. 1985, p. 24).

Dewey believed strongly that the attitudes that an individual brings to bear on the act of reflection can either open the way to learning or block it (Rodgers 2002). Dewey (1933) saw our tendency to jump to conclusions, the failure to examine our own attitudes, and the powerful social influences of parents or the beliefs of a group one belongs to as influences that could inhibit reflective thinking. He named three main attitudes that lead to a readiness to engage in reflective thinking: (1) open-mindedness, (2) whole-heartedness and (3) responsibility (Dewey 1933). Other attitudes mentioned by Dewey as encouraging a readiness to engage in reflection are directness (1916), curiosity (1910, 1933) and a sense of playfulness in one's work (1933). Dewey felt that an interest exclusively in the outcome could lead to drudgery (1933). Pointedly, he wrote,

> For by drudgery is meant those activities in which the interest in the outcome does not suffuse the process of getting the result. Whenever a piece of work becomes drudgery, the process of doing loses all value for the doer; he cares solely for what is to be had at the end of it. The work itself, the putting forth of energy, is hateful; it is just a necessary evil, since without it some important end would be missed. (Dewey 1933, pp. 285–286)

Engaging our students in the reflective process and helping them to get the most out of their reflection on practice was a major goal of our DS project. Encouraging a positive attitude towards the process of reflection would be important to our R-NEST redesign. Furthermore, as Jamissen and Skou (2010) have similarly found, we needed to use prompts and tools that would engage our students to work "in a creative mode and a poetic form", which "may bring out reflections and associations that are not relevant in an analytic-rationalistic mode (Kaufmann 2006). There is also a dimension of energy involved in creative work as described by the concept of *flow* (Csikszentmihalyi 1997)" (2010, p. 187). We aimed to redesign the DS process so that it would hopefully facilitate these more profound levels of engagement and thus deeper reflection.

Collaborative Reflection

Reflecting with others can deepen reflection on practice (Dewey 1916; Hatton and Smith 1995; McDrury and Alterio 2002; Moon 2004; Rodgers 2002; Schön 1987). Dewey (1916) firmly believed that collaborative reflection could surface and lead to further understanding of the strengths and weaknesses in one's own thinking. McDrury and Alterio (2002) felt that, in getting their students to tell stories of practice, both tellers of stories and listeners can be transformed, and this story-sharing can bring about changes in the practicum. However, in order for this to happen, they proposed that the manner in which stories are told is of the utmost importance. They suggested a formal setting, with multiple listeners and a predetermined story to tell as the most appropriate format for sharing stories of practice. Following the CDS's DS process, once a rough draft of the digital story is written, it is shared with peers during the "Story Circle" (Lambert 2013). During the pilot project, this was undertaken rather informally, and also during only one class session. Looking back on this part of our DS process in the context of McDrury and Alterio (2002), we felt that students did not get as much out of it as they could have, given the emphasis in the literature on the benefits of reflecting with others. We therefore decided to redesign the "story circle" activity for the second iteration of the DS design completely. A formal story-sharing process was devised, based on McDrury and Alterio's (2002) storytelling pathways, that would allow students to share a predetermined story in a formal setting, and with multiple listeners.

Second-Order Reflection

Moon (2004) defined second-order reflection as techniques that require a learner to look through previous reflective work, such as private reflective journals, and to write a deeper reflective overview. She felt it was better to get students to use these original reflections, or "raw material" (p. 156), as the basis for deeper reflections on the topic or experience. Just as we would not assess students on the notes they take in class, Moon felt we should not assess students on their initial reflective writings. She held that students' second-order reflections are more valuable and are "likely to yield deeper levels of reflection with improved learning" (Moon 2004, p. 156). Affording opportunities to expand their original reflective writing through working with others to share their ideas, standing back from oneself to take a broader look at the situation, and investigating different viewpoints of the same situation can assist students in deepening their primary reflections.

In redesigning the DS assignment, we felt it was necessary to create a specific opportunity for students to engage in second-order reflection. Students were asked to choose a critical incident from their reflective journal that they originally wrote about while off-campus on their teaching practice in schools.

Outcomes of Reflection

There can be many outcomes of reflection when used for learning, depending on the purpose of the reflective activity. Moon saw one of the possible outcomes of reflection as action: "To reflect on action is to reflect on an event in the past, reprocessing or reorganising the meaning that has been made of that event with the possibility of improving future performance" (Moon 1999, p. 157). Boud et al. (1985) felt that some of the benefits of reflection may be lost if they are not linked to action or application. They stated that the "outcomes of reflection may include a new way of doing something, the clarification of an issue, the development of a skill or the resolution of a problem" (1985, p. 34). They discussed how outcomes can also be of an affective nature, which allow us to continue on to future learning, change our emotional state, attitudes and even values.

The redesigned critical incident analysis assignment asked students to investigate an incident from their teaching practice that subsequently changed their views and or actions in the classroom. It was hoped that deep reflection on a particular, significant incident would lead students to taking action on the situation, prompting a change in their practice.

Evidencing Depth of Reflection

While reflection is a goal in most teacher education programmes, difficulties lie in describing what different levels of reflection actually look like (Hatton and Smith 1995). While educators have noted a lack of depth of reflection in student work (Calderhead 1989; MacLeod and Cowieson 2001; Moon 1999), sometimes it is difficult to describe what "depth" of reflection looks like. Moon (2004) discussed the difficulties that educators can encounter in getting their students to achieve a measure of depth in their reflections. She stated that, the idea of depth has become more important as reflective activities have been increasingly applied in formal education and professional development. There is a frequent observation that while an initial struggle of getting learners to reflect can be overcome, it can be difficult to persuade them to reflect in other than a superficial manner—which might be little different from descriptive writing. (Moon 2004, p. 95)

Hatton and Smith (1995) and Moon (2004) created models to elucidate depth of reflection. These frameworks proved instrumental in our redesign of the digital storytelling process, particularly in terms of characterising what depth of reflection entails.

In their work creating a model against which evidence of reflection in student teachers' reflective writings could be evaluated, Hatton and Smith (1995) identified four types of writing, three of which can be described as reflective:

- *Descriptive writing*: this writing is not reflective at all, but merely reports events or literature;
- *Descriptive reflection*: attempts to provide reasons based often on personal judgement or of the students' reading of the literature;
- *Dialogic writing* is a form of discourse with oneself, a stepping back from and mulling over, an exploration of possible reasons;
- *Critical writing*: involves "reason giving for decisions or events which takes account of the broader historical, social, and or political contexts" (Hatton and Smith 1995, pp. 40–41).

Moon (2004), building on Hatton and Smith's (1995) earlier framework, investigated the concept of depth in students' written reflections. Moon's generic framework for reflective writing described four levels of reflective writing in a continuum, from superficial and descriptive, to deep levels of reflective writing (Moon 2004). At the highest level of her generic framework, Reflective (2), Moon characterised deep reflective writing as including key elements, such as:

- a brief description of the event, covering the issues for reflection and noting their context;
- a standing back from an event, there is mulling over and internal dialogue;
- the account incorporates a recognition that the frame of reference with which an event is viewed can change;

- a metacognitive stance is taken (i.e. critical awareness of one's own processes of mental functioning—including reflection);
- recognition that events exist in a historical or social context that may be influential on a person's reaction to them. In other words, multiple perspectives are noted;
- self-questioning is evident, deliberating between different views of personal behaviour and that of others.

In the redesigned DS brief, students were asked to choose an incident from their reflective journal to expand upon, and to present this in the structure of a personal narrative. As advocated by Moon (2004), students were provided questions in the new DS brief to help them to include all aspects of the critical incident analysis. These questions were structured in a way that emphasised the reflective elements of the critical incident, and illustrated for the students what reflective writing should include. Students were guided to include alternative viewpoints, consider the academic literature related to their topic, and to contemplate the incident along different time frames, among other things. The assessment rubric was also changed completely, both to include assessment elements for the critical incident/reflective content and in order to incorporate elements of the DS rubric devised by the CDS, which is based on their seven elements of an effective digital story (Center for Digital Storytelling 2010).

FINDINGS

The redesign of the DS assignment resulted in many positive outcomes. The completed digital stories showed significantly deeper levels of reflection. The students found the DS process a different and engaging way to reflect, and a refreshing alternative to the traditional essay assignment (Thompson Long 2014).

As part of the DS assignment, students in the second implementation were asked to include a reflective feedback piece on what they thought about creating their digital stories. This gave us valuable feedback on how the students experienced the assignment, as well as what they thought about the process and the product, their completed digital stories. Many students reported that the DS enabled them to reflect more deeply than they had done in other reflective assignments on the course. They noted different reasons for this additional depth to their reflection, such as

- taking more time to reflect on the incident;
- the self-questioning required during the process;
- reflecting on the incident as a whole; stepping back, seeing the bigger picture;
- looking at the incident from different time frames and from different perspectives;
- learning from listening to their own story over and over again;
- creating multiple story drafts;
- bringing up hidden themes, issues;
- assessing personal beliefs;
- connecting theory to practice;
- causing a deeper assessment of their own actions (Thompson Long 2014, p. 231).

Not only did students feel that the DS process added to the depth of their reflection, but they also felt it helped them to understand the reflective process better. Many felt that it gave them the skills needed to be reflective practitioners in the future.

Finally, students articulated the way they felt the use of multimedia, such as images, music and sound, as well as the recording of their own voice, added significantly to their reflection. Describing the different ways they reflected while incorporating multimedia into their DS, students used terms such as "focused", "intensified", "greater clarification" and "greater insight" (Thompson Long 2014, p. 234). The words of one student aptly sum up the comments of many:

Throughout the entire year, doing all of the hundreds of reflections we have done, I have used written words to reflect. Yes, I had to think about what happened, and what would happen, etc. but I did these using words. In this way, I could write down the words, and that would be the reflection done. However, with doing the Digital Story I went deeper into the reflection than I think I ever have done, not just in the PGDE, but in general. For each picture that I was looking for I went deeper into my thoughts and, more importantly, my emotions. Instead of simply writing down the words "that made me feel lost", as I would have done in previous reflections, I went deeper and deeper into how I really felt, and what exactly made me feel this way. This was not difficult; however, as I searched and searched through pictures I could measure my emotions by them. For example, I would see a picture portraying anger and think that I felt angrier than that depicted, or perhaps felt less angry than it portrays. Therefore, I was not only reflecting on the emotion of anger, but I was also able to contemplate the extent to which I felt this. (2010–2011 Student 131)

THE DS ASSIGNMENT NOW

The analysis and redesign of the DS project continued for a third year as part of the first author's doctoral research (see Thompson Long 2014). Similarly, positive findings emerged from the third "capstone" year of the research. At the time of writing this article, we have recently completed our seventh year of the DS project with our students. Each year, we ask students for their feedback and we make slight adjustments to the assignment, with the intent of enhancing students' depth of reflection through their engagement with the digital storytelling process.

The DS assignment today is very similar to the second iteration of the design. The formal story circle process has worked very well, in both enhancing reflection for students and building camaraderie within the cohort, an unanticipated bonus. Using a critical incident as the focus of the digital story has proven very successful as well. The most significant change since the second design iteration is the timing of the project. The assignment now takes place much earlier in the year, at the end of the first semester, immediately after the students' first teaching practice block placement in schools. Feedback from the students regarding the reflective skills they gained from the digital storytelling process encouraged us to complete the process as early in their first year of the programme as possible, so as to give them the reflective skills necessary for the remainder of the course. The whole process is also much quicker; students return from their first teaching placement with a rough draft critical incident, and submit their digital story three weeks later. We found that giving them months to work on the project, as we did in the first two iterations, only led to students putting the assignment off, as other assignment deadlines took precedence. The current three-week process is intensive, but manageable.

CONCLUSION

Crucially, teachers are not merely technicians (Zeichner and Liston 1996). As Dewey (1933) has described, they must be able to meet and respond to challenges and problems holistically, with intuition, emotion and passion. This necessitates significant, expansive capacity for deep reflection, practical knowledge, and learning from experience. Under its five main headings or themes, reflection, narrative, engagement, sociality and technology, R-NEST enumerates key criteria and principles for developing and implementing DS to deepen reflection among pre-service teachers (see Fig. 5.2). It also identifies key stakeholders, design informants, and

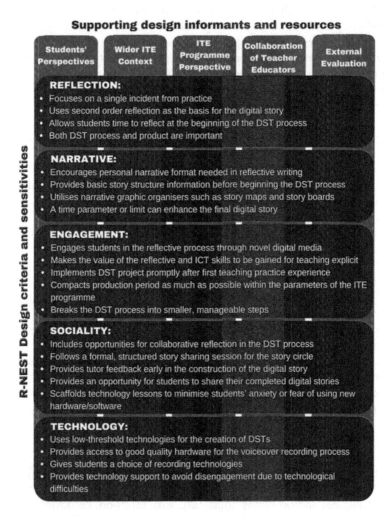

Supporting design informants and resources

| Students' Perspectives | Wider ITE Context | ITE Programme Perspective | Collaboration of Teacher Educators | External Evaluation |

R-NEST Design criteria and sensitivities

REFLECTION:
- Focuses on a single incident from practice
- Uses second order reflection as the basis for the digital story
- Allows students time to reflect at the beginning of the DST process
- Both DST process and product are important

NARRATIVE:
- Encourages personal narrative format needed in reflective writing
- Provides basic story structure information before beginning the DST process
- Utilises narrative graphic organisers such as story maps and story boards
- A time parameter or limit can enhance the final digital story

ENGAGEMENT:
- Engages students in the reflective process through novel digital media
- Makes the value of the reflective and ICT skills to be gained for teaching explicit
- Implements DST project promptly after first teaching practice experience
- Compacts production period as much as possible within the parameters of the ITE programme
- Breaks the DST process into smaller, manageable steps

SOCIALITY:
- Includes opportunities for collaborative reflection in the DST process
- Follows a formal, structured story sharing session for the story circle
- Provides tutor feedback early in the construction of the digital story
- Provides an opportunity for students to share their completed digital stories
- Scaffolds technology lessons to minimise students' anxiety or fear of using new hardware/software

TECHNOLOGY:
- Uses low-threshold technologies for the creation of DSTs
- Provides access to good quality hardware for the voiceover recording process
- Gives students a choice of recording technologies
- Provides technology support to avoid disengagement due to technological difficulties

Fig. 5.2   R-NEST design model: criteria and guidelines

resources that should be consulted in designing DS to enhance reflective practice in teacher education.

Boyer called the informed and principled, transformative possibilities afforded by methodological approaches such as AR and DBR, "the serious study that undergirds good teaching" (1990, p. 23). As we continue to teach and finesse DS as a core element within our teacher education programme, we are constantly striving for what Boyer described as "not only transmitting knowledge, but transforming and extending it as well", where "professors themselves will be pushed in creative new directions" (1990, p. 23). Boyer noted, "good teaching means that faculty, as scholars, are also learners" (1990, p. 24). DBR has enabled us to facilitate our own reflective practice as faculty, alongside the improvement of our student teachers' capacity for deeper, critical reflection through powerful digital storytelling design.

REFERENCES

Barab, S., & Squire, K. (2004). Design–based research: Putting a stake in the ground. *Journal of the Learning Sciences, 13*(1), 1–14. (Special Issue: Design-based research: clarifying the terms).

Barrett, H. (2005). *Digital storytelling research design.* http://helenbarrett.com/. Accessed 16 Apr 2009.

Barrett, H. (2006). *Digital stories in ePortfolios: Multiple purposes and tools.* http://electronicportfolios.org/digistory/purposes.html. Accessed 17 Apr 2009.

Boud, D., Keogh, R., & Walker, D. (1985). Promoting reflection in learning: A model. In D. Boud, R. Keogh, & D. Walker (Eds.), *Reflection: Turning experience into learning.* London: Kogan Page.

Boyer, E. (1990). *Scholarship reconsidered: Priorities of the professoriate.* Princeton: Carnegie Foundation for the Advancement of Teaching.

Calderhead, J. (1989). Reflective teaching and teacher education. *Teaching and Teacher Education, 5*(1), 43–51.

Center for Digital Storytelling. (2010). *Digital storytelling assessment rubric (for educators).* http://www.storycenter.org/. Accessed 19 Dec 2010.

Collin, S., Karsenti, T., & Komis, V. (2013). Reflective practice in initial teacher training: Critiques and perspectives. *Reflective Practice, 14*(1), 104–117.

Dewey, J. (1910). *How we think.* Boston: D. C. Heath.

Dewey, J. (1916). *Democracy and education.* New York: Macmillan Company.

Dewey, J. (1933). *How we think: A restatement of the relation of reflective thinking to the educative process.* Boston: Houghton Mifflin Company.

Gravestock, P., & Jenkins, M. (2009). Digital storytelling and its pedagogical impact. In T. Mayes et al. (Eds.), *Transforming higher education through technology enhanced learning*. The Higher Education Academy: York.

Hatton, N., & Smith, D. (1995). Reflection in teacher education: Towards definition and implementation. *Teaching and Teacher Education, 11*(1), 33–49. http://www.sciencedirect.com/science/article/pii/0742051X9400012U. Accessed 21 Nov 2014.

Heo, M. (2009). Digital storytelling: An empirical study of the impact of digital storytelling on pre-service teachers' self-efficacy and dispositions towards educational technology. *Journal of Educational Multimedia and Hypermedia, 18*(4), 405–428. http://editlib.org/p/30458/. Accessed 16 Oct 2009.

Hofer, M., & Owings Swan, K. (2006). Digital storytelling: Moving from promise to practice. In C. M. Crawford et al. (Eds.), *Society for information technology and teacher education international conference 2006* (pp. 679–684). Orlando: AACE. https://www.learntechlib.org/p/22122. Accessed 16 Oct 2009.

Jamissen, G., & Haug, K. H. (2014). Towards the Digital Storytelling University. In C. Gregori-Signes & A. M. Brigido-Corachan (Eds.), *Appraising digital storytelling across educational contexts* (pp. 1–18). Valencia: Publicacions de la Universitat de València.

Jamissen, G., & Skou, G. (2010). Poetic reflection through digital storytelling – A methodology to foster professional health worker identity in students. www.seminar.net. http://seminar.net/images/stories/vol6-issue2/Jamissen_prcent_26Skou-Poeticreflectionthroughdigitalstorytelling.pdf. Accessed 5 Nov 2010.

Kajder, S., & Parkes, K. (2012). Examining preservice teachers' reflective practice within and across multimodal writing environments. *Journal of Technology and Teacher Education, 20*(3), 229–249. http://www.editlib.org/f/37489. Accessed 14 Jan 2013.

Kearney, M. (2009). Investigating digital storytelling and portfolios in teacher education. In *World conference on educational multimedia, hypermedia and telecommunications 2009* (pp. 1987–1996). Honolulu: AACE. Available at: www.editlib.org/d/31749/. Accessed 16 Oct 2009.

Lambert, J. (2009). *Digital storytelling: Capturing lives, creating community* (3rd ed.). Berkeley: Digital Diner Press.

Lambert, J. (2010). *Digital storytelling cookbook*. Berkley: Digital Diner Press.

Lambert, J. (2013). *Digital storytelling: Capturing lives, creating community* (4th ed.). New York: Routledge.

MacLeod, D.M., & Cowieson, A.R. (2001). Discovering credit where credit is due: Using autobiographical writing as a tool for voicing growth. *Teachers & Teaching, 7*(3), 239–256. http://dx.doi.org/10.1080/13540600120078193. Accessed 3 May 2009.

Matthews-DeNatale, G. (2008). *Digital storytelling – Tips and resources*. http://www.educause.edu/Resources/DigitalStoryMakingUnderstandin/162538. Accessed 16 Apr 2009.

McDrury, J., & Alterio, M. (2002). *Learning through storytelling in higher education*. London: Dunmore Press.

Moon, J. (1999). *Reflection in learning and professional development*. London: Kogan Page.

Moon, J. (2004). *A handbook of reflective and experiential learning: Theory and practice*. London: Routledge Falmer.

Reeves, T. C., Herrington, J., & Oliver, R. (2005). Design research: A socially responsible approach to instructional technology research in higher education. *Journal of Computing in Higher Education, 16*(2), 96–115. http://www.springerlink.com/content/xq235710213h0226/. Accessed 30 Nov 2013.

Rodgers, C. (2002). Defining reflection: Another look at John Dewey and reflective thinking. *Teachers College Record, 104*(4), 842–866. http://www.tcrecord.org/. Accessed 28 Mar 2013.

Sandars, J., Murray, C., & Pellow, A. (2008). Twelve tips for using digital storytelling to promote reflective learning by medical students. *Medical Teacher, 30*, 774–777. http://informahealthcare.com/doi/abs/10.1080/01421590801987370. Accessed 14 Dec 2010.

Schön, D. (1987). *Educating the reflective practitioner*. San Francisco: Jossey-Bass Inc.

School of Education NUI Galway. (2010). Portfolio part B 2009–2010 assignment brief.

Thompson Long, B. (2014). *Designing digital storytelling: Creative technology for reflection in initial teacher education*. Galway: National University of Ireland. https://aran.library.nuigalway.ie/handle/10379/4463?show=full. Accessed 4 Apr 2016.

Tripp, D. (1993). *Critical incidents in teaching: Developing professional judgement*. London: Routledge.

Zeichner, K. M., & Liston, D. P. (1996). *Reflective teaching: An introduction*. Mahwah: Lawrence Earlbaum Associates.

CHAPTER 6

Let's Get Personal: Digital Stories for Transformational Learning in Social Work Students

Kim M. Anderson

INTRODUCTION

In this chapter, the focus is on social work students creating their own digital stories to better understand the production process along with how the personal and professional meet to enhance one's practice. We look at how the production of digital stories can create opportunities to reflect on one's personal experiences with adversity, lessons learned, and how these new-found insights may enhance professional practice.

This chapter addresses the use of digital storytelling to deepen reflective practice for graduate social work students enrolled in an advanced clinical practice course at a Midwestern University. Students ($N = 45$) authored personal stories of adversity digitally, combining voice, music, and images. The end result was a three- to five-minute video that was presented to their peers. They then wrote reflection papers on the process of story selection, the use of multimedia to portray their experiences, and the effect of sharing

K.M. Anderson (✉)
University of Central Florida, Orlando, FL, USA

© The Author(s) 2017
G. Jamissen et al. (eds.), *Digital Storytelling in Higher Education,*
Digital Education and Learning, DOI 10.1007/978-3-319-51058-3_6

their videos within the classroom setting. Findings from thematic analysis of students' reaction papers aligned with Wong-Wylie's self-reflection practice inclusive of Schön's (1983) two modes of practitioner reflection patterns: reflection-in-action, reflecting on responses and actions during production and viewing of one's digital story, and reflection-on-action, reflecting on post-digital storytelling experience regarding impacts on one's personal and professional development. Ultimately, digital story production provided a transformational learning experience (Mezirow 1991) that deepened students' critical thinking, enhanced their self-efficacy, and challenged their personal and professional meaning structures.

DIMENSIONS OF REFLECTION IN LEARNING

Learning through reflection is based on theories of adult learning and teaching as well as models of experiential education (Dewey 1938; Joplin 1981; Kolb 1984). Experiential education underscores how experience coupled with reflection provides the avenue to deeper learning and thus deeper meaning perspectives. "Reflection involves taking the unprocessed, raw material of experience and engaging with it as a way to make sense of what has occurred" (Boud 2001, p. 10). Nursing and nurse education have embraced the reflective process, producing considerable literature on its learning impact (Jamissen and Skou 2010; Stacey and Hardy 2011; Valkanova and Watts 2007). In comparison, social work writings address reflection in a more limited manner, often applied to the field practicum more so than the classroom context (Jenson-Hart et al. 2014). Social work students practice reflection during their internships through journaling and agency supervisory consultation, particularly regarding critical client incidents that may challenge their meaning perspectives regarding self-efficacy and the work they do (Grise-Owens and Crum 2012). Yet, deep reflective practice is not limited to the field experience, as critical thinking can be facilitated in various settings where social work "students engage in doing and thinking about what they are doing" (Jenson-Hart et al. 2014, p. 357). Social work students creating personal digital stories provide such an avenue for synergistic reflection and action, where learning may be transformed and extended beyond the professional realm to include the personal as well.

Reflecting on one's practice promotes greater self-awareness and, therefore, impacts professional growth and development of social work students (Jenson-Hart et al. 2014; Moore et al. 2011). Schön (1983) delineated two types of practitioner reflection patterns: *reflection-in-action* and *reflection-on-action*. Reflection-in-action involves practitioners drawing on tacit knowledge while attending directly to responses and adjusting actions at the time of the event. In contrast, reflection-on-action refers to practitioners analysing post-event, something they have already done, on how they may have acted differently and how to incorporate new-found insights into future practice (Schön 1987). Social work students, therefore, need to not only acquire effective helping skills but also gain ways to better understand and make sense of their practice experiences.

Influenced by Schön's (1983, 1987) work, professional literature of reflective practice is largely focused on the professional self-separate from the personal (Pedro 2005). By contrast, Wong-Wylie (2010) introduced a third pattern—*reflection-on-self-in/on-action*—to refer to practitioners reflecting on the way their personal experiences influence them on a professional level. Such reflection uncovers dimensions of self (for instance culture, life experiences, etc.) that may impact one's helping paradigm. In other words, one's personal experiences are woven into his/her professional practice frameworks. Rooted in the narrative perspective, Clandinin and Connelly (1991) refer to such awareness of the link between personal and professional selves as *personal practice knowledge*. These authors underscore how stories are intricately tied to, and therefore, influence, personal practice knowledge. Stories serve to increase our understanding of personal experiences by promoting awareness and reflection of life circumstances (Anderson 2010).

The class assignment discussed in this chapter consisted of each student creating a brief digital story of encountering adversity that was meaningful in some way to one's life journey. Students did not have to create a story regarding a traumatic experience; instead, they were asked to select one regarding life challenge(s) they had faced. The act of telling the story aloud "externalizes" it, and this externalization allows the story to become an object of reflection. Such experiential learning assisted social work students to transform their meaning structures regarding difficult life experiences and their impact, while helping them connect their personal and professional selves.

CLASSROOM ASSIGNMENT AND CONTEXT

The classroom context involved graduate social work students attending a Midwestern University, who were enrolled in an advance practice course to acquire theory and skill development on psychological trauma and recovery. The clinical practice course was capped at 15 students allowing for intensive instruction, guidance, and experiential learning. Class foci involved learning various evidence-based practice strategies related to trauma recovery for clients; one such intervention was trauma-focused cognitive behavioural therapy (TF-CBT), an intervention for youth with emotional and behavioural difficulties associated with violence exposure (Cohen et al. 2006). Students were taught the core components of standard TF-CBT that make up the acronym PRACTICE (Cohen et al. 2006): *p*sycho-education, *r*elaxation skills, *a*ffect expression and modulation, *c*ognitive coping, *t*rauma narrative development, *i*n-session mastery of trauma reminders, *c*onjoint parent–child sessions, and *e*nhancing future safety and development.

The author, during her role as a clinical coordinator for a rural victim services agency, had initiated, monitored, and evaluated the use of digital storytelling, as a narrative intervention for traumatized youth (N = 16), ages 9–17, receiving TF-CBT (Anderson and Cook 2015; Anderson and Wallace 2015). Digital storytelling was implemented because youth were having difficulty constructing their trauma narratives, as children often do not speak or write plainly about their trauma (Hanney and Kozlowska 2002). We found that children needed to find another mode of expression to discover their voices. Youth used iPads with the iMovie application and worked with therapists to create digital stories of their experiences regarding exposure to domestic violence. It helped youth process and develop their stories of exposure to domestic violence in a less threatening and more approachable manner. As a result, the author developed a curriculum that delineated digital storytelling tasks and stages for clinicians to use in their practice with traumatized youth that was subsequently taught to graduate social work students in the advanced practice course. These students, therefore, produced personal digital stories based on the following prompt:

> Everyone has an experience of facing challenges either for yourself, your family, or your community, where it seemed as if life was too hard to hang in there, but instead of giving up you got through it, and maybe even gained important lessons that helped you grow in areas of your life. Think about how you would turn a true story of a challenge you faced into a short film.

Total class hours for story production and viewing included 12 hours (four class sessions × three hours each). The digital storytelling process began with reviewing the author's digital storytelling curriculum, inclusive of the author and others' video examples. Students then presented their story ideas to each other and the instructor together in one story circle process. Sharing story topics within the three-hour classroom context allowed students to explore story choice and begin planning for story production. Students were given a choice of using their own laptops (often already equipped with digital story media) or they could use the social work computer laboratory that was equipped with Movie Maker software.

Students were provided one additional class session where they worked individually to develop their digital stories. The author's former colleagues/youth therapists at the victim services agency attended these sessions where they and the instructor provided technical assistance to students and shared their digital storytelling experiences with clients. Students often worked on their digital stories outside of the classroom allowing for spaces that were more private and less time-controlled. Upon completion of the videos, two class sessions were dedicated to viewing and processing of each other's videos.

Students were not assessed on their completed digital stories as the learning experience was not focused on production competence, but instead was focused on critical self-reflection. Therefore, students were graded on their reflection papers regarding their digital storytelling process. The intent of the reaction paper was to further process students' digital storytelling experiences while deepening students' reflective practice. Reflection papers were due one week after the classroom viewing of videos and requirements included:

1. Discuss the story you wanted to tell and why.
2. Discuss your reactions regarding creating and completing your digital story.
3. Discuss your reactions upon viewing the digital story with the class.
4. Discuss whether or not this intervention was helpful and why.
5. Discuss how you will use this intervention in your professional work with clients.

DATA COLLECTION AND ANALYSIS

Data collection included a convenience sample of three different class terms resulting in 45 (2 males, 43 females) student reaction papers over the most recent three-year period. Students authored stories of individual, familial, and societal adversity, including topics of sexual assault, domestic violence, substance abuse, mental illness, learning disabilities, death and dying, health challenges, poverty, racism, and homophobia. Reaction papers encompassed students' perspectives on both the process and outcomes of digital storytelling production. The research question was: What insights and impacts does student participation in digital storytelling invoke regarding personal and professional development?

Qualitative data analysis involved the thematic analysis method. This type of analysis allowed the author to examine similarities within the data in order to later organize them into themes (Braun and Clarke 2006). Themes were patterns found across the data set (e.g., insights, effects) that were directly associated with the research question and become categories for analysis (Fereday and Muir-Cochrane 2006). The assignment was not intentionally designed to emulate any particular framework for reflective practice. However, findings from qualitative thematic analysis of students' papers did align with Wong-Wylie's self-reflection practice inclusive of Schön's (1983) two modes of practitioner reflection patterns— *reflection-in-action* and *reflection-on-action*. Reflection-on-self-in-action involved students drawing on tacit knowledge while attending directly to personal responses and adjusting actions during storytelling production and viewing. Reflection-on-self-on-action, in contrast, involved students' contemplations after digital story production, including lessons learned and incorporation of new-found insights into future practice. Gender neutral pseudonyms are used for students' quotes.

REFLECTION-ON-SELF-IN-ACTION

Reflection-on-self-in-action involved students connecting with their feelings, emotions, and prior experiences during digital story production, while also attending to the technical and narrative aspects of digital story creation and dissemination. Four reflection-on-self-in-action themes addressed *how* digital storytelling production promoted transformative learning inclusive of the following elements: (1) selecting a story, (2) learning storytelling components and the narrative process, (3) using multimedia to take ownership of one's story, and (4) recognizing the vulnerability and relief of sharing one's difficult experiences with others.

Story Selection

Students were informed of the assignment at the beginning of the semester and were aware that their finished videos would be viewed by the class as a whole. For many, this influenced their story choice regarding how personal, and thus vulnerable, they wanted to be in sharing their experiences. Often, the courage and support of their classmates helped them to feel safe enough to face their difficult personal experiences.

> I decided to share my story because of the willingness of my classmates to share their own stories. Once I started to conceptualize what I wanted my story to be, I realized that I did not have to dwell on the hurtful part of it. I hoped to communicate in my story, that although I have sustained some personal losses, the loss has made me stronger and I am still standing. (Case, father's death)

For some, story choice was immediate, whereas for others it was an emergent process, or for others it was simply to find meaning and closure.

> The day our class stated our story choices was very difficult for me. When it was my turn to state what I would present upon, I somehow gained the courage to say, "I was attacked and will be exploring the changes that occurred preceding the attack". I had no intention of talking about the attack, but it just came out of my mouth. (Re, sexual assault survivor)

> To be honest, I do not know why I finally chose this story to be a focal point for an assignment, as this story is one of the most painful to tell. Even though I have experienced many other traumas in life understanding how, and why, someone [her brother] is born with such a horrible illness that would later remove him from the lives of his loved ones is something I will never understand. So, I guess I chose this story as a last ditch effort to try and process my feelings regarding his loss. (Tae, brother's death)

Story Production

Learning storytelling components and the narrative process included establishing temporal order and assembling fragments into a coherent narrative. Students had an intuitive sense of how they wanted their stories to develop in regard to the sequencing of images, music selected, and whether or not to record their voice.

I feel as though it helped me put the pieces of my story together, and ultimately helped me pick up the pieces of my broken heart. This story assisted me in establishing exactly what I was feeling. With the combination of music, my voice, and my words, I feel like I accurately portrayed such a complex struggle in my life in just a few short minutes. (Key, break-up with boyfriend)

The digital story process included accepting the feelings that came forth during the digital storytelling process and learning to modulate their emotions as they processed their experiences. Often, an array of both positive and negative emotions occurred during production of their digital stories.

For my digital story I chose to use a song that was sung at the [grandfather's] funeral. I waited until the very end to add in any music. I felt that same feeling listening to it that I did the day of the funeral. I felt my body become full and warm, and as I fought back tears of joy, happiness and sadness, memories flooded my body all over again. I find it amazing how a song can make you feel so much emotion but it is that, simply amazing. (Mar, grandfather's death)

An important aspect of digital story production included balancing technical skills with immersion into difficult story material. The sequential process of script development, audio-recorded self-narrative, selection of photographs, and assembly of the video helped students tell one's story in manageable doses. Such processing allowed them to elaborate and organize their memories while tolerating negative emotions associated with it.

When I wasn't focused on the emotional aspect of creating the story, I was focusing on the technical aspect. After recording, I began putting in photos and adjusting them. I noticed I was very concerned with how things looked and got frustrated with the computer and technology aspect of the story on numerous occasions. However, it was good because this aspect allowed me to focus on something not related to the emotional aspect of creating the story, providing a distraction from becoming too overwhelmed. (DJ, grandmother's cancer battle)

Story Ownership

Students were empowered to address difficult experiences in a deliberate manner while having creative control and a variety of ways to tell their story. They used multimedia to take ownership of one's story through deciding what to tell, convey, and communicate. In doing so, they gained an enriched realization of the power in taking control of one's story.

> The best part about digital storytelling is being able to make your own story. Doing this allowed me to put a personalized touch to it and make me laugh and/or cry when I wanted. This is the good thing about digital stories, because one can put as much or as little as one wants into the story. This was made evident in our class because some had tragic stories, yet they shared the amount they wanted the class to know. (Sutton, grandmother's death)

> The most helpful aspect of the process was typing it out/refining my words and speaking those words aloud. I took ownership of my words and my feelings in a way that I had never done before. It was empowering to put my feelings into words then show peers a very personal part of myself. The entire process, beginning to end, enabled me to let go in a way I hadn't known how to do before. (Reagan, coming out as a lesbian)

Story Viewing

Students' digital stories were not shared with each other until the final film-viewing sessions. Students underscored the vulnerability and relief of sharing one's difficult experiences with others. Students were anxious and concerned about being "emotional" in front of their peers, feeling vulnerable in disclosing something so personal, and concerned regarding how they and their experiences would be received. Ultimately, students felt relieved, supported, and accepted by their peers.

> I believe that sharing the video with the class was so important because it helped me to see what it would be like as a client to share my video with someone I barely know. Just like social workers should, the class made me feel comfortable and supported. I realized how it feels as a client to open up to someone that you barely know. I also think it was helpful to view everyone else's stories and see just how different the digital story videos can be. It was like having many different clients with many different views and values, and seeing what was important to each one. (Jo, mother's breast cancer battle)

Students reported how the entire class signing a contract that each other's stories would not be discussed outside of the class, unless permission was given by the author, helped to ease the discomfort of sharing their personal experiences in a public manner.

I like how we all were able to sign a contract that our stories will not be shared outside of the classroom. Even though it seems like a minute detail, and I most likely would not have shared people's stories with others without signing the contract, it gave me a reminder of the importance of confidentiality and people's right to share their own stories. (Blake, dating violence survivor)

REFLECTION-ON-SELF-ON-ACTION

Reflection-on-self-on-action included students contemplating their reactions to the classroom assignment post-digital story production, and its impact on transformation of self, both personally and professionally. Three reflection-on-self-on-action themes captured such outcomes of: (1) personal mastery over difficult life experiences, (2) enhanced professional wisdom and competence, and (3) use of new-found insights (lessons learned) to guide practice.

Mastery Over Difficult Life Experiences

Students revealed a heightened appreciation of what one has overcome, particularly one's strengths and resilient capacities, along with greater insight regarding the challenges of coping with a difficult experience. Ultimately, they experienced pride on how they persevered despite enduring personal trials and tribulations. These new-found insights affirmed their belief that change is possible regardless of one's circumstances.

By fully participating in such an exercise (with strengths-oriented and resiliency perspectives in the forefront), I was able to not only better view my past experiences as an active gang member as a reflective learning experience, but as a personal narrative of triumph amidst the many environmental barriers and other oppressive forces that I had been directly or indirectly subjected to. Positive change within this population [gang members] cohort *is* possible—I am the living testament to such an ideal. (Sky, former gang member)

During this process I was able to recognize some of the protective factors I had utilized and saw that I had demonstrated resilience which had previously gone unrecognized. For example, I realized that strong connections with my faith and family, as well as my creativity and involvement in extra-curricular activities, helped me to cope with my experience and assisted my recovery. (Ash, dating violence survivor)

Students reported that having ownership of how they wanted to portray the event itself and its impact helped them to gain a sense of control over their personal experiences, which in the past had often rendered them powerless. Students often underscored how creating and producing digital stories was empowering, particularly, as they realized that the event did not have to define them.

> I did not and still do not feel as if I am stuck on the event, and I wanted to focus more on the good experiences I have had in my life, and how I have overcome the [childhood] rape. When the project was completed, and I viewed the video for the first time, I felt victorious. I had succeeded in creating something I felt proud of, and I managed to tell my story how I wanted to. (Jae, childhood rape)

> I found the digital story very helpful because it gave me the opportunity to do some introspective critical thinking. I was able to really think about the struggle that I have been through and critically dissect the ways that it has impacted me. I had the opportunity to not only think about my story, but I was able to choose what should and should not be included in my story and how I wanted my story to look. I felt incredibly empowered by the entire assignment. (Dakota, racism and homophobia)

Students described the relief they experienced in not only finishing the assignment but the catharsis and, for some, closure regarding their difficult life experiences. They gained power over experiences that seemed beyond the possibility of doing so.

> In the days since I presented my digital storytelling movie to class, I have been surprised at the positive difference the experience has made in my life. It is as if a tremendous load has been lifted off of my shoulders. I believe the process forced me to vent emotions that had been held in-check far too long. I recounted out-loud, for others to hear, the heinous acts of terror and abuse he (former son-in-law) committed against our daughter, and gained strength in the process. (Erin, parent of a domestic violence survivor)

> I am eternally grateful for this assignment being put forth for what I perceived as merely being the last and final assignment of this course became the closing and final chapter on a painful memory of my life. Creating a digital story of my experience regarding the rape allowed me to make sense of the event in a way that I had previously not been able to do before. The

creative expression that epitomizes digital stories enables individuals, just as it enabled me, to narrate experiences which are considerably difficult to divulge. I still cannot believe that I was able to take my lack of technological skills and actually produce something that I felt was substantial and meaningful. It is with complete and utter honesty when I say that creating the digital story was the final puzzle piece of this emotionally turbulent and trying time in my life. (River, rape survivor)

Enhanced Practice Wisdom and Competence

Students revealed enhanced practice wisdom and competence (technical and therapeutic skills) due to completing a narrative activity that they would ask of their clients to do. In addition to enhanced critical reflections skills, students reported heightened empathy and compassion for others facing adversity, along with an increased appreciation for the internal struggles one faces in addressing personal hardships.

> I thought this intervention was helpful by having the opportunity to go through the various feelings that other people will experience when completing a trauma narrative. I think it enhances our level of compassion and credibility when we understand the complexity of allowing the hard to surface, but then pressing on to receive comfort and healing. (Emerson, estranged adult relationship with father)

> I think this was an incredibly useful and beneficial assignment. As a clinician, we are asking our clients to open up about very personal and intense things. If we, ourselves, cannot open up about such things, how can we ask our client to do so? The vulnerability that I experienced was very great, but I also think it was character building and helpful for having empathy for my clients, current and future. (Hayden, saved a drowning child)

Lessons Learned

Students reported new-found insights as a result of the assignment that would serve to guide their practice. Lessons learned included the power of digital storytelling to transform difficult life experiences, as individuals own the direction and influence of their stories, and thus their lives.

> This probably was one of the most useful assignments that I have done, and I began to think of the varied uses for this type of intervention. The stories

could encompass many aspects of a client's life that might include trauma or loss and his/her journey through these events. It appears that it could enhance the visualization of strengths that had previously been denied. Powerful tools that can assist clients in recovering their true, healthy, and productive selves are truly profound. (Riley, learning disability)

Individuals are able to use their own creativity to show their story as it has played throughout their life. It is important to note that a lot of individuals who have experienced traumatic events may not have had the freedom to make their own decisions or choose what they want to do. The freedom when creating a digital story helps make this intervention effective, because it allows individuals to take control of their lives and create something to call their own, which many individuals may have never done before. (Remi, parental divorce)

Discussion

Deep learning occurs through the relationship between experience, reflection, and action (Knott and Scragg 2010). This chapter addresses such a process as social work students engaged in the production of personal digital stories, followed by a reflective paper of their experiences. In doing so, they engaged in cognitive, affective, and technical activities to explore their experience resulting in new personal and professional exploration and understanding. Ultimately, the assignment captured Mezirow's "disorienting dilemma" in which the learning experience produced a paradigm shift regarding perspectives of oneself ultimately affecting students' subsequent views of one's professional self.

Initially, the assignment's learning purpose was for students to learn an innovative narrative method they could use to help clients process challenging aspects of their lives. In doing so, students were cultivating an understanding of the technical aspects of the intervention, along with gaining insight and empathy regarding clients' internal processing of difficult personal experiences. The digital storytelling assignment, however, went beyond these initial aims to be a transformational learning experience (Mezirow 1991), a process of challenging, modifying, and/or extending students' meaning perspectives (i.e., one's overall world view). The findings of this study, consequently, underscore the significance of students' critical reflection (Mezirow 1997) going beyond Schön's (1983) two professional patterns of reflection to include the self, as identified by Wong-Wylie (2007).

Yip (2006) discusses how the reflective process for students is enhanced if it includes opportunities for self-analysis, self-evaluation, self-dialogue, and self-observation, which can occur across various educational experiences. An educator needs to go beyond the direction of "reflect on this" for students to gain critical reflection skills; offering a planned activity, as with digital storytelling, is necessary for greater examination of process after, and sometimes during, the learning event (Anderson 1992; Dean 1993). Digital stories, as educational tools used with nurses and other health-care professionals, have found to enhance professional empathy, compassion, and understanding (Hardy 2007; Jamissen and Skou 2010; Stacey and Hardy 2011; Sumner 2009).

The educator's role is to provide a safe and nonthreatening environment for students to develop their digital stories and to support the process. The majority of students in the class were already familiar with the instructor because of prior course involvement. As it was an advanced practice course, students often worked together to discuss readings and practice skills. Thus, there was a familiarity between students and the instructor that enhanced the environment. In addition, students and the instructor signed a contract that the stories would not be discussed outside of the classroom unless permission was sought and given by the story creator.

Perhaps because the students had an informed choice, this allowed them to readily participate, although not without personal struggle, in digital story production and subsequent reflection paper of a difficult life experience. Students were aware of this assignment prior to enrolling in the class, as all students were given information on the content and tasks related to each of the clinical advanced courses to better inform them on their selections. The assignment was also addressed in the first-class session upon review of the syllabus and throughout the semester. In addition, students were provided the latitude to create their digital stories in whatever ways best suited them which provided a sense of control and ownership.

Clinical social work students developing self-awareness is central to competent practice. Therefore, it is necessary to not only increase therapeutic skills but also further address how the personal is professional. Social work education warns students about the hazards of practice, such as vicarious trauma, on one's personhood. In addition, students are asked to reflect on how biases, prejudices, or attitudes may impact practice. If students' difficult life experiences are brought up, however, they are often advised to address them through therapeutic support, or are questioned regarding their suitability for the profession. Thus, little attention is given to how students may impact their personal experiences to positively influence their professional development, as in the case of student digital story production presented in this chapter.

LIMITATIONS

Anonymous written student feedback was sought upon completion of the assignment, 43 of 45 students answered "yes" to the following question: Would you recommend this assignment for other graduate students? Of those who answered, "no", reasons involved the pressure of it being an assignment and therefore needing to complete the process in a specified time period. In addition, students learn in different ways and a multimedia approach may not be the best fit with a student's mode of learning.

CONCLUSION

Mezirow (1997) underscores how significant learning involves critical reflection regarding premises about oneself as a guide to action. Digital storytelling production provided an experiential learning activity for social work students that generated new perspectives and insight to enhance their self-efficacy, along with transforming meaning perspectives, to ultimately benefit their personal and professional development for working with clients facing adversity.

REFERENCES

Anderson, B. (1992). Task and reflection in learning to learn. In J. Mulligan & C. Griffin (Eds.), *Empowerment through experiential learning: Explorations of good practice* (pp. 239–246). London: Kogan Page.

Anderson, K. M. (2010). *Enhancing resilience in survivors of family violence.* New York: Springer.

Anderson, K. M., & Cook, J. R. (2015). Challenges and opportunities of using digital storytelling as a trauma narrative intervention for traumatized children. *Advances in Social Work, 16*(1), 78–89.

Anderson, K. M., & Wallace, B. (2015). Digital storytelling as a trauma narrative intervention for children exposed to domestic violence. In J. Cohen & L. Johnson (Eds.), *Film and video-based therapy* (pp. 95–107). New York: Taylor & Francis/Routledge.

Boud, D. (2001). Using journal writing to enhance reflective practice. *New Directions for Adult and Continuing Education, 90,* 9–18.

Braun, V., & Clarke, V. (2006). Using thematic analysis in psychology. *Qualitative Research in Psychology, 3*(2), 77–101.

Clandinin, D. J., & Connelly, F. M. (1991). Narrative and story in practice and research. In D. Schön (Ed.), *The reflective turn: Case studies in and on educational practice* (pp. 258–282). New York: Teachers College Press.

Cohen, J. A., Mannarino, A. P., & Deblinger, E. (2006). *Treating trauma and traumatic grief in children and adolescents.* New York: Guilford Press.

Dean, G. J. (1993). *Developing experiential learning activities for adult learners.* American Association for Adult and Continuing Education National Conference, Dallas.

Dewey, J. (1938). *Experience and education.* New York: Macmillan.

Fereday, J., & Muri-Chochrane, E. (2006). Demonstrating rigor using thematic analysis: A hybrid approach to inductive and deductive coding and theme development. *International Journal of Qualitative Methods, 5*(1), 1–11.

Grise-Owens, G., & Crum, K. (2012). Teaching writing as a professional practice skill: A curricular case example. *Journal of Social Work Education, 48*(3), 517–536.

Hanney, L., & Kozlowska, K. (2002). Healing traumatized children: Creating illustrated storybooks in family therapy. *Family Process, 41*(1), 37–65.

Hardy, P. (2007). *An investigation into the application of the patient voices digital stories in healthcare education: Quality of learning, policy impact and practice-based value.* MSc dissertation. http://www.patientvoices.org.uk/research.htm. Accessed 20 Oct 2016.

Jamissen, G., & Skou, G. (2010). Poetic reflection through digital storytelling-a methodology to foster professional health worker identity in students. *Seminar: net-International Journal of Media, Technology and Lifelong Learning, 6*(2), 1–15.

Jensen-Hart, S., Shuttleworth, G., & Davis, J. L. (2014). Dialogue journals: A supervision to enhance reflective practice and faith integration. *Social Work & Christianity, 41*(4), 355–372.

Joplin, L. (1981). On defining experiential education. *The Journal of Experiential Education, 4*(1), 17–20.

Knott, C., & Scragg, T. (2010). *Reflective practice in social work* (2nd ed.). Exeter: Learning Matters Ltd.

Kolb, D. A. (1984). *Experiential learning: Experience as the source of learning and development.* Englewood Cliffs: Prentice-Hall.

Mezirow, J. (1991). *Transformative dimensions in adult learning.* San Francisco: Jossey-Bass.

Mezirow, J. (1997). Transformative learning: Theory to practice. In P. Cranton (Ed.), *Transformative learning in action: Insights from practice* (pp. 5–12). San Francisco: Jossey-Bass.

Moore, S. E., Bledsoe, L. K., Perry, A. R., & Robinson, M. A. (2011). Social work students and self-care: A model assignment for teaching. *Journal of Social Work Education, 47*(3), 545–553.

Pedro, J. Y. (2005). Reflection in teacher education: Exploring pre-service teachers' meanings of reflective practice. *Reflective Practice, 61*, 49–66.

Schön, D. A. (1983). *The reflective practitioner: How professionals think in action.* New York: Basic Books.

Schön, D. A. (1987). *Educating the reflective practitioner.* San Francisco: Jossey-Bass.

Stacey, G., & Hardy, P. (2011). Challenging the shock of reality through digital storytelling. *Nurse Education in Practice, 11*(2), 159–164.

Sumner, T. (2009). Inspiring innovation through Patient Voices. *Innovation Expo.* Edexcel London.

Valkanova, Y., & Watts, M. (2007). Digital story telling in a science classroom: Reflective self-learning (RSL) in action. *Early Child Development and Care, 177*(6/7), 793–807.

Wong-Wylie, G. (2007). Barriers and facilitators of reflective practice in counsellor education: Critical incidents from doctoral graduates. *Canadian Journal of Counselling, 41*(2), 59–76.

Wong-Wylie, G. (2010). *Counsellor 'know thyself': Growing ourselves, shaping our professional practice, and enhancing education through reflection.* Saarbrücken: VDM Verlag Press.

Yip, K. (2006). Self-reflection in reflective practice: A note of caution. *British Journal of Social Work, 36*, 777–788.

CHAPTER 7

Navigating Ethical Boundaries When Adopting Digital Storytelling in Higher Education

Daniela Gachago and Pam Sykes

INTRODUCTION

Digital storytelling has been embraced in educational settings because of its potential "to empower participants through personal reflection, growth, and the development of new literacies" (Gubrium et al. 2014). At the university where one of the authors is based, it has increased digital literacies and student engagement, provided a space for reflection and improved management of multicultural classrooms (Condy et al. 2012; Ivala et al. 2013).

However, adopting this emotional and process-oriented practice into an educational context, with its constraints of course objectives, assessment regimes, timetables and large classes, raises ethical concerns. What support and follow-up mechanisms exist to help students cope with any

D. Gachago (✉)
Cape Peninsula University of Technology,
Cape Town, South Africa

P. Sykes
University of the Western Cape,
Cape Town, South Africa

© The Author(s) 2017
G. Jamissen et al. (eds.), *Digital Storytelling in Higher Education*,
Digital Education and Learning, DOI 10.1007/978-3-319-51058-3_7

emotional fallout? Is it ethical to mark these stories? How well equipped are educators to handle strong emotions and difficult dialogues in the classroom (Landis 2008)?

This is an area that is under-researched. This chapter is an auto-ethnographic account (Ellis 2004) in which we reflect on how we have negotiated the boundaries between story work process and pedagogical device when introducing digital storytelling into teaching and learning.

We start by introducing ourselves and our backgrounds to explain our different perspectives, then outline the context of the work we discuss. The main body of the chapter consists of our reflections on a series of "snapshots": short narratives about ethical dilemmas that we have faced in our work, exemplifying how our practice informs our research agenda (Boyer 1990). We have engaged in a continuous dialogue about these issues and have often surprised each other with our different perspectives. These mirror our professional and academic identities and, we believe, represent in interesting ways the tension between pedagogical and therapeutic project that digital storytelling in higher education has to negotiate.

INTRODUCING THE AUTHORS

Daniela Gachago

I am an outsider to South Africa. How to make sense of the complex social and historical phenomenon of apartheid, and the impact it still has today, is one of the biggest challenges I face in my work, my studies and my private life. I was introduced to digital storytelling in 2010 and since then have been supporting digital storytelling projects at my university. I have never undergone formal facilitator training, but have acquired skills mostly through reading, experiential learning and my continuous exchange with digital storytellers such as Pam. My story work is strongly influenced by theoretical approaches framed by the affective turn (Ahmed 2004) and critical emotions studies such as Boler and Zembylas's (2003) work on the pedagogy of discomfort. I introduce digital storytelling into the classroom to allow a different engagement across difference. I have written extensively about my experiences and have made it the topic of my PhD studies (see, e.g., Gachago 2015; Gachago et al. 2013, 2015).

Pam Sykes

I am a child of apartheid. Since 1994 I have lived through both the unreflective enthusiasm of the "rainbow nation" years and the slowly dawning national realisation that the wounds of history are not so easily healed. My personal disillusion with my first-chosen career of journalism—its narrow frames of reference, its tendency to stereotype, its failure to question or disrupt the subtler operations of power—was one of the factors, along with a commitment to personal transformation and process work, that led me to digital storytelling. As a digital storytelling facilitator since 2010, in this profoundly under-storied country, my goal has been to contribute a flow of stories that begins to amplify the voices of ordinary South Africans. I took on some of Daniela's facilitation and other duties temporarily while she was on sabbatical to complete her PhD and have now embarked on my own PhD studies.

CONTEXT

The experiences we draw on for this chapter occurred in the context of pre-service teacher education at a university serving mainly underprivileged students in South Africa. Digital storytelling was introduced to allow final year students to reflect on issues of difference and how to handle conversations about difference in the classroom, one of the programme outcomes. Over the years, this project has become one of very few spaces in the curriculum that allows students to reflect on pasts (and presents) that are often traumatic. Stories of gender-based violence, domestic abuse, drugs, gangsterism, poverty, discrimination and broken families dominate, foregrounding what Frankish (2009, p. 89) calls the "systemic traumas of [South African] contemporary life". Examples of these stories collected between 2011 and 2015 can be viewed on YouTube.[1] In general, the project allowed for an appreciation and recognition not only of the importance of allowing stories of difference into the classroom but also of the difficulties of handling emotions that emerge in this process.

SNAPSHOT 1: DISCOMFORTING THE STUDENT

Pam: In one of the very first workshops I ever facilitated, one of my participants—let's call her Linda—told a powerful story about how the death—the likely suicide—of a business partner had shaken up her life, her career and her sense of her own place and purpose in the world. In the compassionately witnessing space of the story circle, her story flowed. But Linda struggled to transform this story into a script: It came out fragmented and jumpy, incoherent. She couldn't find the thread that tied it all together and sat for long periods paralysed, first over her keyboard and then over a piece of paper. We finally settled on a version of the story that left out large parts of what she had told in the story circle: outside that space, much of it remained unspeakable.

As a facilitator this left me slightly shaken: How had I failed Linda? What could I have done differently to help her tell this story? But when I told the story to a friend who is a clinical psychologist she said instantly: "Oh, but that's trauma. People in trauma can't hold a narrative thread. That's the whole point—they can't make sense of the experience".

So when I read these lines in Daniela's PhD about a story by her student Noni, it had instant resonance: "over the first three days of the workshop, her story jarred and didn't seem to progress. ... She moved from her personal narrative, to discussing inequality in schools, challenging white privilege and finally a lack of engagement across race in South Africa. But the story still didn't emerge".

Later Noni says: "I am a very emotional person. So if I had spoken about some stuff that has happened in my life, we would all have ... I think I would have had to go home because I am that emotional. It wasn't about: How are they gonna look at me? It was about: I know myself, I can only share to this point."

Noni was criticised by her peers in the workshop for not "opening up" more. But by now I've been facilitating stories in South Africa—a country where it's rare to meet someone who has *not* experienced serious emotional and/ or physical trauma—for long enough to suspect that Noni is holding herself together, by who knows how thin a thread, in the face of a life history that threatens to blow her apart. In this context, her decision to distance herself from her own story is wise and sensible: survival trumps storytelling. It is in the decision to withhold, not the decision to share, that Noni most powerfully expresses her agency.

Daniela: In our teacher education project, we adopted a pedagogy of discomfort. Megan Boler and Michalinos Zembylas (2003) stipulate that for educators and students to develop a deeper understanding of their personal and shared pasts and presents, it is necessary for them to move outside their comfort zones. Do Mar Pereira (2012, p. 213) says: "feeling uncomfortable can allow students to notice their surroundings, sometimes for the first time".

This disruption can lead to strong responses, including anger and distress in both students and the educator—who is seldom equipped to deal with these emotions. However, Boler and Zembylas (2003) argue that it is exactly these discomforting emotions and the process of critically reflecting on their origins that is so powerful. They insist that only through this process can dominant beliefs, social habits and normative practices that sustain social inequities be challenged and possibilities for transformation be created: "'inscribed habits of emotional attention' limit, constrain, and/or open possibilities in the process of constructing difference" (Boler and Zembylas 2003, p. 112).

What I have experienced over the years is that the digital storytelling workshop is not equally uncomfortable for every student. Feminist author Sara Ahmed (2004) likens these different levels of comfort to—on the one hand—the ease that certain bodies experience when they sink into spaces that have been moulded to their shape and—on the other hand—the discomfort other bodies experience when having to sink into spaces that do not fit their shapes. I find this a powerful image to understand how dominant structures fit comfortably around certain bodies and not others.

The way student bodies fit, or fail to fit, into the space of the university has a concrete impact on what stories they can and should tell. Within a pedagogy for discomfort, both privileged and non-privileged learners need to feel discomfort, since, Boler and Zembylas (2003) claim, no-one escapes *hegemonic* thought. What does this mean in practical terms? Do we expect the same kind of cognitive and emotional labour, for example, from both students who have various kinds of privilege and those who don't?

Pam: A "pedagogy of discomfort" makes me deeply uneasy, in part because it assumes that students are starting from a position of comfort. The student inscribed here is young, middle class, privileged and relatively untroubled by history. Implicit is the idea that students need to be guided towards turning a more critical gaze on themselves and their relationship to the Other—it does not easily accommodate students who ARE the Other, at least within dominant discourses.

In contexts where students' lives have been marked by discomfort, insecurity and possibly violence, is it not perhaps both arrogant and naive to assume we can teach them anything about discomfort that they don't already know? Is the educator's first job not rather to create spaces of comfort, security and safety? The development of self-awareness and compassion—surely prerequisites for a just society—is a lifelong transformative project, and we must be heard and seen before we can hear and see others.

"Comfort the afflicted and afflict the comfortable", goes the old advice: Is it possible to do both in the same space?

Daniela: Feminist philosopher Iris Marion Young's (2011) work on shared responsibility for justice suggests how to engage with these questions. She contends that to decide who would carry the main responsibility in a fight for a more just society, one needs to consider three aspects: an agent's power, their position of privilege and their interest. I often find my focus shifting towards the experience of white students. Their experience is closer to mine, I understand them better, their narratives are more familiar and, in some ways, I find it easier to challenge them than to challenge black students. Do I expect more from them than from the black students? More work? More engagement with their privilege than black students, for example, with their internalised racism (Adams et al. 1997)? My aim is for white students to recognise their privilege and take responsibility for it. What is there for my black students to learn, apart from finding their voice? The development of their confidence to counter white students' stories with their own? Is it enough, as Berlant (2008, p. ix) argues, to share their stories and to consequently realise a shared humanity, decreasing the feeling of "being alone", for her "one of the affective experiences of being collectively, structurally underprivileged"?

And what about students like Linda or Noni, who are already vulnerable, and for whom a digital storytelling process might trigger even more traumatic reactions? How can we guard against that? What information do students need, to make an informed decision on whether to participate in the project or not? How much do they really want to share? I often have the feeling that the process "takes over" and students share much more than actually planned. Many times, this is a good thing, allowing students to open up about issues usually silenced in the class. But it might also be dangerous.

SNAPSHOT 2: DISCOMFORTING THE FACILITATOR

Daniela: I sit in a story circle with five students. We have heard a number of painful stories. Students have opened up, surprising me with their honesty and willingness to share. There were tears; we had to stop at various points to allow students to compose themselves. Students have hugged, shared tissues and listened intently. So far the group has managed to support each other, to contain the pain. The last student is a white girl. Her story stays on the surface. I try and push her, ask probing questions, trying to help her dig deeper. Still she resists. Suddenly she bursts out in tears and leaves the classroom. I don't know where she has gone. She doesn't come back to any of the workshops. Through the grapevine I hear that she has complained to the department head, arguing that such personal projects shouldn't be part of the curriculum. I worry about her. What if she cannot complete the assignment? What if she won't be able to finish the course because of this project? For the rest of the project I feel vulnerable and uncomfortable. I don't see her again until the day of the final screening where she shows a beautiful movie she did on her own, with the help of one of her peers. A huge wave of relief overcomes me.

Daniela: One of the major tensions in this project, every year we have done it, has been holding the line between therapy and pedagogical intervention. While the most consistent feedback we get from students is the importance of this project for their own personal growth, a space that is usually not created in this very traditional teacher education programme, it also forces us to ask uncomfortable questions about how to support such a process. How we can create uncomfortable yet safe spaces for our students (Freeth 2012)? We are educators, not counsellors or psychologists. The pedagogy of discomfort intentionally moves away from "psychologising" individual students to an understanding of trauma as collective, shared, constructed, inherited experience. How do we negotiate the tension between students' need for "catharsis" and the political project? I believe "in the process", of relying on students to support each other. I agree with Amy Hill (2011, p. 129), trusting her years of digital storytelling work with vulnerable storytellers, that we can and should trust storytellers to tell the story they are ready to tell:

> most people choose to tell their stories, even if doing so is quite challenging, when they intuit that they have the strength and internal resources necessary for doing so and when they sense that someone capable of truly listening is available to hear them.

Each year there have been a few cases where I felt we were pushing our boundaries in terms of ethical student support. This has made us experiment with a number of more or less successful ways of supporting students, such as inviting external support in the form of peer counsellors. We have become more adept at explaining the importance of discomfort, warning students of the challenges and identifying students "at risk". We encourage students to engage with critical readings that destabilise dominant understandings of self and other and challenge some of the assumption we carry about power and privilege, and allow students to see how the personal is always political.

However, is such a distinction really possible? How can one draw the boundaries between storytelling as a therapeutic intervention and a pedagogical activity? How far can students be pushed? What are the limits of discomfort without driving students "crazy"? (Zembylas 2013).

Pam: Based on his experience of teaching a course on the psychology of violence and trauma in a South African university, Collins (2013) suggests a number of ways to integrate strong emotional responses into formal classroom settings. Most significantly, he points to the importance of psycho-education: when people are informed about the reasons for their emotional responses to distressing material, these responses become less confusing and terrifying. Knowing "this is a normal reaction" as opposed to "I'm going crazy" is powerful. Educators who want to include digital storytelling in their curricula need to become psycho-literate themselves so that they can pass this important knowledge on to their students.

Daniela: Zembylas (2013, p. 11) asks some critical questions in this context: "How can critical pedagogues avoid becoming some sort of therapists for their students, when there is pressure in current times to provide therapeutic education?". And do educators need to undergo therapeutic interventions as well to debrief on the often traumatic experiences they encounter in class? South African educator Jonathan Jansen (2009, p. 259) emphasises the critical role of educators in creating a safe space for students to voice, listen to, analyse and reflect on one another's beliefs and assumptions. He points to the need for teacher education programmes to prepare future teachers to consciously create spaces that allow for beliefs and assumptions, often disguised by emotional defensiveness or outbursts, to be disrupted:

> the success of post-conflict pedagogy depends almost entirely on the qualities of those who teach … this means listening for the pain that lies behind a claim, the distress that is concealed in an angry outburst, the sense of loss that is protested in a strident posture. (pp. 263–264)

Can a classroom with its inherent power dynamics ever be a safe space for our learners? Would it not make more sense to recognise and address this lack of safety, for learners and educators alike? And what would that mean for our project?

Pam: Discussions of ethics in digital storytelling focus heavily on the position and rights of participants, especially around consent (see for instance Gubrium et al. 2014). But rarely, if ever, is the ethical lens turned back on practitioners themselves. What personal capacities must digital storytelling facilitators possess or develop to approach, with integrity, the work of asking students to make themselves vulnerable? What processes of supervision and reflection should facilitators commit themselves to? What happens when the stories that surface in a workshop trigger not the students but the educators? Here we need to confront the fact that educators themselves have baggage, which is often unprocessed—universities do not, on the whole, reward efforts towards personal growth. How can these institutions, and the people within them, be expected to provide for students what they can't provide for themselves?

Zembylas asks how educators can "avoid becoming some sort of therapists"—I suggest that avoidance is the wrong strategy. Digital storytelling is both cognitively and emotionally challenging. Supporting students through both kinds of challenge is the facilitator's job, and the task is not trivial. In some ways, undertaking the task in a South African classroom puts us in a position of rare opportunity: because we can legitimately expect every student to have either experienced violence or witnessed it, the issues surface with a clarity and urgency that demands we find solutions. Trauma may be a collective, shared experience, but it is individual bodies that bear its consequences, and individual pain we are called to respond to. How effectively we respond is an ethical issue.

Psychologist Kaethe Weingarten's (2003) work on what she calls "common shock" can provide a useful framework for this discussion: when we witness acts of violence and violation, she argues, we experience a range of emotional and physiological responses that may not be severe enough to be characterised as trauma, but are nevertheless harmful. Stories of violence and violation often surface during story circles, placing all those in the circle in the position of witness and making them vulnerable to common shock. This places particular responsibility on facilitators to manage this response in themselves, because common shock is transmittable. It can pass among members of a community, says Weingarten, "when professionals who have authority over certain areas of our lives have their own common shock reactions that they do not manage well. When this happens, their constituents get "sprayed", as it were, with their inadequate conduct" (p. 91). She warns:

> a professional who witnesses violence or violation, is clueless about its significance or implications, but nevertheless responds as if he knows what he is doing will be misguided, ineffective at best, and guilty of malpractice at worst. (p. 94)

What are the responsibilities of digital storytelling facilitators to manage ourselves in such a way that we are able to avoid the pitfalls of cluelessness and instead act as compassionate, empowered and empowering witnesses? Becoming psycho-literate not only for ourselves but also for our students is a necessary starting point.

SNAPSHOT 3: DISCOMFORTING THE POLITICAL PROJECT

Daniela: It is another Wednesday morning. The class has come together for a final reflection after the screening of the movies and about 50 students are seated in a large circle. I am here as an observer, sitting outside the circle taking notes. For the next hour and a half students talk about what they learnt about themselves and about each other. The strongest theme that emerges is a feeling of connection based on a shared experience of pain and suffering—a recognition that "deep down we are the same". At one point a young white man stands up and, addressing his predominantly black colleagues, tells us that if he has learnt one thing in this process, it is that we are all the same, we are all human. I listen with disbelief. I can feel anger rising, thoughts come up such as "how arrogant of this student to liken his trauma with the everyday trauma his black colleagues have to face on a daily basis". Voices of black activist friends scream in my head … I feel compelled to say something to set this right, but when I look around the room, I just see nodding heads, smiles, support for that student. I bite my tongue and wait for the session to end. I approach one of the more mature African students, who was quiet in the session, and ask her what she felt when her colleague issued his statement: didn't she feel angry? She just looks at me and shakes her head. She explains that this project has allowed her to finally let go of her anger against her father and really all men in general and that she would be eternally grateful for that. Humbled, I turn away, full of confusing thoughts about the tensions between my own political agenda in this project and my students' needs.

Daniela: I consider myself a critical feminist pedagogue. As such I cannot deny having a political agenda when engaging with my students. I want them to change, to be more aware of their own roles in each other's stories. The project is part of a largely apolitical and seemingly uncritical teacher education curriculum, which engages with difference through a celebratory lens, with food and dance exhibitions on diversity days (Hemson 2006). Who gave me permission to challenge these perceptions? What is my students' political agenda, if they have any? Is it fair to subject them to such a potentially painful project? Is that ethical?

These are questions that have cropped up for me over and over again. Especially when students resist discourses such as race and privilege, I have wondered: am I too focused on race? Have students truly just moved on? Is my own personal history biasing me to see my students' narratives first and foremost as raced? Or is it just too painful to engage with the issues? What about gender? What about class? I have had to constantly check myself not just to frame students' experience by race but to focus on the intersectionality between race, class, gender, sexuality, age and so on. Zembylas reminds us that radicalisation of solidarity requires that teachers and learners recognise also their shared complicities, that is, their capacity to injure others and bear responsibility for others' vulnerability. Shantal Ivits (2009) makes an important contribution to this point, when she likens the teacher/student to a psychiatrist/patient relationship. She warns us that in "this context, what may have been issued as an invitation to transform will be heard by desperate ears as something more akin to 'the way out' of the intensely discomforting state" (p.40), coercing the student into transforming in a way suggested by the teacher.

Pam: This raises interesting and difficult questions about the nature of power in the classroom, and educators' responsibility for wielding that power ethically. Sometimes—especially when critical reflection has been explicitly invited into the room—an educator's "I need you to recognize THIS" is going to collide with a student's "but I need you to hear THIS". If one of the aims of digital storytelling is to decentre power, to what extent are we as facilitators required to climb down from our agendas and just listen to what the stories are trying to tell us? The student who valued the storytelling process for helping her to let go of her anger against her father offers an instructive example. Black working-class students have father issues no less than white middle-class ones—clearly, we cannot rule out this experience because it doesn't slot neatly into the metanarrative we have in mind.

Daniela: One of the basic tenets of feminist thought is the recognition that individual pain will not change the world (hooks 2000). It is the linking, or as Ahmed (2004, p. 174) calls it, the "reading" of the relation between individual emotion and structure, between emotions and politics that "undoes the separation of the individual from others" and consequently helps us to as a collective take action. However, this reading always assumes some sort of distancing, a distance between the reader and the text, that may allow the reader to enter into a self-reflexive space, to reflect on her own emotional reactions to the story as much as to the story itself. Boler (1999, p. 167) explains this in the following way: the reader must pay attention "not in terms of 'fears for one's own vulnerabilities', but rather in terms of the affective obstacles that prevent the reader's acute attention to the power relations guiding her response and judgements". How does one achieve such a process within the confines of a digital storytelling process and a classroom? And is that what my students want?

In a pedagogical context, there is another dilemma. As much as I tell my students that we work outside the usual power dynamics of the teacher-student relationship, I am still in a position of power as their teacher (Ellsworth 1989) and the project is still part of the formal curriculum. It has a deadline and it is assessed. The final products are often highly personal stories, not always directly responding to the brief. These stories are also seldom produced in isolation—they are the product of a collaborative process involving peers, peer facilitators, facilitators and lecturers. While in the usual digital storytelling context, there is an expectation that stories are co-authored (Otanez and Guerrero 2015), how can this play out in an educational context where stories need to be individually marked?

Pam: Again, it is exactly this kind of critical self-reflection by facilitators that is lacking in most discussions of digital storytelling—certainly within the academic literature, if not within the informal communities of practice that facilitators have created for themselves.

There's also an argument to be made, perhaps, that there is something missing from an account that says only collective action matters. Daniela and I are working from different theories of change here. For Daniela, drawing on the work of Zembylas and others, the goal is large-scale structural change driven by public activism and solidarity with a more or less defined group of oppressed people. For me, the work of transformation must happen internally or it cannot happen at all. Given this conviction, I am prepared to be patient. Perhaps it is the process of digital storytelling, more than its content or outputs, that is the most important thing at work here. When we do digital storytelling right, we model a way of being with and for each other that is worlds away from the unreflective, authoritarian and inherently violent South African business-as-usual.

Conclusion

In this chapter, we have reflected on a sample of the ethical dilemmas we have encountered in our work with digital stories at a South African university. Our context might seem to be extreme, or outside the boundaries of what is "normal" in the global context. What can the South African experience teach anybody in more resource-rich places, working without the same burdens of history and traumatic memory?

Perspectives from the margins can be illuminating in unexpected ways. A light shone from an unusual angle can expose overlooked features and textures of a landscape—things that were always there but not quite visible. We believe our experience can help to highlight ethical tensions and textures that might otherwise stay obscured.

Issues of power and privilege, agency and voice, are after all global—even in the world's most homogeneous, wealthy and untroubled corners, people may bring histories marked by personal, familial or historical trauma. This will only become more true as global migration brings increasing numbers of students with more obvious and urgent traumas into higher education classrooms.

We also hope to disturb our readers' sense of what is "normal" in the first place. Against what baselines do we measure our norms? Considered globally, is it "normal" for students to come from middle-class families that can afford to pay their fees or subsidise their loans? Is it "normal" for students to be almost exclusively in their late teens and early twenties? Is it "normal" for students to come to digital storytelling workshops with extensive archives of photographs and video dating back to their babyhood? It is "normal" to have lived a life free of violence, deprivation, neglect or involuntary displacement? How many languages is it "normal" for students to speak and study in? What important information might we be missing because we're adjusted to a highly localised version of "normal"?

Our dialogue draws on very different theoretical and practical approaches, highlighting the importance of interdisciplinary collaboration, as Rice (2002) and Boyer (1990) suggest. This is occasionally frustrating, but far more often both useful and necessary to our ability to ask interesting questions about the ethical dimensions we should consider when introducing digital storytelling into higher education contexts.

We ask more questions than we give answers, which seems appropriate. This is new and uncharted territory and we suspect the conversation, although urgently needed, is often avoided. What if one answer to these questions is to leave reflective digital storytelling out of education altogether?

Even within this thicket of ethical questions, we believe in the value of our work. We get consistently good feedback from students, who place digital storytelling workshops among the highlights of their entire educational experience. However, we try always to keep in mind the important questions: Are our existing ethical guidelines adequate to the needs of this project, this classroom, these students? To what extent do we need to adapt them to changing contexts?

We call for a context-sensitive ethical approach that allows digital storytellers and listeners to take control of their lives and position themselves as agentive selves (Hull and Katz 2006) while acknowledging the risks involved when sharing our mutual vulnerability. We also believe educators are ethically compelled to carefully monitor their own capacity to manage the rigours of witnessing students' stories. This may mean always trying to achieve the impossible—creating safety in spaces that cannot be safe, creating connection where connection is a threat—but as all good digital storytellers know, it's the process that counts.

Note

1. www.youtube.com/user/cputstories

References

Adams, M., Bell, L. A., & Griffin, P. (1997). *Teaching for diversity and social justice: A sourcebook*. New York: Routledge.

Ahmed, S. (2004). *The cultural politics of emotion*. Edinburgh: Edinburgh University Press.

Berlant, L. (2008). *The female complaint: The unfinished business of sentimentality in American culture*. Durham/London: Duke University Press.

Boler, M. (1999). *Feeling power: Emotions and education*. New York: Routledge.

Boler, M., & Zembylas, M. (2003). Discomforting truths: The emotional terrain of understanding difference. In P. Trifonas (Ed.), *Pedagogies of difference: Rethinking education for social change* (pp. 110–136). New York: Routledge Falmer.

Boyer, E. L. (1990). *Scholarship reconsidered – Priorities of the professoriate*. Princeton: Carnegie Foundation for the Advancement of Teaching.

Collins, A. (2013). Teaching sensitive topics: Transformative pedagogy in a violent society. *Alternation, 9*, 128–149.

Condy, J., Chigona, A., Gachago, D., & Ivala, E. (2012). Preservice students' perceptions and experiences of digital storytelling in diverse classrooms. *Turkish Online Journal of Educational Technology (TOJET), 11*(3), 278–285.

Do Mar Pereira, M. (2012). Uncomfortable classrooms: Rethinking the role of student discomfort in feminist teaching. *European Journal of Women's Studies, 19*(1), 128–135.

Ellis, C. (2004). *The ethnographic I: A methodological novel about autoethnography.* Oxford: Altamira Press.

Ellsworth, E. (1989). Why doesn't this feel empowering? Working through the repressive myths of critical pedagogy. *Harvard Educational Review, 59*(3), 297–324.

Frankish, T. (2009). *Women's narratives of intergenerational trauma and post-apartheid identity: The said and unsaid.* University of KwaZulu-Natal.

Freeth, R. (2012). *On creating uncomfortable, safe spaces for South African conversations.* Workshop handout.

Gachago, D. (2015). *Sentimentality and digital storytelling: Towards a post-conflict pedagogy in pre-service teacher education in South Africa.* Unpublished thesis from the University of Cape Town. Available at: https://open.uct.ac.za/bitstream/handle/11427/16537/thesis_hum_2015_gachago_daniela.pdf?sequence=1. Accessed 28 Oct 2016.

Gachago, D., Ivala, E., Chigona, A., & Condy, J. (2015). Owning your emotions or sentimental navel-gazing: Digital storytelling with South African pre-service student educators. *Journal of Cultural Science, 8*(2), 18–35.

Gachago, D., Ivala, E., Condy, J., & Chigona, A. (2013). Journeys across difference: Pre-service teacher education students' perceptions of a pedagogy of discomfort in a digital storytelling project in South Africa. *Critical Studies in Teaching and Learning, 1*(1), 22–52.

Gubrium, A. C., Hill, A. L., & Flicker, S. (2014). A situated practice of ethics for participatory visual and digital methods in public health research and practice: A focus on digital storytelling. *American Journal of Public Health, 104*(9), 1606–1613.

Hemson, C. (2006). *Teacher education and the challenge of diversity in South Africa.* HSRC. Retrieved from http://www.hsrcpress.ac.za/product.php?productid=2142. Accessed 28 Oct 2016.

Hill, A. (2011). Digital storytelling for gender justice. In D. Bergoffen, P. Gilbert, T. Harvey, & C. McNeely (Eds.), *Confronting Global Gender Justice: Women's Lives, Human Rights* (pp. 126–140). London/New York: Routledge.

hooks, b. (2000). *Feminism is for everybody – Passionate politics.* Cambridge, MA: South End Press.

Hull, G. A., & Katz, M.-L. (2006). Crafting an agentive self: Case studies of digital crafting storytelling. *Research in the Teaching of English, 41*(1), 43–81.

Ivala, E., Gachago, D., Condy, J., & Chigona, A. (2013). Digital storytelling and reflection in Higher Education: A case of pre-service student teachers and their lecturers at a University of Technology. *Journal of Education and Training Studies, 2*(1), 217–227.

Ivits, S. (2009). *Disturbing the comfortable: An ethical inquiry into pedagogies of discomfort and crisis.* The University of British Columbia (Vancouver).

Jansen, J. (2009). *Knowledge in the blood: Confronting race and apartheid past.* Stanford: Stanford University Press.

Landis, K. (2008). In K. Landis (Ed.), *Start talking: A handbook for engaging difficult dialogues in Higher Education*. Anchorage: University of Alaska Anchorage, Alaska Pacific University.

Otanez, M., & Guerrero, A. (2015). Digital storytelling and the viral hepatitis project. In A. Gubrium, K. Harper, & M. Otanez (Eds.), *Participatory visual and digital research in action* (pp. 57–72). Walnut Creek: Left Coast Press.

Rice, E. R. (2002). Beyond scholarship reconsidered: Toward an enlarged vision of the Scholarly Work of Faculty Members. *New Directions for Teaching and Learning, 90,* 7–17.

Weingarten, K. (2003). *Common shock: Witnessing violence every day: How we are harmed, how we can heal*. Dutton: Penguin Books.

Young, I. M. (2011). *Responsibility for justice*. New York: Oxford University Press.

Zembylas, M. (2013). Critical pedagogy and emotion: Working through "troubled knowledge" in posttraumatic contexts. *Critical Studies in Education, 45*(2), 176–189.

PART 2

The Scholarship of Discovery

CHAPTER 8

Introduction to the Scholarship of Discovery

Grete Jamissen

Boyer describes the scholarship of discovery as "the first and most familiar element in our model, the one that (…) comes closest to what is meant when academics speak of 'research'" (Boyer 1990, p. 17). According to Boyer, "discovery" implies more than research as an activity isolated from teaching and other academic work. It can be conceived as a transgression which "at its best, contributes not only to the stock of human knowledge but also to the intellectual climate of a college or university. Not just the outcomes, but the process and especially the passion, give meaning to the efforts". Discovery, then, has to do with the quest for new and significant knowledge relevant to the professional sphere, informing the relationship between practice and theory, research and teaching.

While Boyer was looking to broaden the definition of scholarship in a scholarly setting, he also embraced wider models of research, from the

G. Jamissen (✉)
Oslo and Akershus University College of Applied Sciences,
Oslo, Norway

© The Author(s) 2017
G. Jamissen et al. (eds.), *Digital Storytelling in Higher Education,*
Digital Education and Learning, DOI 10.1007/978-3-319-51058-3_8

empiricist/positivist tradition to less restrictive and hypothesis-driven models (such as the case study) which were primarily qualitative (Stever 2011)

In spite of the established use of digital storytelling as a way of hearing untold stories (CDS, Capture Wales, Silence Speaks), we find that digital storytelling as a research approach or a methodology in the context of higher education is a relatively new endeavour. The aim of this section of the book is to discuss the opportunities and challenges connected to digital storytelling in relation to research primarily in two contexts: as a mode of collecting and analysing data and as a form for communicating results and sharing knowledge. Other areas of discovery, such as research on *how* digital storytelling affects teaching and learning and digital storytelling as a resource in community-based research, as in the scholarship of engaged collaboration, are discussed in other sections of this book.

DIGITAL STORYTELLING: PROCESS AND PRODUCT—AS RICH DATA

The qualities of digital storytelling, primarily the first-person voice and the multimodal presentation, offer an opportunity for rich data and for hearing the voices of research subjects in a way that is less likely to happen in traditional research approaches such as questionnaires and interviews. Three chapters in this section discuss aspects of digital storytelling as an approach to collecting, analysing and using data.

In Chap. 9, Carol Haigh discusses the evolving role of digital storytelling in health-care research, both as a research method and as a methodology. She speculates upon the ideological shift this evolving role has brought about. Her chapter explores how digital stories can be viewed as a qualitative response to the "big data" approach to research. By introducing the concept of "fuzzy logic", the author discusses the transition of digital stories from learning tool to data collection method and then onto a research methodology in their own right. She argues that digital storytelling can act as a catalyst for change in the established research paradigm and compares the qualities of digital storytelling to main qualities described in the stages of scientific revolution précised by Pajares (1998). Two cases are introduced, one to illustrate the analysis of digital stories as a fine-grained system (Pedrycz 1998), and one to illustrate the qualities of digital stories in overcoming consequences of epistemic injustice on research validity and reliability.

Inger-Kjersti Lindvig, in Chap. 10, addresses the concern for democratic societies when research does not give voice to ethnic minorities, in this case in relation to child welfare services. Lindvig discusses the scientific and methodological potential of digital storytelling to overcome such challenges. Building on Skjervheim's discussion of the relationship between participant and observer positions in research (1996), the author explores whether such an approach meets scientific and methodological requirements. From a theoretical point of departure, and based on a case study involving minority groups, she describes how digital storytelling contributes to dialogic bridge-building between researcher and subject. Her claim is that, when used properly, digital storytelling can function as a methodological approach to qualitative data collection and the dissemination of research in the broadest sense.

In Chap. 11, Satu Hakanurmi builds on a case study where adult workers in a complex organisation share knowledge and build identity through a digital storytelling workshop. These experiences are discussed in light of narrative theory and socio-cultural learning theory in which the construction of the story is a central element of narrative learning in which we can learn from our lives. By analysing the data from interviews with participants, Hakanurmi found the individualistic approach of the interview insufficient to understand the social learning process and the co-construction of knowledge that she had observed. Introducing the dialogue in the story circle as an additional source of ethnographical data enabled her to analyse the storytelling process and its social co-authoring elements. The dialogue was analysed in terms of how participants' contributions and communication in the story circle affected the development of the finished stories in terms of open or closed narratives or ante-narratives, all concepts that are introduced and discussed in the chapter.

RESEARCH DISSEMINATION

In accordance with a general focus on digitised media in all aspects of higher education, and a renewed interest in a narrative approach to knowledge, there is an increasing interest in digital storytelling as a way to communicate research questions, outcomes and new knowledge. In 2012, I was invited to address the annual conference of journalists and research communicators in Norway. The given heading was optimistic: Digital storytelling—research communication in its own right and a door opener for further reading. I added a question mark then, and the conclusion is still open. The answer depends on several dimensions, including aim, content and context. There are still few examples of the use of traditional DS workshops where researchers complete digital stories on their own. One is the Ohio State University where the OSU Digital Storytelling Program has conducted workshops with researchers since 2005. At the University of Nottingham, Christine Gratton, with the support of Chris Thomson of JISC Netskills, works with researchers making their own stories. Oslo and Akershus University College of Applied Sciences (HiOA) invite researchers to produce their own stories in a distributed workshop model building on the traditional CDS workshop.

In a focus group interview, researchers at HiOA describe the qualities of digital storytelling for research communication. They focus, for example, on the short form that supports an effort to get to the essence of the research question or outcome. They also report that the use of several modes of communication contributes to making research findings and issues more easily accessible.

However, they also raise a number of issues and describe the largest challenge as one of "language and voice". Using the personal voice is demanding for researchers who are immersed in the academic tradition of objectivity, in which words such as *I* and *me* are considered signs of a lack of necessary analytic distance.

In this book, we discuss DS as a medium for dissemination of research results from two points of departure: digital stories resembling professional videos produced for researchers and stories produced by the researchers themselves. In Chap. 12, Ragnhild Larsson, a professional research journalist, describes and discusses the experiences of producing digital stories on behalf of, and in collaboration with, researchers. The data underpinning her discussion come from producing stories on behalf of 11 researchers across a multitude of research fields and interviewing 8 of them. Larsson describes the process of producing the stories, and discusses the potential and issues of personalised digital stories for research communication. Her findings confirmed that digital stories produced by a professional can complement traditional ways of communicating in a positive way. Researchers find that digital stories not only capture the driving force behind their research but reach larger audiences, thereby creating new opportunities.

Ida Hydle, in Chap. 13, discusses her experience as a researcher involved in the institutional effort at HiOA and her experiences of developing a digital story to communicate findings and perspectives from research-based evaluation of a Norwegian prison for youth aged 15–18 years. The author introduces perspectives and concepts from visual anthropology to explain the power of the visual. In particular, Hydle discusses the quality of this dimension in communicating new knowledge about how architectural and environmental elements such as buildings and colours can support the aim of prison, that is, reconciliation and rehabilitation. The author describes the digital storytelling workshop as a community of learners. Building on the impact of the story in various contexts, nationally and internationally, she concludes that this method of visualising research serves its purpose.

References

Boyer, E. L. (1990). *Scholarship reconsidered: Priorities of the professoriate.* Princeton: The Carnegie Foundation for the advancement of teaching.

Pajares, F. (1998). The structure of scientific revolutions by Thomas S. Kuhn. A Synopsis from the original. Available at http://www.uky.edu/~eushe2/Pajares/kuhnsyn.html. Accessed 12 Aug 2015.

Pedrycz, W. (1998). Fuzzy set technology in knowledge discovery. *Fuzzy Sets and Systems, 98*(3), 279–290.

Skjervheim, H. (1996). Participant and spectator. In H. Skjervheim (Ed.), *Selected essays. In honor of Hans Skjervheim's 70th birthday* (pp. 127–141). Bergen: University of Bergen, Department of Philosophy.

Stever, G. (2011). Creative ethnography: Boyer's philosophy in action. *Revisiting Boyer. Exploring the Scholarly Work of Empire State College Faculty, 1*(2011), 17–20.

CHAPTER 9

'The Times They Are a Changin': Digital Storytelling as a Catalyst for an Ideological Revolution in Health-Care Research

Carol Haigh

INTRODUCTION

Written from a health-care perspective, the focus of this chapter is to discuss the evolving role of digital storytelling, as a research method. Examples of using stories as a medium to share experiences, to educate, to illustrate the human condition and to provide cautionary examples are as old as humanity itself (Haigh and Hardy 2010). Storytelling has evolved with human ingenuity from pictograms and oral traditions to printed word and other visual media such as film. It is, therefore, unsurprising that digital media and technology are the next natural step in this journey of shared experience. The creation of digital stories allows everyday people to share aspects of their life story and the World Wide Web provides a platform that allows such stories to become part of the shared global consciousness. The media used may include the digital platform equivalent of film techniques (full-motion video with sound), animation, stills, audio only or any of the other forms of non-physical media (material that exists only as electronic files as opposed to actual paintings or photographs on paper,

C. Haigh (✉)
Manchester Metropolitan University, Manchester, UK

© The Author(s) 2017   115
G. Jamissen et al. (eds.), *Digital Storytelling in Higher Education,*
Digital Education and Learning, DOI 10.1007/978-3-319-51058-3_9

sounds stored on tape or disk, movies stored on film) which individuals can use to tell a story, present an idea or communicate an emotion. Thus, it can be seen that digital storytelling is the process and digital stories are the product, and while researchers have been using digital stories as data for some time now, it is the process of storytelling that has a contribution to make to research methodology that is the primary focus of this chapter. However, it must be recognized that a consideration of process without acknowledgment of outcome provides only half a picture, thus the contribution of digital stories will also be considered where appropriate

Digital stories have been used to inform, educate and entertain. The ways they have been used are varied and creative as the stories themselves: they have been used to educate patients, as a part of the interview process for staff of all seniorities and to share experiences (Hardy and Sumner 2014). They have been shown in universities, in clinics, at business meetings and in open community spaces in city centers. They can make people laugh, they often make people cry but they never fail to make a lasting impression.

DIGITAL STORIES AS DATA

While digital stories are widely acknowledged as providing accessible and powerful ways of communicating a health-care experience (Cueva et al. 2015), there is an increasing body of work that actually researches the effect of digital stories on the learning experience, see, for example, the work of Price et al. (2015). Price et al. suggested that nursing students appreciated the use of digital stories in nurse education settings as it allowed them to correlate theoretical information with "real-life" patient experiences in ways that the students believed would impact upon their future practice. It is this link between the theory of a profession and the "real-world" perspective of service users that is seen as the unique selling point of this approach, especially in the teaching and learning domain. Haigh and Hardy (2010) have also explored how digital stories are used in various educational contexts and with different student groups.

This reluctance to exploit a fruitful vein of qualitative data is a strange phenomenon, particularly in the modern research world of "big data". Big data is a term for data sets so large that traditional approaches to data processing are inadequate. Big data is a uniquely twenty-first century phenomenon driven by the expansion of the World Wide Web and mobile technology together with the huge amounts of personal, economic, occupational and health-related data that we share, consciously and unconsciously, every day via our computers, tablets and smart phones. McAfee et al. noted in 2012 that about 2.5 exabytes (one exabyte is one quintillion bytes) of data are being created each day, and that number is doubling every 40 months or so. More data cross the Internet every second than were stored in the entire Internet in 1992. Big data is providing information to pharmaceutical companies (Hu and Bajorath 2014), supermarkets (Smith 2014) and universities (Wixom et al. 2014).

Thus, it can be seen that the scientific and business research communities have been quick to exploit this plethora of data that is being produced every day. This chapter is not the place to open the "hard vs soft/empirical vs anecdotal/quant vs qual debate" (this has been explored admirably by Gustavsson and Hallin in 2014). However, there can be no denying that the number of digital stories that are available on the World Wide Web are a rich source of data for those researchers who are more concerned with the human experience. Kitchen (2014) refers to this as the "digital humanities" and suggests that the use of digital data such as social media or digitized literary/artistic collections allows for a richer and wider understanding with the opportunity of applying "methodological rigor, and objectivity to disciplines that have heretofore been unsystematic and random in their focus and approach". One of the perennial criticisms leveled at qualitative research is the use of small samples to explore a research question. Digital stories have the potential to be a kind of "big data" of the qualitative world, in that they provide a reservoir of narrow, deep information that can be seen as analogous to the wide, shallow information provided by big data sets.

The broad scope and breadth of digital stories mean that they can also be used comfortably with a number of existing research methodologies. It was Barney Glaser who famously stated "all is data" (2007; Glaser and Strauss 1967), and while digital stories would definitely come under that definition within a Grounded Theory approach, their versatility means they can also be viewed as data by phenomenologists, constructivists and those interested in undertaking hermeneutic research. The stories themselves are layered and nuanced to the extent that, in some cases, they can provide data across a wider range of topics and methodological approaches than topic-specific approaches may do. Haigh (2014) has illustrated this by using existing digital stories to obtain insight into patient and carers' experiences of accessing cancer care when access to suitable participants was frustrated by an overly protective approach from professionals. The insights and data drawn from these stories, which were created for many reasons other than an exploration of cancer services, triangulated with data obtained from more traditional means.

There may be critics who would suggest that this type of data mining can only weaken any conclusions drawn from the subsequent analysis. However, data mining is a recognized analytic process designed to explore data in search of consistent patterns and/or systematic relationships between variables, and then to validate the findings by applying the detected patterns to new subsets of data. It is not a method for trolling one's results until data that supports a question or hypothesis is obtained. However, data mining as it exists within the business or market analysis world is very different to data mining in the qualitative research arena. The primary end point of business-related data mining is the production and validation of predictive models, which can then be applied to new data in order to generate predictions or estimates of the expected outcome. The technique is grounded heavily in the quantitative domain of research, even those authors who have explored the concept of qualitative data mining have concentrated upon the methods that can be used to attach numbers to qualitative themes or have at best reduced qualitative data to information that can be inserted into a formulaic type of analysis (Bratko and Šuc 2003). However, digital stories transcend such mechanical scrutiny by bringing the human voice and the human experience into the broader world of data. There is a growing body of literature that focuses upon the effectiveness of the storytelling process although there is little that actually exploits the creation or use of digital stories as data.

Digital Stories as a Methodology

Pedrycz (1998) suggested the application of fuzzy logic to the black and white problem of something being perceived as either true or untrue with no middle ground. Fuzzy logic, articulated in the 1960s by Zadeh, moved theoretical thinking beyond the restriction of Boolean logic, where the truth values of variables may be either 0 (not true) or 1 (true) and suggested that fuzzy logic could extend this stance to handle the concept of partial truth, where the truth value may range between completely true and completely false. This is highly congruent with an approach to storytelling, which may be distinguished at one level from mere narrative.

There are many broad definitions of the difference between a narrative and a story. Some, such as Greenhalgh and Hurwitz (1999), argue that narrative is a cognitive process which acts as a way of organizing temporal events into a form used to inform any subsequent story and that it contains supplementary information that may or may not reflect events as they unfold. Others, such as Hunchman and Hinchman (1997), see a more logical, sequential ordering of events. Haigh and Hardy (2010) suggest that whereas narrative can be defined as predominantly linear and factual, stories are creative and value laden; a narrative may only contain one "truth" but a story may contain many elements of different experiences coalesced into account built of many "truths" but none the less valuable for that. It is this definition which will be used for the purpose of this chapter.

In what could be seen as a backlash against the increasing "scientification" of our world, Pedrycz (1998) noted that "knowledge discovery in databases is concerned with identifying interesting patterns and describing them in a concise and meaningful manner" highlighting that seeking the human experience in large data sets was a key component of knowledge discovery. Pedrycz goes on to emphasize this importance by suggesting that society is data rich but knowledge poor, a situation that has only increased since 1998. The notion of applying fuzzy logic to data systems such as those provided by the anthology of digital stories; the acknowledgment that the sharing of a "truth" which may be placed somewhere on an arbitrary continuum of truthfulness is one that may be appealing to those researchers using the digital story process.

Pedrycz further suggests that when analyzing such data, there must be an element of interaction between data users. This is an important point, especially when using digital stories for research. Proving a clear analytical context is crucial as Case Study 1 highlights.

Case Study 1

I was running a webinar about using digital stories for academics and research students. The audience was multiprofessional and multidisciplinary with health care, engineering, science, business and arts all represented. I picked a digital story from the Patient Voices website by a storyteller named Jean Bailey-Dering (2007) called "Getting to the bottom of things"[1] that I thought would be seen differently by all of the different professional groups.

Nominally a story by a woman with Rheumatoid Arthritis about the difficulty of finding a suitable tool for wiping her own bottom that was as effective as her husband was, I thought it was perfect. I expected the

engineers to see it as a story about design and as a manufacturing problem, that the business students would see this as a marketing opportunity,
the health-care people would see it as a health care problem and the arts
people to be concerned with the aesthetics of the instruments. I showed
the story and asked the webinar group "what do YOU think this story was
about?" One by one, the answers appeared in the dialogue box:

- It's a love story
- It's about how much her husband loves her
- It's about love
- It's about an enduring relationship

The responses were the same across genders, disciplines and age ranges.
    If the question posed at the webinar had been "from a discipline spe-
cific perspective, what do you think this story is about", I may have got
the responses I was expecting rather than the loud message that the storyteller had wanted to share. This demonstrates what Pedrycz (1998) means
when he talks about the granularity of information. Granularity refers to
how divisible a system is. Fine-grained systems, which have high granularity, are broken down into larger numbers of smaller parts, while a coarse-
grained system has a smaller number of larger parts. I had categorized
Jean's story as a fine-grained system, I was expecting the webinar participants to identify a large number of small elements which underpinned
the story; instead, they viewed it as a coarse-grained system with really
just one large part—how much Jean's husband loved and supported her.
Consideration of the granularity of the information is highly important
when using digital stories as data that are being subjected to a post hoc
approach to analysis. It is crucial that all of the analysts are aware that the
story is being treated as a fine-grained system—often fine-grained within
specific parameters—if a trustworthy result is to be achieved. This is an
important distinction when dealing with any data generated by people's
experiences but never more so than when collecting data from digital
stories.
    Digital stories have a clear role in research as a method for the collec-
tion or inspection of data with the aim of answering a direct research question; there is also a case to be made for digital stories to be viewed as an
emerging methodology. Crotty (1998) notes that methodology includes
the strategy that lies behind the selection of method. It is my contention
that digital storytelling is becoming a methodology in its own right. To

facilitate this hypothesis, we will use the example of scientific revolution such as described by Kuhn in 1962.

Kuhn (1962) argued from a strongly positivistic perspective and suggested that science worked on a set of rigidly held and strongly defended beliefs/rules. One of these key beliefs is the assumption that scientists know what the world is really like. In order to maintain this belief, established science will suppress "novelties", that is, new or different ways to approach enquiry. One only needs to consider the disdain with which qualitative research was viewed, especially by the medical and scientific communities in the 1970s and 1980s, to understand Kuhn's point.

If a new way of carrying out research is to be supported, Kuhn argues that a change to these rules is required—resulting in a paradigm shift which will require the reshaping of the previously held assumptions. To illustrate, let us map digital storytelling, as used in health-care research, using the stages of scientific revolution précised by Pajares (1998) to contextualize the development of digital storytelling as a methodology and to illustrate how it can be argued to act as a catalyst for a change in the established research paradigm (Table 9.1).

As the desire to accurately record the participant voice and experiences becomes equally important as the desire to accurately measure a response, the time is right for a paradigm shift and a new ideology of research.

As a new methodology, digital storytelling has yet to make any significant impact, although this is slowly growing. Researchers are often loath to abandon tried and trusted, traditional approaches to research design and, it must be noted that funding bodies are often even more reluctant to embrace new processes. It can be very difficult for such individuals to recognize that, in certain circumstances, as much rich data can be derived from a two- to three-minute digital story as can be obtained from an hour's worth of interview. Camp (1996) has noted that paradigm shifts are often slow and of long duration, citing problem-based learning (PBL) in medical education as an example. Any new development should be evaluated as it progresses and Kuhn's work is suggested as an initial framework for contextualizing any such progress.

As with other qualitative methodologies, so much depends upon what research question is being asked, what the expectations of the researcher are and how the voice of the participant is being mediated. This later point is becoming increasingly crucial—even the most reflexive or culturally immersed researcher cannot help but act as a filter to the message their research participants are attempting to communicate, by insinuat-

Table 9.1   Digital stories in the context of scientific revolution

Kuhn's stages of scientific revolution (1962)	Pajares key points summation (1998)	Digital stories in the revolutionary context
I. The route to normal science	Normal science 'means research firmly based upon one or more past scientific achievements, achievements that some particular scientific community acknowledges for a time as supplying the foundation for its further practice'. These achievements can be called paradigms	Much health-care, education and social science research has sprung from a positivist paradigm. The Boolean notion of truth has only recently been challenged
II. The nature of normal science	When they first appear, paradigms are limited in scope and in precision 'By focusing attention on a small range of problems, the paradigm forces scientists to investigate some part of nature in detail and depth that would otherwise be unimaginable'. When the paradigm ceases to function properly, scientists begin to behave differently and the nature of their research problems changes	The research community has challenged the suitability of the positivist paradigm to reflect the messy real-world problems that need more qualitative approaches to illuminate them
III. Normal science as puzzle-solving	Doing research is essentially like solving a puzzle. Puzzles have rules. Puzzles generally have predetermined solutions. To classify as a puzzle (as a genuine research question), a problem must be characterized by more than the assured solution, but at the same time solutions should be consistent with paradigmatic assumptions	The difficulty of applying the 'puzzle' analogy to qualitative approaches and storytelling in particular is the fluidity of the concept of 'truth' inherent in those methods
IV. The priority of paradigms	The existence of a paradigm need not imply that any full set of rules exists. Scientists are often guided by tacit knowledge—knowledge acquired through practice that cannot be articulated explicitly. Furthermore, the attributes shared by a paradigm are not always readily apparent	Within some disciplines that lean toward qualitative approaches, the positivistic paradigm has been seen as superior. Only in the last decade or so have the so-called softer approaches gained traction

(continued)

Table 9.1 (continued)

Kuhn's stages of scientific revolution (1962)	Pajares key points summation (1998)	Digital stories in the revolutionary context
V. Anomaly and the emergence of scientific discoveries	New and unsuspected phenomena are uncovered by scientific research, and radical new theories have again and again been invented by scientists. Fundamental novelties of fact and theory bring about paradigm change	The recognition that the experience of participants can provide rich and important data. The expectation that best RCTs will have an element of qualitative data to make sense of the numbers
VI. Crisis and the emergence of scientific theories	A change in existing theory results in the invention of new theory is brought about. Failure of existing rules is the prelude to a search for new ones	The growth of mixed-method approaches and the increasing focus upon the need to recognize the complexity of research that includes people

ing themselves as a conduit between the researcher and the consumers of research. An important strength of using a digital storytelling approach is that the "research participant", that is, the storyteller, as a part of creating the data, prior to data collection, I is involved in a process of analyzing what happened. It facilitates turning research participants in part of the research team as is further discussed by Lindvig in Chap. 10.

DIGITAL STORYTELLING AS A NEW RESEARCH IDEOLOGY

If we accept the premise that the rise of digital storytelling as both a new instrument of data collection and a new paradigm of the individual voice—a hybrid of the sole truth of positivism, the insider perspective of constructivism and the researcher/researched status and power issues of the critical postmodernist—the ideological foundations of the approach must be considered.

At its simplest, an ideology can be seen as a set of beliefs that affects how an individual or a group views the world. An individual's ideology is often their most closely held set of values and feelings. An ideology acts as the filter through which we see everything and everybody and color our actions accordingly. In fact, these beliefs are often so close to us that we do not realize that they are there. We simply think that our beliefs are natural and obviously true. Religion is an example of one type of ideology, and religious belief affects a person's views.

Heywood (2003) notes that for much of history, the term "ideology" has been used to condemn or decry opposing ideas and beliefs systems. Authors from Marx onward have identified the oppressive nature of ideology and point to the creation of "-isms": racism, sexism, totalitarianism and so on. An awareness of this potential oppression, which is seen as normal discourse by the dominant ideology, is one of the reasons that men in the 1970s were unable to research the feminist movement, why straight people are not often seen suitable to undertake research in the LGBT community, why white people cannot research BME populations and so on. Thus, ideology is seen as the means by which the sets of social relations operating in a social system are legitimated.

However, one could argue that the crude applications of ideological perspective outlined above weaken research in significant ways. If we accept the notion that ideology is repressive and driven by "otherness", focusing exclusively on the experiences of the "others" as shared with members of the "other" community weakens some of the power of the experience. This is of particular concern for groups and individuals who experience intersectionality. Intersectionality refers to groups who fall between the gaps of various oppressions. Articulated by Crenshaw (1989), it is postulated that various biological, social and cultural categories such as gender, race, social class, physical or intellectual ability, sexual orientation, religion and other manifestations of personal or group identity interact on multiple and often simultaneous levels. Intersectionality holds that the classical conceptualizations of oppression within society, such as racism, sexism and belief-based bigotry, do not act independently of one another. This leads us to consider a specific form of injustice, that of epistemic injustice.

Fricker (2007) suggests that epistemic injustice exists in two forms: testimonial injustice and hermeneutical injustice. Testimonial injustice consists in prejudices that cause one to "give a deflated level of credibility to a speaker's word". This can be linked to a myriad of variables and although Fricker focuses upon gender it can also be affected by the role of the speaker in society (class, nationality, immigration status, etc.). The speaker is perceived as less competent than the prevailing group (or the researcher?) or as an "other", outside of the dominant zeitgeist and therefore their testimony is diluted or disregarded.

In addition to testimonial injustice, which may be argued to occur predominantly at the individual level, Fricker proposes hermeneutical injustice, describing it as the kind of injustice experienced by groups who lack the shared social resources to make sense of their experience. One consequence of such injustice is that such individuals might be less inclined to believe their own testimony.

Such intersectional issues are still prevalent in today's society (e.g., think of the experiences of transgender individuals) and can be easily detected in traditional qualitative research approaches as Case Study 2 demonstrates.

Case Study 2

Our research team was commissioned by a local hospital to talk to patients with cancer about how the hospital staff could improve communications with them. What the hospital wanted was information from people who could be considered as "vulnerable" prior to their cancer diagnosis, that is, individuals with learning difficulties, other long-term conditions or mental health problems. The team only recruited people who had accessed the cancer services of the commissioning hospital. Data were collected via focus groups and, as the information was to be used for teaching purposes, short videos were made highlighting the specific problems the focus groups had identified, illustrated with exemplar quotations from the participants, a sort of modified digital story. The team identified three key themes and selected suitable comments to support them as illustrated in Table 9.2.

The research team was pleased with the information that the groups had supplied. They felt that the aim of finding out how to improve the experiences of these vulnerable people had been met. They presented their findings to the educational team who had commissioned the work and who would be working on how to raise the issues with staff. Their unequivocal responses were:

- No—we don't believe these things happen in our hospital.
- We are a center of excellence, this doesn't happen here.
- The patients must have got it wrong.

Interestingly, we could not detect whether it was the label "vulnerable" or of "patient" that leads to such dismissal of their testimony but it was clear that the answer the patients gave to the question was not the one the health-care professionals were willing to believe, the group's individual experiences being seen as unreliable sources of evidence (testimonial

Table 9.2   Themes and example comments

Theme	Supporting comment
Partnership (?)	'The Doctor told me to think about it [having cancer treatment] and I worried for a week about it. When I told him I had made up my mind to go ahead with the treatment, he told me I had made the wrong decision – he didn't think I should' Person with long-standing mental health problem
Overprotective	'I want to be able to decide what I share with my partner. I don't want the nurses and doctors to tell them everything about me without my say so' Person with learning disability
Misunderstandings	'They told me my options and seemed to expect me to make up my mind on the spot. I need time to think about things and my other stuff [health problems] mean it's not as straightforward for me as for other people' Person with learning disability 'Having a History [of mental health problems] doesn't mean I know the system. The control I have regarding my treatment decisions are very different in physical care' Person with long-standing mental health problem

injustice). However, it was also interesting to note that the focus group participants found comfort in the sharing of their experiences, the phrase "I thought it was just me" being used time and time again when describing unsatisfactory interactions with health-care professionals (hermeneutic injustice).

There are three key elements in the methodology of digital storytelling that can address epistemic injustice in a way that more traditional research methodologies do not. First, and to my mind most importantly, the data that is presented by the storyteller in their digital story can be viewed simultaneously as raw data, that is not data that has been interpreted or thematically analyzed by a third party but also analyzed data via the choice of the storyteller about contact, focus and emotion to be presented. This makes the use of digital stories almost unique among qualitative data methodologies. While the risks and benefits of raw data sharing is one that is being debated among the scientific community, see, for example, Cheah et al. (2015), digital stories have the advantage of offering raw data to the wider research community simply by existing. This addresses the notion of epistemic injustice by ensuring that data is not filtered by a dominant ideology and the voice of the wider community is accessible to those on the edges as well as "other" communities.

A further way in which epistemic injustice is addressed is the notion that once in the public domain the uninterpreted voice of the storyteller exists in perpetuity. Data developed via a digital storytelling approach has the advantage of longevity and historical accuracy, as far as historical accuracy is possible. The clear defining voice of the people telling their story means that a different kind of "truth" can emerge, one that is cemented in the here and now of the storyteller.

In conclusion, it can be seen that digital stories have carved a niche for themselves in the communication of health-related issues; however, they are only now beginning to be viewed, not only as a rich source of research data but also as a potential research methodology. This is an important development since most of the established methods and methodologies used by modern researchers were established in the late nineteenth and early twentieth centuries, for example, Q-sort (Williamson 1935), randomized controlled trials (Streptomycin in Tuberculosis Trials Committee 1948) or Grounded Theory (Glaser and Strauss 1966). A small group of researchers are beginning to explore the application of digital storytelling as a research methodology, attracted by the belief that it represents an ideological shift in the application of power in the researcher/researched relationship.

We live in an open world in which the democratization of health care via participatory media is expanding exponentially. The digital native generation, who were born or brought up during the age of digital technology and who are familiar with the digital world from an early age, will soon begin to access formal health care and become potential research participants. In the main, this is a generation who are accustomed to having a voice and who expect to be heard regardless of their perceived place in society. Digital storytelling as a research method provides a megaphone for the seldom heard from and the oppressed providing an arena in which everyone's story can be heard without prejudice and shared without dilution. This means it is possible to predict that the role of digital storytelling within research will only continue to evolve into an established method in its own right.

Note

1. http://www.patientvoices.org.uk/flv/0110pv384.htm

References

Bailey-Dering, J. (2007). *Getting to the bottom of things.* Available at http://www. patientvoices.org.uk/flv/0110pv384.htm. Accessed 28 Aug 2015.

Bratko, I., & Šuc, D. (2003). Qualitative data mining and its applications. *CIT. Journal of Computing and Information Technology, 11*(3), 145–150.

Camp, G. (1996). Problem-based learning: A paradigm shift or a passing fad. *Medical Education Online, 1*(2), 1–6.

Cheah, P. Y., Tangseefa, D., Somsaman, A., Chunsuttiwat, T., Nosten, F., Day, N. P., & Parker, M. (2015). Perceived benefits, harms, and views about how to share data responsibly. A qualitative study of experiences with and attitudes toward data sharing among research staff and community representatives in Thailand. *Journal of Empirical Research on Human Research Ethics, 10*(3), 278–289.

Crenshaw, K. (1989). Demarginalising the intersection between race and sex. A black feminist critique of antidisceimination doctrine, feminist theory and anti-racist policies. *University of Chicago Legal Forum, 140,* 139.

Crotty, M. (1998). *The foundations of social research. Meaning and perspective in the research process.* London: Sage.

Cueva, M., Kuhnley, R., Revels, L., Schoenberg, N. E., Lanier, A., & Dignan, M., 2015. Engaging elements of cancer-related digital stories in Alaska. *Journal of Cancer Education, 31,* 1–6.

Fricker, M. (2007). *Epistemic injustice: Power and the ethics of knowing* (p. 7). Oxford: Oxford University Press.

Glaser, B. (2007). All is data. *Grounded Theory Review, 6*(2). Available at http://groundedtheoryreview.com/wp-content/uploads/2012/06/GT-Review-vol6-no2.pdf. Accessed July 2015.

Glaser, B. G., & Strauss, A. L. (1966). *Awareness of dying.* Chicago: Transaction Publishers.

Glaser, B. G., & Strauss, A. L. (1967). *The discovery of grounded theory: Strategies for qualitative research.* Chicago: Aldine.

Greenhalgh, T., & Hurwitz, B. (1999). Why study narrative? *BMJ: British Medical Journal, 318*(7175), 48.

Gustavsson, T. K., & Hallin, A. (2014). Rethinking dichotomization: A critical perspective on the use of "hard" and "soft" in project management research. *International Journal of Project Management, 32*(4), 568–577.

Haigh, C. (2014). What really matters to patients? Digital storytelling as a qualitative research tool. In P. Hardy & T. Sumner (Eds.), *Cultivating Compassion. How digital storytelling is transforming healthcare.* Chichester: Kingsham Press.

Haigh, C., & Hardy, P. (2010). Tell me a story – A conceptual exploration of storytelling in health care education. *Nurse Education Today.* doi:10.1016/j.nedt.2010.08.001.

Hardy, P., & Sumner, T. (2014). *Cultivating compassion. How digital storytelling is transforming healthcare*. Chichester: Kingsham Press.

Heywood, A. (2003). *Political ideologies. An introduction* (3rd ed.). London: Palgrave Macmillan.

Hu, Y., & Bajorath, J. (2014). Learning from 'big data': Compounds and targets. *Drug Discovery Today, 19*(4), 357–360.

Hunchman, L. P., & Hinchman, S. (1997). *Memory, identity and community. The idea of narrative in the human sciences*. Albany: Sunny Press.

Kitchin, R. (2014). Big data, new epistemologies and paradigm shifts. *Big Data & Society, 1*(1), 1–12.

Kuhn, T. S. (1962). *The structure of scientific revolutions*. Chicago: University of Chicago Press.

Pajares, F. (1998). *The structure of scientific revolutions by Thomas S. Kuhn A synopsis from the original*. Available at http://www.uky.edu/~eushe2/Pajares/kuhnsyn.html. Accessed 12 Aug 2015.

Pedrycz, W. (1998). Fuzzy set technology in knowledge discovery. *Fuzzy Sets and Systems, 98*(3), 279–290.

Price, D. M., Strodtman, L., Brough, E., Lonn, S., & Luo, A. (2015). Digital storytelling: An innovative technological approach to nursing education. *Nurse Educator, 40*(2), 66–70.

Smith, P. (2014). How can the analytics on big data affect the buying trends of customers in the retail industry? *Enquiry-The ACES Journal of Undergraduate Research, 5*(1).

Stephenson, W. (1935). Technique of factor analysis. *Nature, 136*, 297.

Streptomycin in Tuberculosis Trials Committee. (1948). Streptomycin treatment of pulmonary tuberculosis. A Medical Research Council investigation. *British Medical Journal, 2*(4582), 769–782. doi:10.1136/bmj.2.4582.769.

Wixom, B., Ariyachandra, T., Douglas, D., Goul, M., Gupta, B., Iyer, L., & Turetken, O. (2014). The current state of business intelligence in academia: The arrival of big data. *Communications of the Association for Information Systems, 34*(1), 1.

CHAPTER 10

Building Bridges: Digital Storytelling as a Participatory Research Approach

Inger Kjersti Lindvig

INTRODUCTION

The lack of opportunities for minority-ethnic users of child welfare services in Norway to express themselves in the literature that focuses on them is an increasing cause of concern. Through my experience in using digital storytelling with immigrants involved in training and educational programmes, I have discovered the scientific and methodological potential of the creation and sharing of such stories in minority research. When used judiciously, digital storytelling can function as a methodological approach to qualitative data collection and the dissemination of research in the broadest sense. This includes research activities as an integral part of academic work related to teaching, guidance, research and development, where interaction with the field of practice is part of a social aim. Such an understanding of research in higher education corresponds well to Boyer's concept "scholarship of discovery". I interpret Boyer's ideas concerning "discovery" to cross the boundaries of what one might normally associate with research in the traditional sense: "The scholarship of discovery, at its best, contributes not only to the stock of human knowledge but also to

I.K. Lindvig (✉)
University College of South-East Norway,
Porsgrunn, Norway

131
G. Jamissen et al. (eds.), *Digital Storytelling in Higher Education*,
Digital Education and Learning, DOI 10.1007/978-3-319-51058-3_10

the intellectual climate of a college or university. Not just the outcomes, but the process, and especially the passion, give meaning to the efforts" (Boyer 1990, p. 17). "Discovery" understood in this way deals with the quest to discover significant new practical knowledge and information that can be conveyed in new ways, to help to transcend the gap between theory and practice, and research and teaching. Research understood in this way can also revitalise the research process, results and dissemination in the context of higher education.

To clarify if the use of digital storytelling can be justified for research purposes, I will examine how this approach meets scientific and methodological requirements by using Skjervheim's discussion of the relationship between participant and observer or spectator positions in research (1996).[1] The basis for Skjervheim's theoretical universe is the value premise that even the most complex academic issues can stem from everyday problem areas. The relationship between digital storytelling and the political "giving voice" tradition is clear when it comes to allowing ordinary people and their voices access to the public sphere.

SCIENTIFIC CHALLENGES

The aim of minority research is, among other things, to establish knowledge about relationships between minority and majority populations. The research into contemporary topical issues concerns descriptions, explanations and valid evidence-based knowledge (Fuglerud and Eriksen 2007). Scientifically valid knowledge is based on an epistemological foundation that deals with "systematic reflection upon and study of scientific activities and the results of such activities" (Grimen 2004, p. 173). An epistemological perspective thus relates to the question of what it is possible to have knowledge about, what constitutes valid knowledge and how one can obtain it. Important in this context is the relationship between *descriptive* form, where one studies what scientists do, and *normative* form, where one discusses what requirements should apply to theories, concepts, explanations and methods of science (Grimen 2004).

Minority research, in Norway and elsewhere, should ensure evidence-based knowledge. In addition, research often forms the basis for policy-making and providing information to the relevant authorities about current challenges faced by minorities. The relationship between research, professionals, governmental authorities and the public debate is understandably complex and challenging. Minority research has been criticised for being too politically and economically controlled in addition to being distinctly problem focused and not especially participant oriented (Fuglerud and Eriksen 2007; Fauske and Qureshi 2010).

Based on these critical inputs, there is reason to caution against a type of research that contributes to a recycling of existing stereotypes about minority-ethnic users of child welfare services rather than challenges them. Allowing the voices and stories of minority users, that is, "the many voiceless", to come to expression in research is, as yet, a largely unexplored opportunity. Moreover, it is precisely research-based knowledge about minority-ethnic users' experiences with public services that is called for in the knowledge reports on multicultural child welfare services (Holm-Hansen et al. 2007; Paulsen et al. 2014). Consequently, it is a major challenge to facilitate participatory research for minorities.

The researcher needs to become an active participant in the dialogue with the primary subjects of the research in the process of obtaining emprical data. The challenges concern particularly the question of understanding the relationship between the social scientist and the objects of research, here termed the research subjects and social actors. According to Grimen (2004), the challenges concerning such human-related research is firstly about the attitudes, values and preferences the researcher has regarding the research subjects, secondly how the researcher's use of terms and concepts relate to the actors' terms and concepts, and thirdly if the explanations used by the actors conflict with those of the researcher. Finally, these challenges also involve the way the researcher relates to possible ethical implications implicit in the relationship between researcher and object of research in terms of trust between people who are part of each other's universes of understanding (Grimen 2004, pp. 289–290). Against the backdrop of such challenges, I will discuss my own practice-related research discovery concerning the use of digital storytelling with immigrants, and then go on to consider these experiences in light of epistemological requirements.

THE USE OF DIGITAL STORYTELLING AS A DISCOVERY-BASED RESEARCH METHOD

For the duration of five days in April and May 2014, a colleague and I conducted a participant-based educational programme using digital storytelling for 15 adults whose native countries were Myanmar, Vietnam, the Philippines, China, Afghanistan, Iran, Iraq, Jordan, Ethiopia, Somalia and the former Yugoslavia (Kosovo). They were all participants in a Labour Market Training Course for immigrants with limited or no formal education. Our teaching programme was included as part of the training programme and a local project.[2] The aim was to convey identity and meaning-making life stories in order to enhance the participants' awareness of the importance of their own life. Living is associated with identity, memory and the social and cultural contexts in which they live. For this reason, life stories are dynamic and diverse, consisting of a large amount of knowledge, memories and reflections. These can be selected, combined and interpreted in many different ways, depending on the individual's social context or phase of life. We chose digital storytelling as the appropriate vehicle to enable the participants to relay their life stories. Digital storytelling is not just a physical expression but also a way to process the stages in their stories, from an idea to the finished product. As an introduction, we used sense-based exercises that I describe below. Our intention was to enable the participants to share and give each other feedback on their life stories, from the first sketches to the finalised "film".

One of the chief objectives was to ensure that each participant's voice was projected into the public space. Another aim was to ensure that digital storytelling would help participants to perceive themselves increasingly as fellow citizens and become more active in terms of democracy-building participation in politics and society. In addition, there was a desire to strengthen our knowledge base about people's life challenges and self-understanding as a minority. We also wished to communicate this knowledge to students and staff on the various Bachelor and Master's programmes at our university college focusing on this field of interest.

THE STORYTELLING PROCESS

The reason we chose digital storytelling is based on our previous experiences of it as a successful method, as adumbrated above. Another reason was that digital storytelling has the ability to move the listener through the expression of authentic life stories. The use of digital storytelling can be an *effective*, *affective* and *reflective* way to communicate understanding, meaning and experiences of the individual lives, without being recreated or interpreted by others who are necessarily separated from the context in which the story is created (Sumner 2009). On the first day, we met the participants on a guided tour of the art exhibition at Kunsthall Grenland, at The Cultural Centre, Ælvespeilet. Since this was our first meeting, and we were equal participants as an audience, we had occasion to get to know each other. On the second day, we used sense-based exercises as a way to recall important scenes from our lives, while focusing on today's situation and hope for the future. This exercise was used again on the third day in the digital storytelling workshop, using a sample of their stories in the story circle and working with writing the manuscript, pictures and music. On the fourth day, the participants and their teachers met at the data lab of the University for the final editing of the stories. Some weeks later, on the fifth day of the course, we had the public screening, showing stories of the participants in front of an invited audience. As part of the process to establish a safe framework in the research work of promoting the individual life story, and as a means of bringing to mind what had been forgotten or repressed, we made use of various exercises that I will describe below.

Involving Our Senses

We smelled and tasted warm homemade bread, freshly ground coffee, fresh tobacco and spices from all around the world. Everyone participated, and there were no passive observers. One by one, the participants talked about the struggle to get enough food to survive, or the family's agricultural production and the economic importance of coffee, tea and spice plantations as places of employment. Others had memories associated with not only illness, death and various types of life tragedies, but also births and joyful events. Several recounted memories of their school days and their good teachers or lack of such teachers, while still others reminisced about cuisines and culinary traditions, religious ceremonies, everyday life and special occasions and various celebrations. For several participants, the scents brought back memories of war, flight and refugee camps. Central to all the memories shared were the strong ties to parents and other relatives, as well as their native country, the nature of their native country, indigenous culture and religion. Common to all participants was the balance of happy memories against feelings of sadness and deprivation connected with loss, or being so far away from everything they had known before.

Memory Boxes and Dreams for the Future

We asked the participants to collect objects related to important events and memories in their lives. The Memory boxes were filled with the names of family members, pictures of their family, country and flags, descriptions of nature, native language in poetry, songs and recipes. The participants showed and told each other what they had in their boxes—memories that reminded them of important events in their own lives and that had helped them to create a connection between past and present. The last exercise, called "My dreams and hope for the future", prompted the participants to talk about the different ways in which they viewed their lives while living in another country.

Stories We Heard

One woman brought along a ring that her mother had given her in her early adulthood. The ring was a personal gift that she had treasured throughout her life. Another woman took out a brown hijab decorated with white dots, which was among her most precious memories of her deceased mother. Her mother had worn the hijab shortly before her death, and it was still unwashed and represented a place of comfort and a reminder of a childhood spent with a good mother. When she put on her mother's hijab, she remembered the beautiful song they used to sing to her on Mother's Day, and at the end of the recording of the digital story, she chose to sing in her mother tongue. A fourth participant proudly showed us a yellowed photo of the ship he had captained and that had sailed through international waters in what he described as his "previous life". One of the participant's stories concerned the loss of schooling after just five years of primary education, due to the necessity to escape from the Taliban regime. Central to this story was the message that the Taliban wrested from her the dream of having an education. "But they have not won over me, and I will never let them have the last word about my life!" she exclaimed. Others spoke of the importance of their diaries, described by many as among their most prized possessions, something that secured a sense of continuity in their lives. There were also several stories about fleeing from war and poverty, life in refugee camps and exile, and years of travelling through many transit countries before finally arriving in Norway, where new problems related to applications for residence permits awaited them.

Several participants mentioned the contradictory expectations and dilemmas of being parents of children born in Norway, caused by the disparity between Norwegian society's expectations concerning upbringing, on the one hand, and the expectations of family, relatives and friends in their native country, on the other hand. One single mother with several young children shared a compelling story about what was required of her to be a strong mother for the sake of her children, and to secure their future in Norway. There were also stories of a more humorous nature. For instance, a male participant from Somalia who had never seen snow before recounted his first encounter with it in Norway. When he arrived at the refuge centre it was a snowy cold winter's day, and he was wearing only his sandals! The round of stories elicited both laughter and tears, sadness and hope. Perhaps the most important aspect of the stories were the authentic conversations between equals who revealed their lives to share and communicate their thoughts and life stories; this was experienced by everybody as a meaningful and effective process regarding the opportunities to establish a good life in a new country.

At the end of the session, in which they shared their "dreams for the future", the participants had written down their hopes and dreams for their future lives in Norway. For instance: "I dream about learning Norwegian, because it is the key to a future in Norway for me and my children". Others expressed the wish to learn Norwegian so they could get jobs as cleaners, welders, teachers, drivers, shop workers, IT workers and so on. Some also described the dream of seeing their children get an education and being employed, and living a good life with family and friends without having significant health problems or being exposed to racism. All the participants expressed the wish to participate in Norwegian society using their resources so they could extricate themselves from the voyeuristic position OR as observer they often found themselves in. These activities were the base for further work with the digital storytelling process, from the initial idea to the final text.

MOVING INTO THE DIGITAL STORYTELLING PROCESS

As teachers, we went through the process with them using the CDS model based on the *Story Circle* and the *Seven Elements* (Lambert 2013). As part of the storytelling process, the participants selected one of their life stories that had emerged from the work with "Memory Boxes" and "Dreams and hopes for the future". First, everyone was given the task of coming up with a short, descriptive headline for their story. Then they were given an exercise where the aim was to build on the stories they had told by using free creative writing. In this phase, they wrote down everything that came to mind without erasing, correcting or deleting anything. They were encouraged to note down all their thoughts, feelings, moods, as well as colours, images, sounds and smells. Those who were unable to write got help from the teachers or other capable participants.

They were then divided into different story circles, with three or four in each group. There were two rounds in the story circle, and each group was followed closely by the teachers and researchers. Lambert has described this as the mainstay in digital storytelling. "When you gather people in a room, and listen, deeply listen to what they are saying, and also, by example alone, encourage others to listen, magic happens" (Lambert 2009, p. 86). In the "Story Circles", all the participants received constructive feedback on their unfinished draft from both the other participants in the group and the teachers and researcher. Feedback was also given on the messages and points made in the stories, dramaturgy, the use of emotion and narrative voices, and the use of music, imagery, rhythm and tempo. The process towards the recording of the final digital stories was challenging because it was largely tied to the individuals' life stories, which all included episodes of grief. Many were aware of their own experiences of loss, and several underwent a painful recollection process (Lambert 2013). In the process leading to the completion of the digital story, the participants were encouraged to maintain the authentic quality without opening up themselves to such an extent that they might later regret it.

Sharing Stories in Public-Knowledge Dissemination

On the opening day, all the participants shared their digital stories in the Cultural Centre where families, and friends, representatives from public and private sectors, politicians and media attended.[3] The participants' shared their digital stories, while the teachers' and researchers' reflections contributed to an awareness-enhancing process, giving voice to a group of people who are not usually heard in society, potentially creating greater understanding. On the following day, we read in the editorial in the local newspaper about the screening and the use of digital storytelling, described as "Brilliant integration". The editor commented that digital storytelling used in this way in public, would increase understanding between people from different parts of the world and be a positive part of the integrating process.[4] We saw that using digital storytelling in cooperation with participants with minority background had resulted in the impact we had hoped for.

For us, the teaching programme also functioned as a form of practice-research discovery (Boyer 1990). We discovered how the work with digital storytelling corresponded with key requirements for participant-based research, while we also attained more in-depth knowledge. In what follows, I will clarify and discuss the justification of the research approach.

FROM EMPIRICAL RESEARCH DISCOVERY TO SCIENTIFIC CLARIFICATION

To justify the use of digital storytelling as a research approach in relation to scientific and methodological requirements, I build upon Skjervheim's perspectives concerning participant and observer or spectator positions in research and practice (1996). It is the responsibility of social scientists to tackle particular challenges in research where real people are the research subjects, including their opinions and understanding of reality. Thus, understanding the relationship between the social scientist and the people the scientist wishes to learn something about is crucial. Part of this required clarification relates to the four key challenges regarding human-related research as introduced by Grimen (2004, pp. 289–90) and described earlier in this chapter. As research was not the primary aim in this project, I will discuss these issues primarily from a theoretical point of view and use the experiences from the workshops as illustrations.

Digital Storytelling as a Participatory and Dialogue-Oriented Approach

One of the most important issues concerning the relationship between researcher and research subject concerns the researcher's attitudes towards the research subjects and the kind of relationships the researcher should aspire to have for the research subjects (Grimen 2004). The question of whether the social scientist should engage in the research subjects' world, or whether she should be indifferent to what they think, say and do, is still an open question in the field of epistemology. Should the researcher be an observer or a participant with regard to the research subjects? From the perspective of an observer, humans are examined and treated in the same way as if one was studying natural phenomena. Conversely, a participatory approach involves researchers regarding their subjects of study as qualified dialogue *partners*, where the researcher should take into account the fact that they may be critical of her understanding of concepts and her explanations (Grimen 2004, p. 293).

In our teaching programme, it was precisely the discovery of the participatory and dialogue-oriented potential that was important and that has been called for in minority research. Everyone who attended the class was active in the process towards completing a digital story and the sharing of the story in question. Using digital storytelling functioned as an entry to gaining an understanding and being able to interpret the participants' world, and how they experience and interpret their worlds. Digital storytelling is part of the human sciences with a hermeneutical and phenomenological approach, and has a social sciences orientation with an emphasis on critical theory depending on the theme, problem, purpose and area of use.

The digital storytelling process, in our context, was related to a specific type of digital story, a concrete production process that has its origins in the "giving voice" tradition. In the case of our target group, we worked with the participative digital storytelling, so the process towards the final stories was largely dialogue-based. The participants were the main players through the process. Everyone was involved in the dialogues, especially in the "story circle". We experienced that "allowing more voices to participate brought multiple perspectives and interpretations of what was documented, which helped to clarify and make sense of the story" (Haug and Jamissen 2015, p. 39). In the story circle, all participants were on an equal footing as dialogue partners. None were "spectators or observed" without the opportunity of response. Skjervheim introduces the concept *instrumentalistic error* to describe the consequences of adopting an observer position from the study of natural phenomena into the social sciences, seeing people as objects, something which precludes the option to respond. To avoid this mistake, he focuses on the different ways of meeting people linguistically and illustrates this by presenting relations as either two-part or tri-part. A two-part relationship is characterised by an observer position. This can occur, for instance, where the researcher does not become engaged in the minority-ethnic user and the specific case material the user presents. In other words, the researcher does not treat the research subject as a dialogue partner, but rather as an object, a thing. With such a basis, the researcher can only learn something *about* the research subject, and not *from* her (Grimen 2004, p. 294). Conversely, a tri-part relationship is characterised by a participatory approach, where those studying and those being studied function as interacting subjects. This relationship is described by Skjervheim as a subject/subject relationship, where the researcher and research subjects are together in a relationship with a third party, a case material that binds them together as fellow subjects. The researcher relates and is engaged in what the research subject has to say, and may contribute to what they say and vice versa. Both parties treat each other, and what the other says, with respect (1996). However, this requires a three-part relationship between the researcher, the research subjects and the subject matter in which both parties are involved, such as is potentially the case in digital storytelling. This was exactly what we experienced when we worked with digital storytelling. Throughout the process, the participants' stories functioned as a case material, the neutral "third" that was shared by the two; the research subject and the researcher. Both were engaged in the stories as something that tied us together and provided the basis for a real dialogue. I will share an example. One of the participants, a mother living alone with her three children, shared a story about her fear of the child welfare services. She dreaded they might be able to take the children away from her, thinking that she was a bad mother without understanding her own cultural way of raising her children. In the digital storytelling work, we had an opportunity through the story as a "third" that placed us as participants in a dialogue-based position, to investigate this fear and the background for it, a concern she raised as a life-challenge.

Digital Storytelling as an Approach to Popular or Scientific Concepts and Explanations

Scientific challenges related to *concepts* and *explanations* will largely depend on the researcher's attitudes towards, and preferences for, the people he/she wishes to study. Which concepts should the researcher use for what is to be studied? Should the researcher always apply scientific concepts irrespective of which concepts the research subjects use or understand? Alternatively, should the researcher endeavour to use more popular concepts that the research subjects use themselves? This can certainly result in restrictions regarding scientific conceptualisation. Some of the same research challenges may be found in the question concerning which explanations should be given weight. Should the researcher use the research subjects' explanations, often rooted in popular everyday explanations at the expense of scientific explanations? This is particularly relevant in the research contexts where there are different or divergent explanations.

In the process using digital storytelling with minority-ethnic participants, we conducted conversations where we made an attempt to make concepts intelligible and to clarify explanations. This resulted in the need for everybody to modify the terms and explanations that we initially used in the work. Through dialogue, we had the opportunity to discuss concepts and explanations in a way that contributed to safeguarding the meaning that the participants wanted to communicate through their stories. Our own, more academic and scientific concepts and explanations often had to give way, or be replaced or modified by, those of the participants. At other times, when presented with our concepts and explanations, the participants experienced that their own concepts and explanations were inappropriate, incomplete, and incorrect. One example was the statement from the mother who was afraid of losing her children. Her understanding was based on a knowledge, prevalent among some people, that the reason the child welfare services might take children away from their mother is that they do not understand her cultural values and traditions and consequently see her as a poor parent. From a professional point of view, the concepts and explanations linked to such a case are more complex. Moreover, these are based on the law, the child welfare services' administrative practices, and an understanding that taking a child from its mother is a serious step. The principle of "for the good of the child", "the biological principle" together with extensive examination by the Child Care Office, expert statements and a decision by the County Governor is thoroughly investigated before a care order can be issued. In the dialogue connected to developing her story, we observed a continual conceptual and explanatory development on both sides which helped us develop a mutual understanding of the issue in question, in this case fear of the child welfare services. We observed similar processes with the other participants where we mutually developed concepts that correlated more with what we were all attempting to grasp with respect to their life stories.

Skjervheim believes that the reality the research subjects live in represents a world that has already been interpreted and conceptualised by them, and therefore something the scientist must actively relate to when transforming the subjects' concepts into his/her own language. This view is based on what he calls *the subjectivity principle,* which involves the social scientist describing and studying behaviour by using terms that belong to the subjects' interpretation of situations (Skjervheim 1996). A participating researcher has to include the research subjects' concepts and explanations in his/her scientific practice as a kind of translation process, where conceptual development takes place in the field of tension between experience-related concepts and explanations and the science-oriented ones. It is only in this way that minority research can be given authority, by being rooted in the explanations that the subjects can accept and by adopting an openness about the complexities related to the ethical challenges arising from the relationship between the researcher and research subjects.

Digital Storytelling as an Ethical Challenge: Friend or Researcher

The last epistemological challenge in researching human phenomena addresses *ethical challenges*. These are implicit in the relationship between researcher and research subject and are linked to the issue of trust. It is important to get the balance right between the role of the researcher and friend, inasmuch as the researcher must not lose sight of his/her aim to obtain empirical data and without the research subjects finding themselves used, misused or misunderstood (Israel and Hay 2006).

Everyone who participated in the digital storytelling project came closer to each other as human beings and dialogue partners in what could be defined as a relationship of trust. The participants contributed and shared important life stories with each other through the various exercises, including the Story Circle. In many ways, we created a common universe of understanding while sharing each other's ways of understanding reality. It goes without saying that such communities also have ethical implications. Taking part in human-related research often presents ethical dilemmas that stem from the fact that it is not always possible to attain symmetric relationships. In our case, as course coordinators, we represented a majority among the minorities. Also, we had a special responsibility by the virtue of being professionals with extensive expertise. We also belong to the majority-ethnic/majority-linguistic group in the population and possess a better socio-economic situation than the participants. In sum, this may provide a more or less skewed balance of power that can be used and abused in an unethical manner. One has by virtue of one's position the opportunity to control the narratives in the desired direction, using specialist terms and explanations from the professional field, far removed from the participants' universe of understanding. We were constantly aware of these ethical concerns and also aware of a desire to bring out each participant's authentic narrative without it becoming excessively intimate or going beyond a therapeutic barrier. In some cases, since because the stories were to be used in a public context, we advised participants to select a different situation or event, or take a more distant perspective with respect to their stories. Skjervheim warns against unethical research practices where one objectifies research subjects (1996). Ethically rooted research practices related to the actions and relationships to avoid *the instrumentalistic error* and which are based on tri-part relationships characterised by respect, tolerance, recognition and fairness between researcher and research subjects are necessary.

With reference to the four epistemological challenges in the relationship between researcher and research subjects, where the main concerns are the researcher's attitudes towards those being studied, we find evidence that the use of digital storytelling is a promising approach that may meet research requirements.

DIGITAL STORYTELLING AS A SCIENTIFIC AND METHODOLOGICAL APPROACH

Based on requirements for a strengthened qualitative participant-orientation in minority research, a number of epistemological challenges, and an emphasis of the researcher as a participant in the dialogue with research subjects, I have argued that digital storytelling has a scientific and methodological potential. If used rigorously, digital storytelling is an approach that can exceed the asymmetric relationship that often exists between researcher and research subject. The work involved in making digital life stories assumes that researchers and research subjects enter into a tri-part relationship with the story as the common third (Skjervheim 1996). The case material involved in the digital storytelling work may also lead the participants into larger socio-political discourses. Such critically oriented discourses can deal with questions about the conflicts of interest, power relations and social structures that affect the actual case and provide possible answers to factors that can promote or inhibit life opportunities. According to Lambert, working with digital storytelling has a powerful potential to highlight social and political injustice at the micro as well as macro level (2010). Digital storytelling is at its core based on the human need to tell stories (Bruner 1991), and offers a new way of communicating stories. For research purposes, it may offer a new way of acquiring knowledge and understanding. The process in the story circle towards the formation of meaning that forms the basis for the story of the individual participant is not straightforward. In working with the seven elements, the aim is to bring out the individual narrative, personal involvement and an emotional dimension. In this context, digital storytelling provides a good opportunity for the individual to give both a self-presentation and self-representation. Lundby (2008) describes self-presentation as a form of direct and focused communication between the presenter and the recipients, while self-representation implies that one actively directs a picture of oneself as one wishes to appear and be perceived. This constitutes one of the key parts of the methodological potential of digital stories in securing research subjects a participatory approach and subject status.

Concluding Remarks

In research, digital storytelling may serve as a form of empirical data collection in both the process and the final product. Throughout all parts of the digital storytelling process, a researcher will relate to the participants as participatory dialogue partner. It is also important that the researcher in this process clarifies the professional and ethical premises for the relationship and that the research aspect of the process is presented, understood and consented to. By adopting such an approach, as a minority researcher, one will need to have as a starting point a genuine interest in the participants' understanding of their situation or the specific events one wants to discuss. The researcher may be challenged in the encounter with popular and experience-based concepts. These are then explored and refined in contact with scientific and analytical concepts introduced by the researcher in a dialogue with research participants. Likewise, the work process towards the completed digital stories gives the participants a unique opportunity to reflect on the assertions and facts, and enter into a dialogue about possible explanations in a dynamic process that will often reflect both popular and scientific explanations. The participants' understanding, concepts and explanations based on their experiences will find their final shape in the completed digital stories, together with the researcher's understanding. These will ultimately be presented to invited user groups, professionals and colleagues as an empirical basis for reflective discussions and a basis for further research. Specifically, the completed digital stories may serve as empirical data and be analysed using qualitative methods such as narrative theory, grounded theory and phenomenological approaches. If we choose to record the story circle as an alternative to focus groups, or other qualitative methods, there is a good chance that the data collected is more representative for the research subjects' own understanding.

Through such qualitative, participatory and dialogue-oriented research approaches, minority research on child welfare services will be able to ensure a more valid and credible knowledge of this user group. The researcher will also be able to make digital stories about the research findings from the digital stories of others. The use of digital storytelling offers the researcher a new language, a common language that can help revitalise research, give dignity to teaching, and help higher education to be more responsive (Boyer 1990). Digital storytelling used in this way will accommodate Boyer's wish to create more coherent and comprehensive academic institutions where "discovery, teaching and learning, integration and engagement" are included.

Acknowledgement I want to thank my wise colleague and mentor over the years Bjarne Nærum for challenging me to embrace digital storytelling as a liberating pedagogical approach to teaching, mentoring, research and social responsibility. Without his enthusiastic support, this chapter would not have been written.

Notes

1. Hans Skjervheim (1926–1999), Norwegian Professor of Philosophy, public intellectual debater and critic of the social sciences. http://prabook.org/web/person-view.html?profileId=1121289. Accessed 30 September 2016.
2. "Kunsthall Grenland (Flyt project)...".; Awarded "Institution of the Year" in 2014 for the project, by Norske kunstforeninger [Art Association in Norway]). http://www.norskekunstforeninger.no/?pArticleId=39675. Accessed 30 September 2016.
3. http://www.pd.no/lokale_nyheter/article7424998.ece. *Jeg vil være en sterk mamma*. Porsgrunn Dagblad, 18 June, 2014. Andresen, M. E. (17.6.2014). *Vil integrere med kunst*. Telemark Arbeiderblad. Accessed 30 September 2016.
4. http://www.pd.no/leder/article7427328.ece. *Glimrende integrering*. Porsgrunn Dagblad, 19 June, 2014. Accessed 30 September 2016.

References

Boyer, E. L. (1990). *Scholarship reconsidered. Priorities of the professoriate, Special report*. Princeton: The Carnegie Foundation for the Advancement of Teaching.
Bruner, J. (1991). The narrative construction of reality. *Critical Inquiry, 18*(1), 1–21.

Fauske, H., & Qureshi, A. N. (2010). Empowerment og antiundertrykkende sosialt arbeid. In M. S. Kaya, A. Høgmo, & H. Fauske (Eds.), *Integrasjon og mangfold. Utfordringer for sosialarbeideren.* Oslo: Cappelen Akademisk Forlag.

Fuglerud, Ø., & Eriksen, T. H. (2007). *Grenser for kultur? Perspektiver fra norsk minoritetsforskning.* Oslo: Pax Forlag A/S.

Grimen, H. (2004). *Samfunnsvitenskapelige tenkemåter.* Oslo: Universitetsforlaget.

Haug, K. H., & Jamissen, G. (2015). *Se min fortelling. Digital historiefortelling i barnehagen.* Oslo: Cappelen Damm Akademisk.

Holm-Hansen, J., Haaland, T., & Myrvold, T. (Eds.). (2007). *Flerkulturelt barnevern- En kunnskapsoversikt.* Oslo: NIBR – Rapport 2007 10.

Israel, M., & Hay, I. (2006). *Research ethics for social scientists.* London: SAGE Publications.

Lambert, J. (2009). *Digital storytelling. Capturing lives, creating community. 3. utg.* Berkley: Digital Diner Press.

Lambert, J. (2010). (red.). *Digital Storytelling Cookbook.* San Francisco: Center for Digital Storytelling (CDS).

Lambert, J. (2013). *Digital storytelling. Capturing lives, creating community* (4th ed.). New York/London: Routledge.

Lundby, K. (2008). Introduction: Digital storytelling, mediatized stories. In K. Lundby (Ed.), *Digital storytelling. Mediatized stories: Self-representations in new media* (pp. 1–17). New York: Peter Lang.

Paulsen, V., Thorshaug, K., & Berg, B. (2014). *Møter mellom innvandrere og barnevernet. Kunnskapsstatus.* Mangfold og inkludering. Trondheim: NTNU. Samfunnsforskning.

Skjervheim, H. (1996). Participant and spectator. In H. Skjervheim (Ed.), *Selected essays. In honour of Hans Skjervheim's 70th birthday* (pp. 127–141). Bergen: University of Bergen/Department of Philosophy.

Sumner, T. (2009). *Inspiring innovation through patient voices: Presentation at innovation expo.* London: Edexcel London.

CHAPTER 11

Learning to Work Through Narratives: Identity and Meaning-Making During Digital Storytelling

Satu Hakanurmi

INTRODUCTION

I was commissioned to contribute to a process of organisational change. Among my qualifications was my experience with running digital storytelling (DS) workshops. As I was also a doctoral student, I wanted to use this opportunity to explore the potential of DS as an intervention in an organisational development context and as a research tool. This study will be of interest to those concerned with narrative meaning-making through DS in organisations and those using story work as an alternative method of data collection.

In this chapter I explore the meaning-making process during the story circle in a work context. I use a case study approach to capture the complexities of how stories emerge. The aim of this research is to consider how individual participants felt, what they learned throughout the process and how the story circle contributed to the stories and narratives, for instance, how the social aspect influenced individuals. I introduce a model for analysing stories as "closed narrative," "open narrative" and "ante-narrative."

S. Hakanurmi (✉)
University of Turku, Turku, Finland

© The Author(s) 2017   149
G. Jamissen et al. (eds.), *Digital Storytelling in Higher Education*,
Digital Education and Learning, DOI 10.1007/978-3-319-51058-3_11

My research results provide an increased understanding of ways of learning with storytelling and narratives. The intention is to show how DS can provide new insights into organisational development, and how using DS in this context can give us new insights into how the story circle affects the individual's narrative process and organisational meaning-making. It contributes to the Scholarship of Discovery in that it is empirical, explores theoretical positions and uses DS as a method.

My theoretical position has deep roots in narrative theory, the way people organise their ideas and how they participate in the social contexts of their lives by sharing stories, ideas, culture and communication. In terms of learning theory, this is rooted in socio-cultural theory as discussed by, for example, Vygotsky (Wertsch 1990).

The distinction between story and narrative is often unclear. Story with the function of meaning-making is seen as a narrative with a plot, whereas a story without any meaningful plot is seen as a chronicle or just noise (Czarniawska 2004, pp. 10–11). How researchers use these concepts varies. There is a stark contrast between everyday conversational narrative and sophisticated storytelling. The role of storyteller and listener is not always clear, whereas in the practice of cooperative storytelling, both the storyteller and the listener engage in a joint narrative effort. Oral and conversational discourse draws on many more resources linked to the face-to-face presence of the narrative interlocutors. In oral storytelling, physical presence and interaction are directly connected to the situation, the narrative event and environment, thereby enriching their expressive and communicative registers. Since participants in these highly contextualised narrative events interact in a variety of ways, researchers prefer to use the term "co-narrators" (Brockmeier 2015, pp. 208–209).

My chief aim is to explore how making stories and turning them into narratives give the participants motivation and direction, challenging their identities by challenging and expanding their narratives.

Theoretical Background

A sense of coherence is a prerequisite for learning at work. In order to maintain coherence, identities are continuously under construction, shaped through the way they express feelings and experiences. Individuals' mediated narratives are rough reconstructions of the past and constitute ways of seeking the ontological security of 'being themselves' (Billett 2008, p. 53). Work identities and their renegotiations are necessary elements in professional learning, although it has been argued that workplace learning focuses on participation and building identity rather than learning (Eteläpelto 2009, p. 94, p. 97). Professional development is a collective process in which identity is negotiated and work practices are developed (Hökkä et al. 2014).

Today's business models and management systems need a postmodern management paradigm. This includes the recognition of the relevance of people's experiences, emotions and energy in shaping and influencing the quality and performance of organisations (Schiuma 2011, p. 9).

DS can be seen as an intervention to support learning at work because, as a creative and collaborative method, DS offers a forum for collective identity work based on the community's beliefs and cultural narratives.

A number of researchers have reported the impact of storytelling and narratives in learning (Clarke and Adam 2012; Maddin 2012; Yang and Wu 2012; Coventry 2008a, 2008b; Lundby 2008; Boje 2001; Yang 2013; Biesta et al. 2011). Less attention has been paid to DS and learning in organisations where business stories have usually been oral narratives collected from interviews, discussions or observations (Orr 2006). Recently, there has been a renewed interest in narrative learning, which combines narratives, learning, identity and agency. Previous studies, such as the Learning Lives project in the UK, have shown the importance of stories as vehicles for learning from one's life. Life stories play a crucial role in the articulation of a sense of self, which means that narrative learning is also a form of identity work (Biesta et al. 2011, p. 110).

In the light of recent research on the close connection between identity and agency at work, this issue has assumed greater importance (Eteläpelto et al. 2013; Billett and Pavlova 2005) but there is a lack of research into the use of narrative in work. Educational research has usually concentrated on the finished narratives of learners, employees or teachers, but the storytelling process itself has elicited relatively little interest. Earlier research reveals qualitative differences in life stories, such as the extent of narrative intensity, descriptive–evaluative quality and differing learning outcomes. There appear to be important relationships between styles of narration, forms of narrative learning and agency (Field et al. 2011, p. 110). In closed narratives the meaning-making and reflection are mostly finished; stories represent the existing identity and social impact has a minor role. In open narratives and in ante-narratives, however, narratives are born during the storytelling process, and identity expressions are more co-authored (Boje 2001, 3; Biesta et al. 2011, 68; Brockmeier 2015, 125–126).

SOCIO-CULTURAL THEORY OF HUMAN LEARNING

Social theory under the influence of Vygotsky provides a rich potential source for understanding and developing processes of social transformation such as education (Wertsch 1990, p. 113; Daniels 2001, p. 9). A Bakhtinian "space of authoring" is to a great extent a particular "zone of development"; and one that is extremely important in an explication of the development of identities as aspects of "history-in-person" (Holland 2001, p. 183). The position of storytellers and the context of their narratives are constantly changing. Each story is part of an ongoing dialogue with local, societal and global contours that rearticulate meaning in embedded acts of retrospective sense-making (Boje 2001, p. 78). At the same time, humans are part of figured worlds that consist of human history, the changing positions of humans and an unknown future. Humans also actively modify the social and cultural ecology to which they belong. These figured worlds are socially organised and reproduced (Holland 2001, pp. 41–42).

In the research underpinning this chapter, humans are seen as having an internalised culture within which individual and organisational identities are inextricably linked and affect each other. It is not only the interaction and transformative representations that reshape the understanding of things and individual and social identity but also the joint construction itself that gives shape to expression. Narratives can be seen as an intersubjective attitude to the joint construction of meaning; a commitment to find common ground on which to build shared understanding (Palinscar 2005, pp. 290–294).

NARRATIVE LEARNING THROUGH STORYTELLING

Stories give our lives structure, coherence and meaning. To a large extent, we *are* the stories about our lives and ourselves. The story is not merely a description of life and self: it *constitutes* the life and the story. The *construction* of the story—the storytelling of the life and self—is a central element of the way in which we can learn from our lives through storytelling. This is *narrative learning*. It is more than learning from stories, it is learning while storying. With stories we often build future-oriented narratives unconsciously and as a by-product of our ongoing actions, interactions and conversations (Biesta et al. 2011, pp. 50–51).

Narrative learning theory is interested in the role of stories and storytelling in learning processes, the possible relationships between the characteristics of the stories themselves and the potential of narrative and narration for learning and action (Biesta et al. 2009, pp. 50–51). Narrative learning operates at the intersection of "internal conversations" and the social practices of storytelling. For many, the social opportunities for narrating one's life story are vehicles for narrative learning. A number of studies have emphasised the importance of a "social practice pedagogy" establishing common ground where people's narratives can be heard and valued (Biesta et al. 2011, p. 111). The telling of stories is a future-oriented activity as telling stories is the currency of knowledge-making and knowledge negotiation (Boje 2001, p. 8; Czarniawska 2004, pp. 10–11).

NARRATIVES AS REPRESENTATIONS OF IDENTITY AND REFLECTIONS OF EXPERIENCES

Narratives are representations of identities whereas storytelling is a meaning-making tool for constructing identity; narrative is the language of our identity (Brockmeier 2015, pp. ix, 119). Identity is composed of representations about oneself developed in relation to other people and their own systems of representation. Representation of an identity is a dynamic reality, never fully realised and always in a process of reformulation. Different discourses existing in society and organisations make identity construction a creative endeavour (Glăveanu and Tanggaard 2014, p. 14).

Reflection is a key to learning from experience; a process of internally examining and exploring an issue of concern triggered by an experience that results in a changed conceptual perspective. Theories of workplace learning and professional development have stressed the role of social exchange in professional learning (Billett and Somerville 2004). Reflection as an individual activity is often considered to be less effective than reflection in the context of social interaction underpinned by shared knowledge (Hetzner et al. 2012, pp. 548–549). Dewey saw people as belonging to a "common world," in which the co-construction of knowledge inevitably involves shared understanding and meaning, rather than the diverging individual stances (Biesta et al. 2009, pp. 20–21).

Telling an appropriate story is a means of gaining validation of one's identity from listeners. The function of narrative can vary from gaining approval of the social group to the renewal of culture. Here, the position and ecological condition of one's field of action have an impact. In the course of their [own] development, human beings actively shape the very forces that shape them (Daniels 2001, pp. 1–2). Experiences and stories do not simply happen to us; it is we who make and remake them (Brockmeier 2015, p. 116, p. 119). Similarly, digital stories as a narrative product do not simply represent our existing identities. Instead, storytelling is closer to dialogue, communication and social co-authoring where audience, context and individual spaces of authorship interact. Identity is constantly being performed and reshaped within performance and in the way we react to others (Glăveanu and Tanggaard 2014, p. 13). Stories do not pre-exist in our minds to be expressed as digital stories but they are actively constructed during the storytelling process. In order to tell narratives, stories with meaning, storytellers must go through an active reflection process exploring their experiences in the past, present and future.

WE DON'T FIND NARRATIVES BUT MAKE THEM

Narrative is of crucial importance in understanding the complexities of human meaning-making. It is the primary way of investing human experience with meaning. Human behaviour is generated from, and informed by, this meaning (Polkinghorne 1988, p. 1) Brockmeier proposes that the intricacies of autobiographical meaning-making are not just represented or expressed by narrative but also that they only come into being through narrative. Stories emerge during the storytelling process. Brockmeier calls this the strong narrative thesis. The strong narrative is a kind of action that takes place in acts of narrative meaning construction. A case in point is the capacity of narrative to create complex temporal scenarios that are typical for the autobiographical process. Another phenomenon illustrating the strong narrative thesis is the "what's-it-like quality" of conscious awareness, which Brockmeier describes as a critical property of narrative experience (Brockmeier 2015, pp. ix, 116, 118–119).

Storytellers may speak from different perspectives by separating the narrating and narrated event as far as possible, describing parts of the event in question impartially. They may align narrating and the narrated events, omit the here-and-now from the narrating event and speak from the perspectives of enacted characters inside the narrated events there-and-then. Speakers engage in meta-narration—the overtly and explicitly social interactional elements of discourse—bridging the gap between the narrated event and the storytelling event. When a group or an audience have an impact on the story, co-authoring takes place and it is during the reflection of the storyteller that the narrative is created (Koven 2007, pp. 151–154). The availability to study this co-authoring process, first of all in not only the story circle but also other phases of the production process towards the construction and sharing of the stories, represents one of the most interesting qualities of DS in the context of the scholarship of discovery. This is also discussed in Chaps. 9 and 10 in this book.

Context and Methodology

This chapter takes the form of a case study and narrative analysis of story circle discussions and interviews. The DS project was organised at the end of a two-and-a-half-year organisational staff development project lasting from autumn 2011 until the end of 2013. The aim of the project was to improve customer services, interpersonal and management skills. The company chose a representative sample of storytellers, including men and women, different age groups and positions, such as managers, staff working in customer services, support services, web and call services, contact persons, business services and insurance sales. Some employees over the age of 50 refused to participate because of their limited technical skills and therefore the older age group is under-represented. The stories were produced during February–March 2014 and the premiere took place in April, during the annual celebration of the preliminary report. At this event, 300 employees, including members of the management group, watched the eight stories which lasted 25 minutes altogether.

The workshop started with a one-and-a-half-hour story circle comprising seven storytellers, two HR employees and two facilitators. I was one of two independent workshop facilitators. Storytellers were instructed to tell a story about a learning experience during the staff development project. Each story was discussed for 12 minutes in the story circle. The story circle of 11 people and 7 interviews performed after the screening were audiotaped and transcribed. The research framework is summarised in Table 11.1.

Table 11.1   The research framework

Research question	Data	Concepts used in analysis
1. Individual experience of storytelling What kind of learning and identity work was done during the storytelling? Difference between written and digital stories?	Interviews	Identity Identity work (Eteläpelto 2009)
2. Social co-authoring of stories At what stage were the narratives when they were presented in the story circle? What kind of meaning-making and co-authoring took place during the story circle?	Story circle discussions	Strong narrative thesis (Brockmeier 2015), ante-narrative (Boje 2001), open and closed narratives (Biesta et al. 2011) and functions of discussion episodes (Iiskala et al. 2010)
3. Time dimensions of storytelling Were stories told from the perspective of past, present or future?	Story circle discussions	Here-and-now, there-and-then (Koven 2012), next-in-future (own addition)

INDIVIDUAL EXPERIENCE OF STORYTELLING

Common to the discursive spaces was the experience that the story was based on storytellers' own voice. This is a big narrative of our time; a narrative of the individual over the social and at odds with the idea that our minds are outside our bodies, but in the world (Brockmeier 2015, p. 232). It is a social construct to see life in Western culture mainly through individuals; we live, experience and learn as individuals:

> It was my own story without anyone else's imprint. (Neil, 29)

Personal experiences also acquired meaning from the group and storytellers were conscious of the social presence, context and audience:

> Since this was done at the work place I naturally took certain things into consideration but the story is entirely mine. (Sheila, 56)

The possibility to tell stories with a voice-over and visuals was considered more attractive than written stories. The emotional dimension became natural and things that would otherwise have been difficult to express became part of the stories. Without the visuals the storytellers thought an important and powerful aspect would have been missing. They transformed the workshop into an emotional learning environment, as described by the HR expert of the organisation: "there was a highly charged emotional atmosphere and this made a difference compared with other kind of trainings".

> This visual aspect added more depth to the story. (Paul, 34)
>   There was a far greater feeling of intimacy and the atmosphere was more personal. ... I mean I'm a pretty extrovert person and so I wouldn't want to show to the whole organisation what my home is like or how I was as a child or anything like that but here I had the courage to lead them into my story. (Olga, 28)

The DS workshop allowed an opportunity to reflect on one's own work and identity. All storytellers found DS fruitful and were grateful to have participated.

> at a certain point I didn't really know why we were doing these stories but when we had finished them and especially afterwards when I was discussing the topic with other people I thought that in the end perhaps the aim was to clarify things for myself and say things aloud in public. (Paul, 35)
>   There were a lot of emotions involved in the storytelling. If I had considered the big audience during the process I might have left something out of the story. On reflection it was just as well we had so little time and it was done at full speed. It was not too purpose-oriented. So it wasn't just like a sales pitch. (Neil, 29)

SOCIAL CO-AUTHORING OF STORIES AS ETHNOGRAPHIC DATA COLLECTION

Numerous scholars with an interest in conversation analysis and ethnographic studies have criticised interviews as a mode of data collection, arguing that interviews are, by definition, artificial and lack interaction. By using individual interviews for studying storytelling, I found myself, as researcher, a part of this criticised individualistic paradigm. Based on this self-criticism, I added the one-and-a-half-hour discussion of the story circle as an additional source of data in order to analyse the storytelling process and its social co-authoring elements. Stories told to others are often heteroglossic, and participants' comments connect to each other differently—either facilitating or inhibiting discussion (Koven 2007, p. 165).

The story circle discussions include a total of 448 comments, laughing or a short "hmm." I analysed comments according their function, described in Table 11.2.

Based on the analysis, storytellers presented three types of narratives during the story circle, as described in Table 11.3.

During the story circle, the narratives were at different stages and the quality of social co-authoring varied, as shown in Table 11.4. The ante-narratives and open narratives had more changes, slowing and stops than the closed narratives. Collaborative co-authoring and social meaning-making weaved the open stories into closed narrative plots infused with meaning. In open narratives, there was more space for co-authoring when meaning-making was done between the storyteller and the listeners.

Below I give examples from the comments in the story circle of the various forms of narrative.

Table 11.2 Functions of discussion comments. Modified from the functions of episodes used by Iiskala et al. (2010)

Function	Description	Example
TO FACILITATE	The direction of the discussion remains the same and gets stronger during the episode	
Activate	Activating new constructs in line with previous direction	*The client comes and the computer doesn't work.*
Confirm	Confirming that the previous direction is correct	*Yes working with the client must be difficult if there is no picture in the data-projector and you have to rush round looking for another data-projector so these are live experiences*
TO INHIBIT	The direction of the previous discussion is interrupted during the comment	
Slow	Returning to a previous direction presented in discussion	*and still we have several support services helping us*
Change	Changing the direction of the discussion	*Yes we are like enablers in the background and play an important role so evaluation should not be limited to sales*
Stop	Stopping the direction of previous discussion but a new discussion does not follow in the same direction	*It is good. It is personal*

Table 11.3 Different forms of narratives during the story circle

	Closed narrative—narrative with a plot	Open narrative—narrative without a clear plot from the start	Ante-narrative—missing the theme and/or the plot
Description of the narrative process	Meaning-making was to a large extent already done by the storyteller while the role of the other participants was to listen, confirm and ask questions about the story	The narrative was created during the discussion and there were changes in the discussion. Meaning-making was done collaboratively	Discussion comments were still unrelated to a clear plot or meaningful narrative. Meaning-making was done while the storyteller and other participants were reflecting together on things
Function of meaning – making in story circle	Social meaning-making of the personal story	Social and personal meaning-making of personal experiences	The impact of social meaning-making on the experiences of storyteller's and colleagues'

Table 11.4 Percentage of functions and the amount of different comments (N=) during the 12-minute discussion

	Closed narratives	Open narratives			Ante-narratives	
	Sheila	Berit	Neil	Mia	Paul	Cathrine
Confirming	68% (61)	76% (44)	65% (48)	67% (49)	57% (34)	63% (59)
Activating	23% (20)	10% (6)	15% (11)	12% (9)	10% (6)	11% (10)
Slowing	6% (5)	5% (3)	9% (7)	11% (8)	8% (5)	6 % (6)
Changing	3% (3)	9% (5)	11% (8)	10% (7)	22% (13)	17% (16)
Stopping	–	–	–	–	3% (2)	3% (3)
	(n= 89)	(n = 58)	(n = 74)	(n = 73)	(n = 60)	(n = 94)

Closed Narratives: Individual Re-Evaluation of the Experience

Closed narratives were presented in the story circle in a narrative form, with a sequence of events and meaning-making of the experience.

> it was easy for me [to start storytelling] and with the given materials I was able to start right away and I almost needed to control a bit myself in this

[writing]. Then I had to check the number amount of words so that it wouldn't be too long but basically I just let it go and then afterwards started to count the words and take off some parts so I mean it was a great experience. (Sheila, 56 years)

Open Narrative: A Forum for Social Meaning-Making

When there was a theme for the story without a clear plot, the storytelling process was creative and reflections were shared in a social interaction. Discussions provided different options for the story. Other participants in the story circle were able to identify with the *what's-it-like*—feelings and expanded on the reflections with aspects the storyteller hadn't thought of before:

Berit:	"Do you ever find that you think you have to be better at listening but then, as you are thinking this you find you are no longer listening?" (all laugh together)
Berit:	"So, oh my God…"
Neil:	"Exactly! I think I'm listening but in reality I am concentrating on trying to listen and so I can't listen properly!"
Berit:	"That's what I've found a couple of times"
Neil:	"Well yeah. That's why I wrote that you shouldn't just listen. You need to really stop and think what the other person is saying, and what their words really mean. So really you should listen and not have to think about how well you are listening."
HR-trainee:	"Yeah, it is really good to realize this." (all laugh together)
Mary (HR-employee):	"Do you also find that thinking about what you are going to respond actually stops you from listening properly?"
Neil:	"Yeah, yeah. That's the thing especially you are in a hurry and need to do a report in a certain way. You start thinking about how exactly you're going to do it and then you don't listen properly to what the air traffic control man is saying and what he actually wants you to do (all laugh

> together). And my answer isn't what the air traf-
> fic control man actually asked me about and
> then I have to go through it all over again and
> it's dialogue up there in the air and all kinds of
> Finnair and others have to wait there when this
> guy has finished (raucous laughing together) so
> that they can give their flight report too".

The group reflected on the difficulty of listening, the reasons for this and how one might listen more effectively. The discussion allowed the deconstruction of the expertise and listening skill to take place. It is a skill to know when to listen on a one-to-one basis and when to listen to the customer as a salesman. Laughing together was a strong expression in confirming the direction of the emerging story.

Ante-Narrative: From Discontinuity to Co-Authored Meaning-Making

Ante-narratives leave space for the renewal of the identity. Catherine found it hard to find a story to tell. She worked in the organisation's support services. In the story circle the group tried to define the identity for this unit:

> I'd just like to say that many people working in the support services prob-
> ably think what has this got to do with us [the staff development project].
> (Cathrine 56)

During the discussion, there were 16 changes such as new beginnings, points of views, examples and suggested visuals. The process of meaning-making was not a linear and continuous trajectory, consisting of an accumulation of signs, which are organised progressively (De and Francesca Freda 2016, p. 139). Other people in the group found several concrete instances where the role of support services could be demonstrated:

> Without you customer service and selling would just not be possible.
>   And although you are in the background of every single web-meeting
> you are still there even though you can't be seen.

The discussion was interactive and elicited negotiation while making Catherine see her role in support services differently. At times, it was hard to determine who the primary storyteller was because events were experienced by everyone. The discussions suggested a place for support services in the chain of customer services, and Catherine found her own voice based on a professional identity which was different from that of the others. The value she herself placed on support services became visible. Catherine created a story about the role of support services and the responsibility of each individual to learn to use information technology. This she did by using her own voice.

STORIES FROM THE FUTURE

Narratives involve multiple events and sets of participants and are thus inherently interdiscursive. The storyteller must negotiate at least two speaker roles: narrator (of the narrating event) and a character (in the narrated event). There are a number of ways of orchestrating events and roles, resulting in different types of narrative performances. A speaker's sense of having a coherent "identity" in a narrative emerges from the multivoiced orchestration of different here-and-now, there-and-then, self-and-other roles. When determining which speaker roles are present in a narrative discourse, the general question is "Who is doing the talking?" (Koven 2012, pp. 151–154). "Who" means here an identity of the past, present or future.

Discussion around stories was partly future-oriented, even though the stories dealt with past experiences. A future-oriented way of talking is an extension of reflecting on the present. There are comments on how identity is now and how identity will be in the future. This kind of identity work provides a basis for agency with an impact on practice. The difficulties of the past were helping the next form of identity become visible. A sense of coherence was represented when past, present and future were described, and reflected on, as mixed (Table 11.5).

Table 11.5 Story circle comments classified according to time-scale. The same comment could include several time-scales

	Sheila	Berit	Neil	Mia	Paul	Cathrine
Then-and-there	8% (8)	19% (13)	9% (8)	14% (12)	14% (14)	7% (8)
Here-and-now	84% (82)	74% (50)	74% (62)	74% (61)	60% (59)	82% (90)
Next-in-future	8% (8)	7% (5)	17% (14)	12% (10)	26% (26)	11% (12)
	n= 98	n = 68	n = 84	n = 83	n = 99	n = 110

In the following comment, past, present and future are mixed (present in *cursive,* **past as bold** and the <u>future underlined</u>):

Perhaps you just don't understand what the other person is saying, or with customers you think, is the meeting successful? Will there be any sales or not? Or it may be a situation with a friend—a situation where the other person thinks you aren't even listening you still don't get it so **it was the kind of situation where in reality it suddenly became clear when my friend—who I have known since childhood said that out of all his friends, I am the worst listener. It was a situation I hadn't understood up till then and suddenly I found myself talking about why it is like this and then you get hurtful criticism.** *And in this [staff development] project we were talking about the differences between people and how the ways you can face the facts can differ so much. This was discussed several times* <u>and this inspires you to undertake a development project on yourself.</u>

DISCUSSION

Narratives provide a rich forum for learning. Moreover, they enable individual identity work to be carried out while renewing the values and practices of work. The story circle as a social practice within DS supports the co-authoring of narratives and is also a rich source of data when we seek to understand both the individual and the collective learning processes. Interdiscursive groups provide a forum for social meaning-making. For facilitators it is important to understand that learning occurs while storytelling—not only by the telling of and listening to closed stories. The core of narrative is social, and the more open participants are in the story circle, the more they challenge the existing identities and enable the discovery of new aspects of identity. Telling stories in a group helps them to see and tell more than when alone. Coherence increases at individual and social level when co-authored discovery is part of the process.

The data of this research comprised transcribed discussions, but it is obvious that co-authoring is more than just spoken words. Laughing together, for instance, meant conforming to the narrative, belonging together as a group and sharing similar values. Analysis of video data would highlight further nuances of interactions and co-authoring. The nature of meaning-making in, for example, online interaction, which plays a crucial role in modern working life, is a subject for further research. Storytelling may also differ in groups were people with different backgrounds, values and cultural narratives meet.

In order to be innovative, organisations need to find new ways to support employees in identity work and in the remaking of their own agency. If we extend an educational culture based on individualistic and cognitive practices so that it embraces socio-cultural and embodied practices, storytelling should have a place in the education of adults throughout their working life. It may be beneficial for organisations to consider how they can promote storytelling as part of the organisation's culture. It is not enough to simply organise individual psychologically orientated sessions with therapists or clinical supervisors, or to increase knowledge and skills. Simultaneously, a sense of coherence should be fostered and the identity work of employees should be valued. It is not a question of individually produced stories but rather of co-authored reflections, and knowledge acquired through social discovery of narratives (Boyer 1990, p. 24).

Reformulation of identity is an essential process when employees and organisations are developing their agency and practices. There is evidence that DS has potential in promoting a sense of coherence and a renewal of identities. For storytelling individuals the future-orientation of narratives together with rich expression of DS is a valuable basis for their future. Telling stories about work at work, works.

REFERENCES

Biesta, G. J. J., Fiel, J., Hodkinson, P., Macleod, F. J., & Goodson, I. F. (2011). *Improving learning through the lifecourse: Learning lives.* London: Routledge.

Billett, S. (2008). Learning throughout working life: A relational interdependence between personal and social agency. *British Journal of Educational Studies,* 56(1), 39–58.

Billett, S., & Pavlova, M. (2005). Learning through working life: Self and individuals' agentic action. *International Journal of Lifelong Education,* 24(3), 195–211.

Billett, S., & Somerville, M. (2004). Transformations at work: Identity and learning. *Studies in Continuing Education,* 26(2), 309–326.

Boje, D. M. (2001). *Narrative methods for organizational and communication research.* London: Sage.

Boyer, E. L. (1990). *Scholarship reconsidered: Priorities of the professoriate.* Princeton: Carnegie Foundation for the Advancement of Teaching.

Brockmeier, J. (2015). *Beyond the archive: Memory, narrative, and the autobiographical process.* New York: Oxford UP.

Clarke, R., & Adam, A. (2012). Digital storytelling in Australia: Academic perspectives and reflections. *Arts and Humanities in Higher Education,* 11(1–2), 157–176.

Coventry, M. (2008a). Cross-currents of pedagogy and technology: A forum on digital Storytelling and cultural critique: Introduction. *Arts and Humanities in Higher Education, 7*(2), 165–170.

Coventry, M. (2008b). Engaging gender: Student application of theory through digital storytelling. *Arts and Humanities in Higher Education, 7*(2), 205–219.

Czarniawska, B. (2004). *Narratives in social science research*. London: Sage.

Daniels, H. (2001). *Vygotsky and pedagogy*. London: Routledge Falmer.

De, L. P., & Francesca Freda, M. (2016). The processes of meaning making, starting from the morphogenetic theories of René Thom. *Culture & Psychology, 22*(1), 139–157.

Eteläpelto, A. (2009). Työidentiteetti ja subjektius rakenteiden ja toimijuuden ristiaallokossa. In A. Eteläpelto, K. Collin, & J. Saarinen (Eds.), *Työ, identiteetti ja oppiminen* (pp. 90–91; 142). Helsinki: WSOY Oppimateriaalit.

Eteläpelto, A., Vähäsantanen, K., Hökkä, P., & Paloniemi, S. (2013). What is agency? Conceptualizing professional agency at work. *Educational Research Review, 10*(0), 45–65.

Field, J., Gallacher, J. & Ingram, R. (2009). *Researching transitions in lifelong learning*. Oxon: Routledge, Abingdon.

Glăveanu, V. P., & Tanggaard, L. (2014). Creativity, identity, and representation: Towards a socio-cultural theory of creative identity. *New Ideas in Psychology, 34*, 12–21.

Hetzner, S., Heid, H., & Gruber, H. (2012). Change at work and professional learning: How readiness to change, self-determination and personal initiative affect individual learning through reflection. *European Journal of Psychology of Education, 27*, 539–555.

Hökkä, P., Paloniemi, S., Vähäsantanen, K., Herranen, S., Manninen, M., & Eteläpelto, A. (2014). *Ammatillisen toimijuuden ja työssä oppimisen vahvistaminen: luovia voimavaroja työhön!* Jyväskylä: Jyväskylän yliopisto.

Holland, D. C. (2001). *Identity and agency in cultural worlds* (3rd pr. ed). Cambridge: Harvard University Press.

Iiskala, T., Vauras, M., Lehtinen, E., & Salonen, P. (2010). Socially shared metacognition of dyads of pupils in collaborative mathematical problem-solving processes. *Learning and Instruction, 21*(3), 379–393.

Koven, M. (2007). *Selves in two languages: Bilinguals' verbal enactments of identity in French and Portuguese*. Amsterdam: John Benjamins Pub.

Koven, M. (2012). Speaker roles in personal narratives. In J. A. Holstein & J. F. Gubrium (Eds.), *Varieties of narrative analysis* (pp. 151–180). London: SAGE.

Lundby, K. (2008). *Digital storytelling, mediatized stories: Self-representations in new media*. New York: Peter Lang.

Maddin, E. (2012). Using TPCK with digital storytelling to investigate contemporary issues in educational technology. *Journal of Instructional Pedagogies, 7*, 1–11.

Orr, J. E. (2006). Ten years of talking about machines. *Organization Studies, 27*(12), 1805–1820.

Palinscar, S. (2005). Social constructivist perspectives on teaching and learning. In H. Daniels (Ed.), *An introduction to Vygotsky* (2nd ed., pp. xii, 322). New York: Routledge.

Polkinghorne, D. (1988). *Narrative knowing and the human sciences.* Albany: State University of New York Press.

Schiuma, G. (2011). *The value of arts for business.* Cambridge: Cambridge University Press.

Wertsch, J. V. (1990). The voice of rationality in a sociocultural approach to mind. In L. S. Vygotsky & L. C. Moll (Eds.), *Vygotsky and education: Instructional implications and applications of sociohistorical psychology* (pp. 111–126). Cambridge: Cambridge University Press.

Yang, C. (2013). Telling tales at work: An evolutionary explanation. *Business Communication Quarterly, 76*(2), 132–154.

Yang, Y. C., & Wu, W. I. (2012). Digital storytelling for enhancing student academic achievement, critical thinking, and learning motivation: A year-long experimental study. *Computers & Education, 59*(2), 339–352.

CHAPTER 12

My Story or Your Story? Producing Professional Digital Stories on Behalf of Researchers

Ragnhild Larsson

INTRODUCTION

In this chapter, I share my experiences of producing digital stories on behalf of researchers, building on the method of helping people to create a short, first person, digital story developed by Center for Digital Storytelling, now Storycenter (Lambert 2013). The purpose is to investigate how we can use a personal story approach when producing a story on behalf of others. What are the merits and challenges of such an approach and what do the researchers themselves think of this process and the products?

I had been working as a journalist for 23 years when I became acquainted with Storycenter and digital storytelling (DST) in 2009. It was like entering a new universe and I was amazed by the power in the personal stories. In the constant flood of information, these short stories stood out in a very special way.

After having participated in several workshops producing my own digital stories, I facilitated some workshops on my own. Since I write a

R. Larsson (✉)
Konvoj Produktion, Gothenburg, Sweden

© The Author(s) 2017
G. Jamissen et al. (eds.), *Digital Storytelling in Higher Education*,
Digital Education and Learning, DOI 10.1007/978-3-319-51058-3_12

lot about science, I wanted to arrange workshops for researchers where they could produce their own personal research stories. There was only one problem. It was almost impossible to find a researcher with enough time or interest to spend two or three days in a workshop. Since most researchers are busy with their research and writing research articles to communicate with fellow researchers they seldom have the time to focus on communicating to the public outside academia, even if they realize this is becoming increasingly important.

I then came up with the idea of producing digital stories on behalf of, and in cooperation with, the researchers, drawing as much as possible on the method developed at Storycenter. In 2012 I produced nine digital stories for the Swedish Foundation of Strategic Research. The young researchers had just received funding in a program titled Future Research Leaders. Subsequently, I also produced a digital story with a young researcher who got funding from the Hasselblad Foundation and a story about a sports scientist at the University of Gothenburg. All researchers and their stories are to be found in Appendix 1.

Then, in 2015, I decided to go back to the researchers to find out how they had experienced the process and how they had been able to use the stories. Their answers have also given me the opportunity to improve and develop the method.

Why Digital Storytelling for Research Dissemination?

With the exception of one, the researchers I have worked with conduct basic research in natural sciences. Their stories, however, are not about a specific result or findings, but more about their fundamental research question, their passion and driving forces and, as such, illustrate well Boyer's reflections on the scholarship of discovery: "The probing mind of the researcher is an incalculably vital asset to the academy and the world. Scholarly investigation, in all the disciplines, is at the very heart of academic life. (...) The intellectual excitement fueled by this quest enlivens faculty and invigorates higher learning institutions, and in our complicated, vulnerable world, the discovery of new knowledge is absolutely crucial" (Boyer 1990, p. 18).

There are several different ways to communicate and disseminate science (Bucchi and Trench 2008) and in today's constant flood of information, this constitutes a challenge. For the research to create an impact on society we need new ways to communicate (Negrete and Lartigue 2004). A press release is not enough and facts alone will not do the trick.

Researchers perform research that can change the world, have an impact on their field, or redefine the way we think or look at an issue. They really want to reach out to the public and are also obliged to do so and to explain what they do to both taxpayers and funding organizations. In order to accomplish these tasks, researchers must be able to apply and describe the insights of the research.

Storytelling in general, and digital storytelling in particular, is a powerful way to communicate science outside academia and to create an impact (Margles 2014; Zikovich 2013). "narratives are indeed an alternative and an important means for science communication to convey information in an accurate, attractive, imaginative and memorable way" (Negrete and Lartigue 2004, p. 120). Stories can help people see and understand the science and digital stories are ideal vehicles for reaching the general public (Olson 2015).

We know from research that the human brain has been evolutionarily hardwired to think, to understand, to make sense and to remember in specific story terms and elements (Gottschall 2012; Haven 2007). Emotionally engaging stories affect more areas of the brain than rational, data-driven messages. Stories are more memorable, trigger emotions and inspire people to take action (Boyd 2009; Zak 2012). Storytelling is also a way for researchers to reach new audiences: "The biggest perk is that people actually remember information conveyed in a story format. It's more intuitive than a graph, and the emotional response we have as listeners (or viewers) means the message sticks with us far longer" (Minke-Martin 2015).

THE PROCESS OF PRODUCING A DIGITAL STORY ON BEHALF OF A RESEARCHER

To produce a story on behalf of the researcher I have tried to use the method from a traditional Storycenter workshop in digital storytelling. One of the main differences is the lack of a story circle and the process of producing the stories together in a group which, as anyone who has been part of a workshop can testify, is a transformative experience (Hartley and McWilliam 2009). The story circle is replaced by an in-depth interview conducted by the science communicator, in this case myself.

Another important difference in the way I work with the stories is that the researcher does not participate in the decision as to what images and what music to use. Sometimes the researcher has film clips or photos that are included, but usually a professional photographer is responsible for taking the photos to illustrate the story. I am responsible for finding music. The part where the researchers have the most influence is in developing the script and the story, although the story emerges to a large extent from the questions I ask. Based on the interview, I write the script, which is then reviewed and approved by the researcher.

Both the researcher and I are responsible for recording the script. The voice of the researcher is crucial. I carry out the final editing, while sharing the final story is mandatory. There is no option for the researcher not to screen his or her film as would have been the case had he or she participated in a workshop.

Before discussing the issues, I have identified, it is beneficial to describe the method I have used, step by step:

Interview

After my initial investigations into the background of the researcher we meet for an interview. I explain in detail the stages of the process, producing the digital story, in order for them to know exactly what will happen. Some interviews are conducted by telephone. This usually takes about one hour. I almost always pose the same type of questions:

- How did you end up where you are now?
- Why did you start doing this kind of research?
- What is your main interest as a researcher?
- What do you want to achieve through your research?
- What are the opportunities?
- What are the challenges?
- Why is this research important to you?
- What are you doing right now?
- What makes you get up in the morning and continue your research?
- Can you tell me about a decisive moment/a turning point in your research?
- Tell me about your dream project.

The questions are open and quite loose, in order to provide space for a story. I very seldom ask the researcher specific questions about their research. The risk is that if you ask specific questions, you will get a long answer with factual details that are of little interest to people outside the specific field of research. Besides, I know I will in any case get the necessary factual information when they answer the other questions.

Writing the Script: A First Person Story

I transcribe the interview and typically end up with about 5000 words. I then spend a significant amount of time trying to build an interesting story and reducing the information to a script of 350–400 words in length. During this process, I feel at liberty to change the wording in order to make the script readable and understandable. Additional work is then required to make the story powerful.

The script is always written in first person. In the case of some researchers who are accustomed to presenting their research in a demotic way, this is a straightforward process. Other people not only write, but even talk, in a very academic way.

On completing the script, I send it to the researcher in order that he or she can implement changes and make the story their own. I advise them to read the script aloud to establish whether it feels like their own words. When the researcher is satisfied with the script, it is sent to a photographer who considers the question of images. The photographer also receives the recorded voice-over. Whereas the use of a professional photographer secures high-quality visual elements, it does result in less control and ownership as far as the researcher is concerned.

Recording the Voice-Over and Collecting the Visuals

I meet the researcher to record the script. First, the researcher reads the script aloud until she/he is satisfied. Then, we put the script away and I ask questions based on the script which allows the researcher to answer more freely. I then delete my questions in the editing process. Sometimes, the read script will turn out the best option and sometimes the edited recording prompted by my questions is better.

In the next step, the photographer meets the researcher in a suitable place. This could be their working environment, but it is always preferable to avoid a laboratory or an ordinary office. For instance, in the case of Natalie Barker Ruchti, a sports researcher and senior lecturer at the Department of Food and Nutrition and Sport Science at the University of Gothenburg, the photos were taken at a sports center. The pictures and video footage for the story about Caroline Johnson, a doctor at the Department of Chemistry & Molecular Biology at the University of Gothenburg, were taken at her house and in the woods nearby. In her case, this environment was relevant to the finished story since nature is of great significance to her and is directly relevant to her research into the way nanoparticles affect nature.

On occasions, the researcher may have short-film clips or images available for us to use, as in the case of Marie Dacke, a senior lecturer in Functional Zoology at Lund's University. Her film clips from South Africa were remarkable and illustrated a breakthrough in the department's research by showing how beetles navigate by the moon.

Editing

When the script is recorded and the photo session complete, it is time to edit the story, which involves importing the voice-over and images into the editing program. I always start by editing the voice-over, and since the recording is usually well prepared little work is required. I do not always add music but, if I do, I try to commission someone to compose music customized for the story. During the editing process, I work alone without the researcher's involvement.

Voices of the Researchers

The data supporting my discussion in this chapter come from in-depth interviews with eight of the researchers intended to find out more about their values and opinions regarding their experience of being part of this production process.

My aim is not to draw any conclusions on a general level from these eight interviews. Rather, the aim is to investigate the advantages and disadvantages of using this method. My hope is that this approach will help to improve and inspire future ways of developing this method.

The following questions were sent to all 11 researchers with whom I had produced stories up to April 2015:

How did they experience the overall process and how were they able to use the finished story and for how long?

How did they value a digital story compared to more traditional forms of communicating science?

Did they feel that the stories I produced were *their* stories and would it be a different story if they had produced a story on their own?

How did they feel about being personal, talking about themselves rather than exclusively about facts from their research?

What reactions, if any, did they receive to the story?

Finally, I wondered whether they would like to participate in a traditional digital storytelling workshop, producing their own story.

Of the 11 researchers, eight answered the questions, three in a telephone interview and five by e-mail between May and October 2015. Of the other three, two indicated that, much as they would have liked to participate, they did not have enough time to do so, while one person failed to respond to my invitation.

FINDINGS AND DISCUSSION: WHAT ISSUES ARISE?

Below I discuss the findings revealed during the process and in the interviews. As an introduction to the findings, we start by considering the story of Nathalie Barker Ruchti.

The Story of Natalie Barker Ruchti

Natalie Barker Ruchti is an associate professor in Sports Science at the University of Gothenburg. During the interview I asked her to recount how she ended up at the University of Gothenburg. She then told me the story about her experience as a gymnast in the Swiss National Team in artistic gymnastics. In fact, it was due to these experiences, which were sometimes challenging, that she eventually found herself conducting research into the relationship between the athlete and the coach. Although this was her motivation as a researcher, she had never talked about this before in public. When she first saw the digital story, she was very enthusiastic and told me that we had done an excellent job. She also stated that it was unusual for her to see herself so close up in the photos. It was only when I returned with the interview questions, in 2015, that she revealed that she was unaccustomed to being the focus of attention. She felt a little intimidated when recording the script and found the photo sessions even more demanding. She said it would have helped if the photographer had explained the process in advance. It was clear that she also wished she had had a better understanding about the possible impact of a digital story. "The written script was developed by the journalist and myself. I was aware that the content and wording mattered, and this somewhat complicated the way I formulated the sentences. When recording the script, I felt a little intimidated, but I did not stumble too many times. The focus on me felt unfamiliar. It is not something I am used to" (Natalie Barker Ruchti).

Use of the Stories: Impact?

At the time of the interviews, the researchers had used their digital stories in many different settings. "Sometimes I have used the story to show how I ended up where I am now. Then it becomes much more interesting to know about my personality than about the research itself. It also has a career value. In this setting we were portrayed as the Future Research Leaders, we were chosen because they believed in us as people. Then you need to add something personal. For younger people this is important" (Marie Dacke 2015). Alexander Dmitrijev said he had noticed that people remember the stories much better and can relate to them more than through traditional science communication dominated by facts and figures. He even suggests that the digital stories could sometimes replace press releases in which current research is also reported.

Most of the researchers published their stories on their personal webpages, on their departments' webpages and, in some cases, on the university's home page. Some researchers also included links to their stories in their e-mail signatures, in their presentations of their research and in funding applications.

The stories made on behalf of the Swedish Foundation for Strategic Research have been shown to Swedish students between 16 and 18 years of age. They were produced with the aim of inspiring young people to carry out research and consider a career in the natural sciences, by showing the people behind the research. These stories were also published on the YouTube channel of the Swedish Foundation for Strategic Research where four of these stories are among the ten most frequently viewed videos.

Because of her digital story, Natalie Barker Ruchti has reached out to new audiences and people she did not know before. The Swedish Gymnastic Federation invited her to give a keynote speech at one of their conferences. One of her former students saw the story and sent it to a regional soccer team, who invited her to talk at a conference on how to encourage more female coaches.

Marie Dacke shows her story when she is invited to talk about life as a researcher or to inspire female networks. She appreciates the fact that the story provides a complement to her own real-time voice and says it helps to change the pace in the presentation.

Caroline Jonsson has many international contacts and receives a number of requests from people who want to collaborate with her or to embark on a PhD. She says that her digital story is very useful because it serves to explain her work and research focus in an easily accessible way. The story is a way of promoting herself as a researcher as well as the field she works in. Caroline Jonsson has also sent the story to people she intends to collaborate with and to students who are interested in working with her.

A Digital Story Versus More Traditional Science Communication

The researchers consider the digital story to be a valuable complement for reaching new audiences compared with other ways of communicating science in a popularized way, such as press releases, news articles and traditional films (Bultitude 2011). One of the researchers said that this method resulted in a better story than a more traditional recorded interview would have done. The researchers also felt it was important to give me a degree of professional liberty.

What the interviewed researchers particularly liked was the pace in a digital story, and the fact that it is useful in many different settings. They said that the digital story feels more thoroughly worked through and the message more targeted than a short film where the researcher talks without a script.

Creating a Story Resembles Research

Some of the researchers felt that the digital story was easily accessible and that it was soothing to watch compared to ordinary films where things happen continuously. Even though a digital story may be more time-consuming and more expensive to produce than a short-film clip on YouTube, the researchers still found it worthwhile. They considered it to be a more professional production and therefore more useful in professional settings where a hastily produced film would not be shown. One researcher also mentioned the possibility of using the digital story as a multimedia complement to her CV.

One of the researchers compares the digital story to the way research is done, implying that digital storytelling is a particularly appropriate way of communicating research. "Sometimes it is fast and lively (like a video), but sometimes one pauses and reflects. (...) It actually has this very human pace in it, how the story is told—it's not too fast, and not too slow, you have time to actually look through the illustrative images, and the video adds liveliness when it is just one part of the presentation" (Alexander Dmtrjev).

More Sustainable

Compared with other ways of communicating, the researchers felt that these stories could be used for a longer time, since the focus is on emotion and motivation rather than on facts. Thus, they provide a more general picture of the research in question. One of the researchers pointed out that, since she was involved in basic research, she found the digital story to be particularly useful and sustainable. Many of the stories referred to in this chapter introduce a bigger research question rather than a new finding. The story about engagement in how nanoparticles affect nature is a case in point; another instance is the background for questions on how to change the relationship between a coach and an athlete.

Other stories focus specifically on the researchers' motivation for engaging in a particular research issue, such as the researcher who is working to find methods for effective pain relief. She told a story about her father who had been badly injured in a car accident ten years earlier, and who suffered pain every day thereafter. This story will always be relevant when introducing her field of research.

Some researchers were concerned about the cost of producing a digital story. Not everyone will be able to afford such costs, and if, or when, the film appears to be outdated, it might be difficult to fund a new one. However, when considering that the story will be used for at least three to four years, the production cost is very low compared with that of a more traditional news story.

Reactions from Audiences

Unfortunately, I have not been in a position to interview people who have seen the stories, so this information comes from the researchers' report on the reactions, mostly positive, that they have received. Natalie Barker Ruchti has received positive feedback from several sources. People have said that the story is professional, convincing and strong. She believes it moves people in a compelling way since the message is meaningful. Marie Dacke has noticed that her story gets attention when she shows it, and that people really listen. Some people also comment on the unusual format with still images. Caroline Jonsson is often told that the story is professional, and that it is clear that a great deal of thought has gone into it.

THE PERSONAL STORY: IS IT TRUSTWORTHY IN AN ACADEMIC CONTEXT?

The most obvious difference between a digital story and other, more traditional, ways of communicating research is that it is more personal, focusing on the researcher, rather than the research results alone. In digital storytelling, the storyteller's unique voice is pivotal (Burgess 2006; Lambert 2013; Lundby 2008), but researchers are not used to being the center of attention. In general, researchers talk about their facts and findings, while academic identity and credibility rely on personal distance. You must never say "I" in an academic paper. In a digital story, on the other hand, the personal voice is essential.

Unused to the Personal Focus

Being personal was a challenge for some of the researchers and I do not think they always understood the need for this before they saw the complete story and saw how it affected themselves and others. Also, in my opinion, not all of them understood that the interview would result in such a personal story. Still, only three of the interviewees saw potential disadvantages in using a digital story to communicate research. One of them said that others might not like the fact that it focuses on one person only. Some of the interviewees were concerned that their colleagues and other scholars might not like the personal focus since "research is commonly seen as something that should be done as objectively as possible, and hence talking about your personal connection to a research topic might irritate" (Nathalie Barker Ruchti 2015).

After the process of making the digital story, and in some cases before, most of the interviewees believed that the personal angle is suitable in this context and is good from an outreach perspective. Some of them pointed out that my questions stimulated them to come forward and talk about themselves. One describes it as follows: "The personal touch is very important—and actually I had people (young researchers) quoting my words about this from the video later when they talked to me". "So it obviously made an impression on them" (Alexander Dmitrijev 2015).

In my experience, it is easier for younger researchers to be personal than it is for their older colleagues who were raised in a tradition where it is regarded as non-credible and unprofessional to show one's personality. Also, those researchers who were more used to popular outreach were less uncomfortable talking about their personal driving forces. They had experienced a positive response from making their research available outside academia. In fact, they believed that the personal story was extremely important in order to reach out to the public beyond academia. One researcher felt that the digital story was a pleasing contrast to how he was usually presented in the media where he was often depersonalized and reduced to the "researcher".

My Story or Your Story?

In the traditional way of producing digital stories in a workshop, it is essential that the storyteller produces her own story, with some guidance from the facilitator. In this case, one could say that I took on the role of a very active facilitator and co-storyteller, both writing the script and editing the story.

So how did the researchers feel about this approach? Since none of them had experience of participating in a digital storytelling workshop, they were not in a position to compare the two approaches. Therefore, I was curious to find out if they felt it was *their* story. When asked, some of the researchers had not even considered the option of doing a story on their own. One said that would never happen, due to time constraints and lack of interest. Another researcher said he believed that, if he had done it himself, it would have been fairly close to the story I produced for him. Yet, another researcher said she would focus more on the subject and that she would not dare to focus so much on herself.

Most interestingly, all the researchers interviewed said they felt the story was their own and that they had got their most important message across, although they said they would not have used exactly the same words or highlighted the same parts of the story. In some cases, they felt the story was more specific and targeted than if they had written the script on their own. Since a targeted message often elicits feedback from peers or other readers they were satisfied with the assistance of a professional storyteller. Because the researchers were invited to read and change the script, they felt they were in control and that the script was in their words, even though I changed the order of the paragraphs and omitted some parts.

None of the interviewed researchers made any significant changes to the script I had written. Most accepted my first draft and appreciated my skills as a professional communicator in building a story. They also felt it was important to give me a degree of professional liberty. Overall, I felt there was a great deal of mutual respect, which I believe is a precondition for a good result.

This is perhaps especially true for researchers who are used to writing in a way that is almost the opposite to the way a story is created, starting with the background, ending with the results and then expanding on their doubts. Applying this way of writing would result in a boring story. "A digital story produced in a professional way lessens the likelihood of it becoming boring and reduces the risk of feeling that you are watching an ordinary slideshow" (Marie Dacke 2015).

One advantage, according to the researchers, was that it was easier for me to find a good story behind the facts, than it would be for them. They commented that, with a very deep knowledge of their research themes and outcomes, the challenge of explaining it in an easy and understandable way was far greater.

Nathalie Barker Ruchti did not see the digital story until it was ready and I realize that if she had been more involved she might have made other choices, for instance when it comes to the photos. This is a reminder to the professional storyteller to be wary about challenging the "main character" to reveal things they might not be prepared to share and to be aware that the story can make the person who is in focus realize things they have not previously fully understood themselves. This is also a reason why it is important to allow sufficient time for the process and ensure that the researcher understands the various stages,

Positive Experience of the Production Process

The majority of the respondents mentioned the effectiveness of the production, and the fact that it did not take too much time out of their tight schedules, while allowing them to feel they were in control of the process. One of the researchers compared this process with a film team that spent a week at his office to produce a film of the same length. Using "my" method the researcher contributed three or four hours of their own time.

All the researchers appreciated the planning, having done the preparatory interview and being able to collaborate on the script before we recorded their story. "I felt I had a good overview of the final product, and I was able to contribute with comments, shaping the story. So it was really a collaboration. I liked it" (Alexander Dmtrijev 2015).

Caroline Johnson said that the production process became an excellent learning experience. As a researcher she could focus on the message she wanted to convey while I took care of all other aspects, such as writing the script, building the story and deciding which photos and film clips to use.

No Time to Participate in a Workshop

Most of the interviewees said they would like to participate in a workshop to produce their own story, but that they would not have the time. Natalie Barker Ruchti would like to participate in a workshop to produce a story, not so much about herself, but the individuals she researches, to communicate her research findings through a narrative story of a research participant, for example, a case study of an athlete. If this opportunity could be offered, she would be very keen to attend. On the other hand, Marie Dacke explained that time constraints would prevent her from participating in a workshop: "The way you did it took very little of my time. Since the currency I use is time, I got a lot out of that investment and I would like to do it that way again".

"What If": Would the Stories Be Different?

There are many ways to tell the same story and there will obviously be a difference if I tell your story or if you tell your own story. In the end, it is the researcher who decides what should be included and excluded in the script. So far, I have not experienced any disagreements concerning the finished script.

I wish every researcher could have the opportunity to experience being part of a digital storytelling workshop, since it is only through such a workshop that you can fully understand the power of creating your own story. I am convinced that researchers would benefit from sharing their stories with others in a research group or collaborative setting as described by Hydle in Chap. 13 in this book; it is necessary to experience a story circle in order to understand its power.

PROFESSIONALLY PRODUCED DIGITAL STORY: A USEFUL ALTERNATIVE

To conclude, I find that producing digital stories on behalf of others, building on the method of a classical digital storytelling workshop, is a useful alternative when working with researchers who do not have time to participate in a workshop. Obviously, the stories will not be the same as they would have been if the researchers had completed their own stories in a workshop. As a journalist, I am used to telling other peoples' stories, and these are always filtered through my eyes. When producing digital stories on behalf of researchers, their stories will also partly be my stories, colored by what fascinates me in the stories they share. These researchers have not experienced the challenge and possibilities of workshop participants in deciding what to tell and how to tell it. Workshop participants have the final say even though the facilitator plays an active part in the process. On the other hand, many of the digital stories described here would never have been told if I had not created them. It is possible to claim that I have tried to combine the journalistic method with the traditional DST method, adapting it to the reality of the demanding lives of researchers.

Producing stories on behalf of researchers and inviting researchers to create their own stories are two different methods of communicating. One is not necessarily superior to the other. I believe we can learn a great deal from both methods in an attempt to develop new ways to promote research through meaningful personal stories and create impact.

One advantage of using the skills of a professional journalist or storyteller, who is trained in finding and writing stories, is that the finished stories may be more powerful. When facilitating a workshop, you will always help participants develop their stories, but with a larger group the focus on each individual will necessarily be less intense.

Also, since most researchers are not used to being in focus as individuals, I believe their stories might become more personal when a professional storyteller helps them to find and shape the story.

To develop this method, there are several aspects worthy of further exploration. For example, it would be interesting to try and increase the researcher's involvement in the process of developing the script, finding the photos and choosing the music. It is impossible to tell how these particular stories would have turned out if the researchers had produced their own. Therefore, as a research design, it would be interesting to produce stories on behalf of researchers in the way described above, and as a control, arrange for researchers to produce their own stories and observe the differences, both in process and in product.

APPENDIX 1: LIST OF INVOLVED RESEARCHERS AND LINKS TO THE DIGITAL STORIES

Alexander Dmitrijev, Associate Professor, Bionanophotonics, Department of Physics Chalmers. http://www.chalmers.se/sv/forskning/vara-forskare/Sidor/Alexander-Dmitriev.aspx

Natalie Barker Ruchti, Associate Professor, Sport Science, Faculty of Education Gothenburg University. http://iki.gu.se/english

Marie Dacke, Associate Professor, Functional Zoology, Department of Biology Lunds University. https://www.youtube.com/watch?v=LeSgdzMm16c

Caroline Jonsson, Doctor, Nanoparticles, Department of Chemistry & Molecular Biology, Gothenburg University. https://vimeo.com/150806315

Johan Mauritsson, Associate Professor, Atom Physics, Faculty of Engineering, Lunds University. https://www.youtube.com/watch?v=fFNCDX2bqlE

Johan Malmström, Associate Professor, Infection Medicine, Faculty of Medicine, Lunds University. https://www.youtube.com/watch?v=j9sghCazy50

Martin Högbom, Associate Professor, Structural Biochemistry, Department of Biochemistry and Biophysics, Stockholm University. https://www.youtube.com/watch?v=Nmp2mNiawr8

Peter Nilsson, Professor, Chemical Biology, Department of Physics, Chemistry and Biology, Linköping University. https://www.youtube. com/watch?v=_h6GeLOfZt8
Camilla Svensson, Assistant Professor, Molecular Pain Research, Department of Physiology and Pharmacology, Karolinska Institutet. https://www.youtube.com/watch?v=LFmtbxHfDZQ&list=PLAwDfLn MNIOZ4kG0OKmE1fy6ey1bgsU53&index=15
Sebastian Westenhoff, Associate Professor, Membrane Proteins, Department of Chemistry & Molecular Biology, Gothenburg University. https://www.youtube.com/watch?v=cqp7u6NGlww&index=5&list=PL AwDfLnMNIOZ4kG0OKmE1fy6ey1bgsU53
Rickard Sandberg, Associate Professor, Cell and Molecular Biology, Department of Cell and Molecular Biology, Karolinska Institutet. https:// www.youtube.com/watch?v=hU_DzpK3ZMw&index=6&list=PLAwDf LnMNIOZ4kG0OKmE1fy6ey1bgsU53

REFERENCES

Barker Ruchti, N. (2015, August). *E-mail exchange between the author and Nathalie Barker Ruchti.*
Boyd, B. (2009). *The origins of story evolution cognition and fiction.* Cambridge, MA: Harvard University Press.
Boyer, E. (1990). *Scholarship reconsidered: Priorities of the professoriate.* Princeton: The Carnegie Foundation for the Advancement of Teaching.
Bucchi, M., & Trench, B. (2008). *Handbook of public communication of science and technology.* London/New York: Routledge.
Bultitude, K. (2011). The why and how of science communication. In P. Rosulek (Ed.), *Science communication.* Pilsen: European Commission.
Burgess, J. (2006). Hearing ordinary voices: Cultural studies, vemacular creativity and digital storytelling. *Continuum Journal of Media and Cultural Studies, 20*(2), 201–214.
Dacke, M. (2015, August). *Telephone interview between the author and Marie Dacke.*
Dmitrijev, A. (2015, September). *E-mail exchange between the author and Alexander Dmitrijev.*
Gottschall, J. (2012). *The storytelling animal, how stories make us human.* Boston: Houghton Mifflin Harcourt.
Hartley, J., & McWilliam, K. (2009). *Storycircle. Digital storytelling around the world.* Chichester: Wiley-Blackwell.
Haven, K. (2007). *Story proof: The science behind the starling power of story.* Westport: Libraries Unlimited.

Lambert, J. (2013). *Digital storytelling capturing lives creating community.* New York: Routledge.

Lundby, K. (2008). *Digital storytelling, mediatized stories: Self representations in new media.* New York: Peter Lang.

Margles, S. (2014). *The mahi-mahi & the map: Digital storytelling for science.* Cool Green Science. http://blog.nature.org/science/2014/02/18/themahi-mahi-the-map-digital-storytelling-for-science/.

Minke-Martin, V. (2015). *Narratives of nature: Use storytelling to reach new audiences with your research.* Canadian Science Publishing. http://www.cdnsciencepub.com/blog/narratives-of-nature-use-storytelling-toreach-new-audiences-with-your-research.aspx.

Negrete, A., & Lartigue, C. (2004). Learning from education to communicate science as a good story. *Endeavour, 28*(3), 120–124.

Olson, R. (2015). *Houston, We have a narrative: Why science need story.* Chicago: The University of Chicago Press.

Zak, P. (2012). *The moral molecule actions. The source of love and prosperity.* Dutton: Penguin Group.

Zikovich, B. (2013). Telling science stories. *Scientific American.*

CHAPTER 13

The Power of the Eye and the Ear: Experiences from Communicating Research with Digital Storytelling

Ida Hydle

INTRODUCTION

The media department at the University College of Oslo and Akershus for Applied Sciences (HiOA) offered a workshop in digital storytelling for researchers during 2013–2014. This coincided with a commission from the Norwegian Ministry of Justice to evaluate a new prison for young people aged from 15 to 18 years. In the workshop, I learned how to use narrative and visual skills to convey some impressions from my ethnographic fieldwork in relation to the quality and design of the prison. First, I made a Norwegian version. To my great astonishment, the heads of the prison at three administrative levels understood the audio-visual story and, with my consent, used it as part of their own presentations. They felt that I, through the combination of personal visuals and vocals, had articulated many of the dilemmas related to the imprisonment of young people. They requested an English version and the story has since travelled to China, Kazakhstan, the USA, Germany and the Baltics: "Every time I see

I. Hydle (✉)
Oslo and Akershus University College of Applied Sciences, Oslo, Norway

© The Author(s) 2017
G. Jamissen et al. (eds.), *Digital Storytelling in Higher Education,*
Digital Education and Learning, DOI 10.1007/978-3-319-51058-3_13

your little film, I feel like crying", said the vice-director of the regional Norwegian correctional services.

Elements of this evaluation are difficult to convey and disseminate by words alone. The method of digital storytelling in this project proved more effective than I could ever have envisioned. One of my conclusions is the same as the American educator Ernest L. Boyer, who conveys in his report *Scholarship reconsidered* (1990, p. 17) the process of discovery as a commitment to knowledge and freedom of inquiry.

Based on my experiences of digital storytelling, this chapter will discuss the power of the visual and the challenge of the emotional. My ambition is to build bridges between:

1. teaching, learning and dissemination of research results as a visual and dialogical process,
2. the emotional challenges and responses to this dialogical process explained with neurophysiology and psychology, and
3. the experienced impact of a particular digital story from a Norwegian youth prison.

With a cross-disciplinary background as a medical doctor and a social anthropologist, I combine intrapersonal skills and interpretations that might be useful for a deeper look into the benefits and challenges of using digital storytelling for research dissemination.

Previously, I had no experience of the audio-visual tools and programmes of either PC or Mac. Thus, part of this chapter focuses on the complexity of acquiring the practical skills and knowledge necessary to construct a digital story. A second part relays the unexpected outreach of the story. The third part analyses the viewers' reaction to the story—and the impact this had on its continuing dissemination.

BACKGROUND AND CONTEXT: THE PRISON EVALUATION RESEARCH

The background and arena for my first digital story experience is a research-based evaluation of the Norwegian youth prison conducted for the Norwegian Ministry of Justice. The assignment was to investigate whether the prison and its interdisciplinary team fulfil the requirements of the UN Convention on the Rights of the Child. Since 2012, there have been a

Fig. 13.1 The finished prison building

number of legislative amendments concerning youth in conflict with the law in Norway. The new youth penalty aims to reduce the number of imprisoned young offenders between the ages of 15 and 18 and to help them to understand the consequences of their acts. A new type of youth prison, *ungdomsenheter* (two special units for 15–18-year-old offenders outside Oslo and Bergen[1]) was planned according to the needs of young people.

Upon the establishment of these youth prisons, the Norwegian Parliament demanded a research-based evaluation of the first unit in Bergen. The purpose of the evaluation project was to enable the Ministries to make decisions about continuing the existing unit while planning a new unit in the Oslo area. In addition, it was to provide a knowledge base for the various legal and administrative changes needed to implement the UN Convention on the Rights of the Child within the various support systems for young people in prison or probation (health and social care, child protection and education).

Through fieldwork, interviews and photos, I studied the new implementations at all levels, together with a legal scholar—Elisabeth Gording

Stang. We reported to a committee of senior advisers from four ministries: Justice and Public Security; Education and Research; Health and Care Services and Children, Equality and Social Inclusion, in addition to the Directorate of Norwegian Correctional Services (Hydle 2014; Hydle and Stang 2016).

During the prison evaluation fieldwork, I observed how many different actors, including some young inmates, had been involved in the careful planning of the prison. They were concerned with a wide variety of practical, ethical and aesthetic details, as well as the desire to achieve a balance between the young people's safety, security and well-being and their need for a normalised life, albeit within prison walls. The need to find good design solutions to all these issues is regulated by legislation. A number of details in the physical environment had both practical and symbolic importance.

I was present at various stages of construction, listening to discussions and questioning the choice of colours, walls, security safeguards, space selections, decoration, outdoor space and playgrounds. I witnessed how this delicate balance between care and control was gradually taking physical form. These were findings and issues that are not easily conveyed by words alone, and therefore I was looking for alternative approaches to research dissemination, building on my knowledge and previous experiences of working with visual media (as I describe below). This led me to explore digital storytelling as a method of research communication.

My Theoretical Background for the Entry to the Field of Digital Storytelling

I have been interested in the visual and auditory approach to communication through video for a long time. Since 2000, I have collaborated with visual anthropologists, in particular at the Department of Visual Culture Studies at the University of Tromsø and at the University of Bergamo. I had thus dug deeply into important theoretical contributions by Christina Grasseni (2007, 2009), Sara Pink (2012), David MacDougall (2005) and Tim Ingold (2002, 2010, 2011).

In the current era of multimodality, a visual cultural approach belongs to newer anthropological knowledge about the senses and their contribution to new perspectives regarding the role of vision. This approach is not "as an isolated given, but within its interplay with the other senses, and with the role of mutual gestuality", as Grasseni explains, based on her fieldwork among Italian cow farmers in the Alps. Her studies focused on efforts to perfect cow breeding for the production of the famous Taleggio and Strachitunt cheeses. She continues: "Moreover, it explores vision as a ductile, situated, contested and politically fraught means of situating oneself in a community of practice" (Grasseni 2007, p.1)—both for data gathering and for dissemination—or as David Howes conceptualises it, "Cross-talk between the senses" (2010).

Film is used as a strategy for discovering coherences in the world, for improving dialogue and for dissemination of knowledge. Film as a disseminating tool for ethnographic knowledge can reveal best or unique knowledge or expert knowledge (Holtedahl 2006). The cognitive effect of the viewing or filming process may be a tool for education and change. When words are insufficient, vision may replace sound and speech. Film creates a reflective space between man and the world on one level, or between partners in a dialogue on another. Thus, the visual representations from research sites may be rich sources of meta-knowledge that contribute significantly to alternative interpretations of the research process and of the dissemination methodology of a project.

That said, there are further complexities to be unravelled. What does it mean to "cross-talk between the senses"? Pictures and video/film used for research nowadays may be seen as a recapturing of a particular approach to vision, look and gaze in more than one sense. Firstly, the observation, that is, the gaze or the look, is one of the main tools in the collecting, ordering, analysis and presentation of data. Yet, it is often taken for granted or regarded as so obvious that one does not even register it. Bourdieu (1977) called this doxa, that is, the syntax that guarantees a common understanding when people talk with each other. In everyday speech, people do not explain their grammar; it is taken for granted. Latour, by observing and analysing the behaviour of natural scientists in their laboratories, named all the material and social processes that contribute to scientific results as "blackboxing"—taken for granted by researchers themselves (Latour 2012; Grasseni 2009). Within the field of anthropology, in which both Bourdieu and Latour have a central place, vision and gaze are in use as active tools in the expression and development of critical self-understanding. This is especially relevant when informants become co-researchers and co-producers, when they themselves are behind the camera (Holtedahl 2006;

Waage 2007), or when they are involved in directing and editing film. Vision is thus an instrument for information, for the development and dissemination of ideas, for thoughts and practices.

Researchers often describe situations in which they are present themselves, whether they are observing and recording what happens in a laboratory (Latour and Woolgar 2013), or interviewing or observing what other people do or say. They therefore participate in something of which they are partly co-producers. Researchers are never invisible observers as storytellers. "We do not just observe those whose story we will tell, they also observe us and take in their impressions of us. We affect both how people speak when they suffer and how they speak about their suffering. We become part of their suffering. In addition our description turns from what we interpret from them to be our own story" (Sachs 2003). In my project, the informants are well cared for legally by the NSD—Norwegian Centre for Research Data. The rules for protecting personal data are strict. Therefore, I "told" the story of the prison building, which is possible to do without showing individuals up-close, and still conveyed some of the context and content of the study subject.

Visual representations are similar to speech or text in the sense that they are not neutral. Recent anthropological knowledge about the senses contributes to new perspectives on vision, not "as an isolated given", but within its interplay with the other senses, and with the role of mutual ways of showing gestures. Moreover, visualisation also shows how the researcher's vision, by leading the camera's eye, is a ductile means of situating oneself in a community of practice (Grasseni 2007). This relates not only to still pictures but even more to film.

In the critical scholarly discussions of documentary filming, visualisation may be seen as more than a recapturing of an approach to vision, look and gaze. One should also be aware of the interplay with other senses and how it is situated in a practice community.

The deaf anthropologist, Hilde Haualand, claims that anthropology is phonocentric, that is, we take *sound* for granted (Haualand 2002). Do we also take light for granted? What about the living picture(s) and the ability and power of the look and the gaze (film, television, worldwide web, smart telephones, etc.) to attract and create new forms of communication, new spaces, new times and new places? Film creates a space between the man and the world, or between partners in a dialogue. When we watch, see, observe or view, we meet light, with the look or the gaze. Light is the necessary condition for human sight, look or gaze. The gaze or look is what we cannot see ourselves, but what others can see and meet. The gaze or look is thus a dialogical term and tool in the sense that *I* am dependent upon *your* seeing for the registration of a gaze or a look. Is it accidental that the term vision refers both to a physical and to a metaphysical phenomenon?

THE COMPLEXITY OF SKILLS AND KNOWLEDGE IN THE CONSTRUCTING OF A DIGITAL STORY

These theoretical basics created an analytical context for understanding the digital story construction as a complex learning experience. However, my own practice was lacking when it came to creating a digital story with the use of light, sound and translation of complex content into pictures, with voice-over (my own) and music. From that point of departure, I was introduced to the methodology of digital storytelling in a workshop offered by the Media section at Oslo and Akershus University College of Applied Sciences (HiOA) in 2014. The workshop, based on the model developed by Storycenter (Lambert 2010), was adapted to meet the busy schedules of the researchers.

We were a group of ten scholars from different academic and practical disciplines (e.g. health care, nursing, physiotherapy, education, social work, creative arts) organised in "story circles". Over two days, we explored various learning methods. Building on theoretical and practical introductions and demonstrations, group discussions, training and practice development, we shared our stories.

We were at different stages in the process of learning about digital storytelling and story making. The facilitators instructed us kindly to share as much as possible of the individual learning and working processes, and show partial results of the digitalisation to each other, creating a community of learning in relation to visual skills (Wenger-Trayner et al. 2014). In this community, I felt inspired and challenged; we all asked useful questions and offered advice to one another, as is the aim of such learning communities (Hydle 2015).

We then had access to individual guidance, tailored to our specific needs, in structuring and developing our stories, choosing pictures or video clips, recording the voice-over, selecting music and working with the technicalities related to all of these. After a couple of months, about half the original group joined a second workshop to finish and share the stories, and to reflect on our experience in a focus group discussion.

Here, I finished the prison story and took part in a focus group where we showed and discussed the stories, offering constructive criticism and advice on the various aspects of the story construction process: purpose, audience, dramatic question, voice, music, images and so on. In the focus group, we also discussed opportunities and challenges involved in using a personalised digital story for research dissemination, including issues such as the use of the personal, "subjective", voice as opposed to the academic, "objective" voice. All of us, to varying degrees, found it challenging—yet stimulating—to change our language and use the personal voice—in both senses of the word.

DEVELOPING NEW VISUAL AND SCIENTIFIC SKILLS: PRODUCING MY STORY

In the workshops, I learned how to create a digital story based on still images and a voice-over in iMovie. Together with the other media community members, I was invited to imagine and synthesise the best story, the best images and the best script—read as effectively as possible in my own voice. Inspired by the multivocal nature of realising and then disseminating my research results in this way, I came to feel that I was creating a work of art. This may be because the personal multivocality of the process—the pictures and videos selected or taken through one's own lens, the reflection on one's own written text and choice of music—comes together within the assembled digital story to create an immediacy that is greater than the sum of their parts.

Even if a digital story has, necessarily, a formal structure of time, sequence and narrative, and iMovie layers on top of this its own programmatic rules and conventions, there is still, for the storyteller, creative freedom in the selection of time, sequence, narrative, images, sound qualities, voice and music.

My focus on communication across the senses is based upon *dialogism* as a theory of knowledge which is embodied in the works of the Russian theorist of culture, Michael Bakhtin (1981) and the Swedish linguist Per Linell (2009).[2] Gradually, during this selection process, I discovered how their theoretical approaches work in practice: Bakhtin's terms "dialogism" and "polyglossia"[3] are tools for understanding the layers upon layers of events and actions in a research project.

My second approach for understanding the digital storytelling process is actor-network theory as described by Latour, which explains how man and machine *together* construct a result (2005, 2012), in this case a digital story. Picturing or filming is thus understood as a collaborative process between man and matter, between the person(s), that is, the researchers and the informants, and the technical and material tool(s) —that is, the cameras, smartphones, computers and so on. I realised how the construction of the digital story "skills the vision", to use the expression from Grasseni's book, *Skilled Visions* (2007)—in a dialogical perspective. This particular dialogical perspective led me to the argument of the anthropologist Tim Ingold (2002, p. 245) that "we see things before light, and hear sound before things". Ingold hardly knew then how his anticipation of how we see and hear would later be documented by neuroresearch. The discovery of mirror neurons, which may enable the brain to react and "mirror" outer visual stimuli even before the reaction reaches the cognitive parts of the brain (i.e. before we even acknowledge that we react), explains how we learn through mimicry and why we are able to feel empathy with others before we become consciously aware that we should do so.[4] One may describe and interpret mirror neurons as dialogical tools without which humans would not be able to develop the necessary communication skills from infancy onwards. However, vision is also embedded in environmental circumstance. Ingold's description widens the understanding of the use of vision, thus also disseminating the effectiveness of digital storytelling.

In practice, we were asked to write the story in 200–300 words, a catastrophic demand for a researcher whose expertise is to dig deep into complexities and explanatory models. How could I possibly convey a message in 200–300 words from the complex project of the evaluation of the activities in a youth prison in the context of children's rights? I did not know then why I had selected the building of the prison to represent the professional and emotional content of the whole issue, the task (mine as well as the task of the correctional authorities) and my results. However, I did know that physical environments cannot be taken for granted.

Then, we were asked to imagine illustrating images—again a foreign feeling for someone used to working in the social-scientific arena. We worked as a mutually supportive and advisory group and helped each other in this new practice of research dissemination.

We were then asked to find images or short video clips to illustrate, deepen, translate or explain the messages of our story. We could have used our own pictures or videos, others' pictures or videos if they were legally free to use, drawings or figures—a wide range of possible imaginative illustrations.

The whole experience was so inspiring, fun and creative that I—even before I finished the digital prison story—made two other stories. They were linked to another issue and focus on conflicts in the Northern Sami areas of Norway, and research into restorative justice in conflicts in reindeer herding (Henriksen and Hydle 2016) as well as Sami child protection and family welfare areas. My Sami colleagues at the Arctic University of Tromsø and I have used both digital stories for education and dissemination purposes on several occasions. I regard this as a discovery regarding the effectiveness of the digital story learning experience. The digital story experience has taught me a new way of translating a cognitive "text" into a multivocal message. Firstly, I experienced how the idea of using digital stories spread rapidly from one field of my research into another. Secondly, I experienced the usability for colleagues, in being able to display and share a research area by means of a three-minute digital story to support their presentations. In one instance, a colleague brought my Sami story to the international conference of indigenous social work in Darwin, Australia.

Thanks to the skills and vision of our teachers, we were led through the complex process of digital story construction. My pictures were partly taken by me (the building details of the prison), and partly taken from the Internet, free to use (displaying a Norwegian courthouse and prison). I was struck for the first time by the artistic aspect of the work—in the sense of expression or application of human creative skill and imagination, typically in a visual form such as painting or sculpture, producing works to be appreciated primarily for their beauty or emotional power. The invitation for a researcher literally to use imagination to express a scientifically based message was striking and compelling.

I had told the story with my own voice recorded in the studio. Now, I wanted a particular piece of music to play the background "mood". Music has an important contribution to the impact of a digital story. The brain processes music or musical sounds differently from other sounds. Music constructs another layer of meaning and thus conveys other emotional messages than text or pictures (Clynes 2013). I wanted to use a particular piece, *60 Seconds*, of mixed electronic and instrumental music made by the Tunisian-born French musician and DJ Claude Challe. Since the piece is available on YouTube[5] and iTunes, I tried it out without his written permission In spite of several efforts I have not yet been able to obtain permission from Challe, and therefore may only share my story with audiences in closed spaces.

The story ends with some questions on a scrolling text: Care? Punishment? Reconciliation? Restoration? Reparation? While the music fades out. The spectators are left to reflect.

ADVOCACY THROUGH DIGITAL STORYTELLING?

As I mentioned earlier, neither images nor sounds are neutral. Individuals will always add a personal touch via all the decisions and selections that are made in the process of constructing the digital story. It is not possible to believe in objectivity or neutrality. Even if the images are taken by camera, there is an eye behind it, and a new eye to interpret the result. The famous press photographer Cartier-Bresson wrote in his book *The mind's eye, writings on photography, and photographers* (1998):

> For me the camera is a sketch book, an instrument of intuition and sponta-
> neity, the master of the instant which in visual terms, questions and decides
> simultaneously. In order to 'give a meaning' to the world one has to feel
> oneself involved in what one frames through the viewfinder. This attitude
> requires concentration, a discipline of mind, sensitivity, and a sense of
> geometry—it is by great economy of means that one arrives at simplicity of
> expression. One must always take photographs with the greatest respect for
> the subject and for oneself. (p. 13)

To involve oneself is to become visible as a personal process. This may, in a somewhat old-fashioned epistemology, be regarded as "un-academic" or "too emotional" to be a good research or dissemination approach. But many leading science theorists have argued against the so-called objective scientific approach. Latour is one of them, dissolving the artificial distinction between objective and subjective. We are all subjects in relationships. Objectifying "the other" is an act of power. As soon as you have "othered" another person, you have distinguished yourself as something other and above. In anthropology and philosophy, this othering is often linked to "orientalism", that is, colonialism (Said 1978) or sexism (de Beauvoir 1949).

However, there is a clear distinction between personal and private. Thus, the construction of a digital story is not a private matter. I used my biological senses, as well as my voice, in the construction of the film. A wide variety of spectators commented that it was in fact my voice that made the biggest impact and contributed most to their understanding of

the underlying story. Other spectators have commented that the introductory images of the Millennium Boy sculpture by the Australian artist
Ron Mueck[6] together with my wording made a great impression on them,
introducing the main intention of the story. Again an example of my personal interest in the relationships between art and science. I share this
interest with many others, thus I do not regard this as private, but indeed
personal. This interest influences my personal life and I can use it for professional purposes—without revealing my private life at all.

The photograph, as an example of Cartier-Bresson's "simplicity of
expression", will always be in a context, open for interpretation. Gullestad
shows, through careful analysis of photographs, how the images of
"African natives" taken by Norwegian missionaries in the 1900s convey a
colonial perspective and view upon the "other" (2007). The missionaries
acted in good faith in taking and distributing the photos.

With this adapted critical view, what did I advocate through the digital story? The spectators, that is, the receivers of my messages through
the digital story, have so far been in closed spaces (within the context of
teaching and learning about the youth prison in Norway in general, and
especially through my research). First, my cross-disciplinary community of
digital storytelling colleagues gave the impression of having received new
knowledge about youth committing crimes, about the Norwegian prison

Fig. 13.2 This photo shows inmates and employees in front of the new prison
building under construction, discussing details and outlines of the building

system and about this particular youth prison. Through my selection of words and pictures, I was able to convey the suffering and trauma of being an adolescent in this precarious situation and the cross-disciplinary challenges of their helpers, caretakers and guards.

My informants within the Norwegian correctional service took the digital story as if it were *their* story, signifying the impact on feelings and thoughts that this kind of visualisation can have on an evaluation project. Some of them asked to show the story to other closed audiences, both in and outside the country. A variety of students including Chinese law students and Norwegian child protection and social work students have seen it. So have civil servants in Estonia as well as the Kazakhstani ministry of justice and university teachers of social work and child protection. I did not have to use many words and explanations to convey my experiences from the project: this three-minute digital story made up for a long description, analysis and conclusion—an amazing experience.

My reflections upon the messages in the digital story continue with new disseminating experiences. The inner dialogue that Bakhtin describes as part of the human dialogism is enriched by this outer medium (and result of the inner), the digital story. The translation from a personal—but not private—experience to a personal (and still not private) account through a finished digital story of research results has a basis in knowledge theory, as outlined by, for example, Bakhtin, Linell and Latour,[7] as described above.

Another aspect of my reflection is how people perceive a digital story in general. Referring back to the spontaneous comment of the vice-director of the regional correctional services, quoted first in this chapter, it is interesting that he—as most other people—refers to the story as "film". There is not one single moving image in the digital story. Again, I am thrilled by the power of the visual, for example, that impressions from one part of the brain transfer over to another in terms of widening the static visual representation to an impression of something that is dynamic and moving.

CONCLUSIONS

Having made the digital story and shown it several times to different audiences as part of my research-based evaluation of the prison, I realise how the planning and construction of the environment surrounding the inmates and their caretakers expresses ideologies, knowledge and feelings. Both my audience and I found that the digital story condensed a complex message in an honest and accurate way. The story also contributed to parts

of the conclusion of the research-based evaluation: the prison and its professionals find themselves within the framework and requirements of the
UN child convention.

Digital storytelling is an important new field for researchers who want
to or need to disseminate complex interrelationships between realities. In
addition, it is effective as a visual and auditory methodology in showing
research projects and results within a wide range of disciplinary fields and
practices. There are many more mysteries to discover and analyse in this
complex field. Thus, as such, digital storytelling may be part of a basic theory of knowledge of science in new eras of digitalisation and visualisation.

Notes

1. The two largest cities in Norway.
2. I have developed this theoretical viewpoint in two ALTERNATIVE
   publications, Delivery. 2.1. and Delivery. 2.4, see http://www.alter-
   nativeproject.eu/assets/upload/Deliverable_2.1_Report_on_
   conlicts_in_intercultural_settings.pdf [Accessed 5 October 2016] and
   http://www.alternativeproject.eu/assets/upload/Deliverable%20
   2.4%20Final%20research%20report%20on%20conflict%20and%20
   RJ%20(1).pdf [Accessed 5 October 2016].
3. The literary and culture theorist Michail Bakhtin develops in his
   work "The Dialogic Imagination" (1981) a theory of how the
   meaning of a text always is generated in a context, in Bakhtins term
   heteroglossia. Language is of a hybrid nature, in terms of polyglossia
   and there is always a relation between different utterances, that is, an
   intertextual relation. Texts are always build upon other texts,
   whether oral (auditory), written (visual) or visualised (e.g. pictures,
   films).
4. http://www.apa.org/monitor/oct05/mirror.aspx [Accessed 5
   October, 2015].
5. https://www.youtube.com/watch?v=Wnywh99mvwk [Accessed 5
   October, 2015].
6. http://en.aros.dk/visit-aros/the-collection/boy/ [Accessed 5
   October, 2015].
7. Another support for this knowledge theory approach emerged years
   ago from the famous story of the anthropologists Michelle and
   Renato Rosaldo. She died by an accident during their fieldwork
   among headhunters. Her husband, Renato, wrote an article "Grief

and a Headhunter's Rage" (2004). In an interview he focused on personal experiences leading to how "the visceral, the disruptive, and the violent should be at the centre of cultural analysis. Culture should not be limited to what is normal, routine and expected. It may be that we should seek out the unexpected and the atypical as a way of apprehending other human lives". See http://www.uc.pt/en/cia/publica/AP_artigos/AP24.25.12_Entrevista.pdf [Accessed 5 October, 2015].

REFERENCES

Bakhtin, M. (1981). *The dialogic imagination: Four essays.* Austin: University of Texas Press.

Beauvoir, S. D. (1949). *Le deuxième sexe.* Paris: Gallimard.

Bourdieu, P. (1977). *Practical reason. On the theory of action.* Stanford: Stanford University Press.

Boyer, E. L. (1990). *Scholarship reconsidered: Priorities of the professoriate.* Princeton: Princeton University Press.

Cartier-Bresson, H. (1998). *The mind's eye. Writings on photography and photographers.* New York: Aperture foundation.

Clynes, M. (Ed.). (2013). *Music, mind, and brain: The neuropsychology of music.* Berlin: Springer Science & Business Media.

Grasseni, C. (Ed.). (2007). *Skilled visions. Between apprenticeship and standards.* Oxford: Berghahn Books.

Grasseni, C. (2009). *Developing skill, developing vision: Practices of locality at the foot of the Alps.* Oxford: Berghahn Books.

Gullestad, M. (2007). *Picturing pity. Pitfalls and pleasures in cross-cultural communication. Image and word in a North Cameroon Mission.* Oxford: Berghahn Books.

Haualand, H., 2002. *I endringens tegn.* (In the sign of change, my translation). Oslo: Tanum forlag.

Henriksen, J. E., & Hydle, I. (2016). Participatory handling of conflicts in Sámi areas. *International Social Work, 59*(5), 627–639.

Holtedahl, L. (2006). Klovn; klovnen som model for kulturformidling (The clown as model for culture dissemination, my translation). *Rhetorica Scandinavica, 40,* 78–92.

Howes, D. (Ed.). (2010). *Empire of the senses: The sensual culture reader.* Oxford/New York: Berg.

Hydle, I. (2014). *Evaluering av prøveprosjektet med Ungdomsenheten og det tverretatlige teamet ved Bjørgvin fengsel. Delrapport 1.* (Evaluation of the trial project with the youth unit and the cross-disciplinary team at Bjoergvin prison, my translation). Oslo: NOVA. Available at: http://www.hioa.no/About-HiOA/ Centre-for-Welfare-and-Labour-Research/NOVA/Publikasjonar/ Rapporter/2014/Evaluering-av-proeveprosjektet-med-Ungdomsenheten-og-det-tverretatlige-teamet-ved-Bjoergvin-fengsel. Accessed 5 Oct 2016.

Hydle, K. M. (2015). Temporal and spatial dimensions of strategizing. *Organization Studies, 36*(5), 643–663.

Hydle, I., & Stang, E. G. (2016). *Evaluering av prøveprosjektet med Ungdomsenheten og det tverretatlige teamet ved Bjørgvin fengsel. Sluttrapport.* (Evaluation of the trial project with the youth unit and the cross-disciplinary team at Bjoergvin prison. Final report, my translation). Oslo: NOVA rapport nr. 1.

Ingold, T. (2002). *The perception of the environment: Essays on livelihood, dwelling and skill.* London: Psychology Press.

Ingold, T. (2010). Ways of mind-walking: Reading, writing, painting. *Visual Studies, 25*(1), 15–23.

Ingold, T. (2011). Worlds of sense and sensing the world: A response to Sarah Pink and David Howes. *Social Anthropology, 19*(3), 313–317.

Lambert, J. (2010). *Digital storytelling cookbook (revised).* Berkeley: Digital Diner Press.

Latour, B. (2005). *Reassembling the social – An introduction to actor-network-theory.* Oxford: Oxford University Press.

Latour, B. (2012). *We have never been modern.* Harvard: Harvard University Press.

Latour, B., & Woolgar, S. (2013). *Laboratory life: The construction of scientific facts.* Princeton: Princeton University Press.

Linell, P. (2009). *Rethinking language, mind, and world dialogically: Interactional and contextual theories of human sense-making.* Charlotte: Information Age Pub Inc.

MacDougall, D. (2005). *The corporeal image: Film, ethnography, and the senses.* Princeton: Princeton University Press.

Pink, S. (Ed.). (2012). *Advances in visual methodology.* New York: Sage.

Sachs, L. (2003, April 2). Lidandet har blivit en global handelsvara (Suffering has become a global commodity, my translation). Stockholm: *Svenska Dagbladet,* Under strecket.

Said, E. (1978). *Orientalism.* New York: Vintage.

Waage, T. (2007). Om bilders potensial i samfunnsforskning. (About the potential of pictures in social research, my translation). *Sosiologi i dag, 36*(1), 105–116.

Wenger-Trayner, E., Fenton-O'Creevy, M., Hutchinson, S., Kubiak, C., & Wenger-Trayner, B. (2014). *Learning in landscapes of practice: Boundaries, identity, and knowledgeability in practice-based learning.* London: Routledge.

PART 3

The Scholarship of Integration

CHAPTER 14

Introduction to the Scholarship of Integration

Yngve Nordkvelle

The Scholarship of Integration is a way of performing scholarships so that our students and the public are able to make connections across disciplines, relate isolated facts to each other and put them in context, illuminate data in revealing ways, and relate the teaching and learning to the everyday lives of students. In the academic world, prestigious prizes are awarded primarily to researchers who do exemplary work within their disciplines. Prices for integration would be awarded to those who are able to connect their research to the significant issues and problems that students and the public users of higher education deal with. Placing the knowledge in the broader context and connecting the dots of related information is the core activity of this academic scholarship. Integrating knowledge for students means that the academic addresses meaning first and foremost: what does this knowledge mean? Integration has become increasingly important because of the huge increase in knowledge and emerging

Y. Nordkvelle (✉)
Inland Norway University of Applied Sciences, Lillehammer, Norway

© The Author(s) 2017
G. Jamissen et al. (eds.), *Digital Storytelling in Higher Education*,
Digital Education and Learning, DOI 10.1007/978-3-319-51058-3_14

specialties and sub-disciplines are immense. Philosophers of higher education describe how the entire ontology of our knowing is different from
only a few decades ago. Teaching in higher education tries to solve this
question in a variety of ways, by invoking multidisciplinary, intraprofes-
sional, cross-curricular working methods. Catering for interdisciplinary
and interpretive practices will allow students to integrate their knowledge.
In this section we will see how scholarly knowledge and personal knowledge, which are bodily and often unreflected, meet and how digital storytelling helps students to produce those meanings in critical ways. In this
section we try and demonstrate how useful a tool digital storytelling is
for teachers and students in higher education to produce such integrating
connections.

DIGITAL STORYTELLING: LEARNING TO BE IN HIGHER EDUCATION

In this chapter written by Sandra P.M. Ribeiro of the Polytechnic Institute
of Porto, the focus is on the importance of philosophical and personal
development of the student. The title, "Digital storytelling: learning *to
be* in higher education", opens a line of arguments about the importance
of developing interpersonal relationships and emotions through studies
in higher education institutions. Her point of departure is the need to
make education which prepares students for a competent and responsible
way of *being* in society. Education needs to be redesigned to cater for an
integration of all aspects of human learning. The author aligns Boyer's
Scholarship of Integration with similar strands of thinking in Europe, such
as in the Delors Report published in 1996. This report endorses the idea
that education is based upon four pillars: *learning to know, learning to do,
learning to live together* and *learning to be.*

REFLECTIVE INFORMATION SEEKING: UNPACKING RESEARCH SKILLS THROUGH DIGITAL STORYTELLING

In this chapter Brian Leaf, National Network of Libraries of Medicine,
South Central Region in the US, and Karen R. Diaz, of West Virginia
University, take a closer look at how digital storytelling can play a role as
an instigator of a more profound and immersive notion of literacy—or
multiliteracy, as it is called. They take as their context a working university

library—a place where all academics, staff and students find a place that contains thousands of books, each one of them filled with information representing the soul of the author and the culture they have grown out of. Libraries are designed to signal the sacred and traditional dimension of higher education. They communicate prestige and respect for knowledge, as well as everything that unites all sorts of studies at a university: a place to find information, to study, read and write. It is a demanding task for librarians to teach students all those tricks of the trail, which will open the Pandora's Box of the library. What Karen and Brian have done is to use digital storytelling as a vital part of their teaching of this complex matter.

"Now I See": Digital Storytelling for Mediating Interprofessional Collaboration

Grete Jamissen and Mike Moulton work at the Oslo and Akershus University of Applied Sciences and the Norwegian University of Life Sciences, respectively, as a professor and a senior consultant. The chapter grew out of a particular experience of two groups of academics who created a joint Masters degree on "Public Health". The groups represented diverse professional groups at two separate higher education institutions. Since the group worked so seriously to engage with each other in a professional and friendly manner their progress was slower than anticipated and they did not reach their goals in time. They sought digital storytelling as a method to explore their deeper conflicts and problems in communicating about their mutual interest.

Narratives of Age. Embedding Digital Storytelling Within the Curriculum of Health and Social Care with Older People

Tricia Jenkins is the director of Digitales Ltd. and a PhD candidate of Middlesex University, London. Her chapter presents insights from research projects that involve digital stories on several levels. It discusses the benefits of participation in digital storytelling both by active older people and by those who are living with conditions that limit their capacity, such as dementia. It also looks at the learning that can be gained from the stories produced by older people and the benefits of using digital storytelling as a reflective learning tool. It examines the potential for the digital stories to be used within teaching and learning as resources in nursing education, or as rich qualitative data for research—the potential "afterlives", of the stories once they have been produced.

THE SCHOLARSHIP OF INTEGRATION AND DIGITAL STORYTELLING AS "BILDUNG" IN HIGHER EDUCATION

Yngve Nordkvelle, Yvonne Fritze and Geir Haugsbakk work at Inland Norway University of Applied Sciences, Norway. Their chapter introduces a framework in which to see digital stories and the scholarship of integration in the relation to theories about pedagogy and didactics. The use of digital stories for instruction, collaboration and reflection in various contexts of teaching and learning is considered in a European context. The authors describe how using digital stories can be understood as both a method for teaching and a "signature pedagogy" for a course or a programme.

CRITICAL STORY SHARING: A DIALECTIC APPROACH TO IDENTITY REGULATION

Mari Ann Moss is the director of Dreamcatcher Ltd., New Zealand. Her chapter considers the use of digital storytelling as a way of investigating personal and professional identity. She applies a different lens that helps to make sense of the challenges and opportunities of digital storytelling in organisations. The chapter focuses on an exploratory digital storytelling intervention within an organisation and draws lessons that are pertinent to higher education.

CHAPTER 15

Digital Storytelling: Learning *to Be* in Higher Education

Sandra P.M. Ribeiro

INTRODUCTION

Societal changes have pushed the long-established boundaries of higher education (HE). Despite the changes, teachers still hold in their hands the power in learning, not as a bound book of scientific knowledge but as facilitators and instigators of life-long learning and ultimately human development. Promoting active student involvement in the teaching and learning process, improving the communication through responsible interaction has advantages for all stakeholders in education. Admitting that it is through interpersonal relationships and social interaction that meaning is made and that emotions are part of each individual and cannot be dissociated from the learning process will lead to unchartered, yet necessary paths.

As technology and media merge with education in a continuous complex social process with human consequences and effects, teachers aspire to understand and interpret this volatile context that is being redesigned at the same time society itself is being reshaped as a result of the technological evolution. Thus, we sustain that education is about learning to competently and responsibly *be* in society, where each person is unique albeit

S.P.M. Ribeiro (✉)
ISCAP: Instituto Superior de Contabilidade e Administração do Porto, Porto, Portugal

© The Author(s) 2017
G. Jamissen et al. (eds.), *Digital Storytelling in Higher Education*,
Digital Education and Learning, DOI 10.1007/978-3-319-51058-3_15

part of a larger social community. We acknowledge the prominent role of technology in this fast-paced, evolving society and the need for personal development to meet the unforeseen challenges.

By establishing an intrinsic and unbreakable connection between reflection and twenty-first-century skills, Digital Storytelling (DS) has gained momentum in HE. While emphasising twenty-first-century skills, it also forges a controversial path in academia. DS is capable of linking HE and emotion, encouraging self-direction and personal initiative, for overall learning and engagement. In practice, however, while reflection is acceptable and even desirable within the HE community, personal or emotional aspects create barriers that are more difficult to overcome.

We argue "Digital Storytelling" is a *process* which foments positive student development in HE, enhancing interpersonal relationships and self-knowledge while improving overall digital literacy.

EDUCATION IN A FRAGMENTED SOCIETY

Within an educational setting, but specifically for teachers, especially unsettling is Roger Shank's webpage logo that reads: "There are only two things wrong with the education system: 1. What we teach; and 2. How we teach it." Education is a myriad of interlacing threads, multifaceted and complex that educators have for centuries tried to comprehend, in order to piece together and obtain a clearer understanding of the overall puzzle. More understanding will lead to the advocated coherent articulation and integration.

Societal changes bring forth changes in education. Witnessing these changes and recognising that education and society are intertwined and interdependent, as each influences and is in turn influenced by the other, the literature regarding HE has, over the last several decades, attempted to contemplate the changing landscape so as to make sense of these evolving needs.

Boyer's special report, "Scholarship Reconsidered", published in 1990, advocates this need for an integrated view of education. In line with Bruner (1986), Boyer alerted to the shift in the hierarchy of knowledge, claiming that given that the "boundaries of human knowledge are being dramatically reshaped" (p. 21), the need for "integration" to address intellectual questions and human problems was paramount. Indeed, a quarter of a century ago Boyer confronted higher education institutions (HEIs) by stating that the educational paradigm had to be reconsidered so as to include in their mission "an integrated learning approach", to foster students' personal development. That is to say, HEIs mission should be to prepare their students for a life as responsible citizens of the world, capable of "arrang(ing) relevant bits of knowledge and insight from different disciplines into broader patterns that reflect the actual interconnectedness of the world" (p. 19).

Later, Delors (1996) published a report in Europe, insisting that education needed to be viewed in the broader context of its interaction with society, also proposing a humanistic and integrated vision of education. Despite the time lapse, Boyer's "Scholarship Reconsidered" and the Delors Report remain a timely and challenging agenda for shaping education. Indeed, these authors viewed education as all-encompassing, arguing that education is based upon four pillars: "learning to know", "learning to do", "learning to live together" and "learning to be". These four pillars may be regarded a relevant guiding framework for education development in today's world: learn and know in order to interact within a social context, with direct influence on the individual self, that is, "on being".

Hence, education should be regarded first and foremost as a means to endow a person's ability to guide and adjust his/her own development. Education is not just about educational institutions but also about life in general, and more specifically each individual life in a search for meaning, so as to make sense of a person's own life, to integrate the self, context and subject matter into a meaningful, personal learning experience (Baldacchino 2009). This is not a solitary process. It is a relational dialogue, where teachers and students, within a specific context, construct meaning about themselves as well as about their social and cultural context. Lave and Packer (2008) sustain that learning uncovers, describes and fosters human relations. Consequently, learning is not about transferring well-defined knowledge packages, but rather about social/contextual adaptability that derives from personal interpretation and critical reflection. Thus, learning *is* identity development.

THE PARTICULAR CASE OF HIGHER EDUCATION

In a fragmented, postmodern society, where people are faced with, "a noxious, painful and sickening feeling of perpetual uncertainty in everything regarding the future" (Bauman 1997, p. 193), specific content knowledge and technical skills are considered to be no longer sufficient. HE needs to enable students to successfully manage uncertainty to act in society and to cope with the unbounded, exponential knowledge and information, so as to expand the understanding of the world and their own self-understanding, in a reflexive practice (Giddens 1991). Within fragile and shifting boundaries, which Bauman coined as "liquid", the labour market creates new demands. Employers seek new skills and qualities: forgotten seems to be the need for book-bounded knowledge, to be replaced with personal and interpersonal skills coupled with digital and media literacy, creativity and imagination in order to create and adapt to new ideas, as well as readapt old ones and apply them to unfamiliar contexts (Boyer 1990). HEIs are therefore compelled to provide flexible programmes and teachers are asked to redesign curricula and develop practice-based peda-gogical approaches, while students are asked to assume a more active and responsible stance in their own learning. Institutions and teachers need to challenge students to develop critical reflective appraisals regarding them-selves, their interactions and that of the world around them. Deeply and intrinsically rooted in the individual, education is more than instructing, it is about *being*.

Twenty-first century skills postulated across the globe identify the need for an interconnected learning process. Literature on HE reflects this movement, arguing in favour of "rethinking" (Laurillard 1993), "re-envisioning" (Lin et al. 2013), "transforming" (Mayes et al. 2009) or even "revolutionising" (Altbach, Reisberg and Rumbley 2009) HE. The need to probe "established boundaries" (McMahon and Claes 2005) and "renew" (Palmer et al, 2010) HE, in a world that is unpredictable and where knowledge is supplanted by "being" (Barnett 2004), with focus on future technological trends (see, e.g., The Higher Education edition of the Horizon Reports) is clear, direct and well documented.

These trends are built on the premise that the student is pivotal in all educational activities and that the role of HEIs is to help students establish and develop emotional connections to learning. This educational frame-work derives from a humanistic vision of education, from educators such as Dewey, Freinet and Freire, and that of Piaget and Vygotsky's constructivist perspectives and collaborative learning approaches. The problem perhaps lies in the gap between thinking, expectations, pedagogical approaches and what is done in practice in each HEI. Elmore (1991) argues:

> The aim of teaching is not only to transmit information, but also to transform students from passive recipients of other people's knowledge into active constructors of their own and others' knowledge. The teacher cannot transform without the student's active participation, of course. Teaching is fundamentally about creating the pedagogical, social, and ethical conditions under which students agree to take charge of their own learning, individually and collectively. (pp. xvi–xvii)

Student-centred approaches imply establishing closer interpersonal relationships as opposed to sitting in the classroom filtering rendered information. Through dialogue, teachers and students express and discuss their needs and interests, as well as learning material and experiences, creating a continuous feedback loop, through teacher–student interactions, as well as student–student interactions, allowing for the construction, deconstruction and reconstruction of meaning.

These approaches to teaching and learning also acknowledge that despite the massification of HE, each student is unique, with unique personality and experiences. Learning is about personal development in interaction; it is about the self—that of teacher and students—embedded in a social context. Higher educational contexts are rich in challenges and development opportunities, in terms of autonomy, identity construction, development of interpersonal relationships, the development of ideas and developing integrity (Chickering and Reisser 1993). Academically, students need to adapt new teaching, learning and assessment strategies. Socially, challenges emerge in establishing and developing relationships with teachers and colleagues, as well as coping with nest leaving and the restructuring of family relations. The personal domain encompasses identity development, greater self-awareness and that of the world around. Lastly, the vocational domain relates to the development of a project and a professional identity. Within this perspective, HE extends well beyond specific content knowledge and cannot be dissociated from learning to be.

Illeris (2008) draws on the work developed by Vygotsky and describes learning as a three-dimensional interplay—meaning, personal and contextual. Ideally, it integrates two processes—an external interaction process between the learner and his or her social, cultural or material environment, and an internal psychological process of acquisition and elaboration—and three dimensions—the content dimension, usually described as knowledge and skills, but also many other things such as opinions, insight, meaning, attitudes, values, ways of behaviour, methods, strategies and so on; the incentive dimension, which comprises elements such as feelings, emotions, motivation and volition and whose function is to secure the continuous mental balance of the student; and the interaction dimension, which serves the personal integration in communities and society and thereby also builds up the student's social dimension.

While cognition is embraced and nurtured in HE, emotion and close interpersonal relationships are aspects that, despite the literature advocating their relevance, still tend to be disregarded in favour of more traditional approaches to teaching and learning, as these are considered private and beyond the scope of HE. Thus, regardless of the current emphasis on student-centred learning approaches, considerable effort is made to maintain the established boundaries and the distance deemed necessary.

SITUATING EMOTION AND INTERPERSONAL RELATIONSHIPS IN HIGHER EDUCATION

Emotions are essential for human survival and adaptation as they affect the way we see, interpret, interact and react to the world that surrounds us. However, they are underexplored in education.

Emotions are embodied and situated, in part sensational and physiological, consisting of actual feeling—increased heartbeat, adrenaline—as well as cognitive and conceptual, shaped by beliefs and perceptions. Over time, they have been conceived as private experiences that people are taught not to express publicly; they are a natural phenomenon people must learn to control; and are an individual (intimate) experience. Emotion has been excluded from the HE's pursuit of truth, reason and knowledge because they have been associated with "'soft' scholarship, pollution of truth and bias" (Boler 1999, p. 109), despite the proliferation of findings from the neurosciences advocating that emotions are natural and universal, and intimately connected to cognition and the process of meaning making, or learning (Damasio 2000).

Emotions are part of the interpersonal dynamics, which comprise any learning context. Interpersonal relationships within educational contexts, whether they are teacher–student or student–student relationships, are complex and rooted in social perceptions of teaching and learning. Humans are social beings, thus, learning to be implies the development of interpersonal competencies. Within this scenario, emotions, interpersonal relationships and learning cannot be disassociated, nor can we disregard any one of these aspects as they are intertwined. There is incontestable evidence among the literature that states that interpersonal relationships are vital for persistence learning and overall success in HE.

In the field of neurosciences, Cozolino and Sprokay (2006) emphasise the need for a close link between learning and interpersonal relationships in educational settings, arguing that human brain needs social interaction to make meaning, to shape and reshape its connections, to adapt and readapt to an ever-changing world. The brain is thus a social organ, designed to learn through shared experiences. At a time when roles are shifting in HE, it is important to be aware of the boundaries in these interpersonal relationships that seem to be getting closer due to the frenetic use of social networks, especially between teachers and students. Teachers need to find a sustainable personal and professional balance, to understand when and how to rim the boundaries to serve the student and their relationship.

In HEIs where traditional teaching and learning approaches predominate, interpersonal relationships may be devalued. However, as we have been postulating, HE is about learning and student overall development is the work of HE. If science has proven and validated the connections, establishing the framework for teachers to work with, the option lies in their hands. Closer interpersonal relations, whether between students or between students and teachers, step beyond the confines of what has traditionally been deemed as appropriate for HE. Personal or emotional aspects are met with mental resistance that needs to be managed.

Personal Storytelling in Higher Education

Stories as a means of making sense of experience have proliferated across many different subject fields. If education is the re-contextualisation of what has been learned in a continuous process of meaning making, that is, to learn how to use the knowledge and skills in different contexts throughout life, then storytelling is, by far, the best tool humans possess.

Indeed, the art of telling stories, whether orally or in the form of artwork, is one of the oldest methods of communicating ideas and learning. As Ricoeur states a narrative "construes significant wholes out of scattered events" (as cited by Walker 1994, p. 296). Stories evoke in all engaging participants unexpected emotions, ideas and ultimately unexpected selves, shifting perspectives on experience, constructing and deconstructing knowledge. It is through stories that experiences gain meaning and, through reflection and interpretation, is then transformed into knowledge. Storytelling derives from the recollection and interpretation of an experience that has been significant otherwise it is not remembered. It is this dialogic activity in the storytelling process that enables learning and thus human development. Learning occurs when reflection on experience is transformed into a logical, meaningful story that is shared with others. This frames leaning as a social, experiential, reflective process the cognitive, emotional and social dimensions that Illeris (2008) identifies as essential to learning.

Personal stories motivate and engage the author in the act of creation. To create a coherent and effective story, the author must reflect, select, prioritise and organise what he/she wants to say and how this can be conveyed. As the story is told, the audience interprets, reflects and connects to their own personal experience, construing new (mental) stories or reinterpreting older stories, in order to construe new ones. Furthermore, if interaction is possible between author and audience, or among the audience this (social) interaction fosters discussion and further reflection. The entire process is mediated by the intervenient's prior knowledge, his/her feelings in addition to the social and cultural context

The advantages of storytelling are often associated to a particular timeframe—childhood. Stories are subjective and emotional. However, whereas some regard the emotion in storytelling as powerful, others deem emotion as a weakness, particularly in HE. While the value of story writing is uncontested, the academy often devalues narrative.

It is in this duality that recent perspectives in HE have forged a new, if somewhat still fragile path. We argue that reflection is key in HE. The emergence of the reflective paradigm in this specific context has advanced storytelling as a learning tool (McDrury and Alterio 2003; Mezirow 1990; Walker and Nixon 2004). Bruner (1986) and Damasio (1994), for example, argue that cognition and emotion is united in story. Storytelling in HE draws on this to forge and establish a solid path as this contrasts to the reasoning that is traditionally valued in this context. This requires that we look at education from a different perspective not only for knowledge acquisition, but knowledge construction through interpersonal connections, affection and dialogue. This view is grounded in story and storytelling as a primary structure for making meaning and as a metaphor for the developing self. Time constraints impose deep reflection on what to say and how to say it, hinting at metaphorical and creative escapes. Storytelling could then be regarded as a *process* which fosters personal, professional and academic development, encouraging self-awareness, self-identity and self-authoring. Engaging in the storytelling process, students are guided through the stages of learning, ultimately reaching the last stage where deeper level of critical reflection, as is envisioned in HE, is required. At the same time, current technological trends have put a new spin on storytelling.

INTEGRATING DIGITAL STORYTELLING IN HIGHER EDUCATION: A CASE STUDY

The idea that technology is critical in educating the twenty-first-century student has aroused the interest of many researchers around storying skills, as an essential requirement for effective communicating in new technological media. Storytelling coupled with media and digital literacy skills, coined as Digital Storytelling, addresses most, if not all, of the twenty-first-century student outcomes identified. The fact that stories can be created using today's technology enables teachers and students to, together, strive towards better information, media and technology skills, namely in terms of information literacy, media literacy and Information and Communications Technology literacy (Ribeiro 2015).

Digital Storytelling is an umbrella, a global concept to refer to any type of media that facilitates the act of telling stories. Despite the widespread use of the concept, not all Digital Storytelling tells stories the way and with the intent of the Center for Digital Storytelling (CDS). Nonetheless, we feel this Californian model (CDS model) best fits our approach and intentions as its emphasis is on personal voice and workshop-based teaching method, although we recognise it is not the preference in the field of education. Many of the studies in this field refer to its origins and founders (CDS and Joe Lambert and Dana Atchley and Nina Mullen) but in practice the more personal elements are, more often than not, disregarded. The model chosen implies a *process* that, despite not being strict, has a set of recommended elements that are considered essential.

Exploring the intersection of identity and DS, we analysed student self-perception and self-representation in HE contexts, which we intersected with teachers' own perceptions of their students. We considered both teachers' and students' perspectives, in an exploratory case study through the analysis of data collected throughout the DS process—Story Circle, Story Creation and Story Show—and crossed that information with the students' personal reflections and teacher perceptions. Finally, we questioned the influence of DS on teachers' perceptions of students.

Grounded on an interpretative/constructivist paradigm, we chose to implement a qualitative case study to explore DS in HE. In three successive and cumulative attempts to collect student data, we were able to gather detailed observation notes from two Story Circles: 12 written student reflections pertaining to the creation process; 14 Digital Stories and detailed observation notes from one Story Show. We carried out three focus groups with the participants, a total of 16 teachers, where we discussed their perceptions of each student prior to and after watching the Digital Stories. We also asked them about their opinion of DS in HE as a teaching and learning method, as well as their opinion on the influence of DS on interpersonal relationships in HE. Given the vast amount of data collected, we began with an inductive content analysis. Additionally, we also analysed the intent of their discourse and tried to figure out the reasoning behind their choice of words. The multimodal nature of the Digital Stories also impelled us towards a multimodal analysis in an attempt to comprehend the semiotics underpinnings of the modes used to create the story.

Finding Interconnected Threads

We were able to identify a continuum throughout the DS process implemented, that is to say, student self-perception almost always coincides with teacher perception of the student, indicating that perhaps everyday teacher–student interaction is enough to obtain the adequate insights into who our students are. Teachers admit they were able to identify traces of their perception of the students in all the stories and, in this regard, we might be fooled to believe DS does not add value to the interpersonal relationships in the educational context. Nonetheless, all participants admitted that DS had a significant impact on them (author and audience), essential to fill in the blanks, to provide the missing pieces. After one of the focus groups, one teacher claimed,

> Lets say ... we had separate pieces of the puzzle and now they came together. Everything became clear. We had fragments. We have many students and we have to pay attention to all and cannot dedicate ourselves to one person. But if we had been aware of some of the details revealed here.[1]

The teachers admitted that watching the Digital Stories influence the teacher–student relationship. In a particular story, a student discloses a serious health problem, which shocked the teachers, as was evident by their physical reactions. After watching this story, one of the teachers admits "This story has greatly influenced me. From the moment X decided to disclose her problem, I am here for her."

Teachers and students professed having undergone a deeper reflection process and understanding regarding their own lives, motivations and behaviours and that of others, confirming the pivotal position of DS in personal and social development. Another participating teacher explains this as such,

> this type of approach is very important because it allows today's students to get to know each other and share. Today's students have great difficulty in sharing, in opening up. They receive and receive and give back very little. This would allow them to give back a bit of their life, to share things that are relevant to them. .[…] This would bring them closer, foster tolerance and understanding. […] It would help them become people, **people**.(emphasis in original)

For students to talk about what is socially perceived as private is hard because they are afraid to be criticised. Students, like everybody else, worry about what impression they make on others and each element of the story is selected and organised to disclose what they want. The DS process enabled them to undergo a process of self-reflection on who they are and what they wanted to show, whether they then disclosed their thought or not.

Students' reflections may shed some light on this:

> Creating this Digital Story was a gratifying experience because it allowed me to, firstly recall my journey until today and the obstacles I had to overcome and secondly, be aware that although my decision to invest in myself was done rather late, it was one of the best decisions in my life.

> Even if we don't create a very personal Digital Story, …, we always end up reflecting on who we were when we began and who we are now.

> We must be imaginative and think about what we want to show. If we want to disclose more, and what aspect we want to show, because that is very

important too. We should show what we want. What the viewers are going to see is what we decide and choose.

I learned that sometimes we don't see all we believe we see. I was surprised to see how my colleagues were able to show their sensitivity, their life, their innermost self.

Public sharing was an obstacle, seen by the number of stories erased and the number of students that did not deliver the final story. In fact, in the three attempts and of the 58 students who were invited to participate, only 14 consented. Our findings acknowledge that identity, when focused on the more personal issues, is not an acceptable topic to discuss in HE. Four students revealed the reasons for not wanting to hand in their stories, stating:

Sometimes we find it difficult to talk about ourselves. We are still discovering ourselves and so it is a bit difficult.

I prefer to talk about others. (…) Speaking about ourselves is always complicated because we never know if someone is judging us or not, if they agree with what we are saying or not.

If I open up too much, I am afraid people will hurt my feelings.

It is complicated to talk about myself because I am not at ease. I believe it is easier to talk about others than to talk about ourselves. We are never completely aware of who we are or what we are doing. We are testing new limits, talking about things we never thought we'd talk about.

One student who chose to participate in the study situates Identity in HE and the role of DS as follows:

To talk about the self is something we do not do in our daily life, not in this HE context. We must focus on what we are listening to and learn in class, focus on what we must do, on the tasks and often we don't have time to talk to this or that person to understand what we are feeling, who we are. Obviously there is always a part of us that is disclosed, but to talk about ourselves this way is something deeper, more personal and something I truly enjoyed doing, [it was] very interesting and useful, because it also allowed us to understand our colleagues better.

[…] It makes us reflect, structure, think about what we are going to disclose, what we don't want to disclose and, of course, articulate it with sound and images, which makes it much more interesting and relevant in HE. We must learn how to articulate for future jobs or interviews. This helps because it makes me reflect on who I am and what I want to present to others. HE is a good time for something like this, although it is not common. Therefore, I thought it was a fantastic way to get us to speak, to make things a bit more personal and make us reflect on who we are.

For the students present, these moments seem to have been important, in the sense that students knew they were sharing stories, private moments and feelings that were meant for the group only. Furthermore, it was interesting to see that, although unique, there are universal aspects to these stories. Students discovered commonalities, recognising their own life experience in the story of others.

The DS creation process in itself implies the development of effective communication skills and it engages the author and audience in a great amount of reflection. As such, it can be applied to every subject. However, as we have stated elsewhere, the reflection involved in the DS process, whether from the perspective of the author, or the audience, transpires the personal perspective, enriching and creating depth to the final story, as each layer mirrors the self—a story with personal meaning. While research on reflective teaching and emotional intelligence is abundant, the truth is that it remains a challenge to bring this practice into HE classroom.

> The value of integrating reflection and emotion in our teaching and learning is sometimes hard to recognize and even harder to practice. (Lambert 2013, p. 184)

The largest obstacle in incorporating DS in HE challenge is to get teachers to recognise its value, to recognise that student reflection and expression of emotion enrich the learning process. Teachers need to acknowledge the alignment between DS and the intended learning outcomes in HE: DS encourages student inquiry, deeper analysis, critical thinking skills, visual literacy skills, visual and oral communication, team work, as well as global and civic knowledge, rooted intentions in higher educational levels.

DS focuses on the personal and therefore often challenges the way we traditionally think about student and teacher roles in HE, where the teacher still assumes his/her role as the active deliverer of informa- tion and content. This personalised approach in DS creates situations where the student assumes a more visible and active role throughout the entire process. Besides, as DS emphasises how we engage stu- dents in their own learning process, it is also capable of overturning the carefully planned and controlled lessons from the teachers' hands. Additionally, what is valued in today's ever-changing world is not knowledge as a tidy, transferable package, but adaptable knowledge that derives from personal interpretation and critical reflection. In that sense, DS foments reflection and evaluation of experiences by creat- ing opportunities in the classroom for such activities, as an interac- tive and collaborative process where students offer suggestions, argue and question points of view and ultimately rethink ideas. We would argue that the process develops essential but tacit skills that challenge the objectivity, argument, distance and reason currently valued in HE, especially because it is difficult to assess and quantify. Thus, teachers may perceive DS as lacking rigour and "objectivity," despite the sub- stantiated evidence in the field of DS that question this idea. In DS, learning has the power to abolish indifference generated by faceless, student numbers and it invites teachers and students to embark on a new, unprecedented journey, but change is daunting. Our study, in line with Lambert, confirmed it is difficult to break out of the formal, well- established educational discourse despite the proven value of DS. To be fair, we would probably react similarly if confronted with a novel and/ or unusual pedagogical practice that had the potential to challenge our deep-rooted beliefs and routines.

CONCLUSION

Our integrative, interdisciplinary and interpretative approach revealed that Digital Stories are puzzles. Authors and audience use Digital Stories to create consistency, clarification and coherence of the self, through a con- tinual process of subjective interpretation. Each story presents one of the many possible self-representations, inseparably connected with the micro-, meso- and macro-context. Grumet (1991) summarises this idea by stat- ing: "Our stories are the masks through which we can be seen, and with every telling we stop the flood and swirl of thought so someone can get a glimpse of us, and maybe catch us if they can" (p. 69).

Our journey began within the field of education and, in seeking a deeper understanding of DS in HE, we travelled the path of identity development and self-representation, student development as well as objectives and practices in HE. We focus on the connection of identity, emotion and interpersonal relationships to DS as the basis to humanise HE and prepare our students for the world to come. Our own story intends to argue that although the three pillars—identity, education and DS—present a real challenge to the dominant assertions in HE, when interwoven, may potentiate learning experiences.

Crafting a personal story is a complex and engaging activity for meaning making that couples cognition and affection, and links the self to others. Stories are used to create consistency, clarification and coherence of the self, through subjective interpretation. Some criticise emotional and personal content in HE. However, research has demonstrated that the emotional content at the core of personal storytelling is connected to intelligence and higher cognition. It is a reflexive and recursive process, which incorporates the essence of human development, identity and education. By adding the digital to personal storytelling, we are able to incorporate the technical aspects, which drive the information society we live in. While we perceive Digital Storytelling as chaotic, DS imposes rigour. The DS process cements interpersonal relationships and deep critical reflection, which leads to transformation, which lacks in Digital Storytelling.

HE today is not about transferring consolidated or developed knowledge. There is a need for a range of generic skills that are relevant for society, essential for employability and overall citizenship such as applying knowledge in practice, adapting to new situations, information management skills, autonomy, team work, organising and planning, oral and written communication, without ignoring interpersonal skills. The Story Circle and the Story Show are about listening, promoting community, trust and closer emotional ties between teacher and student and among the students. The content is personal and emotional, and thus empowering, motivating and engaging. Digital Storytelling offers more than an opportunity to incorporate technology. As a process, Digital Storytelling demonstrates the capacity to weave the essence of HE: human (personal) development, social relational development and technology, thus fostering Boyer's integrated learning approach.

NOTE

1. Full transcript of the focus groups can be found in Ribeiro (2015).

Acknowledgements The work presented derives from a PhD project on *Digital Storytelling in Higher Education* carried out in Universidade de Aveiro, Portugal, between 2009 and 2014. Parts of the present chapter have been presented in conferences and published in Journals.

REFERENCES

Altbach, P. G., Reisberg, L., & Rumbley, L. E. (2009). *Trends in global higher education: Tracking an academic revolution.* Chestnut Hill: Boston College, Center for International Higher Education.

Baldacchino, J. (2009). *Education beyond education: Self and the imaginary in Maxine Greene's philosophy.* New York: Peter Lang.

Barnett, R. (2004). The purposes of higher education and the changing face of academia. *London Review of Education, 2,* 61–73.

Bauman, Z. (1997). *Postmodernity and its discontents.* New York: New York University Press.

Boler, M. (1999). *Feeling power emotions and education.* New York: Routledge. http://search.ebscohost.com/login.aspx?direct=true&scope=site&db=nlebk&db=nlabk&AN=122655. Accessed 20 Oct 2016.

Boyer, E. L. (1990). *Scholarship reconsidered: Priorities of the professoriate.* Princeton: Carnegie Foundation for the Advancement of Teaching.

Bruner, J. (1986). *Actual minds, possible worlds.* Cambridge, MA: Harvard University Press.

Chickering, A. W., & Reisser, L. (1993). *Education and identity.* San Francisco: Jossey Bass.

Cozolino, L., & Sprokay, S. (2006). Neuroscience and adult learning. *New Directions for Adult and Continuing Education, 2006,* 11–19.

Damasio, A. R. (1994). *Descartes' error: Emotion, reason, and the human brain.* New York: Putnam.

Damasio, A. R. (2000). *The feeling of what happens: Body and emotion in the making of consciousness.* London: Vintage.

Delors, J. (1996). *Learning: The treasure within – Report to UNESCO of the International Commission on Education for the Twenty-first Century.* Unesco.

Elmore, R. F. (1991). Foreward. In R. Christensen, D. A. Garvin, & A. Sweet (Eds.), *Education for judgment: The artistry of discussion leadership* (pp. ix–xix). Cambridge, MA: Harvard Business School Press.

Giddens, A. (1991). *Modernity and self-identity: Self and society in the late modern age.* Stanford: Stanford University Press.

Grumet, M. (1991). The politics of personal knowledge. In C. Witherell & N. Noddings (Eds.), *Stories lives tell: Narrative and dialogue in education* (pp. 67–77). New York: Teachers College Press.

Illeris, K. (2008). *Contemporary theories of learning: Learning theorists... in their own words.* London/New York: Routledge.

Lambert, J. (2013). *Digital storytelling: Capturing lives, creating community.* New York: Routledge.

Laurillard, D. (1993). *Rethinking university teaching: A framework for the effective use of educational technology.* New York: Routledge.

Lave, J., & Packer, M. (2008). Towards a social ontology of learning. In K. Nielsen, S. Brinkmann, C. Elmholdt, L. Tangaard, P. Musaeus, & G. Kraft (Eds.), *A qualitative stance* (pp. 17–46). Århus: Aarhus University Press.

Lin, J., Oxford, R. L., & Brantmeier, E. J. (Eds.). (2013). *Re-envisioning higher education: Embodied pathways to wisdom and social transformations.* Charlotte: Information Age Publishing.

Mayes, T., Morrison, D., Mellar, H., Bullen, P., & Oliver, M. (Eds.). (2009). *Transforming higher education through technology enhanced learning.* New York: Higher Education Academy.

McDrury, J., & Alterio, M. (2003). *Learning through storytelling in higher education: Using reflection & experience to improve learning.* London/Sterling: Kogan Page.

McMahon, F., & Claes, T. (Eds.). (2005). *Probing the boundaries of higher education.* Oxford: Inter-Disciplinary Press.

Mezirow, J. (1990). *Fostering critical reflection in adulthood: A guide to transformative and emancipatory learning.* San Francisco: Jossey-Bass Publishers.

Palmer, P. J., Zajonc, A., & Scribner, M. (2010). *The heart of higher education: A call to renewal.* San Francisco: Jossey-Bass.

Ribeiro, S. (2015). Digital storytelling: An integrated approach to language for the 21st century student. *Teaching English with Technology (TEwT), 15,* 39–53.

Walker, P. (1994). The necessity of narrative in William Least Heat-Moon's "Blue Highways and Prairyerth". *Great Plains Quarterly.* http://digitalcommons.unl.edu/greatplainsquarterly/802. Accessed 30 Oct 2016.

Walker, M., & Nixon, J. (Eds.). (2004). *Reclaiming universities from a runaway world.* Buckingham: Society for Research into Higher Education & Open University Press.

CHAPTER 16

Reflective Information Seeking: Unpacking Meta-Research Skills Through Digital Storytelling

Brian Leaf and Karen R. Diaz

INTRODUCTION

Libraries are made of books, and books are filled with stories. These are stories of dreams, insights, ideas, and research. The uninitiated view libraries as simply the repository for these stories; however, a deeper look reveals libraries' active role in not only sharing these stories but also creating new ones.

Storytelling is not a term traditionally used to describe activities relevant to the academic library or even the academy. But in fact, the academy is all about telling stories—to students, to researchers—for the advancement of society as a whole. While department faculty and lecturers engage students with discipline content expertise and related discourse, librarians are tasked with helping students navigate this content and discourse across disciplines as well as within their majors. At times, this task requires a form

B. Leaf
National Network of Libraries of Medicine South Central Region,
Fort Worth, TX, USA

K.R. Diaz (✉)
West Virginia University, Morgantown, WV, USA

© The Author(s) 2017   225
G. Jamissen et al. (eds.), *Digital Storytelling in Higher Education*,
Digital Education and Learning, DOI 10.1007/978-3-319-51058-3_16

of teaching information seeking, gathering, and sharing, not based within disciplinary confines.

Studies such as Ethnographic Research in Illinois Academic Libraries (ERIAL 2012) and Project Information Literacy (PIL 2015) demonstrate that information-seeking behaviours observed in a variety of populations are complex and require more attention than is traditionally given in the classroom. Effectively teaching "the ability to find, use, and evaluate information" requires thoughtful design that is best served when aligned with primary-course objectives and course assignments. Librarians facilitate successful instruction via classroom visits, short-term collaborations with faculty, and, at some institutions, through for-credit courses.

Furthermore, libraries provide many distinct disciplines a common support structure, which makes Boyer's *scholarship of integration* (1996) a compelling frame for this chapter. Braxton et al. (2002) state "the scholarship of integration often involves doing research at the boundaries where fields converge" (p. 47). Enabling this function has been for many years a growing trend among academic libraries, for example, the development of spaces such as the "commons" in the early 1990s, or subject librarians as facilitators of cross-campus collaborations (Daniels et al. 2010; Knapp 2011). Boundary erasure can also be seen in new library facilities and programming designed to bring researchers together to intersect ideas and expertise. Research commons create spaces for consultation, education, and collaboration space for novice and expert researchers across campus. The spaces and programming of research commons are mapped around the concept of a "research cycle" that is universal to all disciplines and thus provide a common ground for everyone (Research Commons n.d.). The research cycle is a story itself that we use to make the very chaotic and messy research process a bit more understandable and approachable.

Having already fulfilled the roles of non-disciplinary, cross-disciplinary, and interdisciplinary support around the finding, delivering, and creation of information in the past, libraries provide the ideal venue for the community building, collaborative, transformative, and cross-disciplinary work of digital storytelling and positions digital storytelling as a potential signature pedagogy in the libraries. The purpose of this chapter is to position digital storytelling within the developing and transformative literacy(ies) work of libraries by contextualizing it within Boyer's ideas of scholarly integration.

The Origins of Metaliteracy

Libraries encourage, develop, and, by their very nature, demand literacy. In a library context, literacy is not simply the ability to read content, but also the ability to find it, determine if it is the right content, and then to use it properly. In addition to the "back room" work of organizing content to make it findable, libraries also do "front room" work to help users decipher and understand those organizational structures. A brief review of this work will give better context to the values and perspectives librarians give to this view of literacy.

In the 1980s, libraries began teaching programmes called *bibliographic instruction*. Bibliographic instruction taught library users to locate information quickly and effectively and often covered the library's system of organizing materials. Such instruction made sense in a print-based world when most archival, especially scholarly, information was housed in libraries. As information became digital, prolific, and began to "leave" the library, bibliographic instruction proved limiting and ineffective. Libraries then evolved instructional programmes into *information literacy* instruction: this method is a format and location neutral instructional approach to the skills of finding, using, and evaluating information. Information literacy focuses on conceptual notions of the information landscape, the information cycle, and various threshold concepts necessary to become truly proficient in our information-rich world. Information literacy is a concept and pedagogy that has gained international recognition and effort.

Information literacy is a global concept, with many international college and university library organizational definitions. In the UK, the Standing Conference on National and University Libraries (SCONUL 1999) organization developed a framework called the *Seven Pillars of Information Literacy*. National Institute of Library & Information Sciences of Sri Lanka provides the *Empowering 8*, or E8 (Wijetunge and Alahakoon 2009). In the USA, the Association of College and Research Libraries (2015) has quite recently introduced the *Information Literacy Framework* document that stands alongside their *Information Literacy Standards* (ACRL 2000). The Council of Australian University Libraries and Library and Information Association of New Zealand published a position paper on information literacy that addresses the ability to access, process, and use information effectively as a key enabler for society as a whole (Australian and New Zeland Institute for Information

Literacy 2004). Baro (2011) identifies several studies regarding the use of information literacy in various African libraries and universities although there is no continental or official African statement on information literacy.

Beyond these regional documents and studies, the International Federation of Library Associations (IFLA 2015) produced guidelines on assessing information and its role in lifelong learning. UNESCO (2003, 2006) has sponsored two meetings of experts from which were issued statements known as the *Prague Declaration* (Towards an Information Literate Society) and the *Alexandria Proclamation* (Beacons of the Information Society). These documents address the notion of information literacy outside of the academy and focus on lifelong learning that affects societies.

Primary and secondary educational organizations also recognize the concept of information literacy. Two American educators, Mike Eisenberg and Bob Berkowitz (n.d.), devised the *Big 6* model of information literacy that is used in many K–12 schools and much of which has been adopted in the USA in the educational programme known as the Common Core. Often at the primary and secondary levels, information literacy is referred to as either media literacy or Information, Communication, and Technology skills. This approach often conflates the notions of technology skills and information skills.

While information literacy is not always associated with libraries in mainstream contexts, the ability to find, evaluate, and use information is generally recognized as an important competency. In *Informing Communities: Sustaining Democracy in a Digital Age*, a report of the Knight Commission on the Information Needs of Communities in a Democracy, the importance of information literacy is emphasized as an important component of democracy itself. The Executive Summary of this report states that it can only do so when "digital and media literacy are widely taught in schools, public libraries, and other community centers" (Knight Commission 2009).

MOVING TOWARDS METALITERACY

Metaliteracy finds its foundations in Lippincott (2007) and Bobish (2011). Mackey and Jacobson (2014, pp. 21–22) define it as a meta-cognitive approach to information literacy, stating that they both draw upon constructivism for framing this intersection. A theory of learning, constructivism was developed by Piaget (1973) and later defined by Gergen (1999, as cited by Talja et al. 2005; Oldfather and Dahl 1994) "as a view in which an individual mind constructs reality but within a systematic relationship to the external world" (p. 60). Psychologists Lev Vygotsky and Jerome Bruner refined the concept as social constructivism, which states that learning is a "mental process" that is "significantly informed by influences received from societal conventions, history and interaction with significant others" (Talja et al. 2005, p. 80).

And, indeed, Bobish (2011) states explicitly that in constructivism, the "learning is in the doing" and "[doing] promotes active learning. Learners construct their own knowledge, individually, and in a social context" (p. 63). While he invokes the ageing term "Web 2.0" in his discussion, these principles are reflected in such platforms as Wikipedia, YouTube, Facebook, and other tools where users are able to collaborate, learn, and share information. This thread of constructivism is evident in the approach offered by metaliteracy. Its goals echo long-valued information literacy principles but include new goals that reflect today's evolving information environment—one that emphasizes and lends itself to social interaction made possible by today's information technology infrastructure. Metaliteracy is defined as promoting:

> critical thinking and collaboration in a digital age, providing a comprehensive framework to effectively participate in social media and online communities. It is a unified construct that supports the acquisition, production, and sharing of knowledge in collaborative online communities. Metaliteracy challenges traditional skills-based approaches to information literacy by recognizing related literacy types and incorporating emerging technologies. (Mackey and Jacobson 2011)

Metaliteracy recognizes that the information landscape has become increasingly participatory due to social media and the resulting sharing and collaborations happen in many formats and venues. One does not need to look much further than the popularity of apps like Vine or Snapchat that allow users to create and share short videos, or more significantly Twitter's role as a communication channel for the Arab Spring. Thus, the information landscape has become quite complex. Metaliteracy involves more than possessing the technical skills to navigate this complex territory, but also requires deeper understandings to become active, productive, and contributing members of this landscape as well.

The metaliteracy framework can be represented as a series of goals and objectives. These goals include:

1. Evaluate critically, including dynamic online content that changes and evolves, such as article preprints, blogs, and wikis
2. Understand personal privacy, information ethics, and intellectual property issues in changing technology environments
3. Share information and collaborate in a variety of participatory environments
4. Demonstrate ability to connect learning and research strategies with lifelong learning processes and personal, academic, and professional goals (Metaliteracy, n.d.)

These goals can be parsed out for a total of 33 learning objectives. These goals and objectives account for a variety of literacies such as digital, visual, media, and information fluency. Focusing on these goals provides an adaptive model that does not suppose skill sets that are technologically dependent, but is instead one that is flexible in the face of technological innovation and changes in policy. It's a framework that, like basic story structure, can remain fundamentally the same no matter future forms of technologies or interaction. See Fig. 16.1.

The model of metaliteracy provided by Mackey and Jacobson in Fig. 16.1 shows the complex levels of all that is included in this literacy. The outer ring highlights the outputs. Information is used, shared, incorporated, and produced. The second ring in the model highlights some of the tools that allow this work to happen, including social media, mobile technology, online access, and open education resources (OERs). The next ring indicates the cognition required to use the tools effectively—accessing, determining, evaluating, and understanding. However, beyond these cognitive skills, metacognition is needed—the ability to recognize the cognitive skills which are being employed and the ability to use each cognitive skill appropriately. Because these layers of understanding are growing increasingly complex, collaboration must span all of this work. Complex technological and cognitive tasks, such as producing, sharing, using, and incorporating information, are best accomplished through collaboration. Just as building a house requires a complex set of skills and

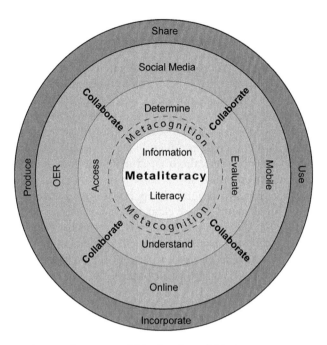

Fig. 16.1 The metaliteracy model by Jacobs and Mackey

collaboration, so does building truly literate outcomes require a complex set of skills and collaboration.

Furthermore, Mackey and Jacobson (2011) mapped each metaliteracy objective into domains of learning: behavioural, cognitive, affective, and metacognitive. *Behavioural* learning refers to the skills and competencies students should gain after engaging in learning activities. *Cognitive* learning is the knowledge students should acquire. The *affective* domain encompasses the changes in emotions or attitudes that occur as a result of participating in learning activities. *Metacognitive* refers to what or how students think about their own thinking vis-à-vis reflection on their own learning and knowledge. While many aspects of metaliteracy are evident in digital storytelling workshops, it is the affective and metacognitive domains of metaliteracy that connect so well to its practice. And while metaliteracy is not yet an internationally recognized term, it is a recent evolutionary term with roots in a widely accepted international programme of instruction.

Digital Storytelling as a Pedagogy for Metaliteracy

Digital storytelling is focused on process, evidenced by core components such as the story circle and the emphasis facilitating a community environment in which individuals can safely voice their stories. Metaliteracy, as inherent in its key prefix *meta*, is intended to be a unifying concept "about" the ways people consume, share, and produce in the digital age. It's not focused on any single product, but how people get there. Digital storytelling is, arguably, less about producing the final story and more about the journey to produce it.

Digital storytelling is a facilitated experience with a distinct pedagogy composed of four elements. These elements do not have to only take place in a workshop, but can be integrated into the classroom as well. These elements of *community, storytelling, technology,* and *sharing* have not only been successful in helping numerous participants produce impactful stories over the years, but they also contribute to the development of a metaliterate learner.

Community

One intentional practice of digital storytelling is the use of a story circle. Forming a literal circle of participants provides not only support for the storyteller, but security. It signals a closed and trusted group in which the storyteller can be vulnerable, explore emotions, and begin articulating what he or she deems important about the story. It provides a safe space in which to begin to hear the sound of his or her voice. The story circle is a time for making all voices equal. Circle guidelines, such as stepping up to speak if you have not yet spoken, or stepping back if you have spoken a lot, allow for every voice to be heard and signal that every voice is important.

The story circle also provides those who are listening the opportunity to practice active listening, empathy, and their own emotional and connectional response to the story being shared. This give and take allows the point of the story to emerge and to uncover engaging elements. Listeners learn to provide feedback that honours the storyteller's ownership of the story even as clarifications are made and new ideas emerge.

Finally, reflection on the effect on audience is an important component of metacognition, especially in regard to writing. The story circle is the beginning of building awareness of audience, and what parts of the story are important and will connect with audience. Storytellers need to reflect on not only the emotion or idea that they want to convey but also the best way to reach the audience to whom they are speaking

Storytelling

When storytelling is practiced first through writing, the storyteller is engaging in the most basic of literacies. The practices of organizing thoughts, economizing the text, developing tone, and tightening the narrative are each important writing skills. The act of writing engages the storyteller to reflect on what has been learned, or accomplished, or felt, that is, metacognition. It is in this reflection that the storyteller develops insights. In academic contexts, the incorporation of content knowledge into experiential writing requires even further synthesis and a deeper layer of understanding in order to communicate it effectively to any given audience.

Technology

As the storyteller moves from script to video editing, s/he engages with new literacies. First come visual literacies in selecting images that enhance or magnify the text of the story. Sometimes, the images are "found" objects that are literal reflections of the story. Often impactful moments that make up stories have not been documented visually, and the storyteller must look for or create metaphorical images that enlighten, colours that enhance, or other even abstract images that enhance the tone or meaning of the text.

When the storyteller needs to search for images that can be used in the story, s/he must exercise skillfulness in searching through the use of appropriate terminology, locating images that comply with copyright restrictions, and finding images of high-enough resolution that keep integrity in both large- and small-screen viewing of the final video. This process of discovery requires creatively generating keywords for discovery in online environments and/or visual composition for those who take their own pictures. Even if the storytelling is relying on personal images or creating their own, it's important to understand his or her legal rights. This stage also presents an opportunity to address issues such as personal digital asset management, even if it is a different scale than searching the larger web. Sustainable metadata (e.g. could be as simple as file naming practices) and version control of one's own media are still important considerations. These are not trivial processes or skills easily learned; being unable to manage assets effectively or shallow search may result in frustration in later stages that aren't completed, or stories that look duplicative if multiple participants are using the same images from generic keyword searches.

Next the storyteller works on pacing the images appropriately in the story, recognizing when to slow down and spend time on an image, and when to rapidly move through images to match the tone and the emotion of the story. What transitions are needed and how can they be judiciously applied? Is it appropriate to zoom in or zoom out of a picture? And how can all of these video-editing techniques work together for a coherent and seamless flow?

Finally, the storyteller has the opportunity to go even a step further and find or create music that elicits the mood intended and that draws the listener in emotionally. What are the sounds that will provide the same emotional connection to the audience as exist with the storyteller? This technical versatility cannot be downplayed and addresses so many aspects of the literacies that make up metaliteracy.

Sharing

The beauty of digital storytelling is the flexibility and far reaching that digital media can have in our web 2.0 world. Storytellers can practice sharing their stories in appropriate contexts. Does this story stand alone? Does it sit in a larger web context? How can it be embedded in the right place for most impact? What social media venue will host this story?

When stories are shared in publicly accessible ways, the storyteller needs to ensure not only that s/he is abiding by copyright restrictions but also that s/he is aware of her/his own rights as author of the work. Will s/he let others use her/his story? If so, in what contexts, for what reasons, and at what costs?

Each of the pedagogical elements of digital storytelling—community, storytelling, technology, and sharing—provides opportunity for storytellers to develop and broaden both hard and soft skills. They are technical, and they are non-technical. They are the full circle of skills that make up what we know as "metaliteracy" and are modelled in Fig. 16.2.

Case Study of Affect and Metacognition in Digital Stories

In the fall of 2014 and the spring of 2015, a digital storytelling workshop was offered to Second-Year Transformational Experience Program (STEP) students. STEP is a co-curricular programme designed to redefine the student experience and, as the name suggests, transform their lives by

The Pedagogy and Skills of Digital Storytelling

•Courage/Vulnerability
•Listening
•Feedback
•Emotion
•Empathy

•Writing
•Reflection
•Insight
•Tone

Community

Storytelling

Technical

Sharing

•Visual literacy/image
 selection
•Video/audio editing
•Pacing
•Searching/Creative
 Commons

•Context
•Social media
•Copyright/Fair Use
•Author's rights/Creative
 Commons

Fig. 16.2 Pedagogy and skills of digital storytelling

engaging in opportunities outside the classroom such as study abroad, service learning, and independent research. In addition to working one on one with a faculty member, one of the requirements of the programme is to report out on their experiences through a poster, presentation, blog, or other means. After the programme coordinator of STEP had attended a faculty/staff workshop with the OSU Digital Storytelling Program, the programme worked with her to develop a workshop especially for students. The following STEP stories demonstrate how digital storytelling easily supports affective and metacognitive learning domains.

Filling a Gap in My Confidence

This student tells the story of her formative journey to become a doctor. She recounts the lessons learned from spending two weeks abroad

shadowing internal medicine and surgery doctors and what she discovered about her own interests. Using the framework often taught in digital storytelling workshops, the *context, crisis, change,* and *closure* in this is
evident. The student is seeking real-world experience in medicine because
she is not sure if this is the right career path for her. The change is in the
STEP experience itself during the time she spends in Iringa, Tanzania, and
realizes that surgery fascinates her. The closure is in understanding that
new possibilities have been opened up, and that she needs to continue to
be active in pursuit of a specialty. The emotionally charged language and
visual selections from the "Science Kills" sign to talking about the "peace
of mind" she gained from the experience clearly represent a change in her
attitude as well as reflection on this change in articulating it (OSU Digital
Storytelling 2014b).

City Roots, Country Heart

A double major in environmental policy and agriculture, a Fall 2014 participant tells of her time in Brazil and an eventual internship in Cleveland.
Her views of the country and personal view of herself as a "city girl"
changed after her STEP experience. The pictures and narration juxtapose
urban and agricultural landscapes as she experiences new environments
and begins to develop a passion for farming practices. The change in her
story comes from an innate desire to go beyond seemingly natural divides
between the city and the country as well as when her perceptions of Brazil
change as she continues to study there. The closure comes from how
small-scale farming practices could exist in the city, or as she says "her own
backyard." The initial view of the city and the country as being separated
entities was transformed when she realized that they could be wedded.
This was reflected in the images of crops located in vacant lots around the
city. This student was able to reflect on how her learning abroad and in
a summer job helped change her perspective (OSU Digital Storytelling
2014a).

CASE STUDY OF METALITERACY IN DIGITAL STORIES

In the fall of 2014, a digital storytelling course focused on the Medical
Heritage Center (MHC) at OSU was developed. The MHC is the special
collection of the Health Sciences Library, and contains over 16,000 items
including rare books dating back to 1555 and medical artefacts from the
1800s. Until the course was offered, this unique collection had been the

purview of primarily genealogists and visiting scholars. While other special collections may be used as primary sources to support classroom learning for student research, the MHC and its primary artefacts was used as the focal point for undergraduate engagement in its special collections.

Life in Moments

In the course, each student was asked to select from a curated set of MHC artefacts to research and eventually tell a digital story. They needed to complete broad research around the artefact, determine a specific story that could be told about that artefact based on deeper research, and then connect that story to a personal experience or their own unique experiences. It was an open-ended project in which instructors would help guide the scope of a student's research and try to ensure a cohesive story that embodied the elements of digital storytelling, but ultimately the student had to determine how they would hook their audience and what details to share in order to communicate the larger story (OSU Digital Storytelling 2014c).

The author of *Life in Moments* selected a trephined skull to research. In her story, she explains the theories and myths surrounding the practice of trephination, and she also focuses in on one man's theory and his inability to prove his ideas. The student uses her findings as a jumping-off point for waxing philosophically about identity and the peace she has made about never finding certainty even while she tries to seek out answers in her chosen field as a pre-med student. The story ends as a celebration of life and all the questions it can bring about for someone like her.

One metaliteracy objective is to "use self-reflection to assess one's own learning and knowledge of the learning process." This story explicitly reflects on her research, the sources she explored, and gives them context with additional information she found in other sources:

> though the learning of trephining practices interested me a lot, it wasn't enough. I wanted to know more. So in hopes of finding further information on my anonymous friend, I decided to seek out clues from the other two skulls mentioned in Dr. Bartholemew's letter. These skulls were different though.
>
> [...]
>
> With this newfound thread, I decided to dive further into researching this practice.

Another objective is to "demonstrate the ability to think critically in context and to transfer critical thinking to new learning." By the end, one can infer she has taken what she has learned from this and transferred them to her own understanding of the world

> His case helped me realize that many questions we have in life will go unanswered. And that's okay. I may never know the name, gender, or age of the skulls I research. Just like I will never know why bad things happen in life or why I was put here on this earth. But all I can do is speculate, accept, and be at peace with the uncertainty of life.

Our Family's Pacemaker

A three- to five-minute story is enough to tell a story, but not enough to deliver every piece of information a student might discover in the course of his or her research. For this reason, students were required to give an oral presentation on their research findings alone. This gave students a greater range of flexibility to choose a story of their own without the burden of having to prove that they had a deep understanding of the artefact at the same time. This was the case for a student who examined an old Medtronic pacemaker for his story. While he describes the function and some of the history of this pacemaker, he uses its function as a device to assist the heart as a metaphor for his grandma's role in his family. This relationship is emphasized by the parallel phrasing the student uses when describing both

> Even though they may be small, they are instrumental in the health of those who use them.
> [...]
> Coincidentally, my grandmother is quite the tiny individual, but she plays an instrumental role in my family (OSU Digital Storytelling 2014d).

The story is a very personally revealing one in contrast to *Life in Moments*. One can infer that being able to share this story with classmates as well as on a public platform helps meet another objective: "Demonstrate self-empowerment through interaction and the presentation of ideas; gain the ability to see what transferable, translatable, and teachable (learners are both students and teachers)." The story circle process speaks to this objective as well as the objective to "participate conscientiously in collaborative environments."

It can be seen in both sets of stories how digital storytelling can be assessed according to metaliteracy goals and objectives while also supporting both the affective and the metacognitive domains of learning and that it can be used in any discipline. While the approach and content of each story varied, they each told a reflective narrative that was infused with emotion and honesty that were more than just a dry delivery of information. Being able to do this required a multitude of processes beyond just introspection as well, such as effectively researching artefacts online, discovering assets that adhered to intellectual property laws, and synthesizing all of this information into a coherent product.

Conclusion

So often disciplinary teaching assumes a set of skills around using information that are not articulated. Disciplinary experts absorb information skills in implicit ways through a variety of academic experiences, making it easy to lose sight of the fact that novice learners may not have yet absorbed these skills. Digital storytelling provides a process for uncovering many of these unspoken, unobserved, and yet critical skills for developing the meta-skills needed in our complex information environment. More importantly, it can do so in the most authentic of ways, by incorporating personal reflection and metacognition into the information creation process itself.

Academic libraries have sat between disciplines since their inception, and in a way, have served as untapped grounds for the scholarship of integration. Institutions such as the Ohio State University and Purdue Indiana University offer data management, geographic information system services, and provide collaborative spaces for researchers to work. Metaliteracy serves as yet another common practice that can be adopted into digital storytelling practice no matter the context. Information literacy in itself has its practices within every discipline and understanding how it functions in other fields would seem to be an important outcome when engaging in interdisciplinary work.

The academic library role has always been to facilitate scholarly communication across time and distance. As the information landscape grows increasingly complex, libraries seek ways to not only facilitate the communication, but to help researchers and learners navigate their own role in it. Digital storytelling is an appropriate vehicle for these tasks, similar in its neutrality while providing a pedagogically rich framework. These case studies are only a small sample of the possibilities, but they demonstrate the potential of digital storytelling as something that not only supports content learning, but a growing awareness of process and the time it takes to seek out quality information sources.

References

ACRL. (2000). *Information literacy competency standards for higher education.* Available at: http://www.ala.org/acrl/standards/informationliteracycompetency. Accessed 23 Sept 2015.

ACRL. (2015). *Framework for information literacy.* Available at: http://www.ala.org/acrl/standards/ilframework. Accessed 23 Sept 2015.

Australian and New Zealand Institute For Information Literacy. (2004). *Australian and New Zealand information literacy framework: Principles, standards, and practice.* Available at: http://www.caul.edu.au/content/upload/files/info-literacy/InfoLiteracyFramework.pdf. Accessed 23 Sept 2015.

Baro, E. E. (2011). A survey of information literacy education in library schools in Africa. *Library Review, 60*(3), 202–217. doi:10.1108/00242531111117263.

Bobish, G. (2011). Participation and pedagogy: Connecting the social web to ACRL learning outcomes. *Journal of Academic Librarianship, 37*(1), 54–63.

Boyer, E.L. (1996). *Scholarship reconsidered: Priorities of the professoriate.* Carnegie Foundation for the Advancement of Teaching.

Braxton, J., Luckey, W., & Helland, P. (2002). The scholarship of integration. *ASHE-ERIC Higher Education Report, 29*(2), 45–53.

Daniels, W., Darch, C., & de Jager, K. (2010). The research commons: A new creature in the library? *Performance Measurement and Metrics, 11*(2), 116–130.

Eisenberg, M. B., & Berkowitz, R. E. (n.d.) *The Big 6: Information and technology skills for student success.* Available at: http://big6.com/. Accessed 23 Sept 2015.

ERIAL Project. (2012). Available at: http://www.erialproject.org/. Accessed 23 Sept 2015.

Gergen, K. J. (1999). *An invitation to social construction.* London: Sage.

IFLA. (2015). *Guidelines on assessing information literacy for lifelong learning.* Available at: http://www.ifla.org/publications/guidelines-on-information-literacy-for-lifelong-learning. Accessed 23 Sept 2015.

Knapp, J. (2011). Plugging the 'Whole': Librarians as interdisciplinary facilitators. Social Science Libraries Section, 2011 *International Federation of Library Associations and Institution Conference Proceedings,* p. 142.

Knight Commission. (2009). *Informing communities: Sustaining democracy in the digital age.* Washington, DC: Aspen Institute. Available at: http://www.

knightcomm.org/wp-content/uploads/2010/02/Informing_Communities_Sustaining_Democracy_in_the_Digital_Age.pdf. Accessed 25 Sept 2015.

Lippincott, J. K. (2007). Student content creators: Convergence of literacies. *Educause Review., 42*(6), 16–17.

Mackey, T. P., & Jacobson, T. E. (2011). Reframing information literacy as a metaliteracy. *College & Research Libraries, 72*(1), 62–78.

Mackey, T. P., & Jacobson, T. E. (2014). *Metaliteracy: Reinventing information literacy to empower learners.* Chicago: ALA Neal Schuman.

Metaliteracy. (n.d.). Available at: http://metaliteracy.org/. Accessed 23 Sept 2015.

Oldfather, P., & Dahl, K. (1994). Toward a social constructivist reconceptualization of intrinsic motivation for literacy learning. *Journal of Reading Behavior., 26*(2), 139–158.

OSU Digital Storytelling. (2014a, October 29). *City roots, Country heart.* Available at: https://www.youtube.com/watch?v=N4jS_qWOaj0. Accessed 1 Sept 2015.

OSU Digital Storytelling. (2014b, October 29). *Filling a gap in my confidence.* https://www.youtube.com/watch?v=TrdAywoHhq4. Accessed 1 Sept 2015.

OSU Digital Storytelling. (2014c, December 12). *Life in moments.* Available at: https://www.youtube.com/watch?v=1eEE1-UrdWA. Accessed 1 Sept 2015.

OSU Digital Storytelling. (2014d, December 12). *Our family's pacemaker.* Available at: https://www.youtube.com/watch?v=IWO3tDTHcAw. Accessed 1 Sept 2015.

Piaget, J., & Piaget, J. (1973). *To understand is to invent: The future of education.* New York: Grossman Publishers.

Project Information Literacy. (2015). Available at: http://projectinfolit.org/. Accessed 23 Sept 2015.

Research Commons. (n.d.). Available at: http://www.lib.washington.edu/commons/about/what; https://library.osu.edu/researchcommons/about/; http://library.case.edu/ksl/aboutus/researchcommons/; https://www.lib.ncsu.edu/spaces/faculty-research-commons-hunt; http://www.lib.sfu.ca/about/branches-depts/rc. Accessed 23 Sept 2015.

SCONUL. (1999). *The SCONUL Seven pillars of information literacy core model for higher education.* Available at: http://www.sconul.ac.uk/sites/default/files/documents/coremodel.pdf. Accessed 23 Sept 2015.

Talja, S., Tuominen, K., & Savolainen, R. (2005). "Isms" in information science: Constructivism, collectivism and constructionism. *Journal of Documentation, 61*(1), 79–101.

UNESCO. (2003). *Prague declaration.* Available at: http://www.unesco.org/new/fileadmin/MULTIMEDIA/HQ/CI/CI/pdf/PragueDeclaration.pdf. Accessed 23 Sept 2015.

UNESCO. (2006). *Alexandria proclamation*. Available at: http://portal.unesco. org/ci/en/ev.php-URL_ID=20891&URL_DO=DO_TOPIC&URL_ SECTION=201.html Accessed 23 Sept 2015.
Wijetunge, P., & Alahakoon, U. (2009). Empowering 8: The information literacy model developed in Sri Lanka to underpin changing education paradigms of Sri Lanka. *Sri Lankan Journal of Librarianship and Information Management, 1*(1), 31–41. doi:10.4038/sllim.v1i1.430.

CHAPTER 17

"Now I See": Digital Storytelling for Mediating Interprofessional Collaboration

Grete Jamissen and Mike Moulton

INTRODUCTION

Boyer's Scholarship of Integration is "the attempt to arrange relevant bits of knowledge and insight from different disciplines into broader patterns that reflect the actual interconnectedness of the world" (Boyer 2004 cited in Jacobsen and Jacobsen 2004, p. 51). Scholarship of Integration often demands interdisciplinary collaboration and implies interpretation, "fitting one's own research – or the research of others – into larger intellectual patterns" (Boyer 1990, p. 19). It requires that the critical analysis and review of knowledge be followed by the creative synthesis of views and insights in such a way that what is known speaks to specific topics or issues.

G. Jamissen (✉)
Oslo and Akershus University College of Applied Sciences,
Oslo, Norway
M. Moulton
Norwegian University of Life Sciences,
Ås, Norway

243
G. Jamissen et al. (eds.), *Digital Storytelling in Higher Education*,
Digital Education and Learning, DOI 10.1007/978-3-319-51058-3_17

In this chapter, we describe and discuss the outcome of introducing digital storytelling (DS) as a tool to strengthen collaboration in an interprofessional faculty group from two Norwegian universities, the Norwegian University of Life Sciences and Oslo and Akershus University College of Applied Sciences, involved in developing an interdisciplinary Master of Science program in Public Health. After one year of planning of the Master's program, the authors were engaged, as educational specialists, to design a process of continuous formative evaluation to support the collaboration. Two main steps were taken. We introduced time for reflection as part of the group meetings, and we introduced a DS workshop as an arena for developing and sharing professional understanding. Our hypothesis was that DS, based on the model developed by Center for Digital Storytelling (CDS), now Storycenter (Lambert 2013, p. 53), would give faculty the opportunity to express and share their engagement and scientific understanding. In previous projects, we have found the process and products of DS promising as tools to negotiate professional identities (Jamissen and Skou 2010; Jamissen 2012). We wanted to examine the potential effect of DS as a boundary object to strengthen a mutual understanding of the program being developed and of collaborators' own contributions. The concept boundary object describes both physical objects, like treatment forms following a patient moving between hospital departments, and designed processes to facilitate interprofessional collaboration (Heldal 2010; Star 2010). We therefore consider this a relevant analytic approach to discuss DS as a tool to strengthen an integrative scholarship understood as interprofessional collaboration and knowledge development.

The questions discussed in this chapter are whether it was possible to observe signs of a better understanding of the knowledge contributions of the self and others within the Master's program development process and what role DS may have played as a boundary object in this process.

Boundary Objects and Challenges in Interprofessional Collaboration

In our discussion, we draw on concepts from several theoretical traditions to explore how they contribute to an understanding of DS as a tool to mediate interprofessional collaboration.

Willumsen (2009, p. 21) suggests that the prefix "inter" (in interpro-fessional) can be used when there is a large degree of interaction and inte-gration of ideas and activities between collaboration partners. Partners are engaged in common decisions, which entail an integration of knowledge and skills across disciplines. Together, they create new knowledge, through the synthesis of the contributions of each partner, something partners cannot achieve alone. Almås (2009, p. 163) introduces the concept of interprofessional capability, stressing the ability to adapt to change and generate new knowledge and refers to WHO's discussion of this concept, highlighting the need for "(…) a sense of identity, based on knowledge and insight of what the team is to do, and on a personal commitment by each member to the common goal" (WHO 1988, p. 8). Almås (2009, p. 166) identifies identity as something that evolves through social interac-tion. Similarly, Goffman (e.g., 1971) argues that interaction with others creates and sustains identity.

Casto and Julia (1994, p. 20) refer to Kane (1983), who summarizes several definitions of interprofessional collaboration in three points, com-mon objective, differential professional contributions and a system of com-munication, which correlate well with Boyer's Scholarship of Integration. The authenticity of research in Boyer's view is dependent upon integra-tion, developing connections across disciplines that place knowledge in a broader context (Boyer 1990, p. 18).

Heldal (2010) refers to common tasks or concepts receiving attention from a collaborative group as *boundary objects*. Within collaboration, with participants representing well-defined disciplinary boundaries, boundary objects invite boundary-crossing initiative from the group. The objects become interacting components of the system, and as Hislop (2005) states, they bring about or form relationships. Actors negotiate mean-ing through the objects. Heldal (2010), however, warns that boundary objects, depending upon their nature, can both improve and impede pro-fessional integration. Objects with plasticity, which invite different inter-pretations in different situations, will tend to enhance interprofessional collaboration, while objects rigidly kept within one perspective are likely to hinder such collaboration. Star (2010), reflecting on the origin of the boundary object concept, describes how interpretive flexibility – how dif-ferent groups may have a different use and understanding of the same object – has become the most frequent use of the concept. She emphasizes that a boundary object is not necessarily a physical object and that "what is important for boundary objects is how practices structure, and language emerge, for doing things together" (Star 2010, p. 602). Both Star (1989, 2010) and Akkerman and Bakker (2011) stress that the usefulness or aim of boundary objects does not lie in creating consensus but in *finding productive ways to build a working combination of diversity and unity* (our highlighting).

The question arises whether or not we can consider a digital story or, more precisely, DS, inclusive of the process of constructing the story in a collaborative setting, as a boundary object. Interesting enough, organizations are now exploring the potential of storytelling as a method for knowledge sharing. Sole and Wilson (2002) point out the dichotomy of knowledge forms within organizations, those that are abstracted through classification, calculation and analysis, and those that synthesize through narrative and anecdotal information. Modern organizations have traditionally favored abstracted knowledge forms but are increasingly finding that knowledge conveyed in abstract forms is inadequate. They see stories as a means to synthesize, communicate and share knowledge (Gabriel 2000). From a review of the literature, Sole and Wilson (2002) identified key knowledge-sharing goals for storytelling in an organization: (i) conveying norms and values, (ii) sharing tacit knowledge, (iii) building trust and commitment, (iv) facilitating unlearning and change and (v) generating emotional connection.

REFLECTION AND STORYTELLING IN ORGANIZATIONS

After analyzing stories in organizations, Gabriel (2000) describes how one incident can be reconstructed and recounted in different ways, either as "facts as information" or "facts as experience". In each case, he says, story-work leads to a different "reading" of the incident. "Story-work then involves the discovery of an underlying meaning to the events" Gabriel states (2000, p. 35), and he refers to these discoveries as *poetic interpretations*. In his elaboration of *poetic interpretation*, he states that interpretation is core to story-work in organizations and necessary to understand how events are "infused with meaning" or meaning is discovered in facts. He describes metaphors and other effects used to convey a specific interpretation or meaning, what he calls poetic *tropes* of story-work. We see possible parallels to Heldal's emphasis on the importance of boundary object plasticity and the possibility of adapting different meanings as a mediating factor for interprofessional collaboration (Heldal 2010).

Knowledge sharing through storytelling, however, assumes a cognitive process of negotiation and interpretation for both the individual story-teller and the group or organization in which the storyteller tells his story. Indeed, as Amulya (2004, p. 3) states, "The most powerful "technologies" for examining experience are stories (narrative accounts of experience) and dialogue (building thinking about experience out loud)". This is in line with what John Dewey (e.g. 1997) insightfully pointed out: "We do not learn from experience. (…) we learn from reflecting on experience".

In creating a digital story, the storyteller is both invited and challenged to use a broader means of communication. To understand the learning processes and outcomes of DS, Jamissen and Skou (2010) introduce the concept of poetic reflection characterized by the three dimensions of nar-rativity, creativity and multimodality. We find this relevant also in the con-text of reflection in interprofessional collaboration. As Bruner states, "a good story and a well-formed argument are different natural kinds" (1986, p. 11). Within academia, it is our contention that collaboration sooner adheres to a logical argumentation approach: seeking the truth, explain-ing how things are and analyzing causal relations. This mirrors Sole and Wilson's (2002) point that organizations tend to favor abstracted knowl-edge forms. Stories, on the other hand, add a new and "poetic" dimen-sion. Through the narrative process, attention is focused on meaning and how experiences can be understood and interpreted. Multimodal texts, in addition, involve our visual and auditive senses, and in combination, they affect our emotions (Tønnessen 2012). A large body of research indicates that visual cues, that unlike the abstract character of words, are concrete and help us to better retrieve and remember information. Kouyoumdjian (2012) remarks that these findings make sense considering that our brain is mainly an image processor and not a word processor. Ultimately, the goal is to tap creative energies that emerge in the meeting of different perspectives heightened through multimodal expression and interpreta-tion. In this meeting, new perspectives, relationships and understanding are formed (Csikszentmihalyi 1997; Amulya 2004).

Clark (1994) stresses the importance of explicit training that would enable professionals to understand what he calls the "cognitive maps" and "value maps" of others, and to do so, they must master the skills that allow them to become reflective practitioners, according to the concept devel-oped by Schön (1983). A central task of a reflective practitioner is to seek out connections between thoughts and feelings. As Amulya points out:

By locating when and why we have felt excited or fulfilled by an experience, we gain insight into the conditions that allow our creativity to flourish. Now we can become more purposeful – not just about our learning but about how to work in more creative and sustaining ways. (Amulya 2004, p. 1)

The use of reflection as a tool for understanding and insight focused initially on personal application, where individuals could draw upon contextually related influences such as feelings and emotions and give these a place in the learning process. Reflective practice as a collective endeavor has grown with the acceptance of learning as a social construction. Learners construct their own knowledge within a social context (e.g. Engeström et al. 1999; Wenger 1998). In fact, individual and group reflection can be mutually supportive within the same learning process (Amulya 2004).

THE DIGITAL STORYTELLING WORKSHOP

Our approach was explorative and heuristic with traits of action research (Carr and Kemmis 1986) and reflective practice (Amulya 2004; Boud et al. 2006).

We based our approach on two assumptions. Firstly, to capture the essence of integrative scholarship and to realize a holistic interprofessional program is easier if there is a mutual understanding among involved faculty members for one another's subject areas as well as insight into each member's professional motivations for their involvement. Secondly, to develop this kind of understanding requires room for a reflective process in addition, and parallel, to the discussions focused on program design and content. Enabling this reflective process was at the core of the project's formative evaluation design.

The development process lasted for two years and the team of researchers represented Health Science, Physical Education, Social Geography, Horticulture and Animal Science, initially highly autonomous and weakly integrated disciplines. Thus the team may be understood as a loosely coupled system (Heldal 2010; D'Amour et al. 2005), meeting on irregular intervals and with their primary professional identity in their respective faculties. Specific to this group was their shared ambition to build a foundation for a holistic, interprofessional program where students experience a near seamless integration of disciplines across universities and university departments.

In the reflection sessions, we gave feedback, based on participatory observation, intended to help the group stay aware of and take action according to identified collaboration issues. In the DS workshop, faculty members developed and shared a story about their personal and professional engagement in public health issues. Our approach to DS varied from the CDS model with regard to both process design and the role of the narrator. The actual workshop consisted of three half-day meetings. We chose to limit the demands on the researchers' participation in the actual production of the digital stories to a minimum – without reducing the situations where the participants shared and listened to each other's reflections. To relieve them from the technical production, we employed bachelor students from the University's Media and Communication Program. We also engaged two consultants from Jazzmontør as process leaders.[1]

DATA COLLECTION AND ANALYSIS

The data underpinning this discussion come from three main sources.

(i)   We both followed the entire process as participating observers taking systematic field notes.
(ii) All meetings, including the feedback sessions in the three DS workshop meetings, were audiotaped. These recordings were analyzed to support our field notes.
(iii) Author one interviewed the six participants involved in developing stories in a semi-structured telephone interview that took place after the stories were finished and shared.

This chapter builds mainly on data from the process of producing and sharing digital stories. However, we also utilize observations from project periods before and after story development and production to inform our reflections on possible changes.

Our focus is on how the group communicated and worked together and how content and focus of the discussions developed. In analyzing the data, based on our theoretical underpinnings, we chose to operationalize these issues in the following points and looked for (i) signs of trust, commitment and emotional connection, for example, engaged participation and expressions of disagreement (Sole and Wilson 2002), and (ii) signs that indicate a more in-depth understanding for their own and each other's contributions to the whole (Boyer 1990). Such signs could include participants referring to or using core concepts from each other's subject areas or expressing recognition of the contribution of the others.

In addition, we were looking for referrals to experience with the stories and the storytelling process, and comments on the usefulness of this kind of approach.

OUTCOME AND IMPACT

The most concrete result from the storytelling intervention was the production of six digital stories, now published on the University website as part of the information available to potential students and others interested in the content of the Master's program (Attachment 1). The participants commented on these stories in the interviews.

Communication and Collaboration in the Group

In the group meetings, we observed a change in the level of energy and the degree of participation in the group discussions after the storytelling process and production of the digital stories. We perceived participants as more active and informal in discussions, exhibiting a greater personal engagement. To illustrate this, we have chosen an example related to the story "Healthy Noise". The storyteller was preoccupied with identifying factors that characterize and support human health and well-being, rather than on factors that cause disease. His first draft was a theoretical recount of the salutogenetic perspective on public health as described by Antonovsky (1987). This theory stresses human capacity for mastery, health and well-being as opposed to pathogeneses that emphasize risk factors and causes for disease. Through an active feedback process, he produced his story introducing central principles of Antonovsky's salutogenesis through children's natural play. He replaced academic terms with references to children at play, a real-life activity – in the cosmos of the child – that is enjoyable, meaningful and fundamental for health.

Working with the story changed the way he communicated the concept to his colleagues. This, in turn, made an impact on the other participants. One of them, on listening to the draft story in a story circle process, exclaimed, "Do you really mean this? I totally disagree!" (Participant 1). When interviewed later, the participant in question said that prior to this she did not really know what his work was and that "working with the stories brought forth the diversity in our work. It was very informative". She adds that they still disagree when it comes to the relative meaning of health and illness: "The way I see it you can find something healthy in what is ill and work curatively from there".

Reference and Recognition

In our field notes, we describe how the participants started referring to each other's concepts. *Salutogenesis* and *restorative context* became shared concepts referred to in discussions around course design as well as in the daily organization of the group process as: "we need to find a restorative setting for the group to work in". We also observed a stronger sense of curiosity about fellow participants' contributions. Before the storytelling process, we sensed an uncertainty among the group for how the scientific contributions of certain members fit in. An example is the participant who had just finished her doctorate in therapeutic and prophylactic use of pets. Her story, "Furry Health", made an obvious impression on the group and lead to a strengthening of her position. The group addressed her with more expressed understanding and inclusion. This story tells of a person suffering from depression and angst, links this person's experience with the healing effect of dogs and relates to research findings supporting the importance of pets for psychological well-being.

Epidemiology with an emphasis on geographical information systems was another component that received little attention from the group, and we understood this to be due to a lack of understanding. The epidemiologist chose to tell a story tracing the discovery of the HIV-virus and comparing this to the Spanish disease epidemic in the early 1900s. He clearly defined geographical and spatial elements of public health in the story and this, in effect, placed Epidemiology firmly within the Master's program. Both his personal engagement and the importance of this epidemiological dimension became clear to everybody as he used all the dramaturgic effects of a crime plot to describe the search for the virus.

The Contribution of Digital Stories

We have seen the atmosphere change in the group meetings, participants becoming more active and expressing acknowledgment of the contributions of the others. The participants confirmed this in interviews although they would not attribute the change solely to the DS workshops. Two of the participants confirmed our observations but point to the fact that they had been meeting regularly over a long period and that the time for the first cohort to begin the Master's program was getting close, as important contributions to increased participation.

There were comments in the interviews, however, that support our observations that the DS approach in fact did matter. One says:

> The group process was important, the way we touched on different dimensions in the story (...) There was a lot to learn in the process when we all were unfinished. Through clarification and revisions of the text, I learned something very important: "what is the message, what do you want to communicate?" this was the most important breakthrough for me. (Participant 1)

Another participant commented that working with the story had made her realize how her own professional focus was relevant for public health science.

> I was not sure how my background was relevant, but I agreed to join because there was a good atmosphere in the group, and the field is interesting. Making the story, and working with the students,[2] seeing my contribution through their eyes, made me realize the relevance of my contribution. (Participant 3)

She added that it was challenging to look at herself from a public health perspective:

> It took a while before I felt I could be associated with public health. Now I see that what I am doing has a lot to do with public health, both physically and psychologically. The production of the story was important in this respect. Otherwise, I would not have been provoked to look at my own research from the outside and think about it in other ways. (Participant 3)

The same researcher also attaches importance to the multimodal and narrative approach: "It helps with another dimension, not just the verbal argumentative form (...) that it involves feelings, not just talk". (Participant 3) Other colleagues elaborate: "I definitely understood the other expert contributions. I have seen the stories several times afterwards. It was very useful to listen to the other stories in the process and to contribute to making the message easier for others to understand" (Participant 1). Yet another participant states: "With the stories I experienced the others as experts in a different way. I see them as experts with a strong personal relationship to their area of research. I looked at the stories again and I recognize the persons in the stories" (Participant 2).

The group leader remarks in the closing interview that she has "no doubt that a lot happened in the process (...). It gave us another arena and we know each other better, in general and not particularly professionally". (Participant 4) She also comments that because of the DS process "I experience a better understanding, for instance of participant 2's work. He does not say much in the meetings". (Participant 4)

In spite of this realization, and a realization that "she feels she has learned more", she expresses an uncertainty with respect to time invested compared to other methods they might have used.

DIGITAL STORYTELLING: A PROMISING APPROACH

Our focus is on the potential of DS as a tool for mediating improved understanding and communication. Our postulate is that the creation of room for individual and collective reflection through DS will help improve interprofessional collaboration and be useful with regard to the scholarship of integration.

According to Casto and Julia (1994) and Willumsen (2009), terms like *common objective, differential professional contributions, and a system of communication* are central themes in interprofessional collaboration. Clearly, our group of researchers had a common objective in establishing a Public Health Master's Program, integrating different professional contributions and perspectives. The integration of contributions would depend highly on how well the group could negotiate a system of communication and a common understanding of terminology. We have seen in the comments above that not only did the group represent different academic disciplines; they also had varying personal views on important issues regarding public health. The question then is whether our intervention in general and the DS workshop in particular contributed to a more efficient system of communication and thereby led to a better understanding of each other's contributions.

We find the small comments and the referrals to each other's concepts are important signs of increased trust and shared tacit knowledge, in line with knowledge-sharing goals described by Sole and Wilson (2002). When two researchers, after more than a year of collaboration, through the storytelling process discover they totally disagree on something as fundamental as the relative importance of prophylaxis versus treat-ment or sickness versus health, the alternative approach clearly brought forth knowledge that had previously been uncommunicated. We find the statement "I totally disagree!" quite a strong and direct statement between professionals and an example of what Sole and Wilson (2002) describe as conveying norms and values. Although it may not be cru-cial that they agree, understanding each other's points of view on such important issues and being able to comment on the disagreement so directly influence the ability to build a trustworthy holistic program for the students.

Collectively, many of our observations and registered comments embody a process of identity negotiation and clarification, something that is vital to interprofessional collaboration (Almås 2009). We see identity negotiation on both the individual level and the group level. These efforts to form understanding exemplify how both personal and professional identities develop through social interaction. This is evident, for example, when a participant confides that she first realized the relevance of her own contribution with the help of feedback on her narrative from other par-ticipants. As Boyer points out, connecting one's own expertise to a larger context is vital for scholarly integration (1990, p. 18).

In "Noisy Health", we see an example of how the producer's pro-fessional identity became clearer to the others. Within the story circle's feedback loops of dialogue and interpretation, he transformed the way in which he communicated his scientific passion. This again transformed the way in which the others understood his passion. The digital story, both through the production process and as a product, contributed to a bet-ter understanding of his professional contribution to the Public Health Program. These examples strengthen our belief that the conscious orga-nization of processes for sharing, reflecting and developing knowledge in a collaborative setting will give more focus and transparency, and serve to improve the quality of both individual and collective identity development and disciplinary integration.

Using stories as focal points for individual and collective reflection, interpretation and understanding captures also the intension of Heldal's (2010) boundary objects as mediators of boundary-crossing initia-tives. Particularly, DS embodies the interpretive flexibility of boundary objects stressed by Star (2010, p. 602) and the necessary elasticity or plasticity (Heldal 2010) that allows for, and in fact elicits, different cross boundary interpretations. The *reflective room* established through DS encourages collective learning through a multifaceted flux between the individual and the group and between academic and emotional reflection.

As a boundary object, DS should be perceived as both a process and a product. The role of the boundary object was not, as in the case discussed by Heldal, to create a mediating connection between health professionals in a process of treatment (2010, p. 21) but rather to contribute to increased consciousness and shared knowledge on professional and personal levels between group members. As we have described, the outcome of the DS process was not consensus in the sense of faculty adopting each other's professional understanding or values (Star 1989, 2010; Akkerman and Bakker 2011). Instead, the process served as a catalyst to disclose and expand on diversity and enable a better foundation for building a "working combination of diversity and unity" (Akkerman and Bakker 2011). This, we feel, defines a dynamic boundary object that supports the negotiation of scientific understanding and professional identity, and the expression of personal engagement.

From our observations, the "poetic" qualities found in DS, but often not explicitly targeted in academic and organizational collaboration, appear to have enhanced the facilitation of interpretation. This was particularly evident when researchers presented their final stories. Narratives that were subject to active story circle discussions and interpretations were now given their complete expressions through audio and visual representations. As Tønnessen (2012) points out, the storyteller has the opportunity to build layers of meaning using images, voiceover, music and sound effects. "Whether it becomes a good multimodal story or not depends on our conscious considerations on how these resources best contribute to the whole – and how they interplay with each other" (2012, p. 62). Although media students were instrumental in producing the final stories and story authors were, in a lesser degree, involved with choosing images and sound effects, multimodal features clearly enhanced the message and personal engagement embodied in each story and thereby strengthen the integrative process. We sensed a collective feeling of pride and an emotional connection between colleagues. The digital stories took on the role of program metaphors or what Gabriel (2000) refers to as poetic tropes of story-work, signifying personal engagement and academic diversity within the work group. The stories created an image of a working combination of diversity and unity, similar to what Akkerman and Bakker (2011) stressed as the primary aim of boundary objects.

Through the story circle process, we witnessed a negotiation of both individual and collective professional identities, which we do not believe would have occurred without the introduction of digital stories. The initial uncertainties we sensed with regard to professional roles within the collaboration seemed to be resolved with the presentation of the finished stories. A greater understanding of each other's knowledge and experience prevailed. With the recognition of interprofessional collaboration as an evolving process, this is a good point of departure for the further development of the Master's program, a program that in its form and content represents an example of scholarship of integration in practice.

Concluding Remarks

Based on our previous experiences, we envisioned DS, when understood as both a process and a product, as a potential boundary object for promoting reflection and mediating interprofessional collaboration and a meaningful integration of disciplines. Our belief is strengthened after this project. We must be careful, however, not to claim a definitive causal relationship between DS and improved interprofessional collaboration. Our research design was not rigorous enough to defend such a conclusion. We are convinced, on the other hand, that many of the exchanges referred in this chapter and the understanding embodied in them would not have come forth without the DS intervention. Stories become focal points for individual and collective reflection, and the resulting interpretation and understanding capture the intension of Heldal's (2010) boundary objects as mediators of boundary-crossing initiative. This initiative is stimulated by the inclusion of the "poetic" qualities of DS (Jamissen and Skou 2010) and by encouraging the expression of personal engagement. Within a long-term collaboration such as ours, we hypothesize that the effects of a DS intervention would be more pronounced if the intervention is introduced at the onset of the collaboration. From experience, devoting time to the involvement of participants in the creative or *poetic* process of choosing and implementing images and sounds engages authors and results in an even greater feeling of personal expression and ownership. We find reason, therefore, to continue our exploration of DS as a means of addressing the broad specter of challenges involved in interprofessional teaching and learning.

Notes

1. Oslo University College has developed the DS workshop in cooperation with the company Jazzmontør. See https://jazzmontor.squarespace.com/ Accessed 28 September 2016.
2. Students in this case refers to the students from the bachelor's program in media and communications that were hired to assist the participants in the visualization and technical production of the digital story.

Appendix 1: List of Stories from the Researchers Involved

The stories are all in Norwegian and presented at the University website. The English titles are given by the authors. Two stories have been equipped with English subtitles. All accessed on 28 September 2016.

"Into the learning game", background for and intentions with the pedagogical approach as flexible and based on asynchronous communication over the intranet. https://video.umb.no/player/folkehelse_laringsspillet/sd

"Furry health", the use of pets in therapy and obviating mental health. https://video.umb.no/player/folkehelse_helse_med_pels/sd. with English subtitles: http://film.hioa.no/furry-health

"Text me well", introducing a project where patients with chronic muscle and skeleton issues are being followed up through sms and e-mail. https://video.umb.no/player/folkehelse_tekst_meg_frisk/sd

"Five minutes on the bench", on the influence on our health of restorative surroundings. https://video.umb.no/player/folkehelse_benk/sd

"Health noise", on a salutogenetic perspective on health illustrated by the meaningfulness of children's naturally playful activity. https://video.umb.no/player/folkehelse_helsetoy/sd. with English subtitles: http://film.hioa.no/helsestoy

"The enigmatic disease that became a world epidemic", an epidemiological detective story on the detection of the HIV virus used to exemplify epidemiologic method. https://video.umb.no/player/folkehelse_owe/sd

REFERENCES

Akkerman, S. F., & Bakker, A. (2011). Boundary crossing and boundary objects. *Review of Educational Research, 81*(2), 132–169.

Almås, S. H. (2009). Tverrprofesjonell kapabilitet, sosialisering og helse- og sosialfaglig identitet. In E. Willumsen (Ed.), *Tverrprofesjonelt samarbeid i praksis og utdanning*. Oslo: Universitetsforlaget. Ch. 11.

Amulya, J. (2004). What is reflective practice? Center for Reflective Community Practice: Massachusetts Institute of Technology. Available through: Community Science website. http://www.communityscience.com/images/file/What%20is%20Reflective%20Practice.pdf. Accessed 28 Sept 2016.

Antonovsky, A. (1987). *Unraveling the mystery of health: How people manage stress and stay well*. San Francisco: Jossey-Bass.

Boud, D., Cressey, P., & Docherty, P. (Eds.). (2006). *Productive reflection at work: Learning for changing organizations*. London: Routledge.

Boyer, E. L. (1990). *Scholarship reconsidered: Priorities of the professoriate*. Princeton: Carnegie Foundation for the Advancement of Teaching.

Bruner, J. (1986). *Actual minds, possible worlds*. Cambridge, MA: Harvard University Press.

Carr, W., & Kemmis, S. (1986). *Becoming critical: Education, knowledge, and action research*. London: Falmer Press.

Casto, M. R., & Julia, M. C. (1994). *Interprofessional care and collaborative practice*. Pacific Grove: Brooks/Cole Publ. Comp.

Clark, P. G. (1994). Social, professional and educational values on the interdisciplinary team: Implications from the gerontological and geriatric education. *Educational gerontology, 20*, 35–52.

Csikszentmihalyi, M. (1997). *Finding flow: The psychology of engagement with everyday life*. New York: BasicBooks.

D'Amour, D., Ferrada-Videla, M., San Martin Rodriguez, L., & Beaulieu, D. (2005). The conceptual basis for interprofessional collaboration: Core concepts and theoretical frameworks. *Journal of Interprofessional Care, 19*(Supplement 1), 116–131.

Dewey, J. (1997). *Democracy and education: An introduction to the philosophy of education*. New York: Free Press/Simon and Schuster.

Engeström, Y., Miettinen, R., & Punamäki, R.-L. (Eds.). (1999). *Perspectives on activity theory*. Cambridge: Cambridge University Press.

Gabriel, Y. (2000). *Storytelling in organizations: Facts, fictions and fantasies*. Oxford: Oxford University Press.

Goffman, E. (1971). *The presentation of self in everyday life*. Harmondsworth: Penguin Books.

Heldal, F. (2010). Multidisciplinary collaboration as a loosely coupled system: Integrating and blocking professional boundaries with objects. *Journal of Interprofessional Care, 24*(1), 19–30.

Hislop, D. (2005). *Knowledge management in organisations.* London: Oxford Press.

Jacobsen, D., & Jacobsen, R. H. (2004). *Scholarship and Christian faith. Enlarging the conversation.* New York: Oxford University Press.

Jamissen, G. (2012). Når erfaring blir fortelling. Studenters praksisrefleksjon. In K. H. Haug, G. Jamissen, & C. Ohlmann (Eds.), *Digitalt fortalte historier. Refleksjoner for læring.* Oslo: Cappelen Damm Akademiske. Ch. 6.

Jamissen, G., & Skou, G. (2010). Poetic reflection through digital storytelling – A methodology to foster professional health worker identity in students. *Seminar. net, 6*(2), 177–191.

Kane, R. A. (1983). *Interprofessional teamwork, Manpower monograph* (Vol. 8). Syracuse: Syracuse University School of Social Work.

Kouyoumdjian, H. (2012). Learning through visuals. *Psychology Today.* Available through: Community Science website: https://www.psychologytoday.com/ blog/get-psyched/201207/learning-through-visuals. Accessed 28 Sept 2016.

Lambert, J. (2013). *Digital storytelling: Capturing lives, creating community* (4th ed.). New York: Routledge.

Schön, D. (1983). *The reflective practitioner: How professionals think in action.* New York: Basic Books.

Sole, D., & Wilson, D. G. (2002). Storytelling in organizations: The power and traps of using stories to share knowledge in organizations. *LILA, Harvard Graduate School of Education.*

Star, S. L. (1989). The structure of ill-structured solutions: Boundary objects and heterogeneous distributed problem solving. In L. Gasser & M. Huhns (Eds.), *Distributed artificial intelligence* (pp. 37–54). San Mateo: Morgan Kaufmann Publishers Inc.

Star, S. L. (2010). This is not a boundary object: Reflections on the origin of a concept. *Science, Technology, and Human Values, 35*(5), 601–617.

Tønnessen, E. S. (2012). Digitale fortellinger som multimodal tekst. In K. H. Haug, G. Jamissen, & C. Ohlmann (Eds.), *Digitalt fortalte historier. Refleksjoner for læring.* Oslo: Cappelen Damm Akademiske. Ch. 4.

Wenger, E. (1998). *Communities of practice: Learning, meaning, and identity.* Cambridge: Cambridge University Press.

World Health Organization. (1988). *Learning together to work together for health.* Genève: WHO.

Willumsen, E. (2009). *Tverrprofesjonelt samarbeid i praksis og utdanning.* Oslo: Universitetsforlaget.

CHAPTER 18

Ageing Narratives: Embedding Digital Storytelling Within the Higher Education Curriculum of Health and Social Care with Older People

Tricia Jenkins

INTRODUCTION

In this chapter, I discuss the use of digital storytelling (DS) with older people within the context of the education and training of students in Higher Education who are studying to work with older people in health or social work settings. The application of Boyer's scholarship of integration is well documented in applied subjects such as Health Sciences (e.g., Hofmeyer et al. 2007). I will discuss how the DS process and the stories that are consequently produced are effective tools to stimulate a multi-focal perspective on teaching and learning, and on research. I will illustrate how DS serves integration well through presentation of case study material drawn from the European applied research project Silver Stories,[1] a two-year transnational study that took place between 2013 and 2015, augmented by the discussion of emerging data from my PhD research, which is investigating the evidence of the benefits of DS with older people.

T. Jenkins (✉)
Middlesex University, London, UK

© The Author(s) 2017   261
G. Jamissen et al. (eds.), *Digital Storytelling in Higher Education*,
Digital Education and Learning, DOI 10.1007/978-3-319-51058-3_18

Underpinning this, I discuss the humanistic gerontologists' focus on narrative-based methods as essential means to undertaking research into and learning about ageing and the effectiveness of DS as a tool to achieve this interdisciplinary approach that has been gaining traction within the field of Ageing Studies over the last 30 years or so. I also discuss the power of story-making in relation to issues of identity of older people, of voice, of listening, of being heard and how the integrative qualities of the DS process can help to integrate the perspective of "patients" or "clients" into the training of health and social care professionals, and in their professional practice in the workplace.

The Ageing Agenda

We are all well aware of accelerated population ageing in most advanced democracies. The International Longevity Centre's 2014 report *Europe's Ageing Demography* states that "Europe as a whole must adapt to a new world where it is projected that almost one in three people will be over 65 and more than one in ten will be over the age of 80" (Creighton 2014, p. 3). Rather than seeing this as a success story, though, the persistent narratives that dominate current media discourse focus on the degeneration associated with growing older and "dealing" with the practical problems posed by ageing populations: health, pensions and the cost of care. The language of large-scale disaster dominates the representation of these stories of the "crisis" of ageing, the "demographic time-bomb" and the impending impact of the "silver tsunami". Where are the voices of "older people" in these discourses? Do they tell us anything about the actual process of ageing? How is the experience of ageing articulated in Higher Education curricula designed for those who will become professionals working with older people?

Humanistic Gerontology: The Integration of Medical Science with Social Sciences and Humanities

So, when do we become old? As Anne Karpf points out in *How to Age* (2015, p. 3): "How absurd of us to envisage 40- or 50- or 60 – 100-year-olds as a single cohort – no less ridiculous than conceiving of the ages of 0 to 40 in such a way". Numeric descriptions of age are seen to be necessary in order to create appropriate policy and services and to direct resources via public and private funding agencies' target-group focused agendas. Other definitions include the distinctions between the "young old, the old and the oldest old" (cited by Rooke and Slater 2012, p. 8; Neugarten 1974; Suzman et al. 1992). The third age and fourth age (e.g., Baltes 1998; Laslett 1991) distinguish between the life period of active retirement, which follows the first age of childhood and formal education and the second age of working life, and which precedes the fourth age of dependence, sometimes abbreviated to "active" older people and "frail" older people. The "Life Course" approach to ageing, preferred by the World Health Organization and the think tank on ageing, The International Longevity Centre, encourages discussions of ageing across all aspects of life, at all ages (including financial planning, social well-being and combating negative stereotypes of ageing), not just health (Age UK 2009). Educating people at all ages about the importance of looking to the future and planning for each stage of life is central to the life course approach. However, as Baars (2012, p. 7) points out, there is an underlying assumption in "life course" advocates that supposes that young people and adults are what is termed "prospectively oriented", making plans for the future, whereas it is assumed that older people have "retrospective orientations" "as if they have lived their lives and should keep themselves occupied with memories". This assumption runs deeply in the use of arts-based and therapeutic interventions with older people, hence the dominance of reminiscence as seemingly the only means by which to engage with the elderly.

What is missing in all of these predominantly technical, medical and objective approaches to defining and categorising age that is prevalent in professional gerontology – and in social and policy contexts – is a language that takes account of non-scientific aspects of ageing, the individual experiences of ageing and the social, philosophical and spiritual contexts of those experiences. The scholarship of integration is central in this context, "because it is definitely best equipped to respond to contemporary problems at both an individual and societal level ... moving beyond the disciplinary silos to build interdisciplinary partnerships with capacity to respond to multi-focal, complex human problems" (Hofmeyer et al. 2007, p. 3).

Humanistic gerontology comprises not only interdisciplinary humanities but also human sciences or interpretive social sciences, including anthropology, psychology and sociology, and it prioritises the use of qualitative research methods to re-appropriate "classic humanistic forms of knowing – in particular interpretation, rhetoric and narrative" (Cole et al. 2010, p. 9). The fundamental philosophical question for the humanistic gerontologists was the one that had never been asked: "what does it *mean* to grow old?" (Cole et al. 2010, p. 1).

In his keynote lecture at the 7th International Symposium on Cultural Gerontology, Jan Baars (2012, p. 143) speaks of ageing as being rooted in time, "yet time is usually reduced to chronometric time; a mere measurement that has been *emptied of the narratives that were traditionally part of it*" (my italics). Narrative approaches to research are widely accepted ways in which to provide more expansive and deeper data and the importance of enabling research subjects to foreground their voice in the data capture process is central to many participatory approaches: they enable the articulation and sharing of experiences, emotions and feelings that are not made visible by quantitative methods that prioritise large sample sizes and measurable outcomes. DS focuses on empowering the individual to create and share personal narratives through the process of the Story Circle (with peers and with facilitators) and then through screening of the finished stories with a wider community (family, friends and community), online (if desired by the individual storyteller) and (potentially) within Higher Education or workplace settings as learning materials. This represents not only integration of disciplines and perspectives but also integration of recipients of the data that is gathered and shared through the DS process. It can have the effect of "placing knowledge in a larger context ... illuminating the data in a more meaningful way" (Lindsay and Stroud 2013).

Voice, Listening and Identity

Many DS interventions state that their aim is to "give voice" to those whose voices are not normally heard (Dunford and Jenkins 2015, p. 30). We at DigiTales[2] certainly made such arguments in our case for support of *Extending Creative Practice* (ECP)[3] to the European Commission's Grundtvig funding programme, in which we asserted that by providing older people with the desire to engage with computer technologies and the Internet *and* the skills with which to do so, through DS, we would be giving voice (Dunford and Rooke 2014) to digitally excluded older people. We certainly enabled a large number of "third age" people to use computers for the first time, to create their own personal digital stories and to upload them to social media and the project website. Through the continuation of collaboration with ECP partners in subsequent research projects, we also know that some of those original participants continue to make stories and use Information and Communication Technologies (ICT). We have to ask, though, are the personal micro-narratives produced by older people through DS projects enough to achieve voice amongst the plethora of personal narratives that pervade the Internet through social media?

DS interventions are often one-off, dependent upon the next round of project funding, partly because the practice recognises the importance of facilitation to the process, which is resource-heavy and difficult to fund long term. DS as a "movement" has been consistently criticised for missing the boat in terms of reaching large audiences (Hartley 2008; Hartley and McWilliam 2009). Digital stories do not tend to go viral and sometimes they remain offline, depending on the wishes of the storytellers. Dreher (2012) discusses "voice" as a key indicator in international debates around social inclusion. She applauds participatory media – in particular, DS – as an excellent way in which to provide opportunities for marginalised communities to tell their stories; however, she goes on to argue for greater "political listening" if the promise of voice is to be even partially fulfilled. This echoes Nick Couldry's work on the value of voice, in which he argues that there are many opportunities for voice but not necessarily for listening. "A system that provides formal voice for its citizens, but fails so markedly to listen, exhibits a crisis of political voice" (2010, p. 50). What is the power and possibility provided by "voicing"? Is telling your story automatically transformative – personally and/or publicly? We still ask, what is the potential for the stories to effect change in policy and practice in which older people are centre stage yet generally have no voice in their construction? In this case, as Couldry (2010, p. 146) states, "The issue is what governments *do with voice*, once expressed: are they prepared to change the way they make policy?"

However, as our experience through the research we undertook in both ECP and subsequent studies, notably Silver Stories shows, the impact of DS on individuals should not be underestimated (Shea 2010), and listening to and viewing digital stories as contributors to change may be effective on a range of levels: from the personal (stories providing a means to deeper understanding of individuals by family, friends, neighbours and peers) and by those who have professional caring relationships (for instance, nurses, social workers and therapists). The latter moves such listening into other territories, such as Higher Education and the workplace, as the stories of many individuals that are shared and discussed can influence the ways in which professional practice is developed, simply by presenting perspectives that go beyond the scientific or the medical. As these discussions – and those individuals' digital stories – make their way into research as well as into teaching and learning in Higher Education, then those original voices can become amplified and make an impact on service provision or even policy.

USING DIGITAL STORYTELLING AS AN INTEGRATION TOOL: SILVER STORIES

Background

Silver Stories was an action research partnership spanning nine organisations across six countries between 2013 and 2015. It was funded by the European Commission Lifelong Learning Programme: Transfer of Innovation and built upon the results of our award-winning ECP project, referenced earlier, which ran from 2010 to 2012.

One unexpected finding illuminated by the evaluation report was that: "by uniquely combining storytelling, which uses resources from the past (such as memories, stories, images and photographs) together with digital technology, which is very much of the present, the project has offered older people an opportunity to think about the ways they may wish to narrate their experiences into the future *and* the means of doing so" (Rooke and Slater 2012, p. 21). Following the success of ECP, the partners wanted to continue to promote the use of DS with older people but in a more sustainable way.

An Integrative Partnership

In order to do this, we extended the partnership to bring together Higher Education Institutions providing training to students and existing professionals working with older people in community, education or healthcare settings, with smaller organisations with expertise in DS facilitation with a view to integrating the practice of DS into the curriculum through the designing and testing of modules that could be accredited in Higher Education. By undertaking this project collaboratively, across nations, across disciplines and across institutional conventions and boundaries, we were, in effect, applying Boyer's integrative research, in which we would move or remove "rigid walls of disciplinary paradigm and researcher exclusivity ... allowing for a different light to be shed on areas of interest and concern: a synthesis of experience and understanding, and 'educating nonspecialists'" (Starr-Glass 2011, p. 34) (Table 18.1).

Silver Stories was 75% funded through the European Commission's Lifelong Learning Programme, under the Leonardo da Vinci Transfer of

Table 18.1 Silver Stories integrative partnership

Country	Silver Stories partner	Local partner	Notes
Denmark	Digital Storylab	University of Aalborg	DS facilitator training with healthcare trainees
Finland	Laurea University of Applied Science	Villa Tapiola (home for elderly people with mid-stage dementia) and local Elderly Care Centres	Piloting of modules with social counsellor students
Portugal	Instituto Politécnico de Leiria (IPL)	Alcobaça & Alcobaça Evora Homecare nursing homes, Santo Andre Hospital, São Martinho do Porto Nursing Home	Piloting of modules with nursing and occupational therapy students
Portugal	Media Shots/ Trapézio	As above	DS facilitator training of staff and students at IPL
Romania	The Progress Foundation	National Library Networks	Also working with National University for Political Studies and Administration using DS
Slovenia	Mitra	Alma Mater University	DS with social gerontology students
UK	CUCR, Goldsmiths, University of London	N/A	Evaluators
UK	DigiTales Ltd.	Salvation Army Housing Association (SAHA)	Delivery of workshops in SAHA managed housing schemes for older people in Essex
UK	University of Brighton	SAHA	Project lead and collaboration with digital storytelling workshop delivery (Transfer 3)

Innovation sub-programme. The "transfers" were designed to adapt and transfer learning methods from ECP across the partnership and to two new countries. Whilst the main focus of the activities was within the context of the training of students and professionals in the caring professions with older people, one of the "transfers" was to extend the use of DS with other marginalised groups. This element enabled partners with DS expertise but without experience of working with older people, to share their experience with partners (such as The Progress Foundation in Romania) and in exchange gain insight and experience of DS with older people from those partners with that expertise. In this chapter, however, I will only focus on the "older people" context.

Silver Stories Methodology

The main objective of Silver Stories was to develop and test quality-assured modules to be used in Higher Education institutions in the training or professional development of students or professionals working with older people, both "active" (e.g., within education or community settings) and "frail" (e.g., in residential care homes). The modules were to be developed to test the use of DS as (a) a reflective learning tool for students and (b) as part of their "professional toolkit", to be used with older people as part of their working practice. A facilitation handbook was also produced as a learning resource. The action research elements of Silver Stories were preceded by a period of desk-based research, consisting of a Needs Analysis[4] that would provide an overview of relevant DS interventions from around the world, to inform the design of the modules that were to be piloted. Partners with expertise in DS facilitation provided facilitator training for staff and students within Higher Education institutions in each partner country, who would then use DS with older people in the various settings. Silver Stories culminated in a touring exhibition and a final conference to promote the modules to other institutions.

It is not necessary in this chapter to provide a full account of Silver Stories: the evaluation report, the modules and the facilitation guide can all be downloaded from the website. Instead, I will present a case study that combines the Silver Stories digital stories interventions with my own PhD research, in Portugal, bringing into focus the impact of using DS as a truly integrative approach to teaching and learning and to research.

Case Study: Digital Storytelling at Instituto Politécnico de Leiria, Portugal

Research Methods

DS was introduced to the Department of Health at IPL through the Silver Stories partnership. Lisbon-based Media Shots/Trapézio,[5] a creative communications company inspired by and specialising in DS, provided facilitator training for teachers at IPL, for professionals already working with older people (social workers, nurses and occupational therapists), some of whom were either IPL graduates or Master's students. Facilitator training consisted of running a DS workshop to enable participants to know not only the steps and techniques involved, and some aesthetic considerations, but also to raise awareness of the sensitivities that could be sparked by the process. The one variation on a "standard" DS workshop was that participants were asked to consider making stories relating to age. The Media Shots/Trapézio team brought many years' experience from professional broadcast journalism and documentary film-making, and this is evident through the high aesthetic qualities of the finished stories that emerged from the facilitator training.

Once the facilitator training was complete, new facilitators, supported by Media Shots/Trapézio, ran a DS workshop for active older people, who were students taking part in the IPL 60+ programme,[6] which is designed for students aged 50 and above to access Higher Education, to promote well-being, "contribute to changing attitudes and ideals about the ageing process and reform the role of older people in contemporary society" and "to contribute to the research, development and innovation of gerontology".

Finally, some of these new (student) facilitators piloted DS in their workplaces, at nursing homes in Alcobaça, Alcobaça Evoria and at São Martinho do Porto, supported by the newly trained IPL staff. I also joined the team at the two Alcobaça homes to provide additional support and to gather additional, comparative data for my PhD research through participant observation and interviewing IPL staff and students, and staff at the nursing homes.[7]

Reflections on the Facilitator Training Workshops

The newly trained facilitators described the importance of making their own digital stories before beginning to work with their clients or patients, not only to be familiar with the techniques – both facilitation and technical – but also to understand the impact of sharing personal potentially sensitive or emotional stories with others and committing them to digital media. "We need to do this to understand what we teach We can understand how, when asked to tell your own story, you can feel exposed, so we know that we have to be skilled as facilitators to prevent possible emotional harm", said an associate professor who had undertaken the training at IPL. Facilitators also learnt the power not only of the process but also of the impact of the stories themselves on others. One trainee facilitator's story (in this case, a graduate of IPL) focused on the loss of her grandfather. *Fazes-me falta e eu não sabia*[8] enabled her to share with her mother what they had not discussed. "It did not need any further word … we became more united in that moment regarding the loss of our loved one". Another spoke about needing to go through the process to foresee both the potential of digital storytelling and the difficulties that were likely to present. "We made our stories about a significant person in our lives and many of us chose people who had died: it was a strong and emotional load on us, so we were able to experience how to deal with that". A number of trainee facilitators spoke about their preconceptions, that the workshop would focus mainly on the technical aspect of DS and how the realisation of finding and sharing a story were challenges that they would encounter themselves, when they were to apply their learning to running DS interventions with older people. "I did not focus on the story until I came into the room and we were told you have to write your story and I thought, Oh God, what am I going to do? What do I have to tell?" Others spoke about the process enabling them to develop the empathy that would be needed to support their older storytellers: "If I hadn't built my own story, I would not have the same care, the same love, to help the lady I worked with to tell her own story; I would not have been able to give her the same motivation necessary to go ahead and fight against all the difficulties she had in doing it". Another reflected on learning about the impact of sharing stories with others: "I think it's very important … especially listening to our inner voice. Sometimes we don't know really what we think about something unless we stay very quiet and let the inner voice come out … I think it's very important to look at the others and see the impact in their eyes, in their faces, to see what they think about what we tell, how we tell our story: it's very important to see ourselves in others".

Supported Facilitation: Working with Older Students in IPL's 60+ Programme

Media Shots/Trapézio supported the newly trained facilitators to run a DS workshop with older students who participate in IPL's 60+ programme. The workshop was presented as being a creative way to engage with ICT and an opportunity to produce a personal story. The Story Circle was seen to be the most important element of the process, with the technology as simply the tool by which to create and share; however, it also presented significant challenges, in that the process awakened memories and emotions that were painful in the first instance. One participant made a story of separation from her family as a child, that she had never shared even with her own husband or children until she created her digital story – a family secret finally revealed. Negotiating this painful territory took considerable facilitation skills and underlined the importance of not only expertise in creating stories but also in having sufficient professional experience (clinical or therapeutic in this instance) to support the storyteller to take the brave step to make the story, share it with family *and* upload it to the Internet, without causing harm to the storyteller.

Another 60+ student lives with a degenerative disease and was initially discouraged by her family from participating in the workshop on the grounds that her lack of experience with computers and her medical condition would prevent her from succeeding. However, she was determined to make her story and when it was screened publicly, the family changed their perception of her capabilities and became instead proud of her achievement. The use of DS with 60+ students, then, demonstrated that facilitators can enable their participants not only to use the technology to tell their story but also give them the structure and support they need to do so. Because the stories are drawn from their own lives and the story circle approach is collaborative and co-creative rather than curriculum-led, this moves the intervention beyond providing ICT skills to generating their own self-representations which are consciously constructed with the intent of sharing in public (rather than with only the teacher).

Although the mastering of the technology was seen to be important for this group of students, what was acknowledged, both in the feedback of the students themselves and in interviews with senior staff within the School of Health and the facilitators, was the impact of the story circle process in demonstrating that everyone has a story that is important to tell and to share. The sharing of the stories through one or more events was said to have a very positive impact on well-being and self-esteem. A staff member of the School of Health said: "One student told me that she felt an important person, with her life similar and different from all other lives: she felt that her life was important and that what she has done was important". Although the 60+ students initially experienced some stress particularly with the technology, learning how to put together a multi-modal story was also described as 'positive anxiety' and the challenge was described as a benefit in terms of motivating them to improve and complete their stories before sharing them at public events. In terms of voice and listening, the 60+ students did see the recording and dissemination of their own stories as an important recognition of their lives, their feelings and their achievements. The sharing of the stories at events hosted by IPL shifted perceptions of family and friends, and the group itself felt a greater bond, knowing more about one another, identifying with similar experiences and learning from differences.

Adapted Facilitation: Working with Older People in Residential Care Homes

After the testing of DS with the active older people through IPL 60+ programme, newly trained facilitators who were already working in care homes piloted the use of DS in their respective institutions. I provided some support and attended workshops in two of these. At Alcobaça Homecare, we worked with three participants, each of whom had good cognitive capacity but were unable to construct a written script because of other impairments. In the Story Circle, we did not use games, exercises or explain the "7 steps" approach; instead, we focused on helping the participants to describe an important element of their lives that they wished to tell and to share. They were encouraged to bring photographs or objects to the Story Circle, to help to identify the elements of what they wanted to share. Each participant shared fairly lengthy stories, which were recorded and transcribed. From these transcriptions, the facilitators were able to help participants hone their stories and, through use of agreed prompt questions, construct and record their stories without requiring the participants to read from a script. The stories varied in their form and content, one, for example, focusing on a 25th wedding anniversary party, another on working life in glass-making and a third, made by our oldest participant, a sad but beautifully told story of unrequited love. All of the stories were screened to staff, residents and visiting relatives at the home, and there was a special screening of *Casa Comigo*[9] *(Marry Me)* at our oldest storyteller's 101st birthday party.

At Alcobaça Evora, we worked with four participants who had greater physical and cognitive impairments (advanced multiple sclerosis, dementia and blindness) which required further adaptation of the process to enable them to construct their stories. In both cases, the technical and interpersonal skills and dedication of the facilitators who were also staff at the nursing homes were key to the success of the intervention. Because of the physical and cognitive barriers to full participation in the process, facilitators had to edit audio to produce a coherent story (from the open-question techniques described earlier) and, in the case of working with one participant who was in the advanced stages of dementia, recording short sentences whilst using pictures and music as memory prompts. They would then edit the final stories to present to each participant for their approval prior to a final edit and celebration screening.

Addressing questions of voice and listening within the context of the nursing home setting, though, is possibly even more important. Even though there are greater challenges in incorporating DS in this environment, in which the various schedules and routines are already crowded with nursing and caring tasks, the benefits were seen far to outweigh the problems. One facilitator commented, "When people go to a nursing home, they sometimes feel that they lose their identity – they re-find their identity through digital storytelling". Another observed that "people who work in nursing homes try to work well but sometimes they are disconnected from the person ... they see the list of tasks to do: taking them to the bathroom, helping with meals, doing medication. When those people see the digital stories they value the person more and understand more about the ways in which people act at certain moments". The power of the stories to promote deeper listening within the nursing home environment is hugely beneficial in terms of improving the care of residents, simply through the humanising effect of articulating and sharing personal stories. "They are able to look at themselves again as a person with feelings, with qualities, with expectations, with good moments and bad moments ... it can also help others, [who are watching the stories] to be able to face some difficulties, or grief in their life because they are sharing the same experiences".[10] In the case of using DS with people with chronic illness, it was felt that placing importance on the personal stories, showing an interest in them, was hugely beneficial in terms of attending to the person rather than to the illness. As one of the facilitators described, "We were not talking about oxygen, or wheelchairs, or incapacity or disability ... They need to share everything .... So it was important for them because we were telling them that we are here for you – we are interested in **you**".

Although most of the participants chose to tell a story from their past, one of the residents at Alcobaça Evora was very clear that he wanted to make a story about how the poor state of the roads makes it impossible for him to use his mobility vehicle to do the everyday things he needs to do and maintain some level of independence. At the time of writing, he was planning to take his finished story to show to the head of the local authority; he fully understood the potential of his story to effect change at a local political level. It is evident from this work in Portugal that participants felt that they had been able to 'voice' something of themselves and that they were being listened to within the context of their peers, families and professional carers.

Visible Voices?

Stories made across the partnership are all available on the   Silver Stories website, and many have also been shown at the final international Silver Stories conference at IPL in 2015, and they have been screened at academic conferences in Brighton, Northampton, in the USA and Romania, to name a few. They also featured in a very successful Silver Stories festival in Maribor, Slovenia and a touring exhibition around Europe.

Across the Silver Stories partnership, as recorded by the Silver Stories evaluation, "there is good evidence of positive change in self-perception by older participants and their families ... partners are finding innovative ways of reaching mainstream audiences and academic modes of dissemination... that will help to contribute to addressing fixed perceptions of older people...[who are] being given new platforms for communicating directly with wider audiences" (Levy et al. 2015, p. 20). Getting the voices of older people listened to beyond the audiences generated by specific project dissemination activities, though, remains problematic: if you don't know about the project, you can't find the stories.

Some Conclusions

The take-up of DS in Higher Education, specifically in this field of training people who will be working with older people, is an important step forward to a more sustainable practice. At IPL, one new facilitator, who worked with the 60+ students, will be focusing on DS for her Master's research. There is a growing number of practitioners and researchers who have completed or are currently in the process of PhD research into DS. DS is clearly gaining traction within Higher Education research communities and collaborations between community-based practitioners and universities are also increasingly prevalent (Dunford and Jenkins and Jenkins 2017 forthcoming). Embedding DS into the health and social care curriculum within Higher Education is an embodiment of Boyer's scholarship of integration. The process of story-making together as a student group, whilst undertaking facilitator training, enables each student to reflect on their own practice as caring professionals; using DS in the field (whether as placement activity or in the workplace) enables clients or patients to be seen as more than a series of symptoms; the sharing of older people's digital stories with wider audiences rebuilds identity and, in so doing, contributes to well-being. The use of digital stories created with older people as teaching resources also integrate the personal and experiential with the medical/scientific/professional.

Whilst there are debates to be had about the potential impact of 'institutionalising' DS as a practice within academia, and the value of the continuation and development of digital storytelling through distinct projects, large and small (although the influence of the commissioning or funding agency could also be seen to be a kind of institutionalisation), the continuity afforded by the resources available within higher education (both in terms of teaching facilitation skills and drawing on research council resources) could be an answer to the development not only of voice but also of listening to the stories of older people in order to place them centre stage in terms of policy, service provision and, perhaps most importantly of all, to provide the diversity of representations of age and ageing that is so necessary to challenging perceptions of old age.

Notes

1. http://arts.brighton.ac.uk/projects/silver-stories/silver-stories-home

2. www.digi-tales.org.uk
3. www.extendingcreativepractice.eu
4. Available at: http://arts.brighton.ac.uk/projects/silver-stories/about-silver-stories
5. http://mediashots.org
6. http://60mais.ipleiria.pt/
7. Interviews took place at IPL, Alcobaça and Alcobaça Evora between June and August 2015.
8. Available at https://vimeo.com/102936597 (copy the link into search bar).
9. Available at https://vimeo.com/129659891 (copy the link into search bar).
10. Observation by IPL teaching staff following the pilot in the nursing homes.

Acknowledgement The author would like to thank the team at Instituto Politécnico de Leiria for their wonderful support during May–August 2015, especially Maria dos Anjos Coelho Rodrigues Dixe, whose help, insight and kindness made it all possible.

REFERENCES

Age UK. (2009). Unequal ageing, briefing 5: Identity. http://www.ageuk.org.uk/documents/en-gb/for-professionals/equality-and-human-rights/id8118_unequal_ageing_briefing_5_identity_2009_pro.pdf?dtrk=true. Accessed 22 Mar 2015.

Baars, J. (2012). Critical turns of ageing, narrative and time. *International Journal of Ageing and Later Life, 7*(2), 143–165.

Baltes, M. M. (1998). The psychology of the oldest old: The Fourth Age. *Current Opinion in Psychiatry, 11*, 411–415.

Cole, T. R., Ray, R. E., & Kastenbaum, R. (2010). *A guide to humanistic studies in aging* (3rd ed.). Baltimore: The John Hopkins University Press.

Couldry, N. (2010). *Why voice matters. Culture and politics after neoliberalism.* London: Sage.

Creighton, H. (2014). *Europe's ageing demography*. ILC UK. http://www.ilcuk.org.uk/index.php/publications/publication_details/europes_ageing_demography. Accessed 2 Feb 2016.

Dreher, T. (2012). A partial promise of voice: Digital storytelling and the limit of listening. *Media International Australia Incorporating Culture and Policy: Quarterly Journal of Media Research and Resources, 142*, 157–166.

Dunford, M., & Jenkins, T. (2015). Understanding the media literacy of digital storytelling. *Media Education Research Journal, 5*(2), 26–41.

Dunford, M., & Jenkins, T. (2017 forthcoming). *Digital storytelling form and content: Telling tales.* London: Palgrave Macmillan.

Dunford, M., & Rooke, A. (2014). Extending creative practice. In C. Gregori-Signes & B. Corachán (Eds.), *Appraising digital storytelling across educational contexts* (pp. 205–221). Valencia: University of Valencia.

Hartley, J. (2008). Problems of expertise and scalability in self made media. In K. Lundby (Ed.), *Digital storytelling, mediatized stories: Self representations in new media* (pp. 197–212). New York: Peter Lang Publishing.

Hartley, J., & McWilliam, K. (2009). *Digital storytelling around the world.* Chichester: Wiley.

Hofmeyer, A., Newton, M., & Scott, C. (2007). Valuing the scholarship of integration and the scholarship of application in the academy for health and science scholars: Recommended methods. *Health Research Policy and Systems, 5*: 5. doi 10.1186/1478-4505-5-5.

Karpf, A. (2015). *How to age.* London: Macmillan.

Laslett, P. (1991). *A fresh map of life: The emergence of the third age.* Cambridge, MA: Harvard University Press. Both cited in Extending Creative Practice Evaluation Report (May 2012), p. 8. www.extendingcreativepractice.eu

Levy, C., Rooke, A., & Slater, I. (2015). Silver stories evaluation report. CUCR Goldsmiths. http://arts.brighton.ac.uk/__data/assets/pdf_file/0008/196316/SILVER-STORIES-FINAL-REPORT-shortversion.compressed.compressed.pdf. Accessed 2 Feb 2016.

Lindsay, N., & Stroud, D. (2013). *The broad horizons of scholarship: Applying Boyer's model.* PowerPoint presentation, slide 15. http://www.umkc.edu/umkc-search/?cx=008281657408603500330%3Avpif2cmpa14&cof=FORID%3A10&ie=UTF-8&q=Boyer. Accessed 31 Oct 2016.

Neugarten, B. L. (1974). Age groups in American society and the rise of the young-old. *Annals of the American Academy of Politics and Social Sciences, 415,* 187–198.

Rooke, A., & Slater, I. (2012). Extending creative practice final evaluation report. CUCR Goldsmiths. http://www.gold.ac.uk/media/magrated/media/goldsmiths/departments/researchcentres/centreforurbanandcommunityresearch-cucr/pdf/Extending-Creative-Practice-Evaluation-Report.pdf. Accessed 2 Feb 2016.

Shea, M. (2010). An exploration of personal experiences of taking part in a digital storytelling project. In *Psychology.* Sheffield: Sheffield Hallam. MSc.

Starr-Glass, D. (2011). Boyer's reconsideration: Connections, transformations and the scholarship of integration. *Boyer Revisited, 1*(3), 34–38.

Suzman, R. M., Willis, D. P., & Manton, K. G. (Eds.). (1992). *The oldest old.* New York: Oxford University Press.

CHAPTER 19

The Scholarship of Integration and Digital Storytelling as "Bildung" in Higher Education

Yngve Nordkvelle, Yvonne Fritze, and Geir Haugsbakk

INTRODUCTION

John Dewey, at the age of 70, in a talk given for a newsreel, stated that: *But going to college is not the same as getting an education; although the two are often confused.*[1] Over the years, we have drawn attention to Dewey's remark to illustrate that the problem of going to school is not one merely of gaining access to education but of becoming engaged in, and enthused by, what the opportunity to learn contains. While for obvious reasons digital storytelling (DS) is an entirely modern phenomenon in higher education, its elements are, singly, well rooted in its history. DS fits well the "Scholarship of Integration" especially when we consider the importance of using all our senses on the path to wisdom. In this chapter, we explore the roles DS plays in study programmes—from a simple boot camp stand-alone element to becoming the central piece of a "signature pedagogy" for the entire institution. We will position DS as a didactic method, with the potential to play a vital role in the formation of the future generation of

Y. Nordkvelle (✉) • Y. Fritze • G. Haugsbakk
Inland Norway University of Applied Sciences, Lillehammer, Norway

© The Author(s) 2017
G. Jamissen et al. (eds.), *Digital Storytelling in Higher Education,*
Digital Education and Learning, DOI 10.1007/978-3-319-51058-3_19

279

higher education students. The gap between being a method and being a principle for a liberal education programme or, in a continental European tradition—the ideas of "Bildung"—is vast, and the need to showcase it—both in theoretical and practical terms—has never been greater.

The US filmmaker James Cameron referred to his endeavours in the movie *Avatar* as an experience of "digital storytelling", and in the film industry, the term is most often associated with special effects produced with visual digital means (McClean 2007). A daring parallel would be to consider how close to the ordinary life of film-making—and higher education—digital storytelling can move. While increasing attention is being paid to "special effects studies" in audiovisual training (film and TV schools and multimedia production), it is worthwhile considering what position working with DS might gain in higher education at large. Will conventional professional and disciplinary studies be receptive to audiovisual expressions of teaching and learning?

THE SEPARATED AND THE INTEGRATED

When we relate these matters to the Scholarship of Integration, the question of how the "scholarship of separation" evolved is implicitly addressed. All the reasons that brought about and made the separation between topics and ideas throughout the history of higher education should be taken into consideration. In the medieval university, no more than the seven arts were taught—Grammar, Rhetoric, Logic, Arithmetic, Geometry, Music and Astronomy. Western university curricula grew out of these academic disciplines. However, the need for skills that were useful outside of the learned societies gradually won ground. This change is exemplified in the art of handwriting and the composition of texts. The need for this "new" skill was articulated by the merchant class of Genoa to the university as a potentially useful and commercially viable qualification. "Ars Dictaminis" (the art of writing) was an important stage in the renewal of the humanistic curriculum of the reforms in the coming years. The "doxa" of higher education changed as merchants, military, urban classes, lawyers, "curiales" and doctors sought an arena for developing relevant knowledge, whether in universities, academies or monasteries.

The inherent divisions of forms of knowledge in Ancient philosophy, such as those espoused by Aristotle, between episteme, phronesis and techne, or between theoria and praxis, are still challenging for the academic world. This complexity was compounded by René

Descartes, who added the puzzle about the division between mind and body. The religious beliefs and ideas about what constitute trustworthy knowledge became a key to understanding how images and texts could provide evidence in different ways. This was a battle where "the audio-visual" lost.

In recent decades, there have been a number of initiatives put forward to curb the tendency to create new specialties and divisions in academic subjects. Initiatives to promote interdisciplinary and integrative studies are now commonplace but seldom effective. In order to solve the problems caused by an accumulated complexity in society, we tend to solve this with yet more complexity!

The problem in higher education concerns the exponential growth of new research areas that constantly spawns vast amounts of new knowledge, which will either renew older curricula or prompt new areas of studies. This may be seen as a mishmash of modules and ideologies jostling for attention, mushrooming from an intense competition and quest for new knowledge. Such a tendency is exemplified by University College London, which offers 61 Master's programmes of Education.[2] However, programmes for teaching can never truly reflect a research field. In any given research area, there are conflicting paradigms, conceptions and interpretations that constitute its borders and limits (Mulkay 1979). When the specialists of a given academic area meet and try to draw up or revise a study programme, the modules compete for space and time in the curriculum, so the professors negotiate and make compromises. When the students arrive, they are faced with an amalgamation of the various representations of how the senior stakeholders in the academic community view their field of study and research. First-year students often find themselves confronted with a confusing curriculum—and gradually have to accept its premises. If not, the students reject and start anew in a different area. If they persist and complete the course of study, they become immersed in the many aspects and peculiarities of the subject until they reach a level as a Bachelor, a Master or as a Doctor of Philosophy. If they still "feel" like being a "geographer", a "sociologist" or a "dietician" after completing their training, they will probably have a great sense of "integrated identity" of being at the core of their subject, even if they accept the variety of sub-disciplines.

An overview of degrees in the USA showed that academic subjects are losing ground to professional degrees. The latter increased from 7000 in 1970 to 36,000 in 2005. These degrees comprise of different subjects, the aim of which is to train students for an existing profession. In Europe, for a three year BA programme, a typical nursing school will provide practical training in about half the time. However, the real challenge of such programmes is to integrate insights from the various disciplines into a single body of knowledge, skills and ethically founded dispositions for action.

INTEGRATION THROUGH TEACHING

Barnett et al. (2001) investigated a large number of programmes for undergraduate education and found them to be poorly written and presented. These programmes generally portrayed fierce competition for attention and representation in the group, having devised the programme. There was relatively little focus on what students might expect to find regarding preconceptions, experience and hopes for their future or how they were meant to progress during the programmes. What students would find most challenging in understanding a cohesive and meaningful integration of modules, courses, units, whatever the names or nomenclature, was having to assemble the teaching and learning elements themselves.

In a European tradition, the art of planning a curriculum is called "didactics"—or in German "die Lehrkunst"—the art of teaching (Nordkvelle 2003). While nearly all teachers in primary and secondary education are familiar with, and incorporate insights from, the art of teaching when planning and performing their teaching, higher education has paid only limited attention to training their teachers for their professional activities as teachers.

Didactics implies that the teacher or teachers plan their activities after taking a large number of contexts into consideration. They decide on the aim for the lesson, establish what students know from previous studies, consider the content, the appropriate types of learning activities, the material conditions for the teaching and how are they going to assess the learning the students are embarking upon. They do this by considering each lesson as part of a module, semester or programme, and in line with the ideas or values of the institution or higher education policy (Handal 1984).

Planning a session on DS where the expected learning outcome for 19-year-old first-year students is to understand, for instance, the social origin and context of DS will require a different content, working method and assessment than for a session about DS for an extension programme for mature students. In a media education programme, importance of linking DS to understanding media in society demands a certain degree of theoretical input, such as teaching about DS and how media affects student's lives. A quick workshop for an extension course will require teaching *with* DS.

Three aspects are crucial to an understanding of the versatility and complexity of DS: (a) how it can help us understand the ways media affect people, (b) how Digital Stories demonstrate the ways we can help students learn about media and last (c) how learning DS can be used to teach and learn about other matters.

If we reduce the complexity of a system like teaching a class or a seminar, we may reduce them to six factors: aims, frame factors, content, assessment, learning activities and students.

But then we need to increase the complexity again when we set these factors up in an ecological model, where all factors are connected to each other (Fig. 19.1).

This figure demonstrates how the elements of a didactical planning scenario are connected (Bjørndal and Lieberg 1978). Any given corner of the "diamond" holds a place for a selected element that is worthwhile considering. Changing any values in a corner affects decisions about the other elements. The interactive nature of relations between the elements are

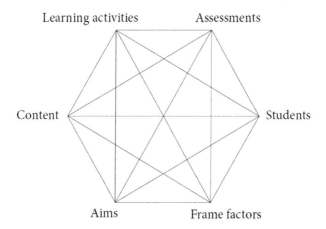

Fig. 19.1 Model of didactical relations

clearly displayed. Some versions add more elements, while others operate with fewer. Copeland and Miskelly (2010) give an interesting account of how these variable factors alter a single course on DS in profound ways.

In the Anglo-American literature, a simpler model designed by Biggs has focused largely on the process of joining up the dots between types of evaluation, presentation of content and the learner's involvement, or what Biggs has called Constructive Alignment (1996). What unites these models is their focus on the process teachers go through when designing a learning environment and on how successful this design is for making students active in constructing their personal and enriched meaning of a subject. Both approaches emphasize that in higher education the outline of the assessment method is the strongest single element influencing how students go about learning their subject. If the teacher's aim is to ensure students learn several new concepts, quickly and efficiently, simply, the content and learning activities need to be selected accordingly. A fair assessment should then measure what has been taught: several concepts learnt swiftly and with limited emphasis on practice. This promotes a learning style that provides students with shallow knowledge.

DIGITAL STORYTELLING AS A DEEP APPROACH

Teaching and learning in higher education is about (both) getting into stuff quickly and defining beginnings and ends, open and closed fields and opportunities and problems, as much as it is about encouraging deep reflection, critical appraisal and innovative and creative thinking. The point is how the ability to detect valuable knowledge as it first appears as "surface" transforms to a desire to study seriously until deeper levels of understanding are attained. The process of assimilating new information and then possessing it as integrated knowledge has been called, inter alia, a "construction of knowledge". The quality of learning increases with every inch of movement of acquired knowledge from the "surface" or atomistic level towards being elaborated and processed to a deep or "holistic level" (Pettersen 2005; Biggs 1996).

Marton et al. (1993) have described this as a process where students initially think studying is a matter of "filling my head". Then comes a phase when they replace it with "swotting for exams and reproducing it", and then, "turning it around and making use of it in other ways", "finding out lots of ways of thinking about things", "opening your mind for new perspectives"—and finally "changing yourself as a person". This ladder of increasing value for the person finds confirmation in many other realms of learning theory, such as Bloom's taxonomy.

Integration of knowledge has at least two meanings. One is the personal learning trajectory from the beginning to end of a degree and the question of how the personal and public meanings, for example, what the programme intended to convey, has been processed. The second meaning is how the programme has managed to teach in such a way as to promote the integration of knowledge in the person, so that the student, as Dewey put it, has not simply attended a college but also got an education.

The potential role of DS in promoting integration rests on several premises. First and foremost, it values *the personal* as a point of departure for any learner's trajectory. Further, it entertains the various steps from an alienated perspective on new information towards a personally interpreted version of public knowledge. It is not a matter of "filling my head" but rather of finding out "what do I have in my mind, and how can I explore it further?" The second is the value DS places on *the narrative*. Having to present a story means that all the mechanisms of trying to understand the spectator, and how she or he might interpret and understand the message, are inculcated in the mental processes of the producer. The third is how the presentation appeals to *several senses* and how the emotions are stimulated by the engagement of sound, voice and images as well as texts. The fourth is how storytelling requires the engagement of skills as well as a physical dimension *engagement* and, last, how it rests on the contribution of a group to develop and validate knowledge and the representation, that is, *the collaborative*.

The importance of creating a culture for teaching and learning that encourages the personal voice, the audiovisual and emotional aspects will be highlighted in the next section. Making knowledge "personal" implies that the learner needs to connect emotions, experiences and values to information. As the French philosopher Merleau-Ponty wrote, "All my knowledge of the world, even my scientific knowledge, is gained from my particular point of view, or from some experience of the world without which the symbols of science would be meaningless" (Quoted from Friesen 2012, pp. 40–41). Most students experience higher education as a place where "the personal" is jettisoned, where they are told to read and adjust to the world of knowledge and ignore the self. Merleau-Ponty addressed the need to "…. [reawaken] the basic experience of the world of which the science is the second-order expression" and thereby connect the learner's "I" to the intersubjectivity of "we".

DS has claimed that it is a method with great benefits for "joining up the dots", in other words, how it enables students to transform the epistemic and accumulated storage of knowledge into wisdom—or integration. In adult education, this is often referred to as "transformative learning", of which adult educators like Jack Mezirow, Oskar Negt and Paolo Freire in particular were exponents for (Illeris 2014). Since teachers in higher education appear to be very dependent on being in control, it is hard for them to assimilate this insight. Leaving so much up to students, and using narratives and images, puts many enthusiastic teachers to the test.

"The narrative is everywhere" is a much used quotation from Richardson (2000). In recent decades, the ability to create narratives has come to be seen as a fundamental feature of our mind. Jerome Bruner has claimed that memory depends on the ability to organize happenings in the form of narratives (1991, p. 4). Narrative has been described as a form of everyday theorizing (van Manen 1994). In keeping with empirical studies, many theorists have described how methods such as "learning journals", learning partners, learning contracts and self-assessment schedules are used to promote reflection in professional study. "Learning exchange" is described as the most powerful method to encourage reflection and learning from peers (Boud et al. 1985; Sampson and Cohen 2001). Learning from peers is a strong source for learning. The personal narrative is fundamental in presenting cases or problem-focused tasks. Teachers who tell stories, both in the immediate sense, for example, for each class and in the way that they are also able to link them together for the entire duration of a course or term, are generally deemed to be first-class teachers (Egan 1989). Narratives are prerequisites for integration of ideas and therefore crucial for the Scholarship of Integration.

Learning which involves several senses is often termed learning via multimodalities. Educational psychologists argue convincingly that the human mind provides a complex set of intelligences, with different abilities to absorb, organize and store impressions, information and knowledge. Theorists of learning styles advocate that different ways of working with learning material will support more learners in diverse ways and facilitate the learning process for a greater number of learners. Kress and Leuwen's (2001) theory of the importance of acknowledging the many modes of perception and orientation and, the various interplays of sound, images, film, texts with its shifting formats has contributed to our understanding of how complex the media have become, as well as the importance of mastering more formats. It has been argued that this change has already taken place. The term "visual turn" indicates that communication in higher education depends on visual expressions to a far greater extent today than in the past, but the battle between images and text is by no means over (Fritze et al. 2016). However, this "turn" calls for more programmes and content that rely in equal measure on the "sayable" and the "seeable".

The case for engaged and collaborative teaching and learning as a key dimension of DS has been made by numerous educational psychologists and learning theorists. A common feature is that telling stories for critical friends leads to more reflection than interaction with staff or by written assignments handed in (Boud and Knights 1996, p. 25). The combined efforts of telling and showing have in many instances shown that self-awareness increases, sensitivity to the environment improves and conceptual perspectives are more prone to change. Critical thinking skills and confidence in a student's own knowledge are more likely to develop through engaged and collaborative processes (Lam et al. 2007).

WHEN THE NARRATIVE IS VISUAL AND AUDITIVE

Liz Anderson and Dan Kinnear describe how sceptical male medical students were when they embarked on a DS workshop. However, their comments after the experience were revealing: "Medical students who don't want to do this should be made to do it as they are probably the ones who it would have greatest effect on. It certainly has on us". These students reported that making a Digital story provided the students with unique experiences to reflect on stories and those of their fellow students: "cathartic and emotional" (2014, p. 118). Kaare and Lundby have argued that a high-quality workshop will potentially produce a connection between "... the authentic "I"—the reflexive "I" who connects its life and its narratives to a community and collective values which give meaning to the life of the individual" (2008, pp. 119–120). Composing a message for broadcasting, even for a small group of classmates, generates higher-order thinking skills.

Media theorists have argued forcefully that most students already make extensive use of media technology for consumption, while an increasing number of students produce media content themselves: from simple social media contributions to webpages, blogs and newsletters for personal or community purposes. Visual and auditive media has therefore gained a lot more interest in the academic community. First and foremost, they claim that we, both students and teachers, are in the state of becoming "mediatized" (Hjarvard 2009). Since, today, people can communicate across time and space, thereby replacing many actions which previously were conducted face to face with virtual activities on electronic media, and that these activities invade our daily activities, we have come to realize that new media set new parameters for what is said, done, felt and communicated. All this is what we mean by "mediatized".

CURRICULUM CONSTRUCTION AND THE "METHOD" OF DIGITAL STORYTELLING

We often take it for granted that students already possess a basic competence in elementary use of digital media. In our programme for general education, a student will encounter one assignment in year one for a digitized presentation of a particular instruction. In year three, they will learn the formal structure and intention of a digital story as an assignment for a module of media education. During the Master's programme they will produce a digital story as an assignment for a module on "Globalization and upbringing". Those who aim to complete a PhD will learn to apply digital stories for the purposes of research dissemination.

In film school, the making of a three-minute film containing a voice-over, a series of still photos or movies, music or other sounds will be the typical format of the introductory genre any student will need to master. A TV- student will learn to expand a three-minute piece into a documentary for the duration of 25 minutes. This is what the students hand in as their final assignment after three years of study, and graduation will allow them into a labour market for film and TV production.

In a continental European context, DS in accordance with the Center for Digital Storytelling-model will be presented as a "method" for teaching and learning. The method does not change substantially whether it is applied to fit a 10-year old pupil, an elderly person or an academic. Any method used may be a recurring element in the curriculum or a vital or structural element of the programme, such as the term "signature pedagogy", as discussed by Shulman (2005). The influence the method has on the curriculum is decisive for the effects it may have on the bigger picture. In keeping with "constructive alignment", the most important and obvious factor is that it counts towards the standard assessment of the course or programme. According to this principle, if you train a student to learn a skill or knowledge, you must assess how it is learnt and how far the student has mastered it. The challenge for many enthusiasts of DS in higher education is that it risks being presented by teachers as an interesting alternative or exploits the opportunity to come up with a new and exciting activity, but fails to understand, or tries its potential in a more holistic sense.

The chief didactical idea of a given curriculum has an impact on the whole professional training. Most programmes employ a variety of methods for different modules yet can still be said to have elements in common. Over the years, many medical schools and nursing programmes, as well as other programmes in the health professions, have adjusted to a "problem based curriculum". In many countries, law education is associated with "case studies" while musical education is often equated with a "conservatoire" model. We are a long way from seeing the successful implementation of DS in mainstream disciplinary or professional fields in similar ways.

To return to film and TV studies: the growing influence of visual effects and of recounting telling stories via digital tools, which are becoming even more affordable, will have a profound impact on training students for the media profession. Newly enrolled students possess personal equipment that, in some instances, is more advanced than the industry standards were five years ago (Fritze and Nordkvelle 2015). The changes that the authors of this book seek are unlikely to be straightforward. Neither will these be directly linked with the technological development of digital technologies, but there will be similar tendencies. Let us explore some of the arguments for a yet deeper change—changes that would ultimately take the way we teach and learn with digital means from the margins to the centre of our activities. This will be a move from a "method" to a "pedagogy", from an activity supported by enthusiasts to a "signature pedagogy" as defined by Lee Shulman. As he specifies, "the types of teaching that organize the fundamental ways in which future practitioners are educated for their new professions" (Shulman 2005, p. 52). Another way of expressing the change in a discipline has been expressed by Gurung, Chick and Haynie. Likewise, they ask, "What does our pedagogy reveal, intentionally or otherwise, about the habits of head, hand, and heart as we purport to foster through our disciplines?" (2009, p. xii). So, why do we think DS will play such an important role?

THE EXISTENTIAL MEANING OF EDUCATION

The Scholarship of Integration was a theoretical construct based on a broad empirical investigation. Its philosophical reasoning is quite implicit and aimed at a diverse group of readers. Philosophy of higher education, however, draws more direct links to its roots in continental philosophy.

Ronald Barnett, one of the most influential British exponents for the field, has written about the context of present-day higher education, which he describes as "supercomplex":

> The key problem of supercomplexity is not one of knowledge; it is one of being. Accordingly, we have to displace knowledge from the core of our pedagogies. The student's being has to take centre stage. Feeling uncertainty, responding to uncertainty, gaining confidence to insert oneself amid the numerous counter-claims to which one is exposed, engaging with the enemy, and developing resilience and courage: these are matters of being. Their acquisition calls for a revolution in the pedagogical relationships within a university. (Barnett 2000, pp. 170–171)

Here he addresses the long-standing discussion concerning the relationship between knowledge in higher education and an individuals' learning and understanding of the knowledge offered. In continental educational theory, this discussion goes back to the German philosopher Immanuel Kant (1724–1804), who asked the same fundamental question in his essay published in 1784, "What is enlightenment?" Obviously, the pile of books, the lectures, lab experiments, fieldworks and practice sessions and simulations students encounter during any course of study are symbols of typical traditions with which one must be familiar before embarking upon a life in the profession and discipline. Undoubtedly, compelling without a doubt the job of coercing students to adapt to, and accommodate, this knowledge has been the most important aspect for teachers in higher education as well as for the institutions they serve. Kant's criticism of this position was similar to that of Barnett, an argument for addressing the individual and personal acquisition of that knowledge. This prompts the question whether the process was one of simply adjusting to the tradition or whether it was a renewal and authentic reinterpretation of the present conditions. Barnett describes in detail what "the present" demands from students: developing courage, engaging with "the enemy", wrestling with difficult questions and finding solutions.

A Revolution in Pedagogical Relationships?

The post Kantian tradition in continental educational theory defined the overall aim of education as the attainment of a state of "Bildung" (Solberg and Hansen 2015). In English, this means a state of mind in which the balance between being a knowledgeable and capable person—in terms of your specific education—has been found by means of critical thinking and reflection as expressions of a profound and authentic engagement. The objective and subjective dimensions of the material learned have reached a balance.

Barnett's statement above gives us an impression of the significance of reaching a state of "Bildung". He implies that in higher education this goal is seldom reached. The Norwegian philosopher, Lars Løvlie, defines "Bildung" as an attitude, disposition, characteristic or a virtue possessed by the individual. He says that these qualities always are in relation to the knowledge and skills one uses in the workplace or in personal life, but it will also be a trait ascribable to the individual. In such times, which he calls "late modernity", individuals are only authentic and consistent if they can have control over their own lives and are able to make decisions that maintain their autonomy. Therefore, to maintain the position as a *gebildete Mensch* of Bildung, the task is largely one of "self-authoring"—to create and constantly recreate—one's autobiography (Løvlie 2009). As we have argued elsewhere, this autobiographical "Bildung" should also benefit from being audiovisual (Fritze et al. 2016).

Much of the criticism of higher education today concerns how—due to financial and political constraints—higher education institutions are constantly drawn into serving societal needs as expressed by the ambitious representatives of the political and business elite. Thus these policies reduce the potential for education while changing the purpose from educating subjects to "producing" objects (Readings 1996; Bok 2003). This results in what the German exponent of "critical theory", Theodor Adorno, has called "Halbbildung" or "half-educated" ("the possession of a smattering of knowledge"), that is, someone with excellent technical skills but lacking an ethical or social compass to direct his/her actions in everyday life. A "halbgebildet[e]" person indicates the typical mental ability that fitted most of the German intellectual elite that chose to follow the fascist, authoritarian leaders and that would fit any student who fails to become considerate, mindful, reflective, and skilled and technically proficient in a discipline or profession (Fritze et al. 2016). The crisis in higher education is that too many students have become compliant, uncritical and market-oriented, without the ethical judgements that critical professional work demands. This is exactly, in our interpretation, what the Scholarship of Integration is the best remedy for.

Mariann Solberg has coined this three-pronged approach in the following advice for following a path towards a state of "Bildung": "Think with, think against, think for yourself" (2010, p. 61). It is of paramount importance that students learn to use their voice to find a "self in academia". Since academe is a community, this voice will need to be developed in a social space of communication, with fellow students and their teachers as "the significant others".

This synthesis of care, sensitivity, knowledge, empathy and wisdom can be described in various ways and is certainly represented differently by a geologist and a nurse. In health professional education, Ballat and Campling (2011) call for an "intelligent kindness" as a much-needed value in health care as one example of what is required to extend a half-fulfilled process to a full-fledged "Bildung". In their study of public health care and students' reflection on placement experiences, Jamissen and Skou (2010) demonstrated that digital stories gained strength and impact when they emphasized the student's personal journey through learning their material. Hence, they coined "the poetic reflection" as the tool that elevated student's thinking of subject matter to a critical and personal engagement.

At the outset, we suggested that DS and its underlying principles of personal, narrative, multimodal, engaged and collaborative dimensions is in itself a sound framework for an education, with the potential for a rounded formation of the personality according to a philosophical "Bildung". Exploring the notion of "Bildung" has brought up many similar ideas to what a Scholarship of Integration ideally deals with, and we suggest that it is worthwhile to use DS as a method to realize such a scholarship, on many levels, in higher education.

NOTES

1. https://www.youtube.com/watch?v=SGjSMqwlP3E&list=PLmgRv T3J00_mtSuIeFVOutpAX_aQ_ax2G (Accessed 15 November 2016).
2. https://www.ucl.ac.uk/ioe/courses/graduate-taught (Accessed 19 September 2016).

REFERENCES

Andersson, L., & Kinnear, D. (2014). They just don't get it: Digital storytelling as reflection with junior doctors. In P. Hardy & T. Sumner (Eds.), *Cultivating compassion. How digital storytelling is transforming healthcare* (pp. 109–120). Chichester: Kingsham Press.

Ballatt, J., & Campling, P. (2011). *Intelligent kindness. Reforming the culture of healthcare*. London: RCPsych Publications.

THE SCHOLARSHIP OF INTEGRATION AND DIGITAL STORYTELLING... 293

Barnett, R. (2000). *Realizing the university in an age of supercomplexity.* Buckingham: Society for Research into Higher Education and Open University Press.

Barnett, R., Parry, G., & Coate, K. (2001). Conceptualising curriculum change. *Teaching in Higher Education, 6*(4), 435–449.

Biggs, J. (1996). Enhancing teaching through constructive alignment. *Higher Education, 32*(3), 347–364.

Bjørndal, B., & Lieberg, S. (1978). *Nye veier i didaktikken?* Oslo: Aschehoug.

Bok, D. C. (2003). *Universities in the marketplace. The commercialization of higher education.* Princeton: Princeton University Press.

Boud, D., & Knights, S. (1996). Course design for reflective practice. In N. Gould & I. Taylor (Eds.), *Reflective learning for social work* (pp. 23–34). Aldershot: Arena Publishing.

Boud, D., Keogh, R., & Walker, D. (Eds.). (1985). *Reflection: Turning experience into learning.* London: Kogan Page.

Bruner, J. S. (1991). The narrative construction of reality. *Critical Inquiry, 18*(1), 1–21.

Copland, S., & Miskelly, C. (2010). Making time for storytelling; The challenges of community building and activism in a rural locale. *Seminar.net International Journal of Media, Technology and Lifelong Learning, 6*(2), 192–207.

Egan, K. (1989). *Teaching as storytelling.* Chicago: The University of Chicago Press.

Friesen, N. (2012). Experiential evidence: I, we, you. In N. Friesen, C. Henriksson, & T. Saevi (Eds.), *Hermeneutic phenomenology in education* (pp. 9–54). Rotterdam: Sense Publishers.

Fritze, Y., & Nordkvelle, Y. T. (2015). Digitalt innfødte eller bare medialiserte? In Y. Fritze, G. Haugsbakk, & Y. T. Nordkvelle (Eds.), *Mediepedagogiske perspektiver: mediesosialisering, undervisning om og med medier* (pp. 67–83). Oslo: Cappelen Damm Akademisk.

Fritze, Y., Haugsbakk, G. O., & Nordkvelle, Y. T. (2016). Visual Bildung between iconoclasm and idolatry. *Nordicom Review, 37*(2), 1–16.

Gurung, R. A. R., Chick, N. L., & Haynie, A. (2009). *Exploring signature pedagogies: Approaches to teaching disciplinary habits of mind* (1st ed.). Sterling: Stylus Pub.

Handal, G. (1984). Hva er fagdidaktikk. *Norsk pedagogisk tidsskrift, 68*(2), 59–63.

Hjarvard, S. (2009). Samfundets medialisering: En teori om mediernes forandring af samfund og kultur. *NORDICOM—Information, 31*(1–2), 5–35.

Illeris, K. (2014). Transformative learning and identity. *Journal of Transformative Education, 12*(2), 148–163.

Jamissen, G., & Skou, G. (2010). Poetic reflection through Digital Storytelling—A methodology to foster professional health worker identity in students. *Seminar. net, 6*(2), 177–191.

Kaare, B. H., & Lundby, K. (2008). Mediated lives: Autobiography and assumed authenticity in digital storytelling. In K. Lundby (Ed.), *Digital storytelling, mediatized stories: Self-representations in new media* (pp. 105–122). New York: Peter Lang.

Kress, G., & Leuwen, T. V. (2001). *Multimodal discourse: The modes and media of contemporary communication*. London: Arnold Hodder.

Lam, C. M., Wong, H., & Leung, T. T. F. (2007). An unfinished reflective journey: Social work students' reflection on their placement experiences. *British Journal of Social Work, 37*(2), 91–105.

Løvlie, L. (2009). Dannelse og profesjon. In: Dannelsesutvalget for høyere utdanning. *Kunnskap og dannelse foran et nytt århundre* (pp. 28–38). University of Bergen website. http://www.uib.no/filearchive/innstilling-dannelsesutvalget.pdf. Accessed 29 Sept 2016.

Manen, M. V. (1994). Pedagogy, virtue and narrative identity in teaching. *Curriculum Inquiry, 4*(2), 135–170.

Marton, F., Dall'alba, G., & Beaty, E. (1993). Conceptions of learning. *International Journal of Educational Research, 19*(3), 277–300.

McClean, S. T. (2007). *Digital storytelling. The narrative power of visual effects in film*. Cambridge, MA: MIT Press.

Mulkay, M. (1979). *Science and the sociology of knowledge*. London: George Allen & Unwin.

Nordkvelle, Y. T. (2003). Didactics: From classical rhetoric to kitchen-Latin. *Pedagogy, Culture & Society, 11*(3), 315–330.

Pettersen, R. C. (2005). *Kvalitetslæring i høgere utdanning. Innføring i problem- og praksisbasert didaktikk*. Oslo: Universitetsforlaget.

Readings, B. (1996). *The university in ruins*. Cambridge, MA: Harvard University Press.

Richardson, B. (2000). Recent concepts of narrative and the narratives of narrative theory. *Style, 34*, 168–175.

Sampson, J., & Cohen, R. (2001). Strategies for peer learning. Some examples. In D. Boud, R. Cohen, & J. Sampson (Eds.), *Peer learning in higher education* (pp. 35–49). London: Kogan Page.

Shulman, L. S. (2005). Signature pedagogies in the professions. *Daedalus, 134*(3), 52–59. doi:10.2307/20027998.

Solberg, M. (2010). Om akademisk danning med utgangspunkt i Kants sensus communis og 'Hva er opplysning?'. In F. Nilsen & L. Dybdal (Eds.), *Festskrift til Hjördis Nerheim i anledning 70-årsdagen* (pp. 51–68). Oslo: Unipub Forlag.

Solberg, M., & Hansen, F. T. (2015). On Academic Bildung in higher education. A Scandinavian approach. In T. Fossland, H. Mathiasen, & M. Solberg (Eds.), *Routledge research in higher education: Academic Bildung in net-based higher education: Moving beyond learning* (pp. 28–54). Florence: Routledge.

CHAPTER 20

Critical Story Sharing: A Dialectic Approach to Identity Regulation

Mari Ann Moss

INTRODUCTION AND BACKGROUND

Higher education is challenged to help students integrate knowledge across professions while building professional identity and relationships with others. Boyer (1990) reclassified the identity of scholars from researchers and teachers to researchers, teachers, collaborators and integrators of knowledge. "By integration, we mean making connections across the disciplines, placing the specialties in larger context, illuminating data in a revealing way, often educating nonspecialists, too" (Boyer 1990, p. 18). One key aspect of integration, which is sometimes overlooked, is the need to develop, integrate and sustain personal *and* professional identity. In order to successfully negotiate the world beyond the academy, students need to know who they are and understand how their personal identity is shaped. As they move through their studies and enter the wider world, the development of professional identity assumes greater importance, and the ability to bridge these two identities will be crucial to survival in both the personal and professional contexts.

This chapter thus considers the use of digital storytelling as a way of investigating personal and professional identity, through a different lens

M.A. Moss (✉)
Dreamcatcher Enterprise Limited, Auckland, New Zealand

© The Author(s) 2017
G. Jamissen et al. (eds.), *Digital Storytelling in Higher Education,*
Digital Education and Learning, DOI 10.1007/978-3-319-51058-3_20

that helps to make sense of the challenges and opportunities of digital storytelling in organisations. It focuses on an exploratory digital storytelling intervention within an organisation and draws lessons that are pertinent to higher education.

Digital storytelling has previously been used to capture the essence of brand identity, but it has not been used to explore how personal identity is entangled with organisational identity. This chapter introduces critical story sharing (CSS) (Moss 2012) as a way to approach the challenges described by Boyer in relation to the scholarship of integration and considers how the process of developing digital stories in a group contributes to clarifying an integrated personal and professional identity. Such clarity of identity is crucial both for higher educational institutions as organisations existing in a competitive world and also for their clients—the students who will engage with multiple organisations during their working lives.

STORIES AND IDENTITY

Digital stories, described by Lundby (2008) as mediatised stories, self-representations in new media, have enabled the age-old practice of storytelling to transcend space and time through the particular constraints and affordances offered by the digital storytelling genre. The "self" is not fixed but inherently social, shaped in relationships and through the stories we tell. "The authenticity of the digital story is not a given. To play with narrative is to play with identity" (Lundby 2008, p. 5).

Narrative and identity are shaped by the processes of management, facilitation and mediation. Digital storytelling can be introduced into an organisation for a number of different purposes, including the need to understand others' identity when multidisciplinary approaches are required for problem solving and innovation.

Lambert (2006) states:

> So our approach to an organization's story always starts with a person connecting their life experience to the organization's mission or branding. It may not be the story that makes it into your next speech, organizational website, or broadcast publication, but until you create it, you probably will not do as good a job of representing other people's stories for the same organization. (2006, p. 105)

When interviewed by Joe Lambert in 1998, Dana Atchley explained how brand identity can be developed:

> I think the important point is that the concept of brand cannot always develop from the top down. People, either as employees or consumers, may invest in brand identity values that you never intended, and allowing their stories to trickle up to the top is what expands and truly defines the brand. (Lambert and Atchley 2006, p. 167)

Brand shapes the identity of organisational men and women.

IDENTITY AND THE ORGANISATION

The intervention was undertaken with WISE Management Services and Women's Wellness, which was composed of The Monastery and Iris, in Hamilton, New Zealand, in 2007, to investigate how digital storytelling could add value to the organisation.

Julie Nelson, Chief Executive of WISE Management Services, chose Women's Wellness to introduce digital storytelling into the WISE Group because of a sense that this organisation was new and evolving. An organisation is a group of people with a common purpose. In this case study, knowledge is integrated across three organisations and multiple professions.

The case study is illuminated by focusing on two participants who were becoming digital storytelling facilitators. This focus highlights the opportunities and challenges of using digital storytelling as a tool to integrate knowledge and build identity across professions and organisations.

The WISE Group was implementing Peak Performance (Gilson, et al. 2000) and Sustainable Peak Performance (Pratt and Pratt 2010), and this underpinned their ethos. Women's Wellness brand identity was captured in their "Peak Performance Organization's (PPO)" dream, focus and spirit which regulated their inspirational women. Women's Wellness organisational dream was "To create transformational wellness services and experiences for women", their focus was "Nurture RICH relationships" and their spirit was "Connections for living well" (Pratt, M., 2007. wise purpose. [email] (Personal communication, 9 July 2007)).

At the time of the intervention, they delivered services through The Monastery and Iris. The Monastery provided retreats for women experiencing stress, trauma or depression. The Monastery women were nurturing and holistic in supporting their clients' health and well-being. From 2011 to 2015, The Monastery supported more than 700 people affected by the Christchurch earthquakes with free wellness retreats. Iris was a mobile service for women and acted as advocates for their clients in securing mental health support. They continue to offer their free service as Women's Wellness through Pathways (Women's Wellness 2014).

Based on my experience with this intervention, I became interested in how the digital storytelling process might be used in working with identity within an organisation and how the process of creating a digital story and the product of a digital artefact might be understood in terms of a dialectic relationship between self and organisation.

Identity Regulation

Higher education institutions regulate the identity of scholars, and organisations regulate the identity of team members through multiple reward systems. Identity regulation was explored within organisations by Mats Alvesson and Hugh Willmott (2002). They critiqued and described identity regulation as a dialectic process of organisational control and micro-emancipation to produce the appropriate organisational man and woman.

> ... we are here concerned primarily with how organizational control is accomplished through the self-positioning of employees within managerially inspired discourses about work and organization with which they may become more or less identified and committed. (Alvesson and Willmott 2002, p. 620)

Organisational men and women embody the characteristics that define the organisation. They think and act from the organisation's perspective in their day-to-day practice in subordination to their professional and personal values and beliefs. Within this dialectic process of identity regulation also exists the seeds of micro-emancipation expressed as small acts of freedom. These act to resist control of identity on a day-to-day basis, as individuals can choose to think, communicate and act based on their professional and personal beliefs and values.

Tempered Radicals

Identity regulation can also be seen as a process that produces "tempered radicals"—persons who challenge professional identity and culture based on their personal beliefs and values (Meyerson 2001, 2004).

> Tempered radicals push and prod the system through a variety of subtle processes, rechanneling information and opportunities, questioning assumptions, changing boundaries of inclusion, and scoring small wins. (Meyerson 2004, pp. 17–18)

Tempered radicals shape their professional identities within the constraints of their organisations, and they have the power to leave if they feel they can make a greater contribution elsewhere. Tempered radicals can use storytelling to share their lived experience, personal beliefs and values. Storytelling can also be a tool to engage in identity regulation.

THE DIGITAL STORYTELLING INTERVENTION

The intervention consisted of eight critical-emancipatory action research steps. Due to the potentially sensitive nature of the study subject and the sensitive nature of sharing lived and personal experience at work, care was taken to draft ethical guidelines as the first step. This was done in partnership with the Waikato Management School's ethics representative, the subject organisation and in discussion with the Center for Digital Storytelling (CDS).

Step two was the first intervention in the form of a three-day digital storytelling workshop intended to teach people how to listen to and share alternative experiences.

Step three was creating a digital storytelling community of practice (Wenger 1999; Wenger et al. 2002) to maintain the knowledge of a discipline through an informal network based on the participation of volunteers.

Step four was a second intervention in the form of a seven-day train-the-trainer's workshop (including a three-day workshop for colleagues). The aim was to build organisational competence in the area of digital storytelling because organisational storytelling was part of their approach and they wanted to see how a digital approach could add value to their practice.

Step five was an interview with the sponsor in order to gain the organisation's perspective,

Step six, which was undertaken after this intervention ended, involved interviews with digital storytelling practitioners to learn from their diverse experiences and to add empirical detail.

Step seven was critical discursive analysis (Broadbent and Laughlin 2008) of the literature to abstract my theoretical framework, which is based on a dialectic conversation that embraces contradictory perspectives to create new knowledge and support the evolving self.

Step eight was more (non-digital) storytelling, which is analytic in itself (Smith and Sparks 2006, p. 185), to illuminate the meaning of my framework.

How Did I Approach the Research?: Reflexivity

When adopting a critical research methodology, it is important to acknowledge the subjective perspective of the researcher and the influence of the historical and social context that influenced his or her thinking. This acknowledges that the lens taken on reality will be shaped by the researcher's theoretical and political views and language (Burrell and Morgan 1979) and that human agency is historically and socially situated (Alvesson and Deetz 2000). The observer focuses his or her attention and interpretation of observations based on individual underlying assumptions and beliefs.

My role as a participant observer within the research project shaped my research question, the data I collected and my analysis. I identified as a tempered radical and embraced digital storytelling based on my belief that an individual's self-representational story of lived experience can make a difference to understanding oneself and to others and that embracing difference can lead to new knowledge.

I was a mature doctoral student with significant management and organisational change experience. I had been involved in several technology-based research and development organisations and in the start-up and sale of an information technology company. I practised participative management and encouraged individuals to lead in their areas of passion and expertise. I had experience of using action research and face-to-face storytelling to uncover issues and support change. I applied a "beginner's mind" (Suzuki 1970) to digital storytelling theory and practice. The data I collected and that underpins the discussion in this chapter includes website profiles, digital stories, interviews, personal communication and online posts.

Reflecting on the Women's Wellness Digital Storytelling Exploration

Six people participated in a three-day digital storytelling workshop and two people, Karen Lund from The Monastery and Tania Rossiter from Iris, participated in a seven-day digital storytelling train-the-trainers' workshop facilitated by the author. Eleven Women's Wellness digital stories were completed. A little over a year after the completion of the intervention, an interview was conducted with the sponsor to reflect on the impact of the intervention on the organisation.

In revisiting the Women's Wellness case study for this chapter, I focus back on Karen and Tania's participation in the intervention because they were becoming digital storytelling facilitators. They were invited to participate, believed they could make a difference to their organisation through the use of storytelling and were both empowered and constrained in their ability to take digital storytelling forward in Women's Wellness. This case study is important because it highlights some of the opportunities and challenges that digital storytelling brings to organisations.

The storytelling prompts chosen by Karen and Tania were "What led you to the organisation and how has the organisation changed the direction of your life?" The prompts acted as catalysts for the participants to engage with who they were in their personal and organisational lives. They shared their stories and images with their colleagues who actively listened and bore witness, asked questions and gave feedback as they co-created stories of lived experience.

Thesis, Anti-thesis and Synthesis

A new critical lens based on the dialectic process of thesis, anti-thesis and synthesis (Fichte and Breazeale 1993) is used in this chapter to reflect on the experience. In this case, the thesis is the dominant discourse of organisational identity: how the organisation saw the professional identity of the participants was published on their website. The anti-thesis is the alternative discourse of self-representations in new media by Karen Lund and Tania Rossiter. The digital stories were shared face to face with Julie

Nelson and the manager of Women's Wellness to see how they could add value to the organisation. And the synthesis was the need for a balanced and integrated personal-professional identity as well as a larger critical conversation to support evolving identity at work.

Karen Lund's website profile before the digital storytelling intervention stated:

> Karen is delighted to be a member of The Monastery team and, as housekeeper, she is passionate about delivering truly exceptional service to guests. (Women's Wellness Ltd. 2007)

Karen's website profile changed after the woman responsible for Women's Wellness branding participated in the second digital storytelling intervention, where Karen facilitated a digital storytelling circle. Here is her updated profile:

> Karen is The Monastery's house manager. She considers her position from a spiritual as well as practical perspective, believing that a caring and nurturing environment enhances healing. Her life experiences include motherhood, special needs teaching, owning and managing a luxury holiday accommodation in South Africa as well as travelling and experiencing diverse cultures. Karen is passionate about delivering truly exceptional service to guests. (Women's Wellness Ltd. 2008, 2009)

Tania Rossiter's website profile, before and after the digital storytelling intervention, stated:

> I believe we are all unique and talented and we are all pupils and teachers. I bring this philosophy to my role at Iris. I feel privileged to be working in such a warm environment, where I get to combine my interests of people, holistic health and well being, and social justice. (Women's Wellness Ltd. 2007, 2008, 2009)

Extracts from the digital stories created by Tania and Karen are included here to exemplify how the digital stories captured the ways in which individuals saw themselves: this forms the anti-thesis in my argument. Writing about and sharing momentous life events led Karen to view herself differently and to represent herself differently via her profile, revealing a more integrated personality; Tania's profile remains the same before and after the intervention but similarly reveals a more integrated, personal-professional identity.

Travelling Light by Karen Lund

In Fig. 20.1, Karen Lund shares "Travelling light". Her story script captures the essence of her journey to The Monastery and her reflections on identity and purpose after working there for one year.

Fig. 20.1 Travelling light by Karen Lund. Copyright 2007 by Karen Lund. Used with permission

After 30 years with the man I had always thought of as my partner for life, the universe intervened. An excruciatingly painful, but necessary, series of events unfolded. The removal of my wedding band obliterated vast chunks of my former life. Nothing would ever be the same again. Slowly emerging from the detritus, this child of Africa began to remember, to learn, about travelling light, about healing.

I found myself in New Zealand, reading a newspaper advertisement for a position in the foundation team at The Monastery, a wellness retreat for women experiencing depression or trauma. I marvelled at the synchronicities which had brought me to this time and place. I had to explore this opportunity to work in an organisation embracing a vision of a programme for healing which I wanted to contribute to. After my first year at The Monastery, I wrote a poem entitled "One Year On".

One Year On

One year on there is deep gratitude for the learning, for the shared wisdom of souls who touch this life. Easing this soul along its path to recognition of serenity. The gift in every perfect moment. I look to the year ahead taking each day as it unfolds. Relishing the opportunities for living, loving and learning. It is my privilege to be of service to the souls who serve me daily abundantly.

K.L., Dec. 2006

I continue to learn and I now know there is nothing quite like travelling light.

"Travelling Light", written and produced by Karen Lund, July 2007. Credits: Photography and assistance with compilation: Mari Ann Moss.

Postcard to Myself by Tania Rossiter

In Fig. 20.2, Tania Rossiter shares "Postcard to myself". Her story script captures the essence of coming to a crossroads in her professional life and the infinite possibilities it could represent which was illustrated by the quote she used from Deepak Chopra (2003, p. 21).

Fig. 20.2   Postcard to myself by Tania Rossiter. Copyright 2007 by Tania Rossiter. Used with permission

> Dear Tania, thought you might like this as you've talked about being at a cross-roads in your life; when I took this image it was to capture the sense of considering what direction to head in and if I'm on the right track. Now I see that the railway line could be a barrier to get across rather than travel along. What is that barrier? I wonder. Does the house signify safety and security? If I come from there across the track, I will be on the open road. From safety on to a main highway, and what if there's a train coming? They say nothing happens by coincidence. Good luck on your journey.
>
> Love Tania
>
> "When you live your life with an appreciation of coincidences and their meanings you connect with the underlying field of infinite possibilities. This is when magic begins …" Deepak Chopra—by Tania Rossiter with gratitude to: Karen Lund, Maree Maddock and Wise Management Services and special thanks to Mari Ann Moss.

"Tania also captured Wise Trust's purpose, inspirational dream, spirit and beliefs around the essence of possibilities. This was also reflected in the Deepak Chopra quote that Tania used at the end of her story" (Pratt, M., 2007., PhD supervisory discussion. [email] (Personal communication, 9, July, 2007)). Tania continues making a difference within Pathways and can be seen as a tempered radical who stayed engaged with the organisation.

Learning from the organisation's perspective was shared by Julie Nelson and Mike Pratt and contributed to my understanding and to the synthesis of my argument. Julie Nelson, the sponsor of the intervention, highlighted a number of things that she learnt:

> ... so, being a bit clearer around when we are doing the 'digital storying' about anchoring it back to the organisation. So I think that was really a significant learning for us. (Nelson, J., 2009. Reflection on organisational learning. [conversation] (Personal communication, 1, April, 2009))

"Digital storying" was valuable to the Wise Group for promoting the organisation's services, people and recruitment.

> ...yes there is a place for staff (stories) ... they were personal to the people they weren't personal to the organisation. And ... I think if we wanted to promote the work of the organisation then we have to actually ... find that balance. (Nelson, J., 2009. Reflection on organisational learning. [conversation] (Personal communication, 1, April, 2009))

She felt that promoting services from the point of view of the people who had experienced them could be powerful. People who had accessed and used the services might need more time, independence and support through the "digital storying" process than staff. Three days was a significant amount of time to invest and she didn't know if organisations could afford that time. She decided to continue to support one day for people to think about how they wanted to present themselves and what they had to say. She reflected that "digital storying" connects to Peak Performance and could capture founder and instigator stories as living memory. She saw this anchoring of "digital storying" back to the organisation as key.

The pilot's focus on personal experience helped Julie connect to employees but she felt participants got more out of digital storytelling than the organisation. She was looking for a balance that represented all stakeholders.

> ...one of the ... lessons for us was ... that ... people ... got more out of it personally ... than ... the organisation.... people talked ... about a very personal story to them, ... but it wasn't necessarily talking about the organisation and what the organisation could do in terms of changing lives. (Nelson, J., 2009. Reflection on organisational learning. [conversation] (Personal communication, 1, April, 2009))

As a result of participating, some people felt motivated to retrain; this supported the organisation's recognition of the need to engage in the conversation looking at both the organisation's and the individual's needs.

> ...one example ... the housekeeper ... decided that she wanted a change of title, ... decided that she actually didn't really want to be a housekeeper any more that she wanted to go on and be ... a wellness consultant ... because she feels that she had a lot to contribute ... I think that's fine but the organisation still needs a housekeeper. ... so it's actually about ... the need for the organisation to have good supports in and for ...... management to be ... clear around ... that's absolutely fine for people to explore in their journey where they might want to go. ... but let's engage in the process that allows people to ... do that but also looking at both the organisational and ... the person's ... need. (Nelson, J., 2009. Reflection on organisational learning. [conversation] (Personal communication, 1, April, 2009))

Finally, Julie reflected that exploratory studies require a considerable amount of time to support and it was important to get the entire management team on board and to agree on the purpose for introducing digital storytelling. After the pilot, she assigned "digital storying" to strategic communications to link to PPO, promotion, recruitment and to anchor it back to the organisation. Wise Management Services modified digital storytelling practice as they felt was appropriate for their organisation. The process was modified to one day, storytellers were given time to think about what they wanted to say and they were filmed and edited by strategic communications.

Mike Pratt was on my PhD supervisory panel and on the WISE Trust board. Mike reflected on the longer term consequences of the intervention,

> "...the big potential learning from this story is how personal stories can relate to the organisation and with what consequences. ... personal digital stories are akin to a personal purpose journey. Wise has committed as part of its wellbeing policy to enabling all staff to develop a personal purpose. ... The connection between personal and organisation purpose is I think a rich field of enquiry." (Pratt, M., 2011., PhD supervisory discussion. [email] (Personal communication, 2, September, 2011))

Understanding Karen's perspective also contributed to my understanding and the synthesis of my argument.

Karen's personal and organisational stories were intertwined and deeply connected. Karen's personal values and beliefs shaped her professional identity. Karen contributed her reflections on participating in the intervention and the potential use of digital storytelling within the organisation in the online community of practice as detailed below:

> … After viewing my first stories, the CEO of Wise Management Services asked me to train as a Digital Storytelling Trainer. A colleague and myself have recently completed a thoroughly enjoyable and very practical trainer's workshop run by Mari Ann Moss. This is a really exciting development in terms of my role at work and I hope the digital storytelling project will gather momentum next year. Those of us who have been involved so far are very keen to develop the project in whatever ways it can be useful within Women's Wellness Ltd and Wise Management Services.
>
> Feedback I have received to date reinforces my sense that digital storytelling can be used in any number of ways within the organisation. A group of us are currently working on developing a story around "Sustainability" allied to the PPO ideals.
>
> We live and work in exciting times!
>
> Thanks to all who support our efforts! (Lund 2007)

Karen highlighted how she felt supported in her desire to learn how to become a digital storytelling facilitator and saw opportunities to take digital storytelling forward in her organisation. Karen's stories highlighted the essence of her identity and her personal experience which led her to support The Monastery's services. Karen left The Monastery in 2009 to pursue special education teaching.

Karen can be seen as a tempered radical who dis-engaged from the organisation. Tempered radicals can help organisations engage in reflexivity and communicative action (Habermas 1984) based on a strong and integrated sense of both personal and professional identity.

CRITICAL STORY SHARING

My experience and synthesis of these insights led me to create CSS (Moss 2012), a dialectic conversation that embraces both the dominant discourse of organisational identity and the alternative discourse of personal identity to synthesise an integrated personal and professional identity to support an ongoing larger conversation about evolving identity at work. CSS is a form of narrative mediation (Winslade and Monk 2000, 2008). Narrative mediation resolves a story of conflict by identifying instances of collaboration and developing them into a new way of interacting overall. It builds on the work of the CDS (Now StoryCenter) and their ethical approach (Harding and Hill 2011; Lambert 2013; Lambert and Hill 2006, 2013) to authoring identity and supporting transformation (Davis and Weinshenker 2012; Lambert 2006, 2013) and on critical management studies to guide critical, autonomous thinkers to participate in identity regulation.

CSS recognises that digital stories need to be shared in a larger conversation outside of the original story circle to include others who did not participate in the co-creation of the digital artefact. CSS as a dialectic approach to identity regulation is affected by the self-identity of the mediator who can limit and empower the participants based on their beliefs about them.

Organisational men, women and tempered radicals need CSS skills to actively listen to each other and share how they see themselves and how others see them and to mediate the difference between their personal and organisational identity. Individuals and organisations can engage in identity regulation through the use of digital storytelling within a larger critical conversation. CSS guides organisational men and women to engage with tempered radicals to co-create evolving identity at work. Developing students as tempered radicals will allow them to move confidently between organisations with a clear sense of self. Encouraging higher education staff to act as tempered radicals and challenge the "status quo" supports innovative thinking.

> I have been on more than one university campus where rather heavy-handed provosts and deans were imposing definitions of scholarship articulated in *Scholarship Reconsidered* and found resistant faculty members complaining of being "Boyerized." (Rice 2002, p. 10)

CSS as a guide to identity regulation mediates the difference between how we see ourselves and how others see us within an organisational context, with the purpose of evolving personal and organisational identity.

The evolving self (Kegan 1982) has been described as a psychological process that favours independence and inclusion.

> What a workplace or organization actually looks or feels like when it can culture interindividuality as well as institutionality ... We can imagine that it creates opportunities to reflect together on "the way we are working," or "the point of our goals," or "how we went about making that decision" as well as insuring that the work gets done, the goals get achieved, the decisions get made. (Kegan 1982, p. 247)

Digital stories make these aspects of identity accessible and can support a larger critical conversation about evolving identity at work. In the context of CSS, identity regulation becomes a reflexive practice based on the dialectic process of thesis, anti-thesis and synthesis.

> (Reflexivity) ... is fundamental to managing organizations in responsive, responsible and ethical ways ... And it's reflexivity that is key to understanding management in terms of *who managers are*. (Cunliffe 2009, p. 817)

The philosophy of the interventionist shapes the outcome of the intervention. A traditional communications management approach controls identity and story. A facilitator's approach helps the storyteller make meaning of their lived experience while a mediator's approach helps the storyteller to embrace and resolve the difference between their organisational and personal identity to recognise their natural authority to make a difference at work.

I see myself as a "tempered radical". There is a photo of me, inspired by M.C. Escher's 1935 "Hand with Reflecting Sphere" (Ernst 1994), that captures how my identity is created in relationship with others, in this case, the photographer who is also captured in the background and a painting by D. Meiring which represents how "I" see myself in relationship with how others see "Me", co-creating my evolving "Self" (Mead 2010).

I regard this photo as a visual metaphor for co-creating an integrated, personal and professional identity in relationship with others (see Fig. 20.3).

Fig. 20.3 Topping, M., 2011. *Co-creating an integrated identity.* [photograph] (Mari Ann Moss's own private collection)

IMPLICATIONS FOR HIGHER EDUCATION INSTITUTIONS

I see a close connection between higher education and organisations in the opportunities and challenges they face. Universities in New Zealand commercialise their knowledge by engaging in innovation parks and spinning out new businesses ventures. I experienced that transformation as the manager of the Waikato Innovation Centre for eEducation at the University of Waikato when we were spun out and successfully sold (as ECTUS) to Tandberg ASA after 18 months of operation. I needed a strong sense of self during the process and it led me to undertake a PhD at the Waikato Management School to make sense of my journey.

The digital storytelling intervention described was the first step in a shared journey between a student, an organisation and the digital storytelling community to bridge the gap between personal and professional identity, purpose and transformation. Although the case that I have presented does not relate directly to higher education, the findings are relevant to the challenges students, academics and administrators meet in their journey to co-create an integrated, personal and professional identity.

Finding the balance between professional and personal identity is specific to a group and to individual members and hence will change over

CRITICAL STORY SHARING: A DIALECTIC APPROACH TO IDENTITY... 311

time as individuals move from one organisation to another. In a group, it is necessary to understand how others see you as well as how you see yourself in order to engage in identity regulation and consciously support who you are becoming. Digital storytelling can be used to co-create integrated, personal and professional identity stories in a group. However, the same integrated professional identity story can feel balanced to the members of the story circle that co-created it and unbalanced to people outside the original story circle. A larger critical conversation that involves more members of the group will uncover this discomfort, while a CSS mediator can guide others to engage in identity regulation to support evolving professional identity.

In addition to a participatory process that can support personal and professional identity development and regulation, digital storytelling can also add value to organisations through the digital artefacts that are created.

Digital storytelling can be used as a tool within a larger CSS conversation by organisations, including those in higher education, who believe their competitive advantage lies within the evolving identity of the critical, autonomous individuals who compose it, while the individuals who create those digital stories benefit from the opportunity to explore, develop and integrate their personal-professional identities. If these individuals happen to be students setting out on a journey that is likely to involve membership of a number of organisations, the opportunities afforded by digital storytelling to integrate not only knowledge across disciplines but also various aspects of themselves are invaluable.

REFERENCES

Alvesson, M., & Deetz, S. (2000). *Doing critical management research*. London: Sage.
Alvesson, M., & Willmott, H. (2002). Identity regulation as organizational control: Producing the appropriate individual. *Journal of Management Studies, 39*(5), 619–644.
Boyer, E. L. (1990). *Scholarship reconsidered: Priorities of the professoriate.* New York: Jossey-Bass.
Broadbent, J., & Laughlin, R. (2008). Middle range thinking. In R. Thorpe & R. Holt (Eds.), *The Sage dictionary of qualitative management research* (pp. 130–133). Los Angeles: Sage.
Burrell, G., & Morgan, G. (1979). *Sociological paradigms and organisational analysis: Elements of the sociology of corporate life*. London: Heinemann.

Chopra, D. (2003). *The spontaneous fulfilment of desire: Harnessing the infinite power of coincidence*. New York: Three Rivers Press.

Cunliffe, A. L. (2009). *A very short, fairly interesting and reasonably cheap book about management*. Los Angeles: Sage.

Davis, A., & Weinshenker, D. (2012). Digital storytelling and authoring identity. In C. C. Ching & B. J. Foley (Eds.), *Constructing the self in a digital World (Learning in doing: Social, cognitive and computational perspectives)* (pp. 47–74). New York: Cambridge University Press.

Ernst, B. (1994). *The magic mirror of M.C. Escher* (J. E. Brigham, Trans., 25th Anniversary ed.). New York: Barnes & Noble.

Fichte, J. G., & Breazeale, D. (1993). *Fichte: Early philosophical writings*. New York: Cornell University Press.

Gilson, C., Pratt, M., Roberts, K., & Weymes, E. (2000). *Peak performance: Business lessons from the world's top sports organizations*. London: HarperCollins.

Habermas, J. (1984). *The theory of communicative action* (Vol. 1). London: Heinemann.

Harding, L., & Hill, A. (2011). Silence speaks digital storytelling—Guidelines for ethical practice. In J. Lambert (Ed.), *Digital storytelling: Capturing lives, creating community* (pp. 191–198). New York: Routledge.

Kegan, R. (1982). *The evolving self: Problem and process in human development*. Cambridge: Harvard University Press.

Lambert, J. (2006). *Digital storytelling: Capturing lives, creating community* (2nd ed.). Berkeley: Digital Diner Press.

Lambert, J. (2013). *Digital storytelling: Capturing lives, creating community* (4th ed.). New York: Routledge.

Lambert, J., & Atchley, D. (2006). *Emotional branding: A conversation with Dana Atchley Digital storytelling: Capturing lives, creating community* (pp. 161–168). Berkeley: Digital Diner Press.

Lambert, J., & Hill, A. (2006). When silence speaks: A conversation with Amy Hill. In J. Lambert (Ed.), *Digital storytelling: Capturing lives, creating community* (pp. 151–160). Berkeley: Digital Diner Press.

Lambert, J., & Hill, A. (2013). Silence speaks: Interview with Amy Hill. In J. Lambert (Ed.), *Digital storytelling: Capturing lives, creating community* (pp. 140–149). New York: Routledge.

Lund, K. (2007). Reflections on sharing my stories outside the workshop. CP2 Course blog. [blog] 10 November. No longer available. Accessed 10 Nov 2007.

Lundby, K. (Ed.). (2008). *Digital storytelling, mediatized stories: Self-representations in new media*. New York: Peter Lang.

Mead, G. H. (2010). The self: The 'I' and the 'me'. In M. J. Hatch & M. Schultz (Eds.), *Organizational identity: A reader* (pp. 30–34). Oxford: Oxford University Press.

Meyerson, D. E. (2001). Radical change, the quiet way. *Harvard Business Review, 79*(9), 92–100.

Meyerson, D. E. (2004). The tempered radicals. *Stanford Social Innovation Review, 2*(2), 14–22.

Moss, M. A. (2012). Critical story sharing as communicative action in organisational change. The University of Waikato, Hamilton. http://hdl.handle.net/10289/6726. Accessed 10 Oct 2016.

Pratt, M., & Pratt, H. (2010). *Sustainable peak performance: Business lessons from sustainable enterprise pioneers.* North Shore: Pearson.

Rice, R. E. (2002). Beyond scholarship reconsidered: Toward an enlarged vision of the scholarly work of faculty members. *New Directions for Teaching and Learning, 90*(Summer), 7–25.

Smith, B., & Sparkes, A. C. (2006). Narrative inquiry in psychology: Exploring the tensions within. *Qualitative Research in Psychology, 3*(3), 169–192.

Suzuki, S. (1970). *Zen mind, beginner's mind.* New York: Weatherhill.

Wenger, E. (1999). *Communities of practice: Learning, meaning and identity.* Cambridge: Cambridge University Press.

Wenger, E., McDermott, R., & Snyder, W. (2002). *Cultivating communities of practice: A guide to managing knowledge.* Boston: Harvard Business School Press.

Winslade, J., & Monk, G. (2000). *Narrative mediation: A new approach to conflict resolution.* San Francisco: Jossey-Bass.

Winslade, J., & Monk, G. (2008). *Practicing narrative mediation: Loosening the grip of conflict.* San Francisco: Jossey-Bass.

Women's Wellness Ltd. (2007). *The monastery—A luxury wellness experience not to be missed I meet the team.* http://web.archive.org/web/20081014042057/http://www.themonastery.co.nz/page/monastery_24.php. Accessed 10 Oct 2016.

Women's Wellness Ltd. (2008). *The Monastery—A luxury wellness experience not to be missed I meet the team.* Retrieved from. http://web.archive.org/web/20081014042057/http://www.themonastery.co.nz/page/monastery_24.php. Accessed 10 Oct 2016.

Women's Wellness Ltd. (2009). *The Monastery—A luxury wellness experience not to be missed I meet the team.* Retrieved from. http://web.archive.org/web/20081014042057/http://www.themonastery.co.nz/page/monastery_24.php. Accessed 10 Oct 2016.

Women's Wellness Ltd. (2014). Where we began—Women's Wellness. http://www.womenswellness.co.nz/history. Accessed 10 Oct 2016.

PART 4

The Scholarship of
Engaged Collaboration

CHAPTER 21

Introduction to the Scholarship of Engaged Collaboration

Heather Pleasants

"Engaged scholarship" is an umbrella term used to describe university/community partnerships oriented toward creating social change. Since Boyer's seminal publications (Boyer 1990, 1996), engaged scholarship has been defined and operationalized in a number of ways—definitions and practices associated with engaged scholarship exist within service learning, community-based research, community-based participatory action research and public scholarship (NERCHE 2016). Engaged scholarship, as embodied in a range of practices and key concepts developed over the last 25 years, has become a central component across the teaching, research and service missions of many institutions of higher learning (Fitzgerald et al. 2012). Leaders of colleges and universities have increasingly recognized that the challenges facing our world demand that we bring the knowledge based in the academic community together with knowledge gained through the lived experience of people in diverse places

H. Pleasants (✉)
University of Alabama, Tuscaloosa, AL, USA

© The Author(s) 2017
G. Jamissen et al. (eds.), *Digital Storytelling in Higher Education*,
Digital Education and Learning, DOI 10.1007/978-3-319-51058-3_21

and spaces. Boyer presciently identified the necessity of moving toward a systematic approach to addressing the civic missions of many public and private colleges and universities:

> But at a deeper level, I have a growing conviction that what's also needed is not just more programs, but a larger purpose, a larger sense of mission … Increasingly I'm convinced that ultimately the scholarship of engagement also means creating a special climate in which the academic and civic cultures communicate more continuously and more creatively with each other, helping to enlarge what anthropologist Clifford Geertz describes as the universe of human discourse and enriching the quality of life for all of us. Boyer (1996)

Building on Boyer, others have continued to think deeply and reflectively about how we might create this climate; see, for example, Strum et al. (2011). As articulated early and throughout this volume, it is our thought that digital storytelling provides a unique means by which we might bring together many aspects of the work of higher education—including outreach or engagement. As the following chapters illustrate, digital storytelling provides us (scholars, researchers and community members) with opportunities to enact concepts that are at the core of successful engaged scholarship processes and projects. These concepts include but are not limited to communication, critical reflection, reciprocity and personal and community transformation. Digital storytelling, as a set of coordinated practices, has the ability to serve as a kind of glue that holds the often very fragile enterprise of engaged scholarship together, given its ability to keep simultaneous focus on our role(s) within our teaching, research and outreach; what students are learning in their making/doing/interacting processes; the ways in which we support and enable reciprocity within university/community partnerships; how we communicate and negotiate problems and processes for addressing them; and how we represent the process and outcomes of our work, including the way each can be used to support those within university and community contexts. In the chapters that follow, each author attends to a variety of issues manifested through the use of digital storytelling work involving researchers, students and community members.

In Chap. 22, Elaine Bliss weaves together longitudinal data from a digital storytelling project conducted over five years, within the community context of a non-profit organization focused on meeting the needs of people with disabilities in order to explore how digital storytelling provides a rich example of collaborative practice (Rice 2003). Further, Bliss uses the concepts of performance spaces and embodied performances to understand how digital storytelling practices reveal the emotional and affective geographies of disability.

In Chap. 23, Darcy Alexandra draws from longitudinal research with asylum seekers in Ireland in order to examine how the process of co-created scriptwriting facilitated and sustained a community of practice for members of the digital storytelling group. In doing so, Alexandra reveals how this group participated in engaged inquiry about asylum and migrant labor regimes, as well as how the group process produced opportunities for multi-layered narrative exchange. In inviting the reader to "listen deeply" (Lambert 2013) to the stories of two participants in particular, Alexandra also highlights the challenges within participatory knowledge production through the new media/new literacies practice of digital storytelling (Lankshear and Knobel 2011).

In Chap. 24, the section shifts from considering the work of individual researchers who are using digital storytelling as an engaged scholarship practice to the work of scholars operating within different levels of the higher education space. In his chapter on digital storytelling within the Greek Context, Michael Meimaris provides details and outcomes from two projects originating from the Laboratory of New Technologies in Communication, Education, and Mass Media at the University of Athens and undergraduate and graduate programs associated with it. Meimaris highlights both the development of a new media tool, *Milia*, which supports online community-based digital storytelling practices, and the benefits of using digital storytelling to provide mutual benefits to young people and elders as they work together to create multimodal intergenerational narratives centered around the concept of work.

In the final chapter of the section, Beverly Bickel, Bill Shewbridge, Romy Hübler and Ana Askoz present multiple perspectives from faculty who use digital storytelling as a central component of their civic engagement work at the University of Maryland, Baltimore County (UMBC). Over the past decade, UMBC has woven digital storytelling into ongoing efforts to create meaningful change in communities, authentic and agentive learning opportunities for students and nuanced research/impact outcomes for faculty. Through exploring faculty perceptions of UMBC's use of digital storytelling, Bickel et al. illuminate the possibilities and challenges inherent in using digital storytelling as an engaged scholarship practice at the institutional level, Further, they discuss how engaged story work has been a critical component of ongoing work to change the campus culture and provide a broad perspective and suggestions for developing, sustaining and promoting publicly engaged digital storytelling work in higher education.

Taken together, these chapters extend an invitation to the reader to consider where the process of digital storytelling begins and ends and to explore the ways in which digital storytelling practices hold us accountable to one another. The chapters also invite us to consider both the limitations and possibilities of digital storytelling as a means by which boundaries between universities and communities can be made more malleable, as multiple sources of knowledge are used to create reciprocal benefits for individuals and groups of people invested in working toward positive change and addressing issues of social justice.

REFERENCES

Boyer, E. (1990). *Scholarship reconsidered: Priorities of the professoriate.* New York: The Carnegie Foundation for the Advancement of Teaching.

Boyer, E. (1996). The scholarship of engagement. *Bulletin of the American Academy of Arts and Sciences, 49*(7), 18–33.

Fitzgerald, H. E., Bruns, K., Sonka, S. T., Furco, A., & Swanson, S. (2012). The centrality of engagement in higher education. *Journal of Higher Education Outreach and Engagement, 16*(3), 7–27.

Lambert, J. (2013). *Digital storytelling: Capturing lives, creating community* (4th ed.). New York/London: Routledge.

Lankshear, C., & Knobel, M. (2011). *New literacies: Everyday practices and social learning* (3rd ed.). Maidenhead/New York: Open University Press/McGraw-Hill.

New England Resource Center for Higher Education. (2016). *Definition of engaged scholarship.* http://www.nerche.org/index.php?option=com_content&view=article&id=265&catid=28. Accessed 2 Nov 2016.

Rice, E. R. (2003). Rethinking scholarship and engagement: The struggles for new meanings. *Campus Compact Reader, 4*, 1–9.

Strum, S., Eatman, T., Saltmarch, J., & Bush, A. (2011). Full participation: Building the architecture for diversity and community engagement in higher education. *Imagining America.* Paper 17. http://surface.syr.edu/ia/17/. Accessed 2 Nov 2016.

CHAPTER 22

Engaged Scholarship and Engaging Communities: Navigating Emotion, Affect and Disability Through Digital Storytelling

Elaine Bliss

INTRODUCTION

In 2010, Joseph participated in a digital storytelling workshop and created a digital story about his life. It provided the inspiration for Joseph to tell his story.

> I was born and lived in Rakanui, near Kawhia, in a tin house with no power and candles. I've been to many schools around Te Kuiti. Now I live in Hamilton. I would like to write a book and a poem to let people know what I'm talking about. (Joseph 2010, Hamilton)

The workshop was part of a research collaboration between myself, a PhD student in Geography at the University of Waikato, and Janelle, Quality Practice Manager at Interactionz, a community benefit organisation in Hamilton that works with disabled persons, one of whom is Joseph. In 2011, Joseph presented his digital story as part of a conference presentation

E. Bliss (✉)
University of Waikato,
Hamilton, New Zealand

© The Author(s) 2017
G. Jamissen et al. (eds.), *Digital Storytelling in Higher Education*,
Digital Education and Learning, DOI 10.1007/978-3-319-51058-3_22

by myself and Janelle at the University of Waikato. Joseph's expression of pride in his digital story, the inspiration he gained through his experience of the workshop and his desire to share his story publicly demonstrate an emotional and affective geography of digital storytelling workshops. In this chapter, I discuss a community-based research collaboration that involved four digital storytelling workshops between 2010 and 2015 that I co-facilitated with Interactionz; disabled and non-disabled participants[1] responded to the question "what would a "good life" look like to them?" to create digital stories.

Collaborative practice is part of a scholarship of engagement where the focus is on "concrete, protracted community-based problems" (Rice 2002, p. 5). I begin by describing the development of this collaborative research and how Janelle and I identified digital storytelling as an appropriate, emotionally embodied methodology for exploring the lives of disabled people. Next, I identify and discuss the scholarly contributions that inform my analysis of emotion and affect in digital storytelling workshops. I then offer vignettes of three of the workshop participants whose co-created digital stories demonstrate workshops as performed spaces of care and empathy. Three points structure my empirical discussion. First, digital storytelling workshops are important collaborative research spaces for conceptualising the lived experience of disability. Second, attention to digital storytelling workshops as performance spaces illustrates the ways in which emotion and affect shape understandings of disability. And finally, the workshop participants' embodied performances created an emotional and affective atmosphere of care and empathy where alternative understandings of disability were constructed.

Space and place is important for understanding how emotion and affect are performed in digital storytelling workshops. According to Rice, "community-based research is of necessity local – rooted in a particular time and setting" (2002, pp. 14–15). As part of this community-based research collaboration, data was gathered and interpreted from the four workshops whose aim was threefold: to explore digital storytelling's capacity as a spatialised, workshopped methodology for understanding the emotional and affective geographies of disability; to capture and evaluate the impact of person-driven practice (PDP)[2] on the quality of life of disabled persons through digital storytelling and to create through the digital stories an empowering community narrative for persons with disabilities.

Making Connections and Creating Collaboration Through Digital Storytelling

I begin this section by explaining how a mutual recognition of the value of digital storytelling contributed to the development of a research relationship between myself and Interactionz. Digital storytelling workshops as a method for creating meaning of "a good life" was the focus of the collaboration, and in this section, I outline our research focus and objectives. I also discuss how we framed the research theoretically within emotional geographies of care work and why this is germane to disabled persons and their communities.

The collaborative research relationship developed between myself and Janelle by way of a personal connection. At the time, I was conducting research on digital storytelling for my PhD, and Janelle was exploring methods for evaluating Interactionz's methods of practice with the people it serves. We arranged to meet and Janelle explained to me that Interactionz was looking at techniques for evaluating its model of PDP. PDP advocates for people with disabilities to have choice and control over the supports they receive and the lives they lead as valued and contributing citizens in their own communities (Bliss and Fisher 2014). Through this approach, Interactionz "endeavour[s] to make long-term, positive and sustainable difference in the lives of the people they serve and the communities they belong to" (Bliss and Fisher 2014, p. 99). As a result of our conversation, Janelle concluded that digital storytelling could provide a valuable method for people with disabilities to create and share their personal stories that have remained largely untold or, at best, communicated by a third party.

We embarked on a collaborative research initiative that involved conducting a series of digital storytelling workshops between 2010 and 2015.[3] We titled the project "The Journey to a Good Life: a longitudinal evaluation of person-driven practice from the perspective of people with disabilities and a community organisation". We had five research objectives: (1) to capture and evaluate the impact that PDP has on the quality of life of the people served by Interactionz, (2) to develop best-practice guidelines of the principles and application of PDP from the research findings, (3) to document and analyse the organisational transition of Interactionz from a service-driven model to a PDP, (4) to facilitate the creation of an empowering community narrative for people with disabilities and (5) to understand the usefulness of digital storytelling as a research method in this context and for possible application in other contexts (Bliss and Fisher

2014, p. 102). The specific methods used in the research project were (1) the creation of digital stories by the participants in a facilitated workshop, (2) interviews with participants and facilitators, (3) focus groups and/or interviews with Interactionz's stakeholders and viewers of the screened digital stories and (4) participant observation by the researchers. These methods are particularly appropriate as social relationships, beliefs and meanings, and critical reflection were the main focus of the research.

Interactionz recruited the workshop participants and asked them to consider what a "good life" would look like to them. The intention of the workshops for both researchers was to map a journey of meaning for each individual with a disability and those who support them, either as family, community or the organisation that would be represented in digital stories. Included in all of the workshops were a variety of people from the Interactionz's community: people with intellectual disabilities, people with physical disabilities, literate and non-literate people, people who are verbal and non-verbal, family/whānau, staff, board trustees, people with advanced technological skills and people who had never used a computer before in their lives (Bliss and Fisher 2014).

The workshops were structured on the Center for Digital Storytelling's (CDS) practice of three-day workshops. The inclusion of people with disabilities and people who support them in the same workshops facilitated an approach to disability that demonstrated the importance of relationships in achieving qualitative outcomes for the people that Interactionz serves. I was particularly interested in how digital storytelling could provide a complementary methodology to other forms of outcome measurement because it offers a relational means for exploring the emotional and affective dimensions of disability. Bondi (2008) argues the importance of attending to the emotional dynamics and geographical contexts of caring and care relationships. Through digital storytelling as a unique methodology, the emotional and affective dimensions of lived experience with disability from a variety of perspectives can be captured and this was important for evaluating PDP within the community and the social justice context of Interactionz's values and vision. The workshops provided a timespace[4] in which the theme "the journey to a good life" could also be explored by the persons they serve. Furthermore, the participation of people who support the disabled persons made the emotional dimensions of care work visible, and the emotional labour of "giving and receiving [of] care is experienced as a deep and deeply rewarding expression of love, pleasure and vocation" (Bondi 2008, p. 250) was expressed.

We recognised that the practice of digital storytelling workshops was in alignment with Interactionz's organisational philosophy of PDP, in other words, putting persons with disabilities in the driving seats of their own lives. Caring for self and others is integral to Interactionz's values and digital storytelling practice. Through the application of emotional and affective geographical theories, we identified the potential of the relational space of digital storytelling workshops for rich meaning-making about how persons with disabilities can lead good lives. In the next section, I examine further the theoretical framework that supports my analysis of emotion and affect in the digital storytelling workshops with Interactionz.

WORKSHOPS AS PERFORMANCE SPACES OF ENGAGED RESEARCH ON DISABILITY, EMOTION AND AFFECT

In this section, I introduce the theoretical foundations that support the digital storytelling workshops carried out with Interactionz. I begin by citing geographers who acknowledge the importance of storytelling and performance as means of giving voice to persons with disabilities. Voice, in this sense, is a practice of meaning-making and knowledge production about disability. I draw primarily on Wood and Smith (2004) and Wood et al. (2007) to argue that the emotional work that takes place in musical performance spaces can be usefully compared to digital storytelling workshops. Like musical spaces, the digital storytelling workshops with Interactionz represent spaces of enhanced emotion where, through their staging and performance, opportunities were created for the researchers to go beyond traditionally disembodied understandings of disability to examine its emotional and affective dimensions.

Smith (2012) highlights the importance of giving voice to people with disabilities, individually and collectively. He argues that stories can provide a personal, inside look at what life with a disability is like and offer alternative understandings to the epidemiological models of disability that favour knowledge at a collective, population level. Digital storytelling also offers an embodied approach to knowledge production about disability, disabled persons and the people that support them in their lives. Digital storytelling is an embodied practice and part of an emerging "performative tradition" (Perkins 2009, p. 128) in geography; social and spatial meaning is conveyed via a range of practices—narrative, gesture, movement, sound, visual and voice—through which discourses can be reproduced or subverted by way of performance. Wood and Smith (2004) explore musical paths to emotional geographies and argue musical settings can help social scientists understand the emotional dimensions of social relations.

Wood and Smith (2004, p. 533) argue that the settings of musical performance spaces where emotions are "deliberately and routinely enhanced" (Wood and Smith 2004, p. 533) provide a space for social scientists to explore emotional dimensions of human life. Emotional knowledge created through musical performance, they suggest, might be relevant for understanding empowerment and the promotion of social well-being and a "good life". Geographies of musical performance are "actively contextualised" (2004, p. 536), being deliberately set through a range of acts on an emotionally charged stage, comprising a performance "infrastructure". Furthermore, geographies of musical performance are improvisational; despite their "infrastructure", musical performances are not fixed and finite. Performances move and sway, expand and contract and, although they are a way of "doing" emotions, musical performances are a way of life in the making. Musical performances that work best are those that create intimacy and emotional bonds, and the spatiality of the performance setting, whether it is "private" or "public", can also have a bearing on how performances "work" emotionally (Wood and Smith 2004).

Digital storytelling workshops, like musical spaces, are performances in which participants, infrastructure and those who view the digital stories are all critical to gain understanding of how emotions "work" and what emotions "do". Workshops are deliberately set timespaces (Wood and Smith 2004) through which emotional experience and relations may be explored and studied, and emotional knowledge may be scrutinised. Digital storytelling provides access to emotion and affect in social life because emotions are both "played up" and "worked on" to create meaning. The digital storytelling workshop performances with Interactionz incorporated a deliberate infrastructure based on the CDS model. They become improvisational when the model's infrastructure was challenged and made flexible to accommodate the range of practical strategies necessary for all participants. The diverse practical requirements of the participants and their unique subjectivities required that the workshops remain living and fluid timespaces that were open to improvisation. Facilitating the digital storytelling workshops with Interactionz required a complex set of skills to manage what I refer to as "guided improvisation", a practical, negotiated strategy within the infrastructure of digital storytelling that acknowledges digital storytelling as "part of a conversation of practices... not a fixed, finite, discreet or finished thing" (Wood and Smith 2004, p. 537).

Wood and Smith state "there is more to emotional geographies than performances which are contextualized, well prepared and rehearsed" (2004, p. 537). The digital storytelling workshops included improvised performances that extended the practical strategies of digital storytelling infrastructure. Wood and Smith (2004) and Wood et al. (2007, p. 872) identify the performing body, "with its own markings, its instrumental extensions, its wiring into technology, and its physical capabilities" (Wood et al. 2007, p. 873), as a site through which to explore the art of "doing" musical performance. Most of the participants in these workshops had a range of cognitive and physical disabilities, and the infrastructure of digital storytelling had to be modified to accommodate these uniquely embodied timespaces.

Wood and Smith's (2004) and Wood et al.'s (2007) geographical analyses of infrastructure and improvisation in musical performance is important for understanding how emotion and affect in digital story-telling make meaning for persons with disabilities and create knowledge about disability. "Guided improvisation", a strategy adopted during the workshops, characterised the ways in which the model workshop infra-structure was modified to facilitate each participant's distinctive capabili-ties. This flexible approach embraced by the researchers was necessary in order to honour and uphold Interactionz's philosophy of PDP. In the next section, I demonstrate how guided improvisation enabled one of the digital storytelling workshops to become a space of care and empathy as participants performed their stories variously to accommodate their respective needs.

Digital Storytelling Workshops as Spaces of Care and Empathy, Agency and Empowerment

In this section, I reflect on examples from one workshop to illustrate how the researchers improvised aspects of the workshop to accommodate par-ticipants. These improvisations were necessary to realise the purpose of creating digital stories with disabled participants as PDP. These examples illustrate ways in which the improvised nature of the participants' per-formances enabled emotional meaning-making. I also examine the sig-nificance of the support received from Interactionz's staff to enable the disabled participants to "voice" their stories verbally and non-verbally through body language. This provoked affective encounters amongst participants that were enlightening and instructive for both researchers' respective but complementary interests.

Joseph is a middle-aged man with an intellectual disability. He has never learnt to read and write; his oral language, however, in English and Te Reo Māori (the Māori language), is well developed and he is a talented orator and singer. Joseph's special needs created a facilitative challenge because he told his story powerfully in the story circle but was unable to write his story script afterwards, which is the conventional workshop sequence of events. My co-facilitator and I decided we would illustrate Joseph's story as a way to prompt him to tell the story again so that it could be audio recorded. Janelle did this by "picturing" Joseph's story as told in the story circle onto a large sheet of paper that was then used to prompt Joseph to retell and audio record his story for use in the creation of his digital story. The improvisational "picturing" became a necessary technique for performing Joseph's digital story.

The methodological challenges that Wood et al. (2007) discuss were met through improvisation and flexibility in Joseph's digital storytelling performance. Joseph's inability to "write" his story into a script that he would later read and record as the audio track for his digital story, which is standard practice in digital storytelling, required the researchers to exercise empathy and active listening to help Joseph determine his story and represent it, pictorially, in preparation for him to perform it as an oral narrative. Emotional meaning and cognitive knowledge, therefore, was co-created improvisationally between Joseph and the researchers. The question for the digital storytelling workshop, "what does a good life look like?", resulted in an embodied story that Joseph performed, interpreted and shared. New meanings were made for Joseph, and new knowledge about Joseph was realised by Interactionz.

The importance of body language in communication is well known and researched in the social sciences (see, e.g., de Gelder 2006). In digital storytelling workshops, body language is important for interpreting emotional knowledge that can then be performed by participants in their digital stories.

> A storyteller needs their whole body to relate a story, their voice may be primary to the telling, but the eyes are necessary to the relating. It is through their eyes that the telling becomes a consensual mutual act, for the voice works in tandem with what the eyes are taking in. They sense with

their skin the emotional atmosphere, its intensity, temperature, energy and mood. Hands mark out the space that together teller and listener populate with characters, and come to inhabit with the story presence. (Cross 2009, p. 100)

Body language is particularly important in the story circle. The spatial arrangement of the workshop infrastructure allows participants to notice corporeal gestures and expressions of emotion that might influence the collective performance of digital storytelling. For example, when Joseph finished telling his story in the story circle, he moved his hands to his face and rubbed his head and his eyes. I could see that his eyes were watery, and the performance of his story had provoked an emotional response in him. Alex, who was sitting next to him, reached over and stroked Joseph's arm to comfort him. Alex's bodily comforting of Joseph demonstrates how digital storytelling can be "heard" socially, generate empathy and prompt emotionally embodied reactions from other workshop participants (Wood and Smith 2004; Wood et al. 2007).

The verbal feedback Joseph received from the other participants in the story circle, however, provoked an empathetic response from him. Not only had Joseph been listening to other people's stories but also had embodied them and, relating them to his own, this contributed to his corporeal actions. Joseph's body language and his verbal reactions to comments and gestures from other story circle participants on his story reflect the "consensual mutual act" of storytelling and how the "emotional atmosphere, its intensity, temperature, energy and mood" are embodied in digital storytelling (Cross 2009, p. 100).

> Well, it made me sad, to think about my family's life, and my parents. And inside me I've got a good heart. I've got good energy. Listening to some of the people in this room here, it make me, I want to cry about it. I don't want to cry. I listen to people and what they're saying. Tegan, she's got a good story. She's got a good life, of her own. I like to listen to people. (Joseph 2010, Hamilton)

Like Joseph, Pam's and Colleen's experiences in the workshop also exemplify the emotionally embodied nature of their digital storytelling performances. Colleen and Pam are both illiterate, and their oral skills not as developed as Joseph's. For Pam and Colleen, their lack of oral and written skills, and the extent of their intellectual disabilities, required a different form of improvisation to enable them to perform their digital stories. Two members of Interactionz's staff who supported Pam and Colleen in the workshop conducted conversational interviews with each of them in order to help voice their stories. Other support staff were present at these interviews to operate recording equipment so as to capture their stories improvisationally. Iterations from the story circle were picked up by the interviewers. These contributed to the development of a linear narrative in the recording process; however, significant editing was conducted one-on-one between one of the workshop facilitators and Pam and Colleen in order to compile their respective audio tracks.

Two examples illustrate the improvisation that was performed in the workshop with Pam and Colleen. Janelle sat with Pam and prompted her with questions and comments about her experience as a person that Interactionz serves and how those experiences have impacted on her "journey to a good life". Janelle typed Pam's "story" into the computer and ended up with a written script that she later used to prompt Pam's digital story during audio recording. The raw recording of approximately six minutes was subsequently co-edited by Pam and a workshop facilitator to one-third the length of the initial recording.

Colleen's storytelling performance was also improvised. Bronwyn, who worked closely with Colleen and prompted her story in the recording session, explained that unlike Janelle and Pam, they did not feel the need to work from a written script because Colleen "knew exactly what she wanted to say" in her story and just needed some encouragement to speak her story (Bronwyn 2011). Wood et al.'s (2007) argument that the performing body can be seen as a site through which to explore the art of "doing" musical performance is applicable to Colleen's digital storytelling experience. In digital storytelling, however, the boundaries of the performing body are often extended to other bodies as "instrumental extensions [of] its physical capabilities" (Wood et al. 2007, p. 873) to create "art" out of a collective, embodied performance, as Colleen's story demonstrates.

The digital storytelling workshop was a performance whereby Joseph's, Pam's and Colleen's body language, mood and emotions were interpreted collectively by storyteller and listener in a co-creative process.

These cues [promptings] mean a teller begins to follow as well as lead in a kind of dance. This dance involves reading the emotional weather whilst one continues to contribute to its creation. Some of the words of the tale are constant but much, much is open to the promptings of the mutual interpretation that the teller senses is possible from the gathered listening. Both teller and listener hold a story, therefore creating the space into which it is told. (Cross 2009, p. 100)

Joseph, Pam and Colleen worked closely with others in the workshop to help them perform their digital stories. In order for this to happen, a caring and empathetic timespace was established and maintained by all participants, and improvisational techniques were applied in the moment to help illuminate the emotionally embodied geographies of disability amongst the workshop participants.

Improvisation in the performance of the digital storytelling workshop was instrumental in enabling Joseph, Pam and Coleen to create their stories. As participants in the workshop, the researchers witnessed the circulation of emotional and affective energies that were captured in stories about what makes a good life for people with disabilities. The embodied nature of digital storytelling that was experienced amongst participants in the workshop enhanced Interactionz's understandings about the people they serve and their support of PDP. Meaning-making about the emotional and affective knowledge production in digital storytelling workshops contributed to geographical understandings of disability and care relationships.

CONCLUSION

Digital storytelling workshops as spaces of emotion and affect are important for making meaning of, and knowledge about, the journey to a good life for people with disabilities. Spatiality was also important in terms of the collaborative nature of researchers who shared a common problem-based interest on how to understand and improve the everyday life of people with disabilities in their shared community. Both Janelle and myself furthered our knowledge and appreciation of the power of digital storytelling to enable the embodiment of previously disembodied discourses of disability through the workshop participants' digital stories. Hegemonic power relations were challenged as diverse participants at all levels of Interactionz created and shared their stories in the same workshop space. This created new knowledge about established power relations in the geographic context of institutions as different voices, able and disabled, made individual and collective meaning about the diverse experience of disability within the same discursive and physical space.

The importance of the improvisational capacity of digital storytelling to create flexibility in expressing the emotional work of disability was emphasised. Examples of three participants' stories illuminated several ways in which the deliberately set infrastructure of digital storytelling workshops must be improvised to allow for different voices of disability to be heard. The digital storytelling workshops became affective spaces of care, empathy, agency and empowerment for participants. Digital storytelling workshops were recognised by the collaborative researchers as safe spaces for knowledge creation about the emotional dimensions of disability.

Attention to emotion and affect in the digital storytelling workshops provided both researchers a unique insight into disability's "entangled terrains of the neurological, personal, familial, cultural and political" (Smith 2012, p. 343). The emotional and affective experiences of the workshop participants enabled alternative care relationships to emerge and contributed to Interactionz's self-evaluation of PDP. Both researchers benefitted from bearing witness to the disabled persons' performances as experts of their own lived experience.

The traditional gap between researchers, community practitioners and people with disabilities was upset in this collaborative research project. Collaborative community-based research recognises that knowledge creation is multidirectional and expertise is shared (Rice 2002). The digital storytelling workshops provided a methodology, situated in a particular time and space, for individuals to voice their own stories. A fluid interpretation of disability and "expertise" into the personal, cultural and political landscape of disability emerged amongst all participants in the digital storytelling workshops. The workshop participants explored individually and collaboratively the "journey to a good life" and the researchers advocated an enabling geography (Chouinard 1997; Kitchin 1997) whereby technical skills, knowledge and resources were shared. The researchers also included workshop participants in reporting research outcomes at meetings, seminars and conferences, as Joseph's experience illustrates. Finally, the engaged, collaborative, community-based scholarship demonstrated in this research project demonstrates how the expression of a good life is navigated through emotion and affect and how (dis)abling geographies of difference can be challenged through digital storytelling.

NOTES

1. Participants in the workshops included disabled persons that Interactionz serves, the Interactionz's staff and Board of Trustees. My co-facilitator and I are both trained in the CDS model of digital storytelling.
2. Interactionz's staff researched models of practice that would enable them to achieve their vision and developed a customised model called person-driven practice (PDP). PDP is a facilitative model of service delivery based on the citizenship model of disability in which people with disabilities have choice and control over the supports they receive and the lives they lead as valued and contributing citizens in their own communities. It is based on a number of principles that recognise that life is different for every person and every situation. The aim of Interactionz's staff is to facilitate decision-making rather than making decisions for the people they serve. Interactionz's staff actively supports the personal capacity of individuals rather than employing an institutional deficit model; they recognise people's gifts and capacities and those of their natural supports (see http://www.interactionz.org.nz/).
3. Four workshops were conducted at the University of Waikato in July 2009, February 2010, August 2010, February 2011 and a fifth at Enderley Community Centre in February 2015.
4. Wood and Smith (2004) draw on Thrift (1996) in their use of timespace, a term which suggests that spatial and temporal processes are impossible to separate.

REFERENCES

Bliss, E., & Fisher, J. (2014). The Journey to a good life: Exploring personal and organisational transformation through digital storytelling. In R. Rinehart, K. N. Barbour, & C. C. Pope (Eds.), *Ethnographic Worldviews: Transformations and Social Justice*. Dordrecht: Springer.

Bondi, L. (2008). On the relational dynamics of caring: A psychotherapeutic approach to emotional and power dimensions of women's care work. *Gender, Place and Culture, 15*(3), 249–265.

Bronwyn. (2011). *Personal communication*. Hamilton.

Chouinard, V. (1997). Making space for disability differences: Challenging abliest geographies. *Environment and Planning D: Society and Space, 15*(4), 379–387.

Cross, B. (2009). Feeling my way into story space: Lessons for research from storyteller Duncan Williamson. *Emotion, Space and Society, 2*(2), 98–103.

de Gelder, B. (2006). Towards the neurobiology of emotional body language. *Nature Reviews Neuroscience, 7*(3), 242–249.

Joseph. (2010). *Personal communication.* Hamilton.

Kitchin, R. (1997). Participatory action research in geography: Towards a more emancipatory and empowering approach. *Disability Studies Quarterly, 21*(4), 61–69.

Perkins, C. (2009). Mapping, philosophy. In R. Kitchin & N. Thrift (Eds.), *International Encyclopedia of Human Geography* (pp. 385–397). England: Elsevier.

Rice, R. E. (2002). Beyond scholarship reconsidered: Toward an enlarged vision of the scholarly work of faculty members. *New Directions for Teaching and Learning, 2002*(90), 7–18. Wiley Periodicals Inc.

Smith, N. (2012). Embodying brainstorms: the experiential geographies of living with epilepsy. *Social and Cultural Geography, 13*(4), 339–359.

Thrift, N. (1996). *Spatial formations.* London: Sage.

Wood, N., & Smith, S. (2004). Instrumental routes to emotional geographies. *Social and Cultural Geographies, 5*(4), 533–548.

Wood, N., Duffy, M., & Smith, S. J. (2007). The art of doing (geographies of) music. *Environment and Planning D: Society and Space, 25*(5), 867–889.

CHAPTER 23

Implicating Practice: Engaged Scholarship Through Co-creative Media

Darcy Alexandra

INTRODUCTION

In political asylum proceedings, the way a story is told determines whether one will be granted refugee status or not—or as Evelyn, one research participant whose monologue is discussed in this chapter, has written, "whether you are in, or out" (Crossing Over 2009). Often what matters is not the veracity of the story, or the ability to communicate it, but the "plausibility" of the story, and the "believability" of the storyteller. The research presented in the chapter draws from a longitudinal (2007–2010) ethnography of media production with political asylum seekers and labour migrants in Ireland (Alexandra 2015).[1] Said research aimed to develop an exploratory and critical practice of inquiry that responded not only to the ethical complexities of research with refugees, asylum seekers, and undocumented migrants, but also to create opportunities for research subjects to interpret, analyse, document, and publicly screen their experiences as newcomers to Ireland. Within a community of practice (Lave and Wenger 1991), participants produced their own media to explore and document their lives as workers, parents, "cultural citizens" (Coll 2010; El Haj 2009; Rosaldo 1994), and artists simultaneously adapting to, and transforming, a new environment.

D. Alexandra (✉)
University of Bern, Bern, Switzerland

© The Author(s) 2017
G. Jamissen et al. (eds.), *Digital Storytelling in Higher Education,*
Digital Education and Learning, DOI 10.1007/978-3-319-51058-3_23

By centring participants from diasporic communities as the primary authors and co-producers of their audio-visual narratives, the research sought to extend and deepen the public discourse of migration. The precarious circumstances of research participants living in the asylum system and/or living without legal documentation, together with the goal of developing digital storytelling as a research method, necessitated a slowing down of the production process. Instead of the standard CDS (StoryCenter) model of a three-day workshop (Lambert 2013), the seminars were constructed as college courses for emergent media producers. Classes were held every week for 2–4 hours over a period of five months with a follow-up phase of approximately four months for collaborative post-production. Great care was given to mentoring participants as emergent media practitioners and to critically exploring the diverse elements of their documentary essays—visual montage, sound design, script development, and video editing.[2] The audio-visual production process—the opportunity to be creative in new ways—contributed to unprecedented engagement among research practitioners who rarely missed a seminar. The development of a longitudinal space for creativity, and, in particular, the act of scriptwriting facilitated relationships of caring and trust. It provided opportunities for dialogue, solidarity, and recognition. Valuing the story that each participant selected through adequate time to develop not only a monologue but also an audiovisual landscape; providing engaged feedback in an affirmative manner; and encouraging each storytellers' practice as author, scholar, and emergent documentarian provided key elements to building a dynamic community of practice (Cammarota 2008; Fine et al. 2000; Freire 1998; Greene 1995; Moll 1992).[3] Through the process, research practitioners—seven women and six men from African, Asian, Eastern European, and Middle Eastern countries—interrogated their daily circumstances negotiating migration policy and revealed the structural violence of asylum and migrant labour regimes.

A scholarship of engagement necessitates collaboration, analysis, and creativity across domains. As a co-creative (Spurgeon et al. 2009) practice, digital storytelling (Gubrium 2009; Nuñez-Janes 2016) can render these domains—the nexus of aesthetic, ethical, political, institutional, and research considerations and questions—tangible and open to consideration. As both researcher and educator in this participatory research and media project at the Dublin Institute of Technology, I ethnographically documented and analysed this production process. It led me outside the seminar to collaborate individually and collectively with research practitioners. Documenting group interactions and one-to-one discussions surrounding the development and production of the audio-visual and written story elements provided concrete in-roads for analysis across domains. In this context, script development emerged as a generative and complex site for knowledge sharing, learning, and production. In contrast to the rules of storytelling enforced in asylum proceedings, the monologues created by research practitioners are more akin to poetic meditations than to legal testimony or political confession. The development and co-creative editing of the monologue served as a vehicle for learning from and about research subjects in new ways—ways that did not entail formal interviews or legalistic questioning. Of equal importance for consideration is the narrative time of the stories that practitioners developed, in terms of the time it took to think through and compose them, and the lifespan and relationships they reveal.[4]

This chapter invites in-depth consideration of co-creative script[5] writing. Following the ethical commitments and methodological contour of the research, the process is slowed down in the chapter, and the analytical assets are opened up for public reflection. The reader is invited to take their time with the work of two research collaborators, and their audio-visual productions. In this way, through the development of *New Ways* by Ahmad and *Crossing Over* by Evelyn, one can observe the emergence of actors toward a framework of engaged scholarship.

NEW WAYS

In the development of their monologues, some participants, like Ahmad, wrote exclusively during the workshop seminars while others, like Evelyn, wrote from the asylum centres and sent in successive drafts via email. Once participants had the sense their script was ready to share with the group, they chose when to present it. By that time, practitioners had had the chance to work alone with their images and ideas, collaborate in the workshop setting, discuss their potential storylines, and examine issues of audio-visual representation through workshop discussions. When participants shared their draft during seminar, they would read the script out loud, and their colleagues and I would discuss different moments in the story, make observations, ask clarifying questions, and suggest possible edits. Some participants welcomed suggestions about possible changes to their monologues, and others were clear about not wanting to make any revisions. I respected this clarity—offering suggestions when they were requested, and within an ethos of supporting the agency of the storyteller.

To demonstrate two different, yet equally co-creative script development and editing processes, we now turn to the work of Ahmad and Evelyn. The following section begins with field notes from the workshop site. The writing situates the reader at the seminar, is arranged in chronological order, and documents how script development unfolded along a circular route of reflection—knowledge sharing—dialogue—reflection.

September 29, 2008

Ahmad arrived early before workshop today. He hasn't decided which story to tell. I assured him he would have time to figure it out. I asked if any of the in-class writing activities had given him ideas.

> "No, not really," Ahmad answers.
> "But you've been doing the group writing activities?"
> "Yes, but there's too much to say, like".

I asked how he learned English. He explained that he had attended courses, but learned most of his English from his ex-girlfriend. He told me that when his application for asylum was refused, he learned his girlfriend "did not value him without refugee status." He felt "inferior." The relationship became "impossible." Eventually they broke up. I asked if I could write down his words, explaining that this might give him some leads, and help him to determine what story he wanted to tell. Ahmad agreed, and I wrote down his complete sentences and fragments of ideas. He talked about his struggles to deal with other people's assumptions about him, and where he comes from.

> When I tell them where I'm from, they assume they know what I think, who I am.

He tells me he is ashamed of his country's politics. He doesn't agree with them, yet people assume he does. I tell him I understand how that can feel. He tells me he grew up Muslim and now identifies as a Christian.

> Which God do I pray to now?

I stop what I am doing and listen. He talks about the Direct Provision Centre where he is "accommodated" in a rural area in Ireland. He shares one room with four other men. Four unrelated people living in one room. He has limited to no control over all aspects of his living quarters.

He can't adjust the thermostat; it's controlled from outside the room. He can't turn off the lights when he wants to sleep. Like in prison. I ask if he has friends outside the hostel, if he is able to get out. He knows some people from church. To keep busy, he volunteers at the hostel repairing washing machines. In Iran, he studied mechanical engineering. Ever since arriving in Ireland, he's been volunteering. It's been three years now. He "hates" the hostel manager. I note the intensity of the word. Ahmad is gentle in his demeanour, careful with his words, considerate of the others in the workshop. The situation with the hostel manager must be unbearable.

Mona, Susan, and the others begin to arrive, and we shift gear. I hand Ahmad the notes. He looks at his sentences in quotation marks, and sets the paper into his folder.

October 27, 2008

Ahmad hasn't shared a script with the group yet, but often stays on after the workshop is over, writing in Farsi, and editing his library of images in Photoshop.

Last week, he came to the workshop with his arm in a sling. Everyone noticed, but when Mona asked him what happened, Ahmad shook his head, smiled, and said nothing. No one insisted. Even during lunch, a more informal time when people often talk and catch up, Ahmad said nothing. Throughout the day, he looked withdrawn, but he listened closely to other people's scripts, and asked questions about their photographs.

November 4, 2008

Tonight, Jimmy, the college porter, knocks on the door like every week— reminding us it's time to leave the building: they're locking up for the night. We know he'll give us those extra ten minutes. Just as I begin turning off computers, Ahmad tells me.

"I punched a wall."

"You punched the wall," I answer back.

"Yeah. I worry about myself." Ahmad alludes to wanting to jump out a window. I listen fast. I hold still. I am conscious of my breathing.

"How did I get here?" he tells me. It is not a question. It is something else of which I am uncertain. It is the third time in two weeks I have heard people in this research project say those words out loud–*how did I get here?*

We walk downstairs to the media centre where I photocopy the notes I've taken from his ideas and our conversation. The director of the centre asks Ahmad what happened to his arm.

> "I don't want to lie, but I feel ashamed to tell the truth," Ahmad answers.
> "In that case," the director replies, "just say: 'It's a long story: I'll tell you some other time.'"

I look at Ahmad. I wonder what he will decide to say now. Which story he will choose? As we walk out the front entrance, I ask if he can speak to a counsellor at the centre, or a friend, someone he trusts. He answers, "not really."

He is visibly upset. I tell him not to internalize something that is outside of his control, not to blame himself for a system that is failing him, and many others who have done nothing wrong. I say I'm worried. I know he has endured a great deal. I know he is a capable man. I am also worried. I want to hug Ahmad—to hug someone in pain, someone who I have come to know and respect, seems the "right" response. But I stop myself. Ahmad is formal, and this relationship of "student" and "teacher," "researcher" and "research participant" is formal. Yet, these roles do not convey the care and kindness that has developed during the workshop. Of course, I am not Ahmad's friend in the traditional sense of the word, but I have come to know him, and I do not know what to do. I feel responsible, and implicated in this practice. We stand outside the building in our silence. The sound of seagulls. The scent of malt from the Guinness factory. A group of adolescents has gathered on the corner talking loudly, laughing. I say I look forward to seeing Ahmad in the workshop next week. He says he will be there. I tell him to call if he needs to talk. We shake hands. He walks north towards the bus station, and I walk south towards my apartment.

November 11, 2008

Mid-way through the workshop tonight, Ahmad told me he had finished his script, and wanted to share it with the group. Reading the final monologue before workshop participants often provided moments of solidarity, recognition, and debate. This was the case with Ahmad. When he read his monologue, people listened closely. I imagine they were curious about this intense, quiet man. He was one of two participants—among nine—who did not have children, and no family members in Ireland. He was one of two participants who did not come from an African country. Although he discussed images and ideas, he talked little about himself. Why exactly was his arm in a cast?

When he read his description of the living conditions at his hostel, the emotions in the room shifted. He read,

> At night when I want to sleep someone is watching television, someone else is snoring loudly and someone else is smoking.

Mona, Marie, and Abazu laughed out loud in recognition. Other participants nodded their heads knowingly.

> "That's it! That's what we live with! That is it. That is it," Ogo asserted, nodding his head in affirmation.

Other participants nodded in agreement. Ahmad observed his colleagues' appraisal of his words. He seemed pleased but did not reply. Following is the monologue that Ahmad read to the group, and later developed into his documentary essay:

New Ways by Ahmad What's going on? What's happening to me? I'm riding in an ambulance. My hand is broken. I'm wondering about the Ahmad I was and the Ahmad I am now! I never expected myself to do something like this.

In Tehran I worked as an engineer. I had a good position in a factory as a tool and mould maker. I belonged to a happy, loving family. I was very patient, a healthy person, always optimistic about the future!

But life became difficult, it was unsafe for me and I had to leave Iran.

Man be in dar na pay heshmato jah amadeham.

(I have not come here seeking prestige or recognition).

Az pase hadeseh inja be panah amadeham.

(Rather, I have come in search of shelter).

Three years ago I came to Ireland seeking asylum. I was placed in the Birchwood House hostel in Waterford City. I live there with about 160 other people. We are not allowed to work, not allowed to study. We are given meals and 19 Euros 10 cent a week.

After a few months, I met a lovely girl. We understood each other well; we had a lot in common. I fell in love with her. We planned to get married.

To get married she said I had to get refugee status. When my application for asylum was refused, I realised she did not value me without refugee status. I felt inferior. It was a very painful period and the continuation of the relationship was unbearable. Finally, we broke up. This had a terrible impact on my already miserable situation.

At the Birchwood House I have to share a room with 4 other men. At night when I want to sleep someone is watching television, someone else is snoring loudly and someone else is smoking. Sometimes the temperature is too hot and sometimes it's too cold. It's impossible to sleep soundly (Fig. 23.1).

I have no one who understands my own language to talk to. I find it really hard to express myself in English. No one is willing to listen.

Fig. 23.1 Screen shot from New Ways (2009) written and directed by Ahmad. In his digital story, Ahmad's photograph of an external view of his "accommodation centre" is animated with a slow pan, and lights that turn on and off as Ahmad narrates the psychologically stressful living conditions of the asylum centre where he lived in rural Ireland

That night I couldn't sleep. The lights were out. But the guy next door had been talking loudly all night. Suddenly we heard water over-flowing from the sink. It smelled terrible. It spilled all over our room, destroying all my books, photographs and documents. I went to ask for help from the Centre's reception, but nobody would help us. Burning with frustration and out of control, I punched the wall and broke my hand.

For a while I looked after my hand and it healed. Now, I need to look after my heart and my life. As an asylum seeker I know my situation won't change quickly. It is difficult, but I have to keep going. As I let go of the old way, a new way is shown to me.

Too Much to Say

As the field notes document, ongoing reflection, knowledge sharing, and dialogue between the storyteller and me, and between the storyteller and a "community" of emergent practitioners animated the script development. Over time, and across this dialogical engagement of reflection—knowledge sharing—dialogue—reflection, Ahmad developed his final monologue, *New Ways*. The collaborative development process that undergirds the monologue illustrates aspects of Ahmad's practice. It materialises his undertaking of reflection, deliberation, and discernment. His observation that there was "too much to say," speaks to the demanding and creative task of conceptualising and editing a brief and purposeful composition. More precisely, it speaks to the challenge of disclosing and analysing a series of traumatic events in Ahmad's life that are both personal and political. What to reveal? What to omit? Where to focus? What might be the repercussions and potential impacts of disclosure? These questions were central to the scriptwriting process—and key to the research process, as well. They are questions that become urgent when a life story unfolds within a broader context of institutional violence, vulnerability, and trauma. As Ahmad examined the "Ahmad (he) was and the Ahmad (he is) now," his monologue reveals the psychological impact of not receiving refugee status and the anxiety of living in legal, professional, economic, and emotional limbo. Who will "value" him without refugee status? Where is the Ahmad he once was? His fear and sadness are tangible. Located in his broken hand, Ahmad's anger is set down in the narrative arc of the story. The physical healing becomes a vehicle for his will to live, his desire to heal invisible wounds—as he writes, "to look after my heart."

The production process of *New Ways*, and the artefact of the monologue raised new points of contact between Ahmad as an engaged scholar and the community of practice, and new questions for consideration. For example, does the "old way" refer to his change of faith, the life decision that set him on a path "seeking shelter?" Or might it represent the collection of moments, family members and friends, daily routines, and site-specific experiences and competencies that have shifted place in relation to his daily existence in Europe? As he wondered during our workshop conversation, where would he find the courage and strength to re/envision his life? Or as he asked, "which God (does he) pray to now?" Where are his lines of continuity and connectivity within a new set of identities, and a new country? Finally, within a community of practice, the field notes document the affective labour of the research—the considered hesitancies, the potential for secondary traumas, as well as solidarity, and the intimacy of the mentoring relationship. They underscore the need for thinking across domains. The monologue—as well as the self-authored images and the final composition—offers multiple pathways for reflection, learning, and engagement.

Due to the unacceptable living conditions described in his monologue, Ahmad requested an accommodation transfer. Nearly a year after filing his request, he was moved to an asylum hostel in Limerick—a former hotel in what he determined to be a violent neighbourhood. Shortly after the transfer, there was a stabbing in the hostel, and Ahmad was transferred from shared accommodation to the newly vacant room. Finally, after so much waiting, accommodation services had responded to his request to live alone, but due to the violent circumstances that led to his transfer, Ahmad did not feel at ease in the new room. When I visited him in the new accommodation centre, he told me he was trying to keep his spirits up; he volunteered for odd jobs through his Iranian social networks, and occasionally travelled to Dublin for different church activities. Nevertheless, two years after the conclusion of the research project, exhausted by the uncertainty of waiting for a response to his claim for humanitarian leave to remain, Ahmad decided to leave Ireland. He moved to London where he enrolled in an English for Speakers of Other Languages (ESOL) course, began an apprenticeship through a job-training programme, and continued volunteering with his church. He hoped London would provide greater possibilities for economic and educational integration as an asylum seeker.

CROSSING OVER

Evelyn is from the Ibibio Clan of Akwa Ibom, Nigeria, and came to Ireland in 2005 seeking asylum. In Nigeria, Evelyn worked as a community journalist. Before participating in the workshop, she was involved with a university-based immigrant women writers' group in Dublin. She had read her prose publicly, and identified as a writer, but noted that she only began to consider herself a poet while developing her audio-visual composition in the college seminar. She is the mother of three sons (aged 12, 9, and 4 at the time of the workshop in 2009). At her accommodation hostel, Evelyn provided counsel to her fellow residents as an active member of the residents' committee. Every week, she travelled several hours by train from County Mayo to Dublin to attend the workshop at the college. These train journeys provided time alone and time to write. She rarely wrote during the workshop sessions; instead, she mentored colleagues with their writing, edited images from her phone, and participated in workshop discussions. Unlike Ahmad, Evelyn had a developed idea about the story she wanted to create—perhaps because of her experience and confidence as a writer. I followed her lead and provided feedback on successive drafts as she sent them via email—entering into editorial discussion with her about potential edits and storylines for further work. In developing her monologue, each draft that Evelyn wrote provided new and detailed information about the asylum system, her experiences of living in direct provision, and the strategies she developed as a community leader. In her writing, she raised a series of questions about asylum policy, institutional brokers, and the complex circumstances that lead people to seek asylum in the first place. She wondered how governments and institutions could be held accountable. She asked which problems, among so many, should be the focus of campaign attention—the boredom arising from social isolation and economic exclusion? The "violent storms and hurricanes of raising children in one room?" The enforced marginalisation and poverty of the direct provision system, and its daily and potentially long-term health impacts on the men, women, and children who seek protection? In making her story, she faced the challenge of how to audio-visually convey the ongoing stress of living with the threat of transfer from one hostel to another, and the often unspoken and pervasive fear of deportation. In her reflections and observations, Evelyn also raised concern about the ways in which Nigerians are stigmatised, and disbelieved, and how the fact of Nigerian citizenship alone can block the pathway to legal status. Evelyn's final monologue takes the reader into her asylum hostel. The narrative is organised around one day of life in the direct provision system. It is the story of one moment that encapsulates many of her questions and observations—the moment of receiving leave to remain, or as Evelyn cinematically recounts in her story, the moment of "crossing over." The monologue highlights the strength of Evelyn's writing. Through her composition, the listener learns about the psychological impact of direct provision and how Evelyn intercepts a failing system by counselling her peers and providing leadership beyond the bounds of her institutionalisation as an asylum seeker. *Crossing Over* developed and grew over several drafts, co-editing sessions, and consideration of the feedback Evelyn received from her community of practice. The following is Evelyn's final monologue, which she recorded and developed into her digital story:

Crossing Over by Evelyn I woke up this morning with a bit of 'hot head' and shivers, even though the room was heated. It is one of those days in Ireland when the sky empties her icy grains. Going to the GP is out of the question. I have seen him five times in one month. I know this is the pulse of frustration–whose height cannot be measured, nor bounds determined by a mere stethoscope.

This is my third year in the direct provision[6] hostel and I have learned that asylum seekers visit the GP four times more frequently than normal Irish people. The pressure in here is so high that everybody seems to be furious over little things. If you ask me, I would say that most of our ailments are stress-related (Fig. 23.2).

I look up; it's Funmi. Not again. It is her 5th year in the hostel so she's a 'bag of trouble.' Being a member of the residents' committee, I am confronted with all kinds of situations. Most times, I get so furious about whom to direct my anger at. Is it the asylum system that piles up people together for years of idleness? Or, our greedy country leaders who send their youth scrambling for safety?

Despite my headache, I counsel Funmi. Just then, Carolyn bursts into my room, raging, swearing and cursing, "What again?" I ask. "Do you know that my solicitor said my case would be great if I wasn't a Nigerian?"

I stare at her, wondering how my country got to be a 'sinful nation' in the eyes of the world.

"Funmi! Funmi! Funmi!" I can hear the lady in room 10 calling out, "You have a registered post!" There is a drop-pin silence. This is one

Fig. 23.2 Screen shot from Crossing Over, (2009) written and directed by Evelyn. The image is in conversation with the following moment in her monologue, "The pressure in here is so high that everyone seems to be furious about little things. If you ask me I would say that most of our ailments are stress related."

moment that every asylum seekers dreads, it is the decider–either you are in, or you are out.

We all cluster around Funmi. Her heartbeat vibrating like a Nokia phone. After five stressful years Funmi received her leave to remain. What a situation! Five years of being on the waiting line, and one minute of crossing over.

How Did We Get Here?

Evelyn and Ahmad developed monologues about the human cost of asylum policies and the mental health impacts of an institutionalised life in the direct provision system. Ahmad outlines the critical incidents that landed him in the hospital, while Evelyn writes about her headache as "the pulse of frustration–whose height cannot be measured, nor bounds determined by a mere stethoscope." Evelyn wrote her monologue in a few afternoons on the train and while living in a one-room apartment with her three sons—her fourth year in the direct provision system while Ahmad wrote his script away from his accommodation centre, in the safety of the workshop setting, and over a period of seven weeks. Evelyn's story ends on a hopeful note—the possibility of receiving leave to remain, the chance to "cross over." The ending of Ahmad's story is also hopeful—"a new way will be shown" to him. However, his conclusion comes so quickly it leaves the reader wondering. How exactly will this "new way" appear? What might it mean to "let go of old ways?" Ahmad is, of course, like Evelyn, writing into an uncertain future.

Evelyn played a key role in framing the discussions regarding impact and dissemination of the documentary essays. Along with the other research practitioners, she expressed interest in screening the essays at the Irish Film Institute (IFI) in Dublin—a preeminent institution for national film. In May 2009, *Living in Direct Provision: 9 Stories* screened as the first collection of short films authored and co-produced by asylum seekers and refugees living in Ireland. There, *Crossing Over* and *New Ways* premiered before an audience of family members, policy makers, immigration scholars, and community activists. The seminar group asked Evelyn to introduce the collection, and she welcomed the audience with a short essay she had written on the train. *Living in Direct Provision: 9 Stories* was well received. One member of a national non-governmental organisation present at the screening told me that Evelyn's story had conveyed in three minutes what their advocacy organisation takes years to convey. An article in the local paper reviewed the videos as a testament to the "scholarship of listening." The collection was invited to the Guth Gafa International Documentary Film Festival and Evelyn and I accompanied the series to Northwestern Ireland for a screening and public discussion. From the seminar, seven of the nine participants released their essays for public viewing and their stories are currently available online.[7]

In 2010, Evelyn and her three sons were among a group of 35 people taken into custody, and deported on a late-night Frontex[8] flight. Approaching Athens, the airplane encountered mechanical failure, and was forced to return to Dublin (Smyth and Mangan 2010). The next day, Evelyn and her family were back in Dublin. Evelyn's friends in Ireland called the technical mishap the "Christmas Miracle." Upon return to Ireland, Evelyn decided to continue building a future there; her sons attended school, she continued writing, she volunteered with a local church, and participated in local and national organising efforts for the rights of asylum seekers. She maintained hope that her case would be positively reviewed and that she and her family would receive humanitarian leave to remain. When I talked with Evelyn in person in 2012, she spoke only briefly about the traumatic deportation and her uncertain legal status. We talked instead about her writing, and the collaborative script writing and editing process. I wanted to know how Evelyn had perceived the process in hindsight. The conversation revealed how Evelyn conceptualised her documentary essay, *Crossing Over* as a means "to tell everybody's story." She saw the workshop as a platform and the production process as one that the participants led as well. Like Ahmad, Evelyn had wrestled her monologue from a place of overwhelming in-articulation, of "too much to say." Through deliberation and discernment, of "knowing what is most important," she shaped her perspective in conversation with a larger collectivity. When I asked her what she took away from the experience, she replied:

> For me it's a stepping stone that in the future could put things down, that is what I hope for because it's a kind of reflection. Maybe in the future things are going to change for individuals, for the country, for everybody, but it's a stepping stone that could document things that happened and people will look back at it, to what Ireland was, or what individuals went through. Positively, it's a kind of strength. I know that I have a story somewhere (Conversation with Evelyn, February 12, 2012).

When asked about how she would describe herself to audiences now, she said:

> I would say this is one individual that the situation in Ireland, the situation I find myself in, has made me a better writer because yes, I never knew I was a poet. So, some bad situations turn out positively. There is a book, and in the synopsis my name is mentioned besides (a prominent Irish politician), you can imagine! It says, (I am) an 'African Irish writer.' If I can now be qualified as an African Irish writer then I should look forward to being one (Conversation with Evelyn, February 12, 2012).

Despite her legal status in relation to the state, Evelyn developed a societal and cultural status as an African Irish writer. Her writing has been published, and her documentary essay, *Crossing Over* has screened at migration and refugee policy meetings, and before Irish legislators and activists. Without having been granted the rights and entitlements of Irish citizenship, she has acted as a "cultural citizen" (Coll 2010; El Haj 2009;

Rosaldo 1994), contributing to the public discourse on migration and asylum policy.

In a complex turn of events, when it became clear that Evelyn would not receive humanitarian leave to remain in Ireland, she made the difficult decision of accepting a "re-location offer" from the Irish government. She returned to Nigeria with her sons. Despite tremendous challenges, Evelyn has recreated a life for herself and her family. At time of publication (2016), her eldest son is beginning studies at a prestigious British university and her two younger sons are excelling in school, as well. Some might conclude that since Evelyn was able to re-build her life in the country she had once fled, her life was never truly in danger. This conclusion would deny the complexities of migration and the continuum of political, social, environmental, and economic reasons that inform the decision, and an urgency, to take flight. The fact that Evelyn has been able to support her family and thrive is testament to her capacity and her courage to build and re-create anew—despite the odds.

Conclusion

Developing a longitudinal, inquiry-based seminar approach provided research practitioners with more points of entry to reflexively engage with, and interrogate, their circumstances. Through this method of engagement, script writing became a form of inquiry. Practitioners had time to consider what they would reveal and to enter into dialogue with one another from the foundation point of their written words and their images. The restriction of the format—the framework of a 3- to 5-minute composition—provided a challenging and useful limitation, a kind of container for practitioners to determine what they know and envision. As Evelyn noted, short-form, creative writing served as a means of telling "your story the way it is for you" (Conversation, February 12, 2012). But as I have aimed to remind us, the telling occurs within both a multi-mediated site of production and learning, and a broader political context. In this way, I have implicitly argued for the benefit of cultivating a reflexive curiosity about one of the most pivotal aspects of our work—its collaborative, dialogical essence. Instead of conceptualising the role of the educator, media mentor, or "story specialist" as a "hands off" position in which one "leaves no fingerprints," we would benefit from recognising the ways in which we influence, shape, and inform the process, as well. To this end, the multi-mediated endeavour of digital storytelling offers a rich landscape of inter-subjective (Jackson 2013) moments as the researcher/educator responds to and interacts with the concerns, interests, and demands of a "community" of practice. Attending to these interactions can make this "implicated" (Stoller 1997; Fletcher and Cambre 2009) endeavour more visible and open to nuance—a potential strategy to counter epistemic violence in the ways in which scholarship can reduce—through reification and/or simplification—human "experience." In this vein, to conceptualise participants as engaged scholars, and emergent media practitioners, could serve to more adequately support the production of heterogeneous stories—stories that express diverse moments shaping diverse lives; stories that might most productively be understood not as "representational" but rather as "embodied." By following the development of two different monologues, and the trajectories of Ahmad and Evelyn, we can observe the emergence of participants as engaged scholars acting within legal and political frameworks beyond their immediate control, and socio-political environments hostile to migration—particularly of Muslims, poor people, and people of colour. Through this slowed down consideration, we begin to glimpse the ways in which *Crossing Over* and *New Ways* are embodied with the heterogeneous, complex, and nuanced experiences of being alive in the world.

NOTES

1. Sincere thanks are due to the research practitioners who participated in the project, and to the Forum on Migration and Communications (FOMACS), Integrating Ireland, Refugee Information Service, and the Dublin Institute of Technology (DIT). An ABBEST Doctoral Fellowship, and a Fiosraigh Research Scholarship supported this research.
2. The research design included discussion and engagement with professional photographers and filmmakers who talked with practitioners about their visual concepts and storyboards, reviewed rough cuts of their videos, and shared their audio-visual expertise. Thanks are due to Aodán O'Coileáin, Siobhán Twomey, and Veronica Vierin.
3. The ways in which I have interpreted Lave and Wenger's original concept are informed by my graduate coursework at the University of Arizona including studies in critical pedagogy and funds of knowledge with mentors Julio Cammarota and Luis C. Moll.

4. Many thanks to Elena Moreo for her keen observations and comments that influenced my thinking about how the artefacts perform.

5. What is called a "script" in digital storytelling practice and literature might be more accurately defined as a "monologue" since it refers to a first-person narrative that is subsequently performed and recorded as the voiceover, which is one element among many in an overall script for video and film production.

6. See Loyal (2011) for research on the Direct Provision regime in Ireland.

7. Please view New *Ways* and *Crossing Over*, Available at: http://www.darcyalexandra.com/practice/living-in-direct- provision-9-stories/

8. The European Agency for the Management of Operational Cooperation at the External Borders of the Member States of the European Union. The simplified term, "Frontex" is derived from the agency's name in French: Frontières extérieures. See Feldman (2012).

References

Alexandra, D. (2015). *Visualizing migrant voices: Co-creative documentary and the politics of listening*. Ph.D. Dublin Institute of Technology.

Cammarota, J. (2008). The cultural organizing of youth ethnographers: Formalizing a praxis-based pedagogy. *Anthropology and Education Quarterly, 39*(1), 45–58.

Coll, K. M. (2010). *Remaking citizenship: Latina immigrants and new American politics*. Stanford: Stanford University Press.

El Haj, T. R. A. (2009). Becoming citizens in an era of globalization and transnational migration: Re-imagining citizenship as critical practice. *Theory into Practice, 48*(4), 274–282.

Feldman, G. (2012). Border control: The new meaning of containment. In *The migration apparatus: Security, labor and policymaking in the European Union* (pp. 78–117). Stanford: Stanford University Press.

Fine, M., Weis, L., Centrie, C., & Roberts, R. (2000). Educating beyond the borders of schooling. *Anthropology & Education Quarterly, 31*(2), 131–151.

Fletcher, C., & Cambre, C. (2009). Digital storytelling and implicated scholarship in the classroom. *Journal of Canadian Studies, 43*(1), 109–130.

Freire, P. (1998). *Pedagogy of hope*. New York: Continuum.

Greene, M. (1995). *Releasing the imagination: Essays on education, the arts, and social change*. San Francisco: Jossey-Bass.

Gubrium, A. (2009). Digital storytelling as a method for engaged scholarship in anthropology. *Practicing Anthropology, 31*(4), 5–9.

Jackson, M. (2013). *The wherewithal of life: Ethics, migration, and the question of well-being*. Berkeley/Los Angeles: University of California Press.

Lambert, J. (2013). *Digital storytelling: Capturing lives, creating community* (4th ed.). New York/London: Routledge.

Lave, J., & Wenger, E. (1991). *Situated learning: Legitimate peripheral participation*. Cambridge: Cambridge University Press.

Loyal, S. (2011). The direct provision regime. In *Understanding immigration in Ireland: State, capital and labor in a global age* (pp. 101–121). Manchester/New York: Manchester University Press.

Moll, L. C. (1992). Funds of knowledge for teaching: Using a qualitative approach to connect homes and classrooms. *Theory into Practice, 31*(1), 132–141.

Nuñez-Janes, M. (2016). When ethnography relates: Reflections on the possibilities of digital storytelling. *Anthropology & Education Quarterly, 47*(3), 235–239.

Rosaldo, R. (1994). Cultural citizenship in San Jose, California. *PoLAR, 17*(2), 57–64.

Smyth, J., & Mangan, S., (2010, December 17). Asylum seekers return after deportation plane breaks down. *The Irish Times*. http://www.highbeam.com/doc/1P2-27495951.html. Accessed 30 Sept 2016.

Spurgeon, C. L., Burgess, J. E., Klaebe, H. G., Tacchi, J. A., McWilliam, K., & Tsai, M. (2009, July 8–10). Co-creative media: Theorising digital storytelling as a platform for researching and developing participatory culture. In *Australian and New Zealand Communication Association Conference*, Queensland University of Technology, Brisbane. http://eprints.qut.edu.au/25811/. Accessed 30 Sept 2016.

Stoller, P. (1997). *Sensuous scholarship*. Philadelphia: University of Pennsylvania Press.

CHAPTER 24

Intergenerational Digital Storytelling: Research and Applications of Digital Storytelling in Greece

Michael Meimaris

INTRODUCTION

During the past eight years, the Laboratory of New Technologies in Communication, Education and Mass Media of the University of Athens (NTLab UoA, www.media.uoa.gr/ntlab) that I direct has offered a number of Digital Storytelling (DST) courses. These have been situated within master's degree programmes at the University of Athens, the University of the Aegean and the University of Fribourg in Switzerland, as well as within an undergraduate seminar in the Department of Communication and Media Studies at the University of Athens.

In addition to the bibliographical research that students are required to do as part of their studies, they are asked to create digital stories in different contexts, such as educational, intergenerational and personal or community-based media projects. Moreover, some of them participate in the research activities on DST undertaken by the NTLab, which, in

M. Meimaris (✉)
National and Kapodistrian University of Athens,
Athens, Greece

© The Author(s) 2017
G. Jamissen et al. (eds.), *Digital Storytelling in Higher Education*,
Digital Education and Learning, DOI 10.1007/978-3-319-51058-3_24

many cases, have resulted in contributions to journal articles and conference proceedings. It is within this academic context that we consider DST as an engaged scholarship practice. Building on Boyer (1996), we define engagement as Welch (2016) does, as "activities benefitting society that are integrated into academic purposes to generate new knowledge through research and to educate in programs of study" (p. 35).

Based on recent publications from the NTLab, and in particularly on the papers by Spanoudakis et al. (2015), Mouchtari et al. (2015) and Meliadou et al. (2012), in this chapter, we focus on two examples that highlight how our work[1] offers a perspective on DST as an engaged scholarship practice, in that our NTLab activities promote the interrelationship of teaching, research and service through theory, action and reflection in response to community needs. Before expanding on these examples, we provide a research context and brief description of a tool that was produced in our laboratory.

MILIA (APPLETREE): AN ONLINE PLATFORM FOR DST

Non-linear storytelling techniques have become much easier to use with the evolution of inherently non-linear media like Web 2.0 DST platforms (see, e.g., Pageflow, Twine). Web 2.0 stories are broad in scope; they can represent history, fantasy, a presentation, a puzzle, a message or some combination of multiple genres of communication. Current online tools for DST often use open structures in order to help users create or launch stories. A major issue in this endeavour, then, is how to design a platform that integrates the storyteller's activity into a framework that respects the basic constituents of traditional narrative, namely, a person or people facing a challenge, trying to overcome it through a sequence of events and, eventually, reaching a resolution (Ryan 2002).

We assert that even if storytelling in general, under the influence of digital media, moves increasingly towards a non-linear model, such a trend does not imply that this sort of narrative coherence should be left out of the equation. Narratives flow through games, platforms and other digital tools widely accessible via the internet, while listening to and reading stories move a "reader" forward from a static activity to an interactive, dynamic process in which the lines between the author and the audience can become blurred. It is within this context that we have attempted to deploy an open platform for socially interactive DST called *Milia*.[2]

The core intentions of this platform are to provide users with the ability to create and share personal stories via social media and to experiment with the possibilities of non-linear stories offered by the branching structure of the platform. By integrating the creation and reading of stories in a non-linear way, the user of the *Milia* platform is meant to be at the same time a reader and a creator, as (s)he imports personal data and also reads the stories of others. A further objective of *Milia* is for the platform to be flexible and powerful enough to support the representation, presentation and collaborative creation of any sort of story in digital format, with intended applications in storytelling, education, publishing and, more generally, in the creation and publication of collaborative digital works. The vision behind the development of the *Milia* platform has been the ability to offer to everyone interested the means to "plant" a story and see it grow into a fruitful tree and to provide an online space where creators can make stories by planting their own trees in publicly accessible "digital fields" or in their own, private, "digital gardens". In this way, the *Milia* platform is intended to enable the creation and curation of a data bank of interactive stories, which readers will have the capability to extend and enrich with their own ideas and alternative versions. *Milia* is thus offered in the spirit of free expression, knowledge and creativity.

Finally, apart from its educational and creative aspects, *Milia* is also intended to afford a medium for preserving stories and narratives from the past, thus safeguarding the collective creations and memories of a community. The challenges, goals and ambitions that sparked the conception and guided the design of the *Milia* platform can be considered, in a sense, to comprise a gap in DST research and applications that this platform is intended to address.

FEATURES AND CAPABILITIES OF THE *MILIA* PLATFORM

Milia is an open platform for social interactive DST. Its implementation is based on the Spiral Model (Boehm 1986), a software development process combining elements of both design and prototyping in stages. *Milia* consists of two main sub-systems: the Storytelling Viewer (Fig. 24.1), where internet users may view posted stories (called *Milia* stories) and the Storytelling Editor where authenticated users create *Milia* stories (Fig. 24.2).

Additionally, in order for *Milia* to be accessible to a wide range of audiences, care has been taken to comply with the Web Content Accessibility

Fig. 24.1 Storytelling viewer interface of the *Milia* platform

Guidelines 2.0 provided by the World Wide Web Consortium (W3C 2008). Examples include the presentation of non-text content of the *Milia* interface with text alternatives, audio control, text resizing capability, keyboard shortcuts and other similar features. A more detailed description of *Milia* features and functions can be found on the platform's website, which is also available in English.[3]

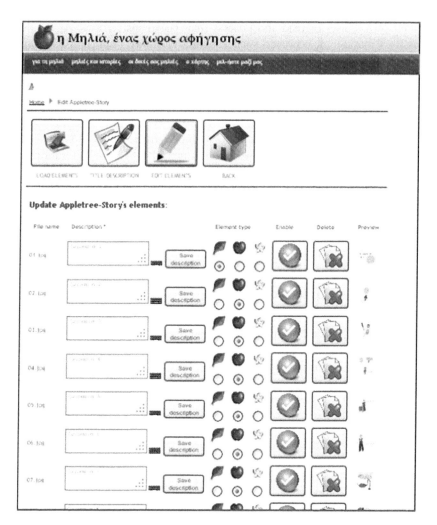

Fig. 24.2   Storytelling editor interface of the *Milia* platform

Milia, as an online digital space for interactive storytelling, can also serve—among other functions—as a useful educational tool. In the domain of education, constructionists emphasize that young users can benefit from systems that are open ended and support creativity and self-expression, given that children (and adults, we may add) *"learn by making"* (Papert 1991). Schoolchildren can use *Milia*, for example, to create their own stories or read and process their classmates' stories. As simple as they may seem, however, such activities can have important learning implications and outcomes. For example, story-making activities provide a way to practice and develop language skills (grammar and syntax), become familiar with the art of mythmaking and narration as well as provide an opportunity to learn and appreciate teamwork, given that students are required to work in teams in order to invent, create and share their stories. At the same time, students can enhance their digital literacy skills through hands-on experience with computers, the internet and multimedia applications.

Last but not least, young people and adults alike can best learn the basic structure of a story by creating one, as well as learning how to present a subject by organizing the main and secondary ideas around it upon the branches of a tree.

Intergenerational Learning and Communication Through Digital Storytelling

We have embarked on research that uses DST and other activities as ways to bring together primary school-age children with retired elderly people, with a view to discovering what the participants learn. For this project, we took stock of learning theories such as constructivism (Vygotsky 1986) and situated learning (Lave and Wenger 1991) that emphasize the creation of an active learning environment in formal education and used DST to establish a framework in which the people involved can actively learn. According to Frazel (2010), DST combines narrative with digital content, including images, sound and video, in order to enrich a basic narration. Digital stories can be historical, persuasive and/or instructional (Robin 2006), promoting communication in all these contexts.

Communication is also a core objective of intergenerational interactions (Winston 2001). On this basis, we have tried to combine DST with intergenerational communication, building on the premise that intergenerational exchange constitutes one of the oldest ways of learning. This project investigates how two different groups, that is, primary schoolchildren and elderly people, attempt to reduce the generation gap through activities that provide knowledge to either group through interactions/communication with the other. At the same time, though not an explicit research goal, this research provides supportive evidence of the way elderly people from local communities can be integrated within the education processes and formal curriculum of primary schools.

The theme we chose for the project was "Jobs of Yesteryear". Computers and automated systems have replaced many traditional jobs, leading entire trades and professions to extinction. Extinct, endangered and so-called old-fashioned everyday jobs, from milkman to iceman, can become better known to children by listening to stories told by elderly people, and they, in turn, are able to maintain their ability to participate in social and cultural interchanges by sharing their stories.

More specifically, this research has investigated the learning exchanges between schoolchildren aged six and seven and elderly people aged 70–80 from local communities, resulting in digital stories made by the schoolchildren. The research project took place in the 15th Primary School of Piraeus, in Athens, Greece, during the 2011–2012 and 2012–2013 academic years. It involved a six-month empirical study and focused on skills such as reading literature, story and song composition and comprehension, painting, digital story creation and improvising through theatrical games. The evaluation tools for the outcomes of this project comprised a questionnaire, participant observation, informal interviews and a video rubric for evaluating the digital creations of the schoolchildren, adapted from the work of Smaldino et al. (2011). Twenty-one primary school students and four elderly people of the local community (members of the first Open Care Centre for the Elderly of the municipality of Nikea, Athens) formed the core participants of the entire project, with many more schoolchildren participating in interim project activities.

The elderly participants in this research were recruited on an ad hoc basis, through existing contacts and networks that the researchers had established with the local community during previous projects on intergenerational communication and learning. This, however, should not be considered as a limitation of the potential of this research design to work in more general contexts since, in all cases, DST and intergenerational communication research requires preliminary work, the establishment of rapport and time devoted to coaching the participants prior to entering the core research activities. In this way, our methodological approach remains consistent with common engaged scholarship practices within higher education (Franz 2009).

Design and Implementation of
the Educational Intervention

The project was structured in four phases. Phase I included preparatory activities for familiarizing schoolchildren with the project. Phase II focused on the initial interchanges between the schoolchildren and the elderly people, using the creation of a digital story as an overarching objective. Phase III of the project was driven by the expressed interest of some 57 more students to participate in a theatrical performance that would take place at the end of the first school year of the project. Finally, Phase IV was the climax of the project: the schoolchildren involved in that phase created a digital story from scratch, through intergenerational interchanges with the elderly people of the local community.

Phase I encompassed activities that prepared children through school lessons according to the school curriculum. Children read about contemporary jobs in their books, then wrote short essays about their parents' jobs and finally dramatized their knowledge through theatrical games, role-playing and pantomime. Later on, the children read a book that referenced traditional jobs of yesteryear in order to compare them with contemporary jobs.

In Phase II, the schoolchildren and the elderly had their first intergenerational contact through DST. Each group of participants was involved in DST from a different angle. The elderly people created short scripts about jobs of yesteryear, bearing in mind that they would be working with primary school students. They chose a place for filming a video based on the script and dressed appropriately. A short film was then shot for the schoolchildren to watch.

In order to motivate children to participate in the creation of a digital story, it was decided that children would only have access to an audio track of the short digital narrative. They were asked to listen carefully and to write down the yesteryear jobs they heard from the audio track. After that, they were divided into four groups. Each group was assigned a specific task. Two groups selected photographs from a readily available digital file of yesteryear jobs that matched the descriptions provided by the elderly people. Another group of children listened to four music tracks in order to select the one that could be used as a soundtrack in the short digital narrative. The last group presented the whole digital story to the other classes of the school. In this way, all the steps of digital story-making (Frazel 2010; Lambert 2009) were accomplished across the work of the groups.

The main objective of Phase III was to create a theatrical performance as a way to end the first school year of the project. The performers were students of the school and the elderly people involved in the project. There were three activities in this phase: firstly, through theatrical games, children chose the character they would portray. Numerous rehearsals were organized in order to have the best possible result for the school performance about yesteryear jobs. The children, with the help of their parents and their teacher, created the scenery for the performance. So, in fact, three generations were involved. Secondly, a meeting was organized between the elderly people and the schoolchildren in order to agree on each group's parts in the performance. This meeting was followed by a full rehearsal of the entire performance.

Finally, the performance took place in the school hall. The performance started with a presentation of the digital story, then the elderly people came in and presented their parts and, at the end, the children presented the scenes they had rehearsed. Students from other classes joined the performance and helped the junior schoolchildren: they danced and sang together.

Phase IV was the concluding and most important part of the project. It was held during the second year of the research. As a motivational activity, the class visited the Benaki Museum[4] in the heart of Athens. The schoolchildren saw old tools and traditional objects that were used in the past. After that, the children formed groups and made paintings of their favourite yesteryear job.

Concurrently, the schoolchildren returned to the idea of creating digital stories. They decided to create a new digital story as a way of thanking the elderly people for participating in the project and to facilitate discussions about yesteryear jobs, the evolution of technology and the changes that are taking place in today's world. The children were divided into groups in order to create the digital stories.

StoryCenter describes "emotional content" as a key component of a digital story. In our research, this was achieved when children decided to use their personal photos from the summer performance in order to make their own digital story. They personalized the story using their voices to help the audience understand the context. For simplicity, they recorded their voices without overloading the viewer with too much information. They also employed a soundtrack that was used in the summer performance as a background to support the storyline. The final digital story lasted approximately three minutes.

The elderly people returned to the school and watched the digital stories with enthusiasm. They thanked the schoolchildren and talked about their experiences when they were young. This led to the last and most important digital story created during this project. All the participants agreed to create an intergenerational digital story with their own spontaneous storyboard about yesteryear jobs. The actors of that story would be one group of children and the elderly participants.

The children used the school hall for shooting the story scenes. In the first group of children, one student used the video camera, another took backstage photographs from the filming and four more students starred in the digital story, together with two elderly participants. The result was an independent digital story that was ready for editing. A second group of children selected photos that would fit with the newly created story. In this way, and keeping in mind guidelines for digital story-making such as the ones provided by Ohler (2008), the digital story was generated, step by step, by the schoolchildren with their own personal touch. A third group of students selected audio effects to recreate a natural outdoor environment and a song to enhance their digital story. The last group of students used Windows MovieMaker to edit the final digital story.

PROJECT RESULTS

DST, combined with in-class activities, was used in the context of this project as an experiential and experimental way of learning. The children successfully completed a digital story; they competently employed digital tools and digital media and were quite excited by their work on the overall project. Collaborative storytelling increased the students' interest in the topic of yesteryear jobs. The activity of creating narratives helped the children develop the power to articulate their own opinions and become heroes and heroines of their own stories. In addition, significant progress was observed in the students' interpersonal relations, whereby their sense of mutual acceptance and esteem was increased.

In this respect, DST was successfully used as a means of communication in a formal education setting. It helped young students become more active and use technology in a more efficient way, within a society that constantly exposes them to numerous media sources from a very young age. At the same time, this effort led to an improved sense of intergenerational solidarity, giving rise to a much more positive view of the elderly by schoolchildren and vice versa.

Through this project, it has been possible to experiment successfully with DST as a mechanism with positive outcomes in terms of digital literacy and in terms of intergenerational acquaintance and understanding.

Observations of participants yielded one other piece of important feedback. Both the schoolchildren and the elderly people were enthusiastic about the project and their participation in it. The schoolchildren cooperated successfully with each other and made good use of the digital tools they were offered. As expected, a number of technical issues came up during the final editing process, but all of these were addressed without disruptive delays. On top of project outcomes related to working with digital media and digital tools, through this project, the schoolchildren used improvisation and dramatization strategies to express their ideas, which enhanced their ability to be creative within a specific context.

Let us now present another example of the implementation of DST in intergenerational communication.

STARS AND PRODUCERS OF DIGITAL MEMORIES

This project workshop was part of a series of activities concerning Intergenerational Communication and Learning, realized by members of NTLab between 2011 and 2013. Students and elderly participants came together to produce videos in pairs. The workshop was designed around the concept of creative learning, which meant that all participants would play an active role in the project and would be encouraged to develop their full potential. In this workshop, technology involved shooting and editing a significant life experience of the elderly people. The added value of this process was the creation of a digital archive of memories available to all.

It was important to observe the part of this process in which participants developed meaningful dialogues with one another. The variety of techniques used in the editing process supported their mutual interest in creating the final video. The workshop was organized in five consecutive sessions in order to provide the participants with a clear idea of the process. First, there was a pre-production session where students became familiar with the use of digital editing tools before the workshop. The first discussion session that took place between the participants involved discussions about the story, the filming and the editing session. Finally, at the viewing session, all participants were able to share their video creations.

Half of the elderly people chose to tell a story from their childhood as presented in the video: *Amalia*[5]; two of them narrated their life stories as immigrants in foreign countries and the other three narrated their own favourite classic tales. During the filming session, the narrator (one of the elderly people) talked directly to the camera while the young person remained silent and did not ask any questions. The editing process was especially creative for both as they cooperated to transform their material into a digital story, by selecting scenes from the footage, scanning photos, downloading music from the internet and composing a cohesive creation. Students accomplished their goal and expressed a sense of pride in having contributed to a piece of work that was very different from their usual assignments. They acquired a growing sense of responsibility throughout the workshop as they interacted with their elderly collaborators. The 14-year-old students admitted that it was only when they actually met the elderly and heard their stories that they changed their attitude towards them and felt connected.

The elderly people were not familiar with the digital artefacts and applications or with computers in general but were eager to learn and connect to the digital world. Their interest was maintained throughout the process and they did not abandon the projects. Their engagement in and commitment to the process was assured by keeping the technology simple; respect for their memories and experiences encouraged them to participate even when technology was involved. There was also enough evidence to conclude that the elderly people enjoyed and acknowledged their double role in the new digital environment as both beneficiaries and contributors; this represents a departure from previous approaches, focusing only on new media literacy as a means of bridging the digital intergenerational divide. In conclusion, technology provides a significant role for elderly users, especially when it is integrated in a meaningful and engaging programme with a clear goal.

Concluding Remarks

The conclusions of this research are promising. We detected an important change in the children's attitudes towards the activities blended with DST. DST was taken up by students as a tool to create their own stories and develop their narrative skills. In addition, students who participated in the creation of digital stories developed enhanced communication skills by learning to organize their ideas and express opinions. Students' progress in developing interpersonal relationships was clear, with DST activities operating as a framework that fostered collaboration and led students to work together in groups. At the same time, this resulted in a significant increase of mutual acceptance and self-esteem, through a feeling of shared ownership and collective accomplishment, since schoolchildren were co-creators of the final digital stories.

DST worked as a whole class activity that increased the groups' sociability. It also created a friendly environment in which both the elderly and the younger people could actively participate. This project actually helped the school open its doors to the local community, interact with groups of elderly people and foster intergenerational literacy that could lead to improved intergenerational solidarity. Both generations had multiple opportunities for success and could experiment with the tools and knowledge they were offered.

As a concluding point, our work within these two projects helps to demonstrate that the rapid development of technology has created new learning opportunities for many different groups. DST, in particular, seems to lend itself to intergenerational communication, especially when it includes elderly people who are ageing actively. It is, therefore, possible to achieve a deeper sharing of knowledge between elder and younger people. In-school educational activities can be used to bridge the gap between generations and create enhanced opportunities for co-operation and cohesion between school and family.

THE WAY FORWARD

Presently, within the Laboratory, research is being completed that aims to record, in the form of digital stories, the experiential relationship between Greek citizens and the media (newspapers, radio, TV and digital media). Approximately 300 participants, coded according to gender, age, education, occupation and place of residence, have created digital stories that we have analysed using qualitative methods, such as Constant Comparison Analysis and Content Analysis (Meimaris 2015), as well as a multimodal approach using the Atlas.ti software.

As far as the *Milia* platform is concerned, although much has been achieved, there is still more to be done in the future. Many new ideas are being discussed for a future updated version of the *Milia* platform. In light of current developments in online social media and online social networks, it is clear that the *Milia* platform lends itself to a number of social extensions. These include enabling *content-centred* social actions such as the ability to "like" and comment on *Milia* stories, as well as sharing these stories via social media outlets such as Facebook and Twitter; we also envisage extensions that enable *user-centred* social actions, namely the ability to "follow" *Milia* story creators as well as subscribe to *Milia* story channels.

Concerning the undergraduate and postgraduate DST courses mentioned above, they are very popular with students and we intend to develop them further. We have adapted the DST model developed by StoryCenter to work with large groups of students (20–40), for instance, by dividing them into smaller groups for the story circle exercise. After sharing stories produced by former students and from other sources, such as StoryCenter and Patient Voices, we invite students to create their own digital stories. We have found that, to really understand what DST is about, it is necessary to create one personally. The first story is a personal story about a crisis, a dramatic situation or a happy event in their life. The second story is a thematic, subject-based story but still connected to their personal experience or motivation related to, for example, mathematics or media studies or social issues such as bullying.

The students who are aiming to become teachers are the ones most likely to follow up the engaged scholarship tradition. They involve the children in their placement schools in creating digital stories that the students bring back to the University; this strengthens the understanding that what Brecht referred as the "historification" of facts enhances their meaning and is part of the construction of knowledge.

Storytelling has a long tradition dating from long before the introduction of digital media and digital tools, and classical oral narrative practices are important sources of inspiration for us. At the same time, we must take into account that our students are digital natives (Prensky 2001), and we have to use the tools of the twenty-first century. We have also seen, as illustrated by the projects and examples discussed in this chapter, how DST has specific qualities enabling it to fulfil the scholarship of engaged collaboration by creating learning communities involving universities, schools, families and communities.

NOTES

1. This work has been developed and conducted by NTLab UoA with the support of the University Research Institute of Applied Communication.
2. http://www.media.uoa.gr/ntlab/milia

3. http://www2.media.uoa.gr/medialab/milia/index.php?lang=en
4. The Benaki Museum ranks among the major institutions that have enriched the material assets of the Greek state. Its collections encompass icons, oil paintings and wood carvings, ceramics, everyday life objects, textiles as well as historical archives. Further information is available on the Benaki Museum's website at http://www.benaki.gr
5. Link to the video Amalia. https://www.youtube.com/watch?v=1 9nEWDbQDP0&feature=youtu.be

REFERENCES

Boehm, W. B. (1986). A spiral model of software development and enhancement. *ACM SIGSOFT Software Engineering Notes, 11*(4), 14–24.
Boyer, E. (1996). The scholarship of engagement. *Journal of Public Service & Outreach, 1*(1), 11–21.
Franz, N. (2009). A holistic model of engaged scholarship: Telling the story across higher education's missions. *Journal of Higher Education Outreach and Engagement, 13*(4), 31–50.
Frazel, M. (2010). *Digital storytelling guide for educators.* Washington, DC: International Society for Technology in Education.
Lambert, J. (2009). *Digital storytelling: Capturing lives, creating community.* Berkeley: Digital Diner Press.
Lave, J., & Wenger, E. (1991). *Situated learning: Legitimate peripheral participation.* Cambridge, UK: Cambridge University Press.
Meimaris, M. (2015, September 25–27). Getting to know the media through the stories told by their audiences. *6th International Digital Storytelling Conference, Voices of Change: Storywork in Activism, Education and Public Service*, Amherst.
Meliadou, E., Nakou, A., Haidi, I., Koutsikos, L., Giannakoulopoulos, A., Gouscos, D., & Meimaris, M. (2012). Technology in intergenerational learning research projects in the Greek context. *3rd International Conference on Elderly and New Technologies* (3ICENT), Castellón.
Mouchtari, E., Meimaris, M., Gouscos, D., & Sfyroera, M. (2015). Learning and intergenerational communication through digital storytelling in the first grades of primary school: Yesteryear Jobs. *Journal of Cultural Science*, special issue on "Broadening Digital Storytelling Horizons", B. Simsek (Ed.), *8*(2).
Ohler, J. (2008). *Digital storytelling in the classroom, new media pathways to literacy, learning, and creativity.* Thousand Oaks: Corwin Press.
Papert, S. (1991). Situating constructionism. In S. Papert & I. Harel (Eds.), *Constructionism.* Norwood: Ablex Publishing.

Prensky, M. (2001). Digital natives, digital immigrants part 1. *On the horizon* 9.5, pp. 1–6.

Robin, B. (2006). The educational uses of digital storytelling. In C. Crawford et al. (Eds.), *Proceedings of society for information technology & teacher education international conference 2006* (pp. 709–716). Chesapeake: AACE.

Ryan, M. L. (2002). Beyond the myth and metaphor: Narrative in digital media. *Poetics Today, 23*(4), 581–609.

Smaldino, S. E., Russell, J. D., Heinrich, R., & Molenda, M. (2011). *Instructional technology and media for learning* (2nd ed.). Upper Saddle River: Pearson.

Spanoudakis, M., Nakou, A., Meliadou, E., Gouscos, D., & Meimaris, M., (2015). Milia (AppleTree), an online platform for digital storytelling. *Journal of Cultural Science*, special issue on "Broadening Digital Storytelling Horizons", B. Simsek (Ed.), *8*(2).

Vygotsky, L. (1986). *Thought and language*. Cambridge, MA: Massachussetts Institute of Technology.

W3C. (2008). *Web Content Accessibility Guidelines* (WCAG) 2.0. http://www.w3.org/TR/WCAG20. Accessed 29 Oct 2016.

Welch, M. (2016). *Engaging higher education: Purpose, platforms, and programs for community engagement*. Sterling: Stylus Publishing.

Winston, L. (2001). *Grandparents, intergenerational learning and civic renewal, K-6*. Portsmouth: Heinemann.

CHAPTER 25

Faculty Reflections at the Intersection of Digital Storytelling and Community Engagement

Bev Bickel, Bill Shewbridge, Romy Hübler, and Ana Oskoz

INTRODUCTION

Educational reformer John Dewey argued in 1916 that democracy requires multidimensional knowledge born of "free interaction" of people from diverse experiences. He proposed that education "must present situations where problems are relevant to the problems of living together and where observation and information are calculated to develop social insight and interest" (Dewey 1916, p. 192). Dewey anticipated what neuroscientists are now arguing is the "natural state" of the human mind where play, flexibility, curiosity, telling stories, and daydreaming open our minds to learning and fuel innovation. This "free play of the mind" was nurtured, Dewey believed, through reflecting on diverse experiences and was critical to imagining democratic communities.

Almost a century later, Ernest Boyer (1990) called on higher education to grow beyond a fragmentation of research, teaching, and service towards a scholarship of discovery, integration, application, and teaching. The discussion initiated by Boyer has evolved into commitments to civically engaged public scholarship that can inspire diverse publics in address-

B. Bickel (✉) • B. Shewbridge • R. Hübler • A. Oskoz
University of Maryland, Baltimore, MD, USA

© The Author(s) 2017   371
G. Jamissen et al. (eds.), *Digital Storytelling in Higher Education*,
Digital Education and Learning, DOI 10.1007/978-3-319-51058-3_25

ing complex, messy, ill-structured problems in our communities. People across communities now draw on powerful digital narrative tools that support knowledge production and connect people from diverse communities. Connected knowledge, when employed to promote participatory democracy as understood by Dewey (1916) as "primarily a mode of associated living, of conjoint communicated experience" (p. 101), can sustain relationships critical to envisioning solutions to our most stubborn social justice problems.

In this chapter, we report on University of Maryland, Baltimore County (UMBC), faculty members' reflections on experiences extending digital storytelling to community projects about pressing social and cultural issues. Our inquiry has been theoretically informed by sociocultural understandings of transformative democratic and dialogic learning and identities (Bakhtin 1981; Dewey 1916; Freire 2003; Weedon 2004), mediatized stories (Couldry 2008; Drotner 2008; Lundby 2008), mediated narratives using material and psychological tools (Vygotsky 1978; Erstad and Wertsch 2008), and story-based agency (Hull and Katz 2006). Our guiding question was this: how are faculty experienced in digital storytelling using and reflecting on story-based projects that support an emerging campus culture of publicly engaged scholarship and democratic, civic agency efforts on campus and beyond? We wanted to hear reflections on challenges and possibilities of using stories in project, place-based community work. We will discuss three emerging themes: (1) how digital storytelling allows faculty, students, and community partners to develop collaborative and inclusive knowledge that extends beyond academic experts; (2) how dissemination of these stories nurtures public scholarship; and (3) how engaged story work is contributing to changing campus cultural practices. We end with suggestions for developing, sustaining, and promoting publicly engaged, digital storytelling in higher education.

ENGAGED DIGITAL STORYTELLING

Since early work of the Center for Digital Storytelling, now Storycenter, led by Joe Lambert and colleagues, story practitioners have understood the potential of stories for personal "transformation through the creative power of biographical story making and storytelling" (Ferguson in Lambert 2013, p. 5) as well as in and with communities telling their own stories for their own purposes in particular historical moments and places

(Davis and Foley 2016). Lambert (2013) and his colleagues understood that story work in higher education could "provide participants with a synthesizing series of metaphors for the continued exploration of human development through the assessment of their own life experience" (p. 160) and that many scholars would extend story work to communities beyond campuses.

Digital storytelling can be "Citizenship-in-Practice" that develops agency among storytellers who recognize the centrality of voice in institutional and community contexts (Erstad and Silseth 2008). As students engage in dialogical activity and take responsibility for knowledge-building, they develop "epistemic agency" which, the authors argue, "might display itself in the student's ability to compose digital stories that consist of different and divergent voices" (p. 219). Couldry (2008) writes that such storytelling can contribute to "a democratization of media resources and widening the conditions of democracy itself" (p. 54).

SCHOLARSHIP OF PUBLIC ENGAGEMENT

Decades of scholars have described an expanding scholarship of engagement (Boyer 1996; New England Resource Center for Higher Education n.d.) and publicly engaged scholarship (Post et al. 2016). In 1982, Derek Bok called for the engaged university to "help address basic social problems, better prepare more teachers, and play a role in societal moral development" (Fisher et al. 2004, p. 4). Ernest Boyer (1990), called on higher education leaders to reconceptualize scholarship and support faculty in "stepping back from one's investigation, looking for connections, building bridges between theory and practice" (p. 16). Recently, scholars have become increasingly insistent about the need for changing dominant cultural practices of knowledge production, and the structures and policies of higher education (Ellison and Eatman 2008; O'Meara 2011). Sturm et al. (2011) proposed that "full participation" in higher education is critical to the integrated success of students, diversity initiatives, and civic engagement missions:

> Full participation incorporates the idea that higher education institutions are rooted in and accountable to multiple communities ... Campuses advancing full participation are engaged campuses that are both *in* and *of* the community, participating in reciprocal, mutually beneficial partnerships between campus and community.

Such engaged public scholarship recognizes and contributes to collaborative, multi-vocal narratives that address problems and envision new futures (Sanchez 2004) and "seeks the public good *with* the public and not merely *for* the public as a means to facilitating a more active and engaged democracy" (Saltmarsh et al. 2009, p. 9).

BACKGROUND AND METHODOLOGY

Opened as the first racially integrated university in Maryland, the UMBC campus has a history of engagement and innovation that welcomes social entrepreneurship, cross-campus collaborations, and innovative technologies with public purposes. Since 2006, UMBC's New Media Studio has facilitated digital storytelling workshops for faculty, some of whom were among the first to receive course redesign grants, supported by the Provost's Office and offered through *BreakingGround,* a civic agency and engagement initiative. With additional campus support from the Hrabowski Fund for Innovation, faculty members started a broader initiative, *Baltimore Traces: Communities in Transition,* involving multiple, cross-disciplinary projects in Baltimore communities.

We talked with these pioneering digital storytellers (who agreed to be identified) and videotaped an interview and then edited transcripts for clarity as we thematically coded and recursively revised for meanings, convergences, and divergences. Our interpretive process drew on other evidence including notes from discussions among faculty and staff storytellers who have gathered at least once a semester since 2006; related events and community viewings; our own reflections as storytelling practitioners; and publicly available stories online through community partners, other public sites, and our *Digital Stories @ UMBC* website (DigitalStories@ UMBC 2016). We worked to understand the impact of engaged story projects (described below) on faculty members and their scholarship; the development of relationships, collaborations, and public dissemination; and the intersections of story work with the developing culture of civic engagement on campus.

EXPLORE BALTIMORE HERITAGE

Denise Meringolo, director of the Public History MA and associate professor of History, was an early adopter of public digital storytelling. Her students used digital storytelling techniques to create short videos, highlighting West Baltimore history (http://tinyurl.com/jh3542) that were integrated into the Explore Baltimore Heritage mobile walking tour app (BaltimoreHeritage 2016).

Mapping Baybrook

Nicole King, chair and associate professor of American Studies and Steve Bradley, associate professor of Visual Arts, collaborated to create Mapping Baybrook (MappingBaybrook 2016), focused on two industrial neighbourhoods in South Baltimore. Highlighting residents' concerns and aspirations, it contributed to fundraising events, exhibitions, and other activities.

Mill Stories

Michelle Stefano, visiting assistant professor in American Studies, and Bill Shewbridge, professor of the practice in Media and Communication Studies, led an effort to protect and publicize the living cultural heritage of steelworkers from the recently closed Sparrows Point mill. Students partnered with former steelworkers to produce over 30 stories about the human side of industrial decline and disinvestment featured on *Mill Stories* (MillStories 2016).

Baltimore Traces

Multiple faculty members collaborated on *Baltimore Traces: Communities in Transition* (BaltimoreTraces 2016a) and were awarded a UMBC Hrabowski Innovation Grant in 2014. The *Mapping Dialogues* project (BaltimoreTraces 2016b), supported by Maryland Humanities, uses maps to launch discussions on the past, present, and future of industrial spaces and local economies. Across projects, faculty members' learning outcomes for students include developing multiple narrative approaches, learning digital production skills, practising deep listening, engaging in dialogues across diverse cultures and communities, developing agency, thinking strategically about public dissemination, and examining how story work can reveal complex, messy problems while imagining and contributing to hopeful futures.

Listening to the faculty storytellers and reflecting on a decade of story work on our campus led to three overarching themes discussed below.

Developing Collaborative and Inclusive Democratic Knowledges

Reflecting on fostering democracy in universities, von Wright (2002) writes, "One of higher education's greatest challenges is to avoid letting facts and knowledge lead to irony, indifference, and detachment. Instead we need to arouse and nurture students' curiosity and interest in the lives and perspectives of other people" (p. 415). Nicole King talked about how she taught the ethics of working with community members during the *Mapping Baybrook* oral history story project:

> Just because someone says something and you find a theme, you have to think critically about how you're going to portray that. Do we need larger context to be able to hear these stories? Are you respecting the agency and the voice of the people's stories, that they are giving to you essentially?

Throughout the work of producing *Mill Stories,* students talked with Michelle Stefano about how the stories of recently unemployed steel-workers affected them and resonated in their own lives. Michelle reported:

> Just going off campus and engaging with real people and real issues that are occurring outside of the UMBC campus really opens their eyes. Most importantly my colleague and I really believe that we're helping students develop empathy and compassion to connect with people.

As students reflect on lived experiences and their own stories and cultural knowledge as meaningful assets (Velez-Ibanez 1988; Heath 1983; Ladson-Billings 1994; Moll et al. 1992), they may also be better equipped to recognize the value of engaging with diverse communities. Over the years, digital storytelling practitioners have talked about the challenges and generative relational work of developing deep listening skills and empathy—what Nicole has come to call radical listening and radical empathy. Scholars across disciplines describe the power of affect or emotion when participating in communities of caring (Ahmed 2004; hooks 1994; Lambert 2013; Noddings 2012) and how reading others' stories and taking others' perspectives can lead students to become citizens of the world as they develop narrative imagination based on compassion, critical thinking, and self-reflection (Nussbaum 1998). Faculty members have focused on empathy in encounters with complex living communities. Michelle described her students' surprise when empathy came back to them from steelworkers concerned about students' struggles to get an education, graduate with loans, but be facing futures without the promise of the union jobs they had relied on:

> It was great to have these rich engagements between the students and the steel workers. The steelworkers were relating their own experiences to the younger generations ... They [were] able to convey these larger processes of global capitalism, deindustrialization, and their impacts not only on their lives, but on the students' lives as well.

Storytelling work in communities under stress can change how students, faculty, and community partners see themselves as they refocus from *what* they know to *how* they are "coming to know" and learning to respect different "ways of being." Steve Bradley described his art students who worked with high school art students in the Baybrook project. "The biggest measurements of success are the bonds that happen with my students and the high school students, and some of those relationships continue!" Faculty members agree that empathy is essential for deep listening and learning about challenges and aspirations of people living in disinvested communities.

Nicole described her students' learning as they listened to diverse voices and previously ignored perspectives from communities not often found in traditional texts.

> The past is not something that is objectively out there that we have to find. The past is something that we negotiate with one another, with our voices, with our memories, with other people's voices and memories. The historical record can, frankly, be wrong. Someone's story can be more precise and tell us more about the research questions or historical questions that we're asking. Often times, working in the communities that we often do with digital storytelling there are people who haven't had a voice.

Like Nicole, Denise reflected new approaches to teaching history:

> My students and I regularly struggle to identify and amplify the desires and interests of people and communities whose stories have not yet been told. We seek balance between the development of practical, marketable skills and the performance of a kind of historical practice that is grounded in a

> philosophy of service and collaboration ... developing interpretations that are forward looking and political rather than strictly grounded in the past and "objective."

This story work in and with community members stretches beyond traditionally valued forms of expertise and objectivity where "social science research must be detached, impersonal and 'objective'" (Mander 2010, p. 252) and instead invites practitioners to expand their epistemological assumptions about what is considered valued and legitimate human experience, who produces knowledge, and how knowledge can be shared widely (Rice 2003).

Michelle explained how students learnt about deindustrialization from steelworkers—"people that they wouldn't generally meet in their lives"—while working at the United Steelworker Local 9477 hall on Dundalk Avenue. "They were able to meet with many steel workers over the course of a couple of days. These interactions were really unbelievable and really valuable for the students, they've told me afterwards." Conversations like those in the union hall highlight von Wright's belief that in order to avoid presumptions about others' lives, "we actually have to be with others" (2002, p. 415). Faculty members believe that this proximity to others might provoke a transformative and connected social hope. As Ganz writes, "Hope inspires us and, in concert with self-efficacy (the feeling that you can make a difference) and solidarity (love, empathy), can move us to act" (2010, p. 518).

DISSEMINATING DIGITAL STORIES AND NURTURING PUBLICLY ENGAGED SCHOLARSHIP

While these storytellers may recognize the power of participatory, public media, and stories for inclusive, democratic communities, most people in higher education work in contexts with the "continued dominance of written text as an academic product" and an underdeveloped appreciation for public scholarship (Gubrium and Harper 2013, p. 198). Revitalizing the humanities, Jay (2011) argues, relies on combining project-based, engaged scholarship with digital media dissemination tools such as those used in this story work.

Faculty members note that using participatory visual methods like interactive mapping with archived and contemporary photos and videos can help academic colleagues recognize their work as legitimate public scholarship while enabling the storytelling faculty to simultaneously disseminate work to broader audiences. Bill Shewbridge explained, "In addition to thinking of our community partners as collaborators and our primary audience, we're constantly surprised about how these stories resonate with a wider audience and how they contribute to broader conversations." Denise described the multiple purposes of *Preserve the Baltimore Uprising 2015 Archive Project* (BaltimoreUprising 2016), where she and her students created an accessible digital public archive that invited people from around the city to contribute stories, photos, and films from diverse perspectives:

> The idea was, here are people who are protesting. Everybody's got a cell phone. They're taking photographs. They're making videos. They're recording their own memory and impression of these events. This is an unusual opportunity and eventually we could create digital stories from this material … and interpretive exhibitions.

The digital archive reveals a collection of different stories lived at one time in diverse sites around the same city that can now be seen, heard, and curated by anyone with an internet connection. The archive website reads in part:

> Share your stories. Upload photographs. Show us what you've seen. Show us the sign you carried. Tell us what you witnessed. When were you there? Where did you stand? Together, we will tell a more complete story.

Nicole imagined how future institutionalization could be significant for wide dissemination and students' learning to be public scholars. "Students are really good at thinking about ways to leverage this work, they want people to see their work. They want to be out there. It's important work."

As public resources for communities and education continue to erode, communities on and beyond campuses are calling for more equitable participation in public life including the recognition of diverse knowledges and media narratives. Couldry (2008) describes a "crisis of voice" in three dimensions of modern global life across three interconnected domains: weakening democratic politics, neoliberal market-centred economics, and "mediated public culture" (p. 57). This "crisis of voice," he argues, is nurtured through unequal social recognition, unequal access to mainstream media and self-representation in the public domain, and the inequities of the public "distribution of narrative resources" that include our human stories (p. 9). Yet, Nicole and her colleagues are extending public narrative resources using a "collaborative engagement paradigm" (Post et al. 2016). Through *Baltimore Traces*, students, community members, professors, and journalists have worked together to shape, produce, and disseminate stories through public community events, online sites, and radio podcasts including *Stories of Deindustrialized Baltimore* (BaltimoreTraces 2016c). Nicole explained:

> The long-term potential is building something that brings the work that faculty and students do, related to digital storytelling, out to a wider audience. We're working with building websites to share, going to conferences to share, and putting the work that we do on the radio with The Marc Steiner show through the Center for Emerging Media.

She hopes that one day the university will create a centre to support dissemination of public scholarship and strategically leverage work to the local public media "because things get picked up from local public radio, and go national."

CHANGING INSTITUTIONAL CULTURES

Boyer (1990) called on higher education to recognize that "theory surely leads to practice. But practice also leads to theory ... The time has come to ... give the familiar and honourable term 'scholarship' a broader, more capacious meaning, one that brings legitimacy to the full scope of academic work" (p. 16). Yet, despite public universities having a public good mission, many infrastructures, policies, traditions, and practices of disciplines are not yet fully aligned with the public aspirations of most campuses (Moore and Ward 2010). Traditional academic practices and structures are stubborn when it comes to scheduling hour-long classes on campus and behind closed doors, relying solely on textbooks and other traditional academic sources of expertise, and directing students' work to a single instructor. Discourses about "the community" too often construct it as a homogeneous place separate from the campus and treat it as a passive recipient of knowledge. Faculty addressed the distance between the university's public engagement aspirations and the expectations of disciplines; promotion and tenure policies that do not recognize integrated or public scholarship; constraints and ethical concerns of single semester courses for sustaining community partnerships; lack of workload recognition for team teaching; and inadequate infrastructures for taking students off campus. Nicole described her needs:

> We need to have access and time to think critically about how to get students out of the classroom. Logistically that can be difficult. We need more infrastructures to get the students out, to make it work for them, to make it work for the professors ... We need flexibility from a university perspective to be able to get students where they need to be ...actually if you've done it, it's quite complicated.

While there is growing understanding about the importance of interdisciplinarity to developing new knowledge—especially knowledge that can help us address society's messy, complex challenges—Nicole discussed the challenges of working across disciplines:

> Students coming from Media and Communication have technology training and background ... They come with a rigorous education in my department[American Studies] on oral history, ethnography, and the methods involved in those disciplines ... If you're coming from different perspectives, and you're blending different methodologies, you have to have some way to bring students from different disciplines together, which in the university structure and silos can be quite difficult to do.

Her experience also echoes scholarship critical of a traditional focus on individual detached knowledge (Hartley and Harkavy 2011) that minimizes self-reflexive, experiential, and collaborative approaches to inclusive knowledge production (Eatman and O'Meara 2015; Ellison and Eatman 2008).

Integration of faculty scholarship depends on how faculty efforts are incentivized, recognized, and rewarded through workload and promotion and tenure policies. Nicole explained:

> We're working with students in some of the research that we do ... and we publish it, and we take students to conferences to present that research. It's something above and beyond [service]. It needs to be quantified in a way that we can better understand it, and better support it.

In spite of constraining institutional structures and practices, collaborating faculty members remain hopeful that their work is slowly shifting campus cultures. As Kezar (2014) argues, "The more that change agents can build upon existing relationships for a change process, the more likely they are to be successful with implementing the change" (p. 99). Steve explains, faculty have relied on relationships developed through networks of digital storytellers and, more recently, the *BreakingGround* civic agency initiative:

> Two, three years ago I would only hear rumours about people doing projects, but now I'm hearing about the actual work ... It's in a different discipline but we really need one another to be aware of what we're doing to be able to address these very complex problems.

Denise also discussed collaborating:

> I was trained in American Studies and I'm accustomed to interdisciplinary work and collaboration. I think that the university is committed to that, but it's challenging for departments. It just is. Being part of the digital storytelling collaborative has been a vehicle for me to maintain those relationships, to have people who are working on similar things, to make connections across classes.

These faculty members are grassroots change-makers whose work contributes to ongoing campus transformation efforts that include shared governance, innovative teaching programmes, and initiatives addressing urgent social concerns on and off campus. While faculty can now see their work reflected in the campus' recently reinvigorated vision statement, they continue to innovate and push the boundaries that constrain deeper, sustained engagement (see recommendations below).

Kezar et al. (2011) argue that institutional change is a complex process that often focuses on senior academic leadership and results in little knowledge about faculty as change-makers. However, as UMBC President Freeman Hrabowski and Psychology Professor Ken Maton (2009) write:

> At the heart of institutional transformation are a campus' culture and the relationships among and within the various groups on campus. To the extent that this culture and these relationships are empowering, institutions will succeed in helping students, faculty, and staff from all backgrounds to excel. (p. 15)

Meyerson (2003) argues that empowered change agents not in positions of formal campus authority can lead change. These "tempered radicals" (Kezar et al. 2011; Meyerson 2003; Meyerson and Scully 1995) are not silent about their objections, do not alter their identities, or leave their institutions but rather temper their actions to change existing norms by working within the university and with its people. Tempered radicals claim the right to create or change their institutions by asserting agency, that is, they "assum[e] strategic perspectives, and/or tak[e] strategic actions toward goals that matter to him/her" (O'Meara 2013, p. 2). When our faculty storytellers expand their projects despite structural barriers, they are not naive. To the contrary, they acknowledge real constraints while finding ways to alter realities, knowing that there is no guarantee of success or sustainability (O'Meara 2013). They come together to share strategies and tools while laughing about quixotic goals and unanticipated outcomes, yet they find deep meaning in the work for themselves, their students, and our communities. They collaborate in a new "third space" beyond their departments, disciplines, campus roles, and the campus itself (O'Meara and Stromquist 2015; Whitchurch 2013). While none of them expect to single-handedly change structures or policies, all of them believe that they are contributing to more participatory, visionary and democratic learning and cultural practices on campus and beyond. Nicole writes:

> When research, teaching, and service in urban history are grounded in civic engagement, the potential for connections are limitless and the possibility for justice enhanced. In the "Preserving Places" course, we look to the past, act in the present, and contemplate the future. (King 2014, p. 439)

While an ability to "imagine otherwise" remains constrained by inequity and segregation, disciplinary compartmentalization, and traditional knowledge paradigms, faculty, staff, students, and community members are going about the work of telling their stories and imagining and enacting new cultural practices.

RECOMMENDATIONS

From the last decade of experiences, we offer the following suggestions for storytelling within collaborative, community engagement projects.

Nurture an Active Community

Bring people from across campus together for storytelling workshops that offer unique opportunities to interact across departments and roles and build new relationships and collaborations. Gather previous workshop participants and storytellers to share resources, consider challenges, explore new ideas, and think together about needed support through meetings, working groups, public websites, active listservs, social media, collaborative publications, and public events with community partners.

Institutionalize Efforts

Support faculty in seeking grants and developing their work as public storytellers. Revise promotion and tenure policies and staff evaluations to recognize public scholarship. Offer credit for students. Recognize and reward high-quality work. Regularly invite community partners to campus as speakers, mentors, and facilitators, and recognize their time and efforts. Provide resources including transportation; support for websites and other dissemination; cameras, recording booths, and portable production gear; staffing for technical questions; technical support from skilled digital storytellers; and experienced practitioners serving as co-instructors or student mentors.

Plan to Plan and Assess

Provide time to prepare with community partners. Help students anticipate unusual scheduling and transportation challenges for work outside of normal class time and spaces. Involve partners and students in assessment planning. Discuss community partners' and students' concerns before, during, and after community work.

Assure Full Community Participation

Allow time for multiple meetings with potential community partners. Build relationships of mutuality and trust. Discuss goals, outcomes, duration, assessment, and possibilities for sustained work. Include critical feedback opportunities with community partners on products and processes. Seek compensation or other recognition for partners' efforts.

Go Public!

With storytellers' permission, find multiple ways to disseminate stories and reflections through websites, campus and community events, academic gatherings, and formal and informal publications.

Seek Funding, But Be Creative

Applying for grants is helpful in conceptualizing collaborations and public impact. But even without fundraising success, creative and flexible thinking in the planning process can move projects forward.

Connect Regionally and Nationally

To sustain the work, connect with others beyond the campus through: national and international digital storytelling conferences and networks, ongoing training, other story initiatives and websites, and collaborative projects that span communities and institutions in a region.

Align with Campus Mission and Plans

Align and narrate the work to support campus values and plans while continuing to *imagine otherwise* and innovate.

CONCLUSION

Reflections from experienced faculty digital storytelling practitioners who are working intentionally with collaborative, publicly engagement story projects speak to collective knowledges and "epistemic agency" on and beyond campuses. At once playful and serious in "third spaces" outside of their disciplines and beyond university classrooms, faculty innovators are generating storied public knowledge. Disseminating and legitimating publicly engaged story projects remain central concerns for faculty who, in spite of constraints, are slowly but steadily changing campus practices and students' expectations for their educations.

While this chapter focuses on faculty experiences, we encourage future inquiry focused on the stories themselves and with the storytellers. Clearly, faculty members do not engage in story-based teaching or public scholarship in isolation from students or community partners, so knowing more about student and community partners' reflections on their experiences will enrich our future understanding of the power of engaged storytelling.

Community-engaged story work is slow and requires "care-full" building of trusting relationships grounded in deep listening, empathy, and openness to each other's diverse stories, knowledges, and skills. When storytellers have learnt to be first person knowledge producers nurtured by serious play, innovation, collaboration, and honest feedback, they want to know that their voices will be heard, that their stories will be useful in public spaces on and beyond the campus. Requiring ourselves to develop equity-based ethics and democratic practices can create storytelling as a potential bridge across decades of distrust between universities and communities too often ignored or misused by academics.

We all live in spaces where we know only incomplete, single stories about each other. Thomas King (2008) reminds us that once a story is heard, it is ours, and our individual stories can become collective stories and new community knowledge. He writes that we may choose to believe a story or not, tell it to a friend, or forget it, "But don't say in the years to come that you would have lived your life differently if only you had heard this story. You've heard it now" (p. 29). The questions become, what are our civic responsibilities beyond engaging with diverse digital stories or being informed by them? How can social action and sustained change be facilitated by publicly engaged story work that is anchored by strong university-community partnerships and democratic commitments?

References

Ahmed, S. (2004). *Cultural politics of emotion*. New York: Routledge.

Bakhtin, M. (1981). *The dialogic imagination: Four essays*. Austin: University of Texas Press.

BaltimoreHeritage. (2016). *Explore Baltimore Heritage*. http://explore.baltimoreheritage.org/ (home page). Accessed 11 Sept 2016.

BaltimoreTraces. (2016a). *Baltimore Traces*. http://baltimoretraces.org (home page). Accessed 11 Sept 2016.

BaltimoreTraces. (2016b). Mapping dialogues. *Baltimore Traces*. http://baltimoretraces.org/mapping-dialogues. Accessed 11 Sept 2016.

BaltimoreTraces. (2016c). Stories of deindustrialized Baltimore on the Marc Steiner show. *Baltimore Traces*. http://baltimoretraces.umbc.edu/projects/stories-of-deindustrialization-on-the-marc-steiner-show/. Accessed 11 Sept 2016.

BaltimoreUprising. (2016). *Preserve the Baltimore uprising 2015 archive project*. http://baltimoreuprising2015.org (home page). Accessed 11 Sept 2016.

Boyer, E. L. (1990). *Scholarship reconsidered: Priorities of the professoriate*. New York: The Carnegie Foundation for the Advancement of Teaching.

Boyer, E. L. (1996). The scholarship of engagement. *Bulletin of the American Academy of Arts and Sciences, 49*(7), 18–33.

Couldry, N. (2008). Digital storytelling, media research and democracy: Conceptual choices and alternative futures. In K. Lundby (Ed.), *Digital story-*

telling, mediatized stories: Self-representations in new media (pp. 41–60). New York: Peter Lang.

Davis, A., & Foley, L. (2016). Digital storytelling. In B. Guzzetti & M. Lesley (Eds.), *Handbook of research on the societal impact of digital media* (pp. 317–342). Hershey, PA: Information Science Reference [IGI Global].

Dewey, J. (1916/1997). *Democracy and education*. New York: The Free Press.

DigitalStories@UMBC. (2016). *Digital Stories @ UMBC*, http://stories.umbc.edu (home page). Accessed 11 Sept 2016.

Drotner, K. (2008). Boundaries and bridges: Digital storytelling in education studies and media studies. In K. Lundby (Ed.), *Digital storytelling, mediatized stories: Self-representations in new media* (pp. 61–81). New York: Peter Lang.

Eatman, T. K., & O'Meara, K. A. (2015). Advancing engaged scholarship in promotion and tenure: A roadmap and call for reform. *Liberal Education, 101*(3), n. p. http://www.aacu.org/liberaleducation/2015/summer/o%27meara. Accessed 11 Sept 2016.

Ellison, J., & Eatman, T. K. (2008). *Scholarship in public: Knowledge creation and tenure policy in the engaged university*. Syracuse: Imagining America.

Erstad, O., & Silseth, K. (2008). Agency in digital storytelling: Challenging the educational context. In K. Lundby (Ed.), *Digital storytelling, mediatized stories: Self-representations in new media* (pp. 213–232). New York: Peter Lang.

Erstad, O., & Wertsch, J. (2008). Tales of mediation: Narrative and digital media as cultural tools. In K. Lundby (Ed.), *Digital storytelling, mediatized stories: Self-representations in new media* (pp. 21–40). New York: Peter Lang.

Fisher, R., Fabricant, M., & Simmons, L. (2004). Understanding contemporary university-community connections: Context, practice, and challenges. In T. M. Soska & A. K. Johnson Butterfield (Eds.), *University-community partnerships: Universities in civic engagement* (pp. 13–34). Binghamton: Haworth Social Work Practice Press.

Freire, P. (2003). *Pedagogy of the oppressed*. New York: Continuum Press.

Ganz, M. (2010). Leading change: Leadership, organization, and social movements. In N. Nohria & R. Khurana (Eds.), *Handbook of leadership theory and practice: An HBS centennial colloquium on advancing leadership* (pp. 509–550). Boston: Harvard Business Press.

Gubrium, A., & Harper, K. (2013). *Participatory visual and digital methods*. Walnut Creek: Left Coast Press.

Hartley, M., & Harkavy, I. (2011). The civic engagement movement and the democratization of the academy. In C. Gibson & N. Longo (Eds.), *From command to community: A new approach to leadership education in colleges and universities* (pp. 67–82). Medford: Tufts University Press.

Heath, S. B. (1983). *Ways with words*. Cambridge: Cambridge University Press.

hooks, b. (1994). *Teaching to transgress: Education as the practice of freedom*. New York: Routledge.

Hrabowski, F. A., & Maton, K. I. (2009). Change institutional culture, and you change who goes into science. *Academe, 95*(3), 11–15.

Hull, G. A., & Katz, M.-L. (2006). Crafting an agentive self: Case studies of digital storytelling. *Research in the Teaching of English, 41*(1), 43–81.

Jay, G. (2011). The engaged humanities: Principles and practices for public scholarship and teaching. *Journal of community engagement and scholarship, 3*(1), 51–63.

Kezar, A. (2014). Higher education change and social networks: A review of research. *Journal of Higher Education, 85*(1), 91–125.

Kezar, A., Gallant, T., & Lester, J. (2011). Everyday people making a difference on college campuses: The tempered grassroots leadership tactics of faculty and staff. *Studies in Higher Education, 36*(2), 129–151.

King, T. (2008). *The truth about stories: A narrative.* Toronto: House of Anansi Press.

King, P. N. (2014). Preserving places, making spaces in Baltimore: Seeing the connections of research, teaching, and service as justice. *Journal of Urban History, 40*(3), 425–449.

Ladson-Billings, G. (1994). *Dreamkeepers: Successful teachers of African American Children.* San Francisco: Jossey-Bass Publishers.

Lambert, J. (2013). *Seven stages: Story and the human experience.* Berkeley: Digital Diner Press.

Lundby, K. (Ed.). (2008). *Digital storytelling, mediatized stories: Self-representations in new media.* New York: Peter Lang.

Mander, H. (2010). Words from the heart: Researching people's stories. *Journal of Human Rights Practice, 2*(2), 252–270.

MappingBaybrook. (2016). *Mapping Baybrook.* http://mappingbaybrook.org (home page). Accessed 11 Sept 2016.

Meyerson, D. E. (2003). *Tempered radicals: How everyday leaders inspire change at work.* Boston: Harvard Business School Press.

Meyerson, D. E., & Scully, M. (1995). Tempered radicalism and the politics of ambivalence and change. *Organization Science, 6*(5), 585–600.

MillStories. (2016). *Mill Stories.* http://millstories.org (home page). Accessed 11 Sept 2016.

Moll, L., Amanti, C., Neff, D., & Gonzalez, N. (1992). Funds of knowledge for teaching: Using a qualitative approach to connect homes and classrooms. *Theory Into Practice, 31*(2), 132–141.

Moore, T., & Ward, K. (2010). Institutionalizing faculty engagement through research, teaching, and service at research universities. *Michigan Journal of Community Service Learning, Fall, 2010,* 44–58.

New England Resource Center for Higher Education. (n.d.). *Lynton Award for the scholarship of engagement for early career faculty.* http://www.nerche.org/index.php?option=com_content&view=article&id=375:ernest-a-lynton-award-for-early-career-faculty&catid=25&Itemid=68. Accessed 27 Oct 2016.

Noddings, N. (2012). The caring relation in teaching. *Oxford Review of Education*, *38*(6), 771–781.

Nussbaum, M. C. (1998). *Cultivating humanity: A classical defense of reform in liberal education*. Cambridge: Harvard University Press.

O'Meara, K. A. (2011). Faculty civic engagement: New training, assumptions, and markets needed for the engaged American scholar. In J. A. Saltmarsh & M. Hartley (Eds.), *"To serve a larger purpose": Engagement for democracy and the transformation of higher education* (pp. 177–197). Philadelphia: Temple University Press.

O'Meara, K. A. (2013). Advancing graduate student agency. *Higher Education in Review, 10*, 1–10.

O'Meara, K. A., & Stromquist, N. P. (2015). Faculty peer networks: Role and relevance in advancing agency and gender equity. *Gender & Education, 27*(3), 338–358.

Post, M., Ward, E., Longo, N., & Saltmarsh, J. (2016). *Publicly engaged scholars: Next-generation engagement and the future of higher education*. Sterling: Stylus Publishing.

Rice, E. R. (2003). Rethinking scholarship and engagement: The struggle for new meanings. *Campus Compact Reader, Fall, 2003*, 1–9.

Saltmarsh, J., Hartley, M., & Clayton, P. H. (2009). *Democratic engagement white paper*. Boston: New England Resource Center for Higher Education.

Sanchez, G. J. (2004). The tangled web of diversity and democracy. *Foreseeable Futures #4, Imagining America, Artists and Scholars in Public Life*, pp. 4–24. http://imaginingamerica.org/wp-content/uploads/2011/07/Foreseeable-Futures-4-Sanchez.pdf. Accessed 11 Sept 2016.

Sturm, S., Eatman, T., Saltmarsh, J., & Bush, A. (2011). Full participation: Building the architecture for diversity and community engagement in higher education, *Imagining America*. Paper 17. http://surface.syr.edu/ia/17. Accessed 11 Sept 2016.

Velez-Ibanez, C. G. (1988). Networks of exchange among Mexicans in the U.S. and Mexico: Local level mediating responses to national and international transformations. *Urban Anthropology, 17*(1), 27–51.

von Wright, M. (2002). Narrative imagination and taking the perspective of others. *Studies in Philosophy and Education, 21*(4/5), 407–416.

Vygotsky, L. S. (1978). *Mind in society: The development of higher psychological processes*. Cambridge, MA: Harvard University Press.

Weedon, C. (2004). *Identity and culture: Narratives of difference and belonging*. Berkshire: Open University Press.

Whitchurch, C. (2013). *Reconstructing identities in higher education: The rise of "third space" professionals*. New York: Routledge.

INDEX

Note: Page numbers with "n" denote notes.

Printed by Books on Demand, Germany